For MacsBug 6.2

MacsBug Reference and Debugging Guide

▲▼
Addison-Wesley Publishing Company, Inc.

Reading, Massachusetts   Menlo Park, California   New York
Don Mills, Ontario   Wokingham, England   Amsterdam   Bonn
Sydney   Singapore   Tokyo   Madrid   San Juan   Paris
Seoul   Milan   Mexico City   Taipei

APPLE COMPUTER, INC.

© 1990, Apple Computer, Inc.
All rights reserved.

No part of this publication or the software described in it may be reproduced, stored in a retrieval system, or transmitted, in any form or by any means, mechanical, electronic, photocopying, recording, or otherwise, without prior written permission of Apple Computer, Inc., except in the normal use of the software or to make a backup copy of the software. The same proprietary and copyright notices must be affixed to any permitted copies as were affixed to the original. This exception does not allow copies to be made for others, whether or not sold, but all of the material purchased (with all backup copies) may be sold, given, or loaned to another person. Under the law, copying includes translating into another language or format. You may use the software on any computer owned by you, but extra copies cannot be made for this purpose.

Printed in the United States of America.

The Apple logo is a registered trademark of Apple Computer, Inc. Use of the "keyboard" Apple logo (Option-Shift-K) for commercial purposes without the prior written consent of Apple may constitute trademark infringement and unfair competition in violation of federal and state laws.

Apple Computer, Inc.
20525 Mariani Avenue
Cupertino, CA 95014-6299
408-996-1010

APDA, Apple, the Apple logo, AppleShare, AppleTalk, A/UX, HyperCard, ImageWriter, LaserWriter, Macintosh, MPW, MultiFinder, SADE, and SANE are registered trademarks of Apple Computer, Inc.

Finder, QuickDraw, and ResEdit, and are trademarks of Apple Computer, Inc.

Classic® is a registered trademark, licensed to Apple Computer, Inc.

FullWrite Professional is a trademark of Ashton-Tate.

ITC Garamond and ITC Zapf Dingbats are registered trademarks of International Typeface Corporation.

MacPaint® and MacWrite® are registered trademarks of Claris Corporation.

Microsoft is a registered trademark of Microsoft Corporation.

Motorola is a registered trademark of Motorola Corporation.

NuBUS is a trademark of Texas Instrument.

POSTSCRIPT is a registered trademark, and Illustrator is a trademark, of Adobe Systems Incorporated.

Varityper is a registered trademark of Varityper, Inc.

Simultaneously published in the United States and Canada.

ISBN 0-201-56767-9 (without disk)
ISBN 0-201-56768-7 (with disk)
1 2 3 4 5 6 7 8 9 -MU-9594939291
First printing, APRIL 1991

LIMITED WARRANTY ON MEDIA AND REPLACEMENT

If you discover physical defects in the manual or in the media on which a software product is distributed, APDA will replace the media or manual at no charge to you provided you return the item to be replaced with proof of purchase to APDA.

ALL IMPLIED WARRANTIES ON THIS MANUAL, INCLUDING IMPLIED WARRANTIES OF MERCHANTABILITY AND FITNESS FOR A PARTICULAR PURPOSE, ARE LIMITED IN DURATION TO NINETY (90) DAYS FROM THE DATE OF THE ORIGINAL RETAIL PURCHASE OF THIS PRODUCT.

Even though Apple has reviewed this manual, **APPLE MAKES NO WARRANTY OR REPRESENTATION, EITHER EXPRESS OR IMPLIED, WITH RESPECT TO THIS MANUAL, ITS QUALITY, ACCURACY, MERCHANTABILITY, OR FITNESS FOR A PARTICULAR PURPOSE. AS A RESULT, THIS MANUAL IS SOLD "AS IS," AND YOU, THE PURCHASER, ARE ASSUMING THE ENTIRE RISK AS TO ITS QUALITY AND ACCURACY.**

IN NO EVENT WILL APPLE BE LIABLE FOR DIRECT, INDIRECT, SPECIAL, INCIDENTAL, OR CONSEQUENTIAL DAMAGES RESULTING FROM ANY DEFECT OR INACCURACY IN THIS MANUAL, even if advised of the possibility of such damages.

THE WARRANTY AND REMEDIES SET FORTH ABOVE ARE EXCLUSIVE AND IN LIEU OF ALL OTHERS, ORAL OR WRITTEN, EXPRESS OR IMPLIED. No Apple dealer, agent, or employee is authorized to make any modification, extension, or addition to this warranty.

Some states do not allow the exclusion or limitation of implied warranties or liability for incidental or consequential damages, so the above limitation or exclusion may not apply to you. This warranty gives you specific legal rights, and you may also have other rights which vary from state to state.

Contents

Figures and Tables / xiii

Preface   **About This Manual / xix**
How to use this manual / xx
Other sources of information / xxi
Notation conventions / xxii

1   **MacsBug and Low-Level Debugging / 1**
Error handling on the Macintosh / 2
Why low-level debugging? / 3
Why MacsBug? / 4
New features in MacsBug 6.2 / 5

2   **Getting Started / 9**
Installing MacsBug / 10
    Installing MacsBug under A/UX / 10
    Displaying MacsBug on a different monitor / 11
        System software versions 3.2 through 6.x / 11
        System software version 7.0 / 12
    Updating the Debugger Prefs file / 13
The MacsBug display / 13
    The command line / 14
    The PC region / 14
    The output region / 15
    The status region / 16
        The stack area / 17
        The status area / 18
        The register area / 19

Invoking MacsBug / 19
    MacsBug when you least expect it / 20
    Using the programmer's switch to invoke MacsBug / 20
    Defining an 'FKEY' resource to invoke MacsBug / 21
    Invoking MacsBug from your source program / 22
        Inactivating user breaks / 23
        Using DebugStr from an assembly-language source program / 24
    Invoking MacsBug under A/UX / 24
Getting out of MacsBug / 24
Saving MacsBug output / 25
Working with the Debugger Prefs file / 26
Exercise: Getting started with MacsBug / 28
    Getting information about MacsBug / 29
    Using the command line to perform calculations / 30
    Displaying memory / 31
    Where is an address? / 33
    Further explorations / 34

3 An Assembly-Language Primer / 35

Compilers and assemblers / 36
Reading assembly-language instructions / 38
    Instruction syntax / 38
    Addressing modes / 40
        Absolute addressing / 41
        Data and address register direct addressing / 42
        Address register indirect addressing / 43
        Address register indirect with predecrement addressing, and address register indirect with postincrement addressing / 44
        Address register indirect with displacement addressing / 46
        Indexed indirect addressing with displacement / 47
        Program counter (PC) relative addressing modes / 48
        Immediate addressing / 49
        Implied addressing / 50
    Assembly-language instructions / 50
        The representation of negative numbers / 50
        Integer arithmetic instructions / 52
        Program control instructions / 53
        Intersegment calls and the jump table / 56
        Stack frame instructions / 58

        A simple assembly-language program / 59
        Comparing assembly-language code to source code / 62
            Assignment statements / 64
            A procedure call / 65
            A loop / 65
    MacsBug's disassembly commands / 66
        Reading the disassembly display / 67
        Determining where to start disassembling / 68

4   Macintosh Memory Organization / 71

    An overview of Macintosh memory space / 72
        The memory map / 73
            Memory units and their representation / 73
            Using MacsBug commands to display and set memory / 75
            Memory map regions / 77
            Using low-memory global variables to draw a memory map / 81
        Memory management under system software version 7.0 / 84
            32-bit addressing / 84
            Virtual memory / 85
        Registers / 88
        Using templates to display memory / 90
            Standard templates / 91
            Using basic and template types to define template fields / 92
            Constructing linked lists using the 'mxwt' resource / 94
            Exercise: Creating your own template / 97
    Application space / 100
    The heap / 101
        Heap blocks / 104
        Displaying information about heap blocks / 107
        Corrupting the heap / 110
        Lost in the heap / 111
        Heap management in a multiple-application environment / 113
            Displaying heaps in a multiple-application environment / 116
            Switching heaps in a multiple-application environment / 117
    Life on the stack / 117
        Looking at the stack / 118
        Allocating space for global variables / 121

        Stack frames / 122
            Stepping out of a procedure / 127
            Displaying a function's result / 127
            Using stack frames to establish a calling chain / 128
        Pascal and C calling conventions / 130
    Application parameters and the jump table / 131

5 The Macintosh Operating System / 133

    Exception processing / 134
    A-trap exceptions / 135
        How the operating system handles an A-trap / 136
    Patches and glue / 137
        Patching an A-trap / 138
        Determining whether a trap has been patched / 140
        Using in-line glue to implement a system routine / 141
    Using the stack to implement A-traps / 142
        Operating system routines / 143
        Exercise: Watching an A-trap call / 144
    Interrupts / 151
        Macintosh interrupts / 152
        Code that runs at interrupt time / 153
        Displaying information about VBL tasks / 154
    MacsBug's A-trap commands / 154
        The A-trap action table / 155
        Using A-trap commands / 156
            Specifying an A-trap name / 156
            Setting an A-trap action on a range of traps / 157
            Restricting A-trap actions to your application / 157
            A-traps in packages / 157
    Macintosh managers / 159
        The file system / 159
            Drive queue / 160
            Finding and displaying information about mounted volumes / 161
            File control blocks (FCBs) / 162
            File I/O queue / 163
            Debugging low-level file system calls / 163
            Synchronous and asynchronous I/O / 163

Drivers / 164
　　Device control entry (DCE) / 165
　　The unit table / 167
　　Desk accessories / 169
　　Displaying information about installed drivers / 170

6 Discipline / 173

How Discipline works / 174
Installing Discipline / 174
　　Installing Discipline as an INIT file / 174
　　Installing Discipline as an application / 175
Reading Discipline output / 177
Using Discipline during application development / 178
　　Using Discipline to test applications / 179
　　Using Discipline to test INITs and other startup code / 179
　　Using Discipline to test DAs and XCMDs / 180
　　Restrictions on Discipline / 180

7 Debugging Strategies / 181

Before the crash / 182
　　Use the compiler's directives / 182
　　Turn trap recording on / 182
　　Check operating system errors whenever possible / 183
　　Use signals and error handler routines / 184
　　Use assertions in your source program / 185
　　Test code on all machines / 186
　　Catch NIL pointers and handles instantly / 186
　　Use SetPort correctly / 187
After the crash / 188
　　Where am I? / 188
　　Who done it? / 189
　　Why did it happen? / 190
　　　　Check the source code / 190
　　　　Other suspects / 191
Common problems / 192
　　The deep freeze / 192
　　The restart surprise / 192
　　Nasty pointers / 193

No room to maneuver / 193
Mind-reading problems / 194
Using MacsBug to control program execution / 194
Controlling program execution / 196
Setting breakpoints / 197
Watching for memory to change / 199
Make it easy on yourself / 199

8 Introduction to MacsBug Commands / 201

The MacsBug command line / 202
Using the command line to enter commands / 203
Specifying command parameters / 204
Specifying an address / 204
Using procedure names / 205
The dot address and the colon address / 205
Using expressions in MacsBug commands / 206
Resolving conflicting name references / 207
Extending the command line / 207
The command line as calculator / 208
Base conversion / 208
Command line arithmetic / 208
Getting help / 210
Command line editing commands / 211
The command line buffer / 211
Using macros / 213
Macro commands / 213
Using 'mxbm' resources to define permanent macros / 214
Standard macros / 214
Creating permanent macros / 217
The FirstTime and EveryTime macros / 219
Using dcmds / 219
Standard dcmds / 220
The printf dcmd / 221
Listing available dcmds / 222
Creating your own dcmds / 223
Passing information to the dcmd / 223
Responding to a dcmdHelp request / 227
Responding to a dcmdDoIt request / 227

Restrictions on dcmds / 228
Building a dcmd / 229
Debugging dcmds / 229

9 MacsBug Commands / 231

ATB — A-trap Break / 232
ATC — A-trap Clear / 236
ATD — A-trap Display / 238
ATHC — A-trap Heap Check / 240
ATP — A-trap Playback / 242
ATR — A-trap Record / 244
ATSS — A-trap Step Spy / 246
ATT — A-trap Trace / 248
BR — Breakpoint / 251
BRC — Breakpoint Clear / 255
BRD — Breakpoint Display / 256
BRM — Multiple Breakpoints / 258
CS — Checksum / 260
DB — Display Byte / 261
DH — Disassemble Hexadecimal / 262
DL — Display Long / 263
DM — Display Memory / 264
DP — Display Page / 267
DSC — Discipline / 268
DV — Display Version / 269
DW — Display Word / 270
DX — Debugger Exchange / 271
EA — Exit to Application / 272
ES — Exit to Shell / 273
F — Find / 274
G — Go / 278
GT — Go Till / 279
HC — Heap Check / 281
HD — Heap Display / 284
HELP — Help / 287
HOW — Display Break Message / 289
HS — Heap Scramble / 291
HT — Heap Totals / 292
HX — Heap Exchange / 293

HZ — Heap Zone / 294
ID — Disassemble One Line / 297
IL — Disassemble From Address / 299
IP — Disassemble Around Address / 301
IR — Disassemble Until End of Procedure / 303
LOG — Log to a Printer or File / 305
MC — Macro Create / 307
MCC — Macro Clear / 309
MCD — Macro Display / 310
MR — Magic Return / 311
RAD — Toggle Register Name Syntax / 314
RB — Reboot / 315
Registers / 316
RN — Set Reference Number / 318
RS — Restart / 319
S — Step / 320
SB — Set Byte / 322
SC6 — Stack Crawl (A6) / 324
SC7 — Stack Crawl (A7) / 328
SHOW — Show / 331
SL — Set Long / 333
SM — Set Memory / 335
SO — Step Over / 337
SS — Step Spy / 339
SW — Set Word / 341
SWAP — Swap / 343
SX — Symbol Exchange / 345
TD — Display CPU Registers / 347
TF — Total Floating-Point Register Display / 348
TM — Total MMU Display / 349
TMP — List Templates / 350
WH — Where / 351

A Command Summary / 353

B Error Messages / 365

C Macintosh Error Codes / 371
    "Sad Macintosh" codes / 372
        Codes for the Macintosh Plus / 372
        Codes for other Macintosh computers / 373
    System Error Handler alerts / 376
    Operating system errors / 380
        OS Event Manager error / 380
        Serial driver errors / 380
        Slot Manager errors / 381
        SCSI Manager errors / 381
        Printing Manager errors / 382
        General system errors / 382
        Color Manager errors / 382
        Device Manager errors / 383
        Macintosh File System (MFS) errors / 384
        Font Manager errors / 385
        Low-level disk errors / 386
        Clock chip errors / 387
        Serial Communications Controller (SCC) errors / 387
        AppleTalk errors / 387
        Scrap Manager errors / 388
        Storage allocator errors / 389
        Hierarchical File System (HFS) errors / 389
        Alias Manager error / 390
        Menu Manager errors / 390
        Color QuickDraw and Color Manager errors / 390
        Resource Manager errors / 391
        Sound Manager errors / 392
        Slot Manager errors / 393
        Notification Manager error / 395
        Device Manager errors / 395
        Edition Manager errors / 395
        Process Manager errors / 396
        Event Manager errors / 397

Memory Manager errors / 397
Data Access Manager errors / 397
Help Manager Errors / 398
PPC Toolbox errors / 399
File ID errors / 400
AppleTalk Name Binding Protocol (NBP) errors / 400
AppleTalk Session Protocol (ASP) errors / 401
AppleTalk Transaction Protocol (ATP) errors / 401
AppleTalk Filing Protocol (AFP) errors / 402
SysEnvirons errors / 404
Gestalt Manager errors / 404
Picture utilities errors / 405
Power Manager errors / 405

D Procedure Names / 407

Procedure definition / 408
Examples of procedure definitions / 409

E MacsBug Internals and Discipline Interface / 411

How MacsBug installs itself / 412
    How MacsBug is implemented / 412
How MacsBug interfaces with Discipline / 414
    Jump table entries / 415
    Calling Discipline / 415

Glossary / 417

Index / 423

Figures and Tables

1 MacsBug and Low-Level Debugging / 1

Table 1-1   Summary of MacsBug 6.2 extensions / 6

2 Getting Started / 9

Figure 2-1   Installation message / 10
Figure 2-2   The Monitor display (system software versions 3.2 through 6.x) / 12
Figure 2-3   Regions of the MacsBug display / 13
Figure 2-4   PC region display / 15
Figure 2-5   The status region / 17
Figure 2-6   Defining an 'FKEY' resource to invoke MacsBug / 22
Figure 2-7   Debugger Prefs file / 26
Figure 2-8   Sample memory map / 33

Table 2-1   Commands used to get out of MacsBug / 25
Table 2-2   Resources in the Debugger Prefs file / 26
Table 2-3   Effects of removing resources from Debugger Prefs file / 27

3 An Assembly-Language Primer / 35

Figure 3-1   Compilers and assemblers / 37
Figure 3-2   Syntax of an assembly-language instruction / 38
Figure 3-3   Absolute addressing / 42
Figure 3-4   Indirect addressing / 43
Figure 3-5   Predecrement register indirect addressing / 45
Figure 3-6   Postincrement register indirect addressing / 46
Figure 3-7   Address register indirect addressing with displacement / 47
Figure 3-8   Indexed indirect addressing with displacement / 48
Figure 3-9   Immediate addressing / 49
Figure 3-10   Conditional branching indicator / 55
Figure 3-11   The jump table and self-relative branching / 57
Figure 3-12   Source code for an assembly-language routine / 59
Figure 3-13   Assembly-language program: disassembled code / 60

Figure 3-14 Registers and memory for sample program / 60
Figure 3-15 Reading the disassembly display / 68

Table 3-1 Addressing modes / 40
Table 3-2 Arithmetic integer instructions / 52
Table 3-3 Branching instructions / 55
Table 3-4 MacsBug's disassembly commands / 67

4 Macintosh Memory Organization / 71

Figure 4-1 Types of Macintosh memory / 72
Figure 4-2 High and low memory / 74
Figure 4-3 Storing a long word / 75
Figure 4-4 Graphic representation of DM output / 77
Figure 4-5 Address space for the 68000 microprocessor / 78
Figure 4-6 A simple Macintosh memory map / 79
Figure 4-7 Memory regions and low-memory global variables / 82
Figure 4-8 Virtual memory in 24-bit mode / 86
Figure 4-9 Virtual memory in 32-bit mode / 87
Figure 4-10 Template fields / 92
Figure 4-11 Linked list field entry in 'mxwt' resource / 95
Figure 4-12 The 'mxwt' template / 98
Figure 4-13 MouseCoords template / 99
Figure 4-14 Application space in a single-application environment / 101
Figure 4-15 Heap zone format / 103
Figure 4-16 The format of a heap block / 104
Figure 4-17 Handles and master pointers / 106
Figure 4-18 Optimal arrangement of blocks in the heap / 109
Figure 4-19 Application space in a multiple-application environment / 114
Figure 4-20 Fragmenting the Process Manager's heap / 115
Figure 4-21 Representations of the stack / 119
Figure 4-22 Stack display and storage in memory / 120
Figure 4-23 Allocating space for global variables / 121
Figure 4-24 A stack frame / 123
Figure 4-25 Part of stack frame built by calling routine / 124
Figure 4-26 Part of stack built by called routine / 125
Figure 4-27 The stack frame / 126
Figure 4-28 Multiple stack frames / 128
Figure 4-29 Application parameters and jump table / 131

Table 4-1 Units of memory / 74
Table 4-2 Commands that display and set memory / 76

Table 4-3   Memory regions / 80
Table 4-4   Memory regions and low-memory global variables / 83
Table 4-5   MacsBug register commands / 89
Table 4-6   Basic types / 93
Table 4-7   Template type names / 94

5   The Macintosh Operating System / 133

Figure 5-1   How the operating system handles an A-trap / 136
Figure 5-2   Patching an A-trap / 138
Figure 5-3   Prepatched A-trap / 139
Figure 5-4   Using in-line glue to implement an A-trap / 142
Figure 5-5   Calling chain for reading from or writing to a disk / 160
Figure 5-6   Device control entry / 166
Figure 5-7   Flag bits in the dCtlFlags word / 166
Figure 5-8   A simplified view of the unit table / 168
Figure 5-9   Detailed view of the unit table / 169

Table 5-1   vbl dcmd information / 154
Table 5-2   A-trap commands / 155
Table 5-3   vol display fields / 161
Table 5-4   file display fields / 162
Table 5-5   High-order dCtlFlags flag bits / 167
Table 5-6   Low-order dCtlFlags flag bits / 167
Table 5-7   drvr display fields / 171

6   Discipline / 173

Figure 6-1   Discipline installation message / 175
Figure 6-2   Sample Discipline output / 177

7   Debugging Strategies / 181

Table 7-1   Low-memory global variables that store operating system errors / 183
Table 7-2   Commands that control program execution / 195

8   Introduction to MacsBug Commands / 201

Figure 8-1   MacsBug command line / 202
Figure 8-2   Base conversion using the command line / 208
Figure 8-3   Command line editing commands / 211
Figure 8-4   Effects of Command-B and Command-V / 212
Figure 8-5   New 'mxbm' template / 218

Figure 8-6 Skeleton dcmd / 225
Figure 8-7 Responding to the dcmdHelp request / 227
Figure 8-8 Responding to the dcmdDoIt request / 228

Table 8-1 Command syntax conventions / 203
Table 8-2 Parameter types for MacsBug commands / 204
Table 8-3 Arithmetic operators / 209
Table 8-4 Macros defined by the 'mxbm' resource / 215
Table 8-5 Standard dcmds / 220
Table 8-6 Conversion characters for the printf dcmd / 221
Table 8-7 dcmd callback routines / 226

9 MacsBug Commands / 231

Table 9-1 Basic memory display types / 265
Table 9-2 Macros for the Find command / 276
Table 9-3 Interpreting the HD display / 285
Table 9-4 Register names / 316

A Command Summary / 353

Table A-1 MacsBug commands by functional category / 354
Table A-2 MacsBug commands in alphabetical order / 357

B Error Messages / 365

C Macintosh Error Codes / 371

Table C-1   "Sad Macintosh" error codes for the Macintosh Plus Computer / 372
Table C-2   "Sad Macintosh" codes for all Macintosh computers other than the Macintosh Plus / 373
Table C-3   System Error Handler alerts / 376
Table C-4   OS Event Manager error / 380
Table C-5   Serial driver errors / 380
Table C-6   Slot Manager errors / 381
Table C-7   SCSI Manager errors / 381
Table C-8   Printing Manager errors / 382
Table C-9   General system errors / 382
Table C-10 Color Manager errors / 382
Table C-11 Device Manager errors / 383
Table C-12 MFS errors / 384
Table C-13 Font Manager errors / 385

Table C-14 Low-level disk errors / 386
Table C-15 Clock chip errors / 387
Table C-16 SCC errors / 387
Table C-17 AppleTalk errors / 387
Table C-18 Scrap Manager errors / 388
Table C-19 Storage allocator errors / 389
Table C-20 HFS errors / 389
Table C-21 Alias Manager error / 390
Table C-22 Menu Manager errors / 390
Table C-23 Color QuickDraw and Color Manager errors / 390
Table C-24 Resource Manager errors / 391
Table C-25 Sound Manager errors / 392
Table C-26 Slot Manager errors / 393
Table C-27 Notification Manager error / 395
Table C-28 Device Manager errors / 395
Table C-29 Edition Manager errors / 395
Table C-30 Process Manager errors / 396
Table C-31 Event Manager errors / 397
Table C-32 Memory Manager errors / 397
Table C-33 Data Access Manager errors / 397
Table C-34 Help Manager errors / 398
Table C-35 PPC Toolbox errors / 399
Table C-36 File ID errors / 400
Table C-37 NBP errors / 400
Table C-38 ASP errors / 401
Table C-39 ATP errors / 401
Table C-40 AFP errors / 402
Table C-41 SysEnvirons errors / 404
Table C-42 Gestalt Manager errors / 404
Table C-43 Picture utilities errors / 405
Table C-44 Power Manager errors / 405

E MacsBug Internals and Discipline Interface / 411

Table E-1 Discipline and debugger information / 414
Table E-2 Contents of register file / 416

Preface About This Manual

This manual describes MacsBug, Apple's assembly-language debugger for Macintosh® programmers. This manual is an updated version of the *MacsBug 6.1 Reference,* and has been expanded to cover

- Extensions and changes to commands introduced in MacsBug 6.2.
- Macros, templates, dcmds, and other resources provided with MacsBug that you can use to make debugging easier.
- Discipline, a tool that tests the validity of parameters passed to and received from system calls.
- Macintosh memory management and the operating system as these relate to low-level debugging.
- Information for high-level language programmers who want to interpret and steer through disassembled code.
- Debugging strategies that you can use to find and cure common bugs.

How to use this manual

The manual contains the following sections:

- This Preface describes the manual and the conventions used in it.

- Chapter 1, "MacsBug and Low-Level Debugging," provides an overview of MacsBug and error handling, including a summary of new features in MacsBug 6.2.

- Chapter 2, "Getting Started," provides installation instructions, including instructions for installing MacsBug under A/UX®. It also describes the MacsBug display and various ways to invoke MacsBug, and includes a hands-on exercise to get you started.

- Chapter 3, "An Assembly-Language Primer," is designed to teach you how to read enough assembly language to interpret MacsBug output and relate this output to your source code.

- Chapter 4, "Macintosh Memory Organization," explains how to use MacsBug commands to examine the heap and the stack, how the stack is used to implement your routines, how virtual memory affects the memory map, how the heap is organized in a multiple-application environment, and how you can build templates to get a more intelligible display of data structures used by your program or by the system.

- Chapter 5, "The Macintosh Operating System," explains exception processing, the implementation of system calls (including packages, patches, and glue), and the requirements of code that runs at interrupt time. The chapter also explains MacsBug's A-trap commands and the standard dcmds: vbl, vol, file, and drvr.

- Chapter 6, "Discipline," describes how to install and use Discipline, a tool used with MacsBug to test parameters passed to and returned by system calls.

- Chapter 7, "Debugging Strategies," describes how you can use MacsBug commands to control the execution of your program and to display values at any point during execution. It also contains tips about how to prevent and also how to find and cure bugs.

- Chapter 8, "Introduction to MacsBug Commands," provides an overview of the use of MacsBug commands, including macros and dcmds.

- Chapter 9, "MacsBug Commands," provides complete descriptions of MacsBug commands, arranged in alphabetical order.

- Appendix A, "Command Summary," provides a summary of MacsBug commands and their syntax.

- Appendix B, "Error Messages," lists MacsBug error messages in alphabetical order and includes a brief description of the possible causes for each error.

- Appendix C, "Macintosh Error Codes," lists error codes returned by the Macintosh system software.

- Appendix D, "'Procedure Names,'" explains how compiler writers should define procedures so that MacsBug is able to accept and return addresses as procedure names and offsets.
- Appendix E, "MacsBug Internals and Discipline Interface," describes how MacsBug installs itself and how it interfaces with Discipline.

Hands-on exercises, to make learning easier and more certain, have been included wherever possible. In some cases, you will need to load the Demo program (from the MacsBug 6.2 distribution disk) in order to do the exercises.

If you are an expert Macintosh programmer and have been working with MacsBug for a while, you should check the descriptions of the commands that have changed, which are listed in "New Features in MacsBug 6.2" in Chapter 1. You should also read Chapter 6, "Discipline," and "Virtual Memory" in Chapter 4.

If you are a seasoned Macintosh programmer, but have stayed away from MacsBug because you cannot read assembly language, you should read Chapters 1, 2, 3, 6, 7, 8, and 9. You should also take a look at "Virtual Memory" in Chapter 4.

If you are new to Macintosh programming, you should read the whole book.

Other sources of information

This manual covers many topics covered in *Inside Macintosh,* but focuses on their relationship to low-level debugging and the use of MacsBug commands. Although it covers some topics that are not covered in *Inside Macintosh,* this manual is not a substitute for that indispensable tome.

You should also get an up-to-date copy of the Macintosh Technical Notes. These notes document special implementation issues, gotchas, updates, and many other details you might need to know in developing an application. They are available through APDA® and from many on-line services, and are mailed out automatically to registered developers.

If you are new to Macintosh programming, you should also read *How to Write Macintosh Software* by Scott Knaster (published by Addison-Wesley). There is no finer book to get you started in Macintosh programming and debugging.

Notation conventions

The following syntax conventions are used to describe MacsBug commands:

literal	Plain text indicates a word that must appear in the command exactly as shown. Special symbols (-, §, &, and so on) must also be entered exactly as shown.
italics	Italics indicate a parameter that you must replace with specific information.
[*optional*]	Brackets indicate that the enclosed elements are optional. Omit the brackets when you enter the command.
...	Ellipses (...) indicate that the preceding item can be repeated one or more times.
		A vertical bar (	) indicates an either/or choice.

Command names and filenames are not sensitive to case.

Your input to MacsBug and MacsBug output use two physically separate areas of the display. Since this separation cannot be conveniently represented in the description of sample commands and their output, input to MacsBug is represented by bold Courier text and MacsBug output is represented by plain Courier text. For example, in the following two lines, BRC is what you enter on the command line, and "All breakpoints cleared" is what MacsBug displays in the output region of the display.

`BRC`
```
  All breakpoints cleared
```

This convention is used throughout this manual.

In the text of this manual, numbers preceded by a dollar sign (like this: $21E8) are in hexadecimal, and all other numbers are in decimal. In any MacsBug display, all numbers are in hexadecimal unless they are preceded by a pound sign (like this: #2148).

Chapter 1 **MacsBug and Low-Level Debugging**

This chapter introduces MacsBug, a Motorola 68000-family assembly-language debugger customized for the entire Macintosh® family of computers. First introduced in 1981, MacsBug has continued to evolve along with the Macintosh. The section "New Features in MacsBug 6.2" in this chapter summarizes changes introduced with version 6.2 of MacsBug.

MacsBug 6.2 runs on all Macintosh computers except the Macintosh XL and computers with the 64K ROM. It is designed to support future members of the 68000 family. It handles the MC68881 floating-point coprocessor and the MC68851 Memory Management Unit (MMU). MacsBug supports external displays for Macintosh Classic® computers as well as various screen sizes and bit depths for monitors used with modular Macintosh computers. There's no need to customize MacsBug for particular configurations, since it determines the attributes of the machine at system startup.

MacsBug 6.2 works with all versions of Macintosh system software. It is compatible with MultiFinder® in system software versions 5.0 and 6.0.

Error handling on the Macintosh

Error handling on the Macintosh is initiated by the microprocessor. When the microprocessor encounters an instruction that it does not recognize or cannot execute, it saves information about its current state and then transfers control to one of several routines whose addresses are stored in low memory and that are responsible for responding to the instruction. The means by which the processor does this is called **exception processing;** the routines to which the processor transfers control are called **exception handlers.**

The Macintosh uses exception processing to implement User Interface Toolbox and operating system routines as well as to handle errors:

- The routine that is called when the microprocessor encounters a system call (that is implemented as an A-trap instruction) is the **trap dispatcher.** Chapter 5, "The Macintosh Operating System," describes how A-traps are implemented using the trap dispatcher.

- The routine that is called when the microprocessor encounters a fatal error is called an **error handler.**

When a fatal error occurs and MacsBug is not installed, the microprocessor transfers control to the System Error Handler, which puts up the bomb box and, optionally, executes a routine that allows the user to resume program execution. If MacsBug (or another resident debugger) is installed, the processor transfers control to it. MacsBug, in turn, displays the debugging screen.

Using MacsBug commands and the information displayed on the debugging screen, you can determine which instruction caused the error, how that instruction came to be executed, and how to change your code to eliminate the error. This process is called low-level debugging because MacsBug shows you the disassembled object code that the machine is executing, rather than the source-level code (if your source code is written in a high-level language).

Why low-level debugging?

If you were a doctor and someone came to you with a fever, a sore throat, and a runny nose, you could make a diagnosis on the basis of this external evidence alone; or you could take a throat culture, look at it through a microscope, and make a diagnosis based on your examination of the biological evidence. A programmer might call the diagnosis based on external evidence source-level debugging, and the diagnosis made with the aid of a microscope low-level debugging.

Obviously, low-level debugging is not necessary in every case. If a man has been run over by a truck, you won't need your microscope. But if the diagnosis you have made on the basis of external evidence hasn't cured the patient, it's time to reach for more precise tools and get a more detailed view.

A low-level debugger is the tool of choice in three situations:

- You have a bug that cannot be analyzed with a source-level debugger either because the bug occurs in an INIT that runs before any applications (including your source-level debugger) are loaded or because the bug crashes the source-level debugger.

- The syntax and logic of your program appear to be perfect, but your program is crashing or behaving erratically nevertheless. It is now necessary to read between your source lines, that is, to look at the instructions the processor is executing and to determine which instruction is causing the problem and what part of your source code is causing that instruction to be executing.

- Your program is running fine, but you want to make sure that you're making efficient use of memory and system resources, and doubly sure that you have eliminated potential bugs. You can use MacsBug to check for fragmentation in the application heap and to force the Memory Manager to move blocks in the heap as often as possible, thus unearthing any bad pointers that haven't surfaced yet.

If you're not familiar with assembly language, a low-level debugger can be rather forbidding. You must learn how to interpret the information it displays and how that information relates to your source-level program and the program's use of system calls before you can use a low-level debugger to find and fix bugs. If you're in this situation, you should read carefully through Chapters 3, 4, and 5. These chapters are designed to familiarize you with assembly language and to give you a better understanding of how MacsBug commands relate to debugging a Macintosh program.

Why MacsBug?

When you're debugging a program, you are interested in the interaction between your code and the system. Any debugger you use also interacts with the system: it makes system calls and uses memory. The less interaction that takes place between the debugger and the system and the less memory the debugger uses, the more certain you can be that the errors you discover are caused by your code. The main advantage of MacsBug over other low-level debuggers is that it does not use the Macintosh system software. The only exceptions to this are the LOG command and whatever system calls are used by a dcmd. MacsBug also takes up very little space in memory: a minimum of 90K or the more standard 140K. If you are a systems programmer, you can debug your software without having to worry about the debugger using the code you're debugging. If you are an applications programmer, and therefore still concerned about the interaction between your application and the system, you'll find MacsBug a powerful tool for debugging applications.

MacsBug is an assembly-language debugger. If you're writing programs in a high-level language like C or Pascal, you'll more often want to use the Symbolic Applications Debugging Environment (SADE®). SADE lets you debug your program at the source-code level, which means you don't need to know assembly language or map object code back to your program's source-level instructions. If you need to, SADE lets you monitor program execution at the machine level as well.

SADE does have its limitations, however, and high-level programmers will find that MacsBug picks up where SADE leaves off. Specifically:

- SADE uses the Macintosh system software extensively, and in the case of a severe crash may not be operable. MacsBug lets you examine the remains to try to determine what went wrong.
- If RAM is severely limited, you may not be able to run SADE. MacsBug is lean and mean.

MacsBug is loaded at system startup and sits quietly in RAM until it's invoked. Unlike debuggers that expect a target program to work with, MacsBug lets you look at practically anything running on the Macintosh—Toolbox and operating system routines, applications, desk accessories, and so on.

You can suspend program execution and invoke MacsBug at any point, either manually (by pressing the interrupt switch or a key that you define) or programmatically (by calling special traps from within your program). And since MacsBug needs so little of the system to operate, it can be used even in the case of fatal system errors. Whenever the System Error Handler is called, or when an exception occurs, MacsBug takes control and lets you look around.

Once MacsBug has been invoked, you can enter commands to

- Display and set memory and registers.
- Disassemble memory.
- Set execution breakpoints.
- Step and trace through both RAM and ROM.
- Monitor system traps.
- Display and check the system and application heaps.

Chapter 2, "Getting Started," explains how you install MacsBug. It also provides specific instructions about how to invoke and leave MacsBug, and how to interpret MacsBug's display. Chapter 2 ends with a hands-on exercise to get you started. The Preface to this manual describes the contents of the other chapters and how to use this manual depending on your experience with programming on the Macintosh and with low-level debugging.

New features in MacsBug 6.2

One of the major changes to MacsBug since version 6.1 is that it now works reliably with all Apple® monitors and all third-party monitors if their slot ROM and driver software have been designed according to the guidelines presented in *Designing Cards and Drivers for the Macintosh II and Macintosh SE*. In addition to its increased portability, MacsBug 6.2 includes the following new features:

- A new display that shows you the name of the current application, the memory management scheme (24-bit/32-bit) currently used, and whether MacsBug can access virtual memory.
- New options for the Find command that allow you to specify the width of the pattern for which MacsBug searches. You can even use one of these options to have MacsBug look for pointers.
- A more detailed heap dump display. The HD command can now display all blocks, even if some block headers are slightly damaged. (Damaged blocks are indicated by a question mark (?) or an exclamation point (!) prefixed to the master pointer.)
- A more detailed heap zones display. The HZ command now indicates embedded heaps and whether a heap is 24-bit or 32-bit. The HZ command also indicates whether a heap contains a damaged block by displaying an exclamation point (!) after the heap zone's ending address.

- An extension to the GT (Go Till) command that allows you to specify one or more MacsBug commands to be executed once the specified breakpoint is reached.
- If an address is in a known resource but not in a known procedure, MacsBug will display information about that resource.
- SC6 and SC7 commands that take optional parameters that you can use to specify the beginning and ending address of a private stack. You can then use either Stack Crawl command to examine that stack.
- A BRD command that tells you whether the microprocessor will step or trace to find the specified instruction.
- A standard printf dcmd (debugger command) that allows you to produce formatted output.

In addition to these specific changes, you should find MacsBug 6.2 easier to use. Whenever possible its output has been made more articulate and its displays more intelligible. Table 1-1 provides a summary of changes and additions introduced with version 6.2.

- **Table 1-1** Summary of MacsBug 6.2 extensions

Item	Syntax	Effect/change
Command-D	Command-D	Displays a menu of procedure names from which you can select a name to insert in the command line. This is not a new command; it is a way of implementing the Command-: command on German and Scandinavian keyboards. See "Determining Where to Start Disassembling" in Chapter 3 for additional information.
Command-B	Command-B	Scrolls the command line buffer up. See Chapter 8, "Introduction to MacsBug Commands," for additional information.
Find command	F *addr nbytes expr* | "*string*"	Returns the address where it finds the specified pattern. See the description of the Find command in Chapter 9 for additional information.

(continued)

■ **Table 1-1** Summary of MacsBug 6.2 extensions (continued)

Item	Syntax	Effect/change
Find command	F[B|W|L|P] *addr nbytes expr*	Returns the address where it finds the specified Byte, Word, Long word, or Pointer. See the description of the Find command in Chapter 9 for additional information.
ATP command	ATP	If ATR is off, the ATP command plays back information from the most recent ATR. See the description of the ATP command in Chapter 9 for additional information.
BRD command	BRD	Output tells you whether the microprocessor has to step or trace in order to break on the specified instruction, and whether the specified instruction is in a relocatable block.
GT command	GT *addr* [';*cmd* [;*cmd*] ...']	Breaks at the specified address and executes one or more commands. See the description of the GT command in Chapter 9 for additional information.
HD command	HD[*qualifier*]	A new qualifier, Q, has been added that causes MacsBug to display all blocks that might have damaged headers. See the description of the HD command in Chapter 9 for additional information.
HZ command	HZ [*addr*]	Indicates whether a heap zone contains a damaged block, whether a heap zone is embedded within another heap zone (by levels of indentation), and whether a heap zone is 24-bit or 32-bit.
SC6 command	SC6 [*addr* [*nbytes*]]	Provides two new parameters, *address* and *nbytes*, that you can use to specify the beginning and ending address of a private stack. See the description of the SC6 command in Chapter 9 for additional information.

(continued)

■ **Table 1-1** Summary of MacsBug 6.2 extensions (continued)

Item	Syntax	Effect/Change
SC7 command	SC7 [*addr* [*nbytes*]]	Provides two new parameters, *address* and *nbytes*, that you can use to specify the beginning and ending address of a private stack. See the description of the SC7 command in Chapter 9 for additional information.
DebugStr trap	DebugStr ("*string* [; *cmd*]...")	Sets a break from within the source program. When MacsBug is invoked, it displays *string* and executes one or more commands. See "Invoking MacsBug From Your Source Program" in Chapter 2 for additional information.
printf dcmd	printf "*format*" *arg* ...	Formatted output command. See "The printf dcmd" in Chapter 8 for additional information.
UserZone variable	UserZone	Identifies the heap whose address you last furnished as a parameter to the HX command. See the description of the HX command in Chapter 9 for additional information.
TargetZone variable	TargetZone	Specifies the zone currently set with the HX command. See the description of the HX command in Chapter 9 for additional information.

Chapter 2 Getting Started

This chapter explains how to install MacsBug and begin using it, including

- How to install MacsBug under both the Macintosh Operating System and A/UX®.
- How to display MacsBug on a different monitor.
- How to interpret the information displayed in the different regions of the MacsBug display.
- The various ways to invoke MacsBug.
- The various ways to get out of MacsBug.
- How to log MacsBug output to a file or a printer.
- The contents of the Debugger Prefs file.

The chapter concludes with a brief exercise designed to get you started using MacsBug.

Chapter 1, "MacsBug and Low-Level Debugging," provides an overview of MacsBug and error handling. Make sure you understand these basic concepts before you read this chapter.

If you have worked with MacsBug before, you only need to read the section "The Status Region," which describes new information shown by MacsBug version 6.2.

Installing MacsBug

To install MacsBug and the Debugger Prefs file, open your distribution disk and drag the MacsBug file and the Debugger Prefs file into your System Folder. Then restart your system. MacsBug is installed at system startup and resides in RAM until shutdown.

After successful installation, the message shown in Figure 2-1 is displayed below the "Welcome to Macintosh" message. The startup application is then launched; this is usually the Finder™.

■ **Figure 2-1** Installation message

To prevent MacsBug installation indefinitely, you can rename the MacsBug file, or move the file from the System Folder. To override MacsBug installation for a single session only, simply hold down the mouse button during startup.

Once MacsBug is installed, it can be invoked in a number of different ways. For additional information, see "Invoking MacsBug" later in this chapter.

Installing MacsBug under A/UX

To install MacsBug, drag the MacsBug document and the Debugger Prefs file into the System Folder. When you are done, you should have the following two files:

```
/mac/sys/System Folder/MacsBug
/mac/sys/System Folder/DebuggerPrefs
```

Then restart your Macintosh.

To invoke MacsBug, press Control-Command-I simultaneously. This will bring up the MacsBug display and allow you to start working with MacsBug. See "Invoking MacsBug Under A/UX," later in this chapter, for additional information.

In most respects, the version of MacsBug that runs under A/UX behaves identically to that running under the Macintosh system software. You can therefore use this documentation for your debugging; however, make sure you read "Invoking MacsBug Under A/UX," later in this chapter, for special considerations.

Displaying MacsBug on a different monitor

If you are working with more than one monitor, MacsBug uses the "Welcome to Macintosh" screen by default. To run your application on one monitor and MacsBug on another, use the procedure that is appropriate for the system software on your Macintosh.

System software versions 3.2 through 6.x

Choose Control Panel from the Apple menu and scroll down until you see the Monitors icon; then press the Option key while clicking the Monitors icon. You will see a display like the one shown in Figure 2-2. Press the Option key to display the "happy Macintosh" icon.

MacsBug displays the debugging screen on the monitor containing the "happy Macintosh" icon. Figure 2-2 shows two monitors installed. To run your application on Monitor 1 and display the debugging screen on Monitor 2, drag the "happy Macintosh" icon to Monitor 2 and restart.

You can use the SWAP command, described in Chapter 9, to keep MacsBug visible at all times on the second monitor. Otherwise, MacsBug is displayed on the second monitor only when it is invoked.

■ **Figure 2-2** The Monitor display (system software versions 3.2 through 6.x)

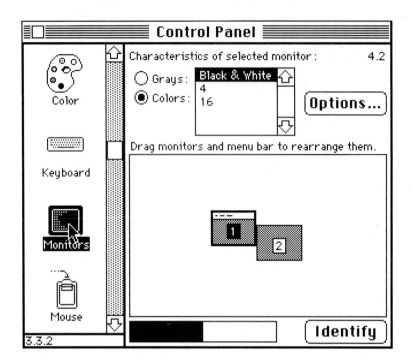

System software version 7.0

Choose Control Panels from the Apple menu or open the Control Panels folder in the System Folder. Then double-click the Monitors icon.

MacsBug displays the debugging screen on the monitor containing the "happy Macintosh" icon. To run your application on Monitor 1 and display the debugging screen on Monitor 2, hold down the Option key and drag the "happy Macintosh" icon to Monitor 2 and restart.

You can use the SWAP command, described in Chapter 9, to keep MacsBug visible at all times on the second monitor. Otherwise, MacsBug is displayed on the second monitor only when it is invoked.

Updating the Debugger Prefs file

If you have used MacsBug before and have created additional macro, template, or dcmd resources, you can use ResEdit™ to copy these resources into the version of the Debugger Prefs file that comes with MacsBug 6.2. For more information, see "Working With the Debugger Prefs File" later in this chapter.

The MacsBug display

Figure 2-3 shows the different regions of the MacsBug display. Normally, when MacsBug is invoked, the status region and the PC region contain information about the current state of the microprocessor. However, these regions are shown blank in Figure 2-3 to make the different regions easier to see.

The sections that follow describe each of these regions, the information they provide, and the MacsBug commands or resources you can use to change the default settings that determine how much information or, in some instances, the kind of information that is shown in each region.

■ **Figure 2-3** Regions of the MacsBug display

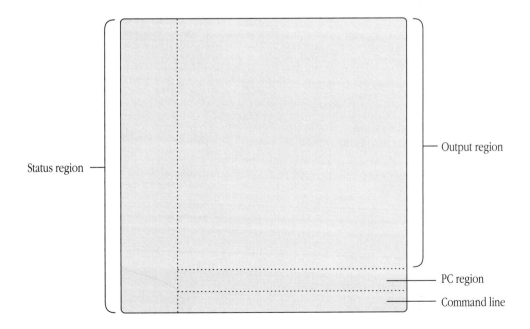

The command line

The **command line** is the area in which you enter commands and perform base conversions and arithmetic calculations. When MacsBug is invoked, the command line is blank. The insertion point is indicated by a blinking cursor in the first position on the command line.

You cannot change the size of the command line. MacsBug contains a command line buffer in which each command that you execute is stored. Command-key combinations allow you to scroll through the buffer and copy a command you have entered before to the command line.

You can use the standard editing keys (Delete, Left Arrow, and Right Arrow) as well as several special functions to edit commands you have already entered.

To enter a command, type the command and press Return. You can enter several commands on the command line by separating them with a semicolon (;), but you cannot continue to a second line.

Please see Chapter 8, "Introduction to MacsBug Commands," for additional information about entering commands and working with the command line.

The PC region

The **PC region** displays the address of the next instruction to be executed as well as the disassembly of that instruction. It is called the PC region because the address of the next instruction to be executed is always stored in the program counter or PC register.

By default only one instruction is displayed in this region. However, you can use ResEdit to change the default setting in the 'mxbi' resource and display several lines. Follow these steps to change the setting:

1. Open the Debugger Prefs file.
2. Open the 'mxbi' resource.
3. Use the Tab key to move to the field labeled "#of PC lines shown" and enter the number of lines that you want displayed.
4. Save the changes to the resource. To load the changed resource, you will have to restart.

Figure 2-4 shows a sample PC region display.

■ **Figure 2-4** PC region display

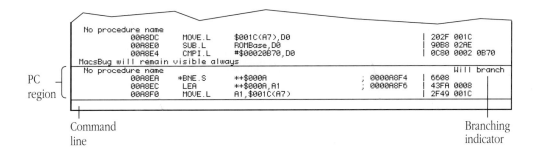

In the sample display shown in Figure 2-4, the PC region displays three lines: the asterisk preceding the first instruction indicates the next instruction to be executed.

The only other information displayed in this region concerns the execution of branching instructions. The branching indicator, shown in the upper-right corner of the PC region, tells you whether the program will branch after executing the next instruction.

The output region

The largest area of the screen is the **output region:** this is the area that MacsBug uses to display information in response to the commands you enter. The size of this area depends on the number of lines you choose to display in the PC region. The more lines you display in the PC region, the smaller the output region.

When MacsBug is invoked, the first line of the output region always displays a message explaining the reason for the break. This could be a microprocessor exception, Macintosh system error, or user-specified break.

In general, MacsBug output falls into three categories, indicated by three levels of indentation:

■ The leftmost line displays the reason for the break.

■ The next level of indentation displays a message for each command you enter, either confirming execution or explaining a failure.

■ The rightmost level of indentation displays command output.

Chapter 2   Getting Started   15

Information shown in the output region scrolls up (and eventually off) the screen as you execute new commands. You can use the Up Arrow and Down Arrrow keys to examine text that has scrolled off the top of the display. If you scroll back to examine some text and then enter another command, the new output is displayed starting from where you are (rather than from the end of the buffer). MacsBug does this on the assumption that you'll more often want to see the new output along with the output at which you were just looking.

Scrollable output is enabled by a history buffer whose default size of 2K you can change using the 'mxbi' resource. You can use ResEdit to change the size of the buffer by following these steps:

1. Open the Debugger Prefs file.
2. Open the 'mxbi' resource.
3. Use the Tab key to move to the field labeled "Size of the history buffer" and enter the number of bytes that you want displayed. An 8K buffer will hold about four pages of output.
4. Save the changes to the resource. To load the changed resource, you will have to restart.

See the section "Saving MacsBug Output" later in this chapter for information on how to log output to a file or printer.

The status region

The **status region,** which is at the left of the MacsBug debugging screen, displays information about the system at the time that MacsBug is invoked. Figure 2-5 shows a schematic view of the status region.

■ **Figure 2-5** The status region

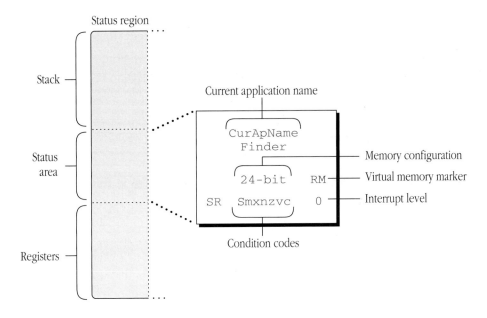

As you can see, the status region consists of three areas:

- At the top of the status region, MacsBug displays an area of memory called the stack.
- In the middle of the status region, MacsBug displays the current application name, the current memory configuration, a virtual memory marker, the setting of the condition codes in the status register, and the interrupt level set by the system.
- At the bottom of the status region, MacsBug displays the contents of the CPU registers.

The following three sections describe the information shown in each area of the status region in greater detail.

The stack area

By default, MacsBug uses the stack area of the status region to display first the contents of the stack pointer (SP) and then memory on the stack starting with the lowest location. The section "Looking at the Stack," in Chapter 4, provides a more detailed explanation of this display.

You can use the MacsBug SHOW command, described in Chapter 9, to display the stack using different formats or to use this portion of the status region to display an entirely different area of memory.

The status area

As shown in Figure 2-5, the first two lines of the status area display the name of the current application. If your application is running in a multiple-application environment (that is, under system software version 5.0 or 6.0 with MultiFinder turned on, or under system software version 7.0), it is possible that one of the background applications has caused the crash. If this is the case, the name of the current application shown in the MacsBug display will *not* be the name of the foreground application.

The third line displays information about the current memory configuration and virtual memory:

- The memory configuration marker indicates whether the Memory Manager is in 24-bit mode or 32-bit mode. Being aware of which mode the Memory Manager is in can save you time and trouble in identifying the cause of some bus errors. (When you try to access a bad address in MacsBug, the error will be "Unable to access that address.") For example, to implement drivers that access a NuBus™ board, you need to switch the hardware to 32-bit addressing mode. If you now dereference an address that uses the high byte to hold data, you will get a bus error because the address does not refer to a valid location.

  It is your responsibility to make sure that your program is not using invalid addresses, either by switching back to 24-bit mode or by using the StripAddress routine to strip the misleading high byte from the address. The marker tells you what memory management scheme the Memory Manager is using. It is then up to you to make sure that your application is behaving appropriately given that state. Please note that the description of the StripAddress routine in the "Memory Management" chapter in *Inside Macintosh,* Volume VI, corrects the description of the routine included in Volume V.

  The virtual memory marker displays one of three codes to indicate whether virtual memory is being used and whether MacsBug can rely on the Memory Manager to swap pages if the program being debugged makes use of virtual memory. The codes displayed have the following meanings:

RM	Virtual memory is not being used (Real Memory).
VM	Memory Manager can swap pages if MacsBug requires it.
vM	MacsBug was invoked while the Memory Manager was swapping pages; now the Memory Manager cannot swap pages for MacsBug.

  For additional information, see "Virtual Memory" in Chapter 4.

The fourth line displays the setting of the condition codes in the status register. The flags used depend on the microprocessor used on your machine. In general, if the letter representing the flag is uppercase, the flag is set; if the letter is lowercase, the flag is not set. The rightmost item on this line is a number from 0 to 7 indicating the interrupt level set by the system at the time MacsBug was invoked. For more information about interrupt levels, see "Interrupts" in Chapter 5.

The register area

The area at the bottom of the status region displays the contents of the CPU registers. As you execute your program, MacsBug updates the register display. If you want to record register values so that you can compare them with their updated values, you can use the TD (Display CPU Registers) command to have MacsBug write their values to the output region of the display.

MacsBug provides two additional commands that display the contents of other registers:

- The TF (Total Floating-Point Register Display) command displays the contents of the floating-point register.
- The TM (Total MMU Display) command displays the contents of the MMU register.

For additional information about these commands, see Chapter 9, "MacsBug Commands."

Invoking MacsBug

Once you have installed MacsBug, it takes control of your system and displays the debugging screen either as the result of a system error or because you invoke it. This section describes the various ways that you can invoke MacsBug and the circumstances under which MacsBug will invoke itself.

▲ **Warning** When you invoke MacsBug, you generate a level 7 interrupt, which means that all interrupts are disabled while MacsBug is running. AppleShare® uses interrupt routines to keep continuous communication going between a file server and a workstation. If you are logged on to a file server, and you enter MacsBug for more than 2.5 minutes, the file server will assume your application has died and you will lose your server connection. ▲

MacsBug when you least expect it

Perhaps the most dramatic and frustrating way to find yourself in MacsBug is as the result of a system error. If you find yourself in this situation, the first thing to do is gather whatever information you can that helps you determine the cause of the crash. MacsBug helps you a little by displaying a message describing the reason for the break in the output region of the display.

You can also get a sense of where your program crashed by looking in the PC region of the display. The instruction displayed in this region is the next instruction to be executed. You can disassemble around that address to find out which routine was executing when you crashed.

Finally, you can use the tilde (~) or Esc key to see what the screen looked like right before the crash. Press any letter key to return to MacsBug.

MacsBug is also invoked if you have Discipline turned on and one of the values sent to or returned from a system call does not meet Discipline's test. MacsBug displays information about the offending call. Having Discipline break in and display diagnostic messages gives you some warning about a situation that might result in a crash. In addition, Discipline displays sufficient information for you to fix the call that caused the break. For more information, see Chapter 6, "Discipline."

If MacsBug is invoked as the result of a system error, you need to be careful about how you get out of MacsBug. See "Getting Out of MacsBug" later in this chapter for additional information.

Chapter 7, "Debugging Strategies," provides additional information on locating the cause of the crash.

Using the programmer's switch to invoke MacsBug

The **programmer's switch** is a two-pronged plastic gadget that is shipped with every Macintosh. If you have not already installed it, please consult the documentation that came with your computer for instructions. The programmer's switch has two parts:

- A reset switch is marked with an arrowhead (or the word "Reset" on the Macintosh Plus). If you are in the Finder, this switch is the preferred way to restart your Macintosh in the event of a crash so bad that you cannot use commands in the Special menu and you can't get into MacsBug.

- An **interrupt switch** is marked with a circled V (or the word "Interrupt" on the Macintosh Plus). Pressing this switch generates a level 7, nonmaskable interrupt, which is why it is often called the NMI key. (On the Macintosh Plus/SE, it can generate a level 4, 5, 6, or 7 interrupt.) The microprocessor handles this interrupt by invoking MacsBug.

If you use the interrupt switch to invoke MacsBug, there is a possibility that the system might be in an uncertain state: perhaps the Memory Manager was in the middle of moving a heap block, or perhaps a ROM routine that used register A5 for its own purposes was executing and the interrupt occurred before the routine restored its value. If this is the case, you might wind up looking at unreliable values. To avoid this possibility when using the interrupt switch, you might want to enter the following commands when MacsBug is invoked:

```
ATB  WaitNextEvent;  G
```

and then

```
ATC  WaitNextEvent
```

This will usually eliminate the problem, and you can continue working without worry. Under earlier systems and applications, use GetNextEvent rather than WaitNextEvent.

Defining an 'FKEY' resource to invoke MacsBug

Another way to invoke MacsBug is to define an 'FKEY' resource using ResEdit or MPW™. Once you have defined this resource, you can use a Shift-Command-key combination to invoke MacsBug.

To define an 'FKEY' resource using ResEdit 2.1, follow these steps:

1. Launch ResEdit.
2. Open the 'FKEY' resource in the System file.
3. Choose "Create New Resource" from the Resource menu to create a new 'FKEY' resource.
4. Type the following numbers into the new resource exactly as shown:

   ```
   A9FF 4E75
   ```

   A9FF is machine code for the _Debugger trap; 4E75 is machine code for the RTS instruction.

Figure 2-6 shows what the resource looks like after you've entered the instruction.

■ **Figure 2-6** Defining an 'FKEY' resource to invoke MacsBug

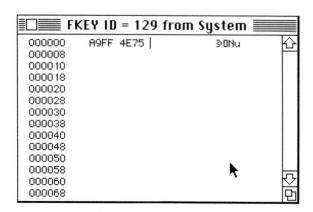

5. Choose Get Resource Info from the Resource menu and set its ID number to a number greater than 4 and less than or equal to 9. Remember to use a number that is not already in use. The numbers 1, 2, 3, and 4 are reserved for system functions.
6. Close and save the System file.
7. To invoke MacsBug, press Command-Shift and the ID number you have assigned the resource. For example, if you've assigned the resource ID 7, press Command-Shift-7 to invoke MacsBug.

This method of invoking MacsBug will only work when the application is calling GetNextEvent or WaitNextEvent regularly, which it might not do if it's hung or frozen.

Invoking MacsBug from your source program

You can call two system routines, Debugger and DebugStr, from your source program to invoke MacsBug.

Calling either of these two routines is also referred to as implementing user breaks.

The Debugger trap simply invokes MacsBug; the DebugStr trap invokes MacsBug and optionally displays a message and executes one or more commands.

If you think that a certain part of your program is causing a crash, you can place the Debugger call in your source code just before the suspect statement. MacsBug will be invoked right before the code in question executes. For example, if your source code contains the lines

```
Begin
        thisnumber := $666;
        Debugger;
        newnumber := thisnumber
End
```

MacsBug is invoked after the instructions for the first assignment statement are executed.

The DebugStr trap pushes a pointer to a Pascal string onto the stack and then invokes MacsBug. If the string contains text, it is displayed by MacsBug as part of its break message. If the first character in the string is a semicolon (;), MacsBug assumes that the string contains MacsBug commands and executes them.

You can include multiple MacsBug commands, separated by semicolons, in the DebugStr call. MacsBug then executes all the commands when it encounters the call. The DebugStr call can also contain text followed by a semicolon and one or more commands, for example,

`DebugStr ('Displaying the heap and application name; HD; DM 910');`

This line in your source code calls MacsBug and passes the string. MacsBug displays the message "Displaying the heap and application name," then does a heap dump and displays memory at location 910. You can embed carriage returns in text that you want to print.

For information on how you can use DebugStr to display variable values when MacsBug is invoked, see "Setting Breakpoints" in Chapter 7.

Inactivating user breaks

If you wish to temporarily inactivate breaks set with Debugger and DebugStr, you can use the MacsBug DX (Debugger Exchange) command. This command turns user breaks on or off. When DX is OFF, MacsBug ignores Debugger and DebugStr calls. You can enter DX again to enable user breaks. Since the FKEY invokes MacsBug by calling the Debugger trap, disabling breaks with the DX command will also disable the FKEY.

Using DebugStr from an assembly-language source program

You can call both the Debugger trap and the DebugStr trap from an assembly-language source program. The Debugger trap (_Debugger) is predefined in the file ToolTraps.a. To use the DebugStr trap (_DebugStr), you need to define it yourself:

```
_DebugStr  OPWORD  $ABFF
```

Before calling the trap, you will also need to include the following instruction:

```
PEA     # ' message '
```

to push the address of the message string on the stack.

Invoking MacsBug under A/UX

To invoke MacsBug under A/UX, you must press the Control-Command-I keys simultaneously. This will bring up the MacsBug display, and you can start working with MacsBug.

The only limitation you will encounter in working with MacsBug under A/UX is that you will not be able to use the LOG command to log output to an ImageWriter®. However, you can still log to a file.

▲ **Warning** Do not press the programmer's switch to invoke MacsBug under A/UX. The programmer's switch is used to break into the A/UX kernel debugger; it will not get you into MacsBug. ▲

Getting out of MacsBug

How you get out of MacsBug largely depends on how you got there in the first place and on what you want to do next. Table 2-1 describes the commands you can use to leave MacsBug.

■ **Table 2-1** Commands used to get out of MacsBug

Command	Action
G	Resumes program execution.
GT	Resumes execution until the program counter reaches the specified address.
EA	Restarts the application from which MacsBug was invoked.
ES	Returns you to the current shell, usually the Finder.
RS	Unmounts all mounted volumes and restarts the Macintosh.
RB	Restarts the system. It unmounts the startup volume before restarting.

If you invoked MacsBug yourself, you can use the G, GT, EA, or ES command, depending on what you want to do next.

If you dropped into MacsBug as a result of a system error, the system might have been damaged. Try to exit using the ES command, then select Restart from the Special menu. If ES fails, use the RB command.

Saving MacsBug output

If you want a permanent record of your MacsBug session, you can use the LOG command to write MacsBug output to a file or to an ImageWriter®. Of course, you will still see the output on the screen.

The syntax of the LOG command is

LOG [*pathname* | Printer]

You can specify a full or partial pathname as a filename. The Printer option specifies that you want the output to be sent to an ImageWriter. The LOG command does not work with the LaserWriter® or AppleTalk® ImageWriter; however, you can send output to a file and then print the file on a LaserWriter.

Working with the Debugger Prefs file

This section describes the Debugger Prefs file included on the MacsBug 6.2 release disk. It assumes that you are using version 2.1 (or later) of ResEdit.

When you open the Debugger Prefs file, ResEdit 2.1 displays a list of resources similar to that shown in Figure 2-7. Note that the display includes information about the number of resources of a certain type (count) as well as the total size of the resources of that type.

Note that *all* MacsBug resources, except for the resource used to provide help information, have been placed in the Debugger Prefs file.

- **Figure 2-7** Debugger Prefs file

Type	Count	Size
c++	1	4988
dcmd	5	15492
mxbc	1	12
mxbi	1	6
mxbm	6	10615
mxwt	3	8054
TMPL	4	401
vers	1	22

Table 2-2 describes the contents of the Debugger Prefs file.

- **Table 2-2** Resources in the Debugger Prefs file

Resource	Contents
mxbi	Specifies the size of the history buffer, the number of traps recorded by MacsBug, and the number of lines displayed in the PC region of the display. See the section "The MacsBug Display" in this chapter for information on how to change the default settings.

(continued)

■ **Table 2-2** Resources in the Debugger Prefs file (continued)

Resource	Contents
mxbc	Specifies color display preferences.
mxbm	Defines the macros you can use to reference low-memory global variables and macros that define useful command lines. See "Using Macros" in Chapter 8 for additional information.
mxwt	Defines the templates you use to obtain a more readable memory display. See "Using Templates to Display Memory" in Chapter 4 for additional information.
dcmd	Defines the dcmds you can use in addition to MacsBug commands. See "Using dcmds" in Chapter 8 for additional information.
C++	Unmangles C++ compiled files so that MacsBug can understand them.

If you *must* save space in memory, you can do so by deleting, moving, or altering resources from the Debugger Prefs file. You should not remove the 'TMPL' resource because this is the resource that ResEdit uses to display the other MacsBug resources.

The effects of moving or altering the resources are described in Table 2-3.

■ **Table 2-3** Effects of removing resources from Debugger Prefs file

Size (K)	Resource	Effect
5	C++	Needed only by C++ programmers for unmangling CFront-generated code.
–	mxbi	MacsBug uses default values. If you reduce the size of the history buffer, you gain some memory but can save less information.
–	mxbc	Uses default black-and-white display.
8	mxbm	If you remove resources 101 and 102, you will no longer be able to reference low-memory global variables by name. Examine the contents of the other mxbm resources before you remove or delete them.
8	mxwt	You will lose the use of templates to make sense of memory display.
1.6	dcmd	You will no longer be able to use these commands. You can remove dcmds individually.

Exercise: Getting started with MacsBug

Follow the instructions at the beginning of this chapter to install MacsBug. For the purposes of this exercise, you need to be working in a single-application environment, which means you must be using a version of system software earlier than version 7.0, and you must have Finder selected in the Set Startup dialog box before you start or restart your Macintosh.

Open the A-Trap Demo application from your MacsBug distribution disk. Choose User Break from the Debug menu. The User Break item contains a call to the Debugger trap, which invokes MacsBug.

Take a few minutes to look over the MacsBug display. Go back to "The MacsBug Display" earlier in this chapter and read over the information provided there while you are actually looking at the display. See if you can answer the following questions by looking at the display:

1. What is the name of the current application?
2. Is the Memory Manager in 24-bit mode or 32-bit mode?
3. Is the current application running under virtual memory?
4. What is the value stored in register A7? Look at the top of the status area; notice that the value for SP (the stack pointer) is identical to the value stored in register A7.
5. What is the next instruction to be executed?
6. What caused MacsBug to be invoked? Look at the output region of the MacsBug display. MacsBug displays a message describing how it was invoked. In this case, it displays the message

```
User break at 00192A4A UserBrk+0008
```

To see the application screen again, press the Esc key. To display the MacsBug display, press any character key.

The simplest way to leave MacsBug is to use the G (Go) command; this resumes program execution exactly where you left off. Type G and press the Return key.

Remember that when MacsBug is invoked because of an unexpected error condition, it might not be possible to resume program execution. See "Getting Out of MacsBug" earlier in this chapter for additional information.

Getting information about MacsBug

Choose User Break from the Debug menu to invoke MacsBug again. Type `help` and then press Return. MacsBug displays the following information in the output region:

```
Return shows sections sequentially.  "HELP name" shows that section.
 Editing
 Selecting procedure names
 Expressions
 Values
 Operators
 Flow control
 Breakpoints
 A-Traps
 Disassembly
 Heaps
 Symbols
 Stack
 Memory
 Registers
 Macros
 Miscellaneous
 dcmds
```

MacsBug lists all the topics for which you can obtain help. To display information for any one of these topics, type `help` and the name of the topic, then press Return.

Try this now. Type `help editing` and press Return. MacsBug displays information about entering and editing commands.

```
Editing
 Type a command and then press Return or Enter to execute it. Typing
 return without entering a command repeats the last command. Multiple
 commands can be executed by separating them with ';'.

   Editing commands
     Command-V            Restore previous command lines for editing.
     Command-B            Command-V the other way.
     Option-Left Arrow    Move cursor left one word.
     Option-Right Arrow   Move cursor right one word.
     Option-Delete        Delete the word to the left of the cursor.
     Command-Left Arrow   Move cursor to begin of line.
     Command-Right Arrow  Move cursor to end of line.
     Command-Delete       Delete the line to the left of the cursor.
```

Chapter 2   Getting Started

Press Command-V. As mentioned earlier in this chapter, MacsBug maintains an internal command-line buffer in which it stores the commands you have already executed. Pressing Command-V moves backward through the buffer, copying the previous command to the command line. The command you entered previous to `help editing` was `help`. This command should now be copied to the command line.

Now press Command-B. This command copies the command you entered after entering `help`. The command `help editing` is now displayed on the command line. Of course, if you're entering commands like Help, it's just as easy to retype them. But in working with MacsBug, you'll often be entering commands that use complex expressions and addresses, which you'll not want to bother to enter again. Using Command-V and Command-B moves you backward and forward through the command-line buffer, and can save you time and eliminate the possibility of error in retyping addresses.

Press Command-Delete to delete the line. The command line should now be blank. Type `DV` and press Return. MacsBug displays displays information about the version of MacsBug you are currently running:

```
MacsBug version 6.2
Copyright Apple Computer, Inc. 1981-1991
  CODE  Leo Baschy, Michael Tibbott, scott douglass
  TEST  Leo Baschy, Keith Nemitz
  BOOK  Joanna Bujes, Bob Anders
  PMGR  Tom Chavez
```

Using the command line to perform calculations

In addition to using the command line to enter commands, you can also use it to perform base conversions and arithmetic calculations.

Type `15` and then press Return. MacsBug displays the following information:

```
15 = $00000015    #21    #21    '····'
```

For any value you type, MacsBug displays its hexadecimal value, unsigned decimal value, signed decimal value, and ASCII value. MacsBug assumes that every number you type is in hexadecimal. To tell MacsBug you are specifying a decimal number, you must prefix the number with the # sign. Type `#15` and press Return; MacsBug displays the following:

```
#15 = $0000000F    #15    #15    '····'
```

Now type `#-15`; MacsBug displays the following:

```
#-15 = $FFFFFFF1    #15     #-15      '••••'
```

Compare the hexadecimal numbers MacsBug displays for the positive and for the negative numbers. They are different, although both appear to be positive. Your compiler uses a special scheme for the representation of negative numbers. For more information, see "The Representation of Negative Numbers" in Chapter 3.

You can also use the command line to perform arithmetic calculations. Type

```
#20 + 40 * 2
```

and then press Return. MacsBug displays the following in its usual hexadecimal, decimal, unsigned decimal, and ASCII formats:

```
#20 + 40 * 2 = $000000A8    #168    #168     '••••'
```

Displaying memory

This section demonstrates some of the commands you use to display memory. For information on how to display memory using templates and how to create your own templates to display memory, see "Using Templates to Display Memory" in Chapter 4.

You can display a selected portion of memory in hexadecimal and ASCII format using the DM (Display Memory) command. Type `DM 910` and press Return. MacsBug displays the following:

```
Displaying memory from 910
 00000910   0646 696E 6465 7220  2020 2020 2020 2020   •Finder
```

The first column displays the address of the first byte of memory displayed. To the right of this address MacsBug displays the first byte of memory, 06 in this case, and then 15 more bytes. The last column of the display shows the 16 bytes of memory in ASCII format. Address 910 specifies a memory location where the current application name is stored. If you look at the ASCII portion of the display, you'll see the name of the current application, Finder.

Now type `DM SysZone` and press Return. MacsBug shows you something like this:

```
Displaying memory from 02A6
 000002A6   0000 1E00 0025 813C  4080 0000 0000 1E00   •••••%•<@•••••••
```

SysZone is a low-memory global variable that contains the address of (points to) the beginning of the system heap. This address (pointer) is always stored at location `02A6`, but you can specify this location using the name SysZone because MacsBug contains a macro resource that defines the string SysZone as `02A6`. If the macro were not installed, you would have to specify the address.

SysZone is a **pointer;** that is, it refers to an address where another address is stored. Since addresses are always 4 bytes long, you need to look at the first 4 bytes displayed to determine the address where the system zone begins. In the example shown, that address is 0000 1E00. This address might be different on your Macintosh, but the address of the low-memory global variable where the address is stored is the same on all Macintosh computers.

Now type `DM ApplZone` and press Return. ApplZone is also a low-memory global variable; it points to the starting address for the application zone. ApplZone is always found at the same address, 02AA:

```
Displaying memory from 02AA

000002AA   0002 D528 4080 0000   0000 1E00 0000 A5F4   ...(@..........
```

According to MacsBug, the application zone starts at 0002 D528 on the Macintosh used for this example.

In a single-application environment, the application heap comes immediately after the system heap, so the beginning of the application heap is also the end of the system heap. To find the size of the system heap, subtract the starting address of SysZone from the starting address of ApplZone. Type

```
@ApplZone - @SysZone
```

and press Return. MacsBug shows something like this:

```
@02AA - @02A6 = $0002B728    #177960    #177960    '...('
```

The system heap is 2B728 bytes long on the Macintosh used for this example. Notice the indirection operators used with the low-memory global variable's names. These (@) operators tell MacsBug to subtract the address stored at location 02A6 from the address stored at location 02AA. Without the indirection operators, MacsBug would subtract the address 02A6 from the address 02AA.

Figure 2-8 shows a standard Macintosh memory map. As you can see, memory in the Macintosh is divided into separate areas. The starting (and sometimes the ending) addresses for each area are stored in the low-memory global variables shown to the right of the memory map. Try using the DM command to determine the address of each area of memory. Then use the command line to calculate the size of each area.

Creating a memory map can be a great help during debugging. For example, by noting the range of addresses that refer to your application's heap, you can determine whether your variable's addresses make sense.

■ **Figure 2-8** Sample memory map

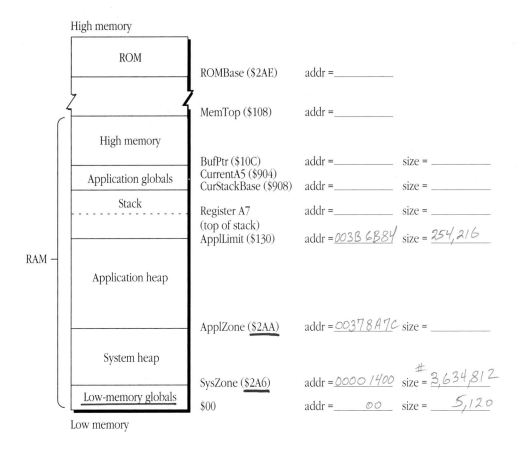

Note that MemTop is only valid in a single-application environment.

See Chapter 4, "Macintosh Memory Organization," for information about how memory is organized on the Macintosh and how to use MacsBug commands to examine memory.

Where is an address?

You can find the name and location of an address by using the WH (Where) command. Type `WH PC`. MacsBug shows you the following information:

```
Address 0002E004 is in the Application heap at USERBRK+0006
It is 000004E8 bytes into this heap block:
     Start      Length       Tag  Mstr Ptr  Lock Prg  Type   ID    File       Name
   • 0002DB1C  00001C52+02    R   0002D634    L   P   CODE  0002   011C
```

Chapter 2   Getting Started   33

If the address is in a heap, MacsBug displays the name of the heap and heap block. In this case, the address is in the application heap. If the address is in a named routine, MacsBug displays the address as an offset from the start of the routine. If MacsBug does not know the procedure name, but the address is in a known resource, MacsBug displays the type of the resource, the number of the resource, the file in which the resource is stored, the name of the resource, and the offset within the resource where the instruction is found; for example:

```
'CODE 0007 0294 Init'+0A3C
```

Now execute the G command to return to the A-Trap Demo application and choose Quit from the File menu to quit the application.

Further explorations

You should now feel more comfortable working with MacsBug. As you read through the chapters that follow, try to duplicate the examples if possible and work through the hands-on exercises. The first step in learning to use MacsBug is to become familiar with it. If you have a very simple program that you've written, use MacsBug to poke around in it; you'll learn more about using MacsBug if you can simplify the object you're looking at and eliminate the fear that you will inadvertently destroy a valuable piece of code.

Chapter 3 **An Assembly-Language Primer**

This chapter covers the fundamentals of assembly language. Its aim is not to teach you how to program in assembly language, but to help you to recognize a program's control structures, system calls (or A-traps), and variables when you use MacsBug to examine your compiled code.

The chapter starts by describing the differences between source code, compiled or assembled code, and disassembled code. It then provides an overview of assembly-language syntax, addressing modes, and instructions. Once you can interpret assembly-language instructions, you can learn to recognize how your program's control structures, routines, A-trap calls, and local and global variables are represented in disassembled code. The chapter concludes with an overview of MacsBug's disassembly commands.

If you are already familiar with assembly language, you do not need to read all of this chapter. If you have not used MacsBug before, you should read through the sections "InterSegment Calls and the Jump Table" and "MacsBug's Disassembly Commands."

Compilers and assemblers

Microprocessors can only interpret **machine language**—that is, the hexadecimal numbers that are stored in memory for direct execution by the microprocessor. When you write a program, you usually write it in a high-level language, such as Pascal or C, and use a program called a **compiler** to translate your source code into machine language. Alternatively, you can write a program in assembly language and use a program called an **assembler** to translate it into machine language.

Although compilers and assemblers both translate source code into object code, the kinds of translation they perform are very different, as the remainder of this section explains.

Every assembly-language instruction corresponds to one instruction in machine language—that is, to the equivalent hexadecimal code executed by the microprocessor. For example, the assembly-language instruction

```
MOVE.L A3,-(A7)
```

means "push the contents of register A3 onto the stack." Once you learn to read assembly language, instructions like this will be relatively easy for you to understand. But the equivalent machine language for this instruction—the code actually executed by the microprocessor—looks like this:

```
2F0B
```

Terms like MOVE and ADD in assembly language represent types of machine operations and are called mnemonics, because they are easier to remember than the equivalent machine language. Terms like A3 and –A7 are called operands. Operands use addressing modes that tell the procesor what to operate on. The assembler translates the mnemonic representation of the instruction into machine code. Another program, called a **disassembler,** reverses the process by converting machine language into a stream of lines; each line contains a mnemonic and, usually, two operands. Since the computer can easily convert between the two, most low-level programmers prefer to work with assembly language. The important thing to note is that there is is a direct, one-to-one correspondence between each assembly-language instruction and each instruction in machine language.

When a compiler translates a Pascal or C program into machine language, there is no direct correspondence between the source-level statements and machine instructions. In fact, the compiler has to generate many machine instructions in order to implement a single Pascal or C statement. One way to describe the difference between what assemblers do and what compilers do is to say that an assembler translates in the way that one would translate a number expressed in words into its numeric equivalent; for example, the numeric translation of one hundred twenty-three is 123. What the compiler does, in contrast, is more like translating an English sentence into German.

Clearly, in the former case, there is only one way to do it (assuming base ten); in the latter case, one could come up with many equivalents. The main thing to remember is that a high-level source statement generates more than one machine instruction.

As Figure 3-1 shows, if you were to use three different compilers to compile your source code, you would obtain three slightly different machine-language translations. The differences between compiler translations are not usually significant. The kinds of disassembled code you'll learn to interpret in this chapter are unlikely to be affected by these differences. The important thing to understand is that when you look at a program using MacsBug, you see the disassembled version of the code generated by the compiler, not the original Pascal or C in which the program was written. There are cases in which you might need to know the peculiarities of your compiler's translations, but these are rare. Realizing that these differences do exist, however, allows you to appreciate how complex the compiler translation is and how much greater the distance between high-level languages and machine language is than the distance between assembly language and machine language.

- **Figure 3-1** Compilers and assemblers

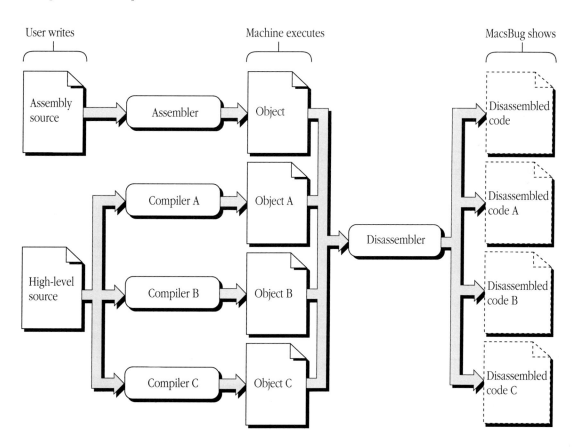

Chapter 3   An Assembly-Language Primer   37

Reading assembly-language instructions

As described in Chapter 4, "Macintosh Memory Organization," the 68000 family of microprocessors can address a large address space that includes RAM and ROM as well as other more specialized areas of memory. Assembly-language instructions tell the processor how to modify parts of memory or change the flow of instruction execution. Each instruction performs a single small task, such as moving data from one place to another, or adding two values. One statement in a higher-level language like Pascal or C compiles into several different assembly-language instructions.

In addition to addressable memory space, the microprocessor itself contains some specialized memory that it can manipulate—a total of 70 bytes in its own registers. These consist of the address registers A0 to A7, the data registers D0 to D7, the status register (SR), and the program counter (PC). Each register is 4 bytes long and holds a single value at a time (with the exception of the status register, which is 2 bytes long).

The sections that follow describe the syntax of assembly-language instructions and how memory locations and register names are used in instructions to refer to values. There are about 60 basic operations in 68000 assembly language, most of which use several of the 68000's 12 addressing modes, providing a wide variety of instructions. Fortunately, you only need to learn a few common operations and addressing modes to use MacsBug.

Instruction syntax

Assembly-language instructions are roughly comparable to high-level language statements. Instructions are composed of an operator, which performs some action on one or more operands. Sometimes the operand to be used is implied in the operator, in which case the instruction takes no operands. Unlike high-level language statements, each of which requires its own syntax diagram, all assembly-language instructions can be generally represented by one diagram, as shown in Figure 3-2.

- **Figure 3-2** Syntax of an assembly-language instruction

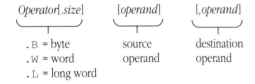

The operator indicates to the processor the simple task to be done, such as adding two operands together, or moving the value of one operand into the memory location specified by another operand. The processor determines the values of the operands by the addressing modes used to specify the operand. The value of an operand refers to an address or the contents of an address in RAM or ROM; it can also refer to the contents of a register.

For example, the instruction

```
MOVE $500(A5),$600(A5)
```

uses the same addressing mode for both the source and destination operands: address register indirect with displacement. To find the value of the source operand, the address in register A5 is added to the displacement, $500. This forms the **effective address,** which is where to find the operand. The effective address of the source operand is the displacement added to the contents of register A5. If A5 contains $10000, then the effective address is $10000 + $500 = $10500. By the same reasoning, the destination operand would be found at $10600. You will frequently see the address register indirect with displacement addressing mode because of the architecture of the Macintosh Operating System.

The operator often includes a suffix that specifies the size of the source operand—that is, how many bytes are being affected by the operator. Operand sizes can be specified as .B, for byte (8 bits); .W, for word (16 bits); or .L, for long word (32 bits). For example, if register A5 contains $10000, the instruction

```
MOVE.B $500(A5),$600(A5)
```

moves 1 byte from memory location $10500 to memory location $10600.
The instruction

```
MOVE.W $500(A5),$600(A5)
```

moves 1 word (2 bytes); that is, it moves the bytes at locations $10500 and $10501 to locations $10600 and $10601, respectively. And the instruction

```
MOVE.L $500(A5),$600(A5)
```

moves a long word, or 4 bytes, from $10500 to four new consecutive locations beginning at $10600. Instructions that do not have a suffix default to the size of a word.

The syntax diagram shown in Figure 3-2 presents a simplified view of the format of an instruction. The representation of operands in actual assembly-language instructions reflects the various ways that values can be manipulated by an operator, as explained in the next section, "Addressing Modes."

Addressing modes

Assembly-language instructions tell the microprocessor how to modify parts of memory. Instructions calculate the specific addresses or values represented by operands using different methods, or **addressing modes.** This section describes the addressing modes you are likely to see when you are reading your disassembled code. If you happen to run across an operand that uses a format different from those described in this section, please consult the Motorola manual for your microprocessor for additional information.

Figure 3-2 shows the syntax of an assembly-language instruction. In that figure, the operands that make up the instruction are shown simply as placeholders:

[*operand*] [,*operand*]

In fact, the representation of operands requires more detailed syntax diagrams that are different for every addressing mode. Table 3-1 summarizes the syntax of operands for different addressing modes.

- The symbols n and d represent any hexadecimal number; d can be negative.
- The symbol An represents an address register; Dn represents a data register.
- The symbol Xn represents either a data or an address register.

- **Table 3-1** Addressing modes

Addressing mode name	Syntax	Meaning
Absolute	$n	The value stored at address $n. If the address can be represented in 2 bytes or less, the addressing mode is absolute word; otherwise it is absolute long.
Data register direct	Dn	The value stored in data register Dn.
Address register direct	An	The value stored in address register An.
Address register indirect	(An)	The value stored at the address in address register An.
Address register indirect with postincrement	(An)+	The value stored at the address in address register n. After use, the value in register n is incremented by the size of the operator suffix.

(continued)

40   MacsBug Reference and Debugging Guide

■ **Table 3-1** Addressing modes (continued)

Addressing mode name	Syntax	Meaning
Address register indirect with predecrement	–(An)	Register An is decremented by the size of the operator suffix. The value at the address now stored in register An is used.
Address register indirect with displacement	d(An)	The value is at the address that results when adding the contents of register An to the 16-bit displacement d.
Indexed address register indirect with displacement	d(An, Xn)	The value is at the address that is the result of the contents of address register An added to the 8-bit displacement d, then added to the index register Xn.
PC-relative with displacement	d(PC)	The value is at the address that is the sum of the address stored in the program counter and the 16-bit displacement d.
PC-relative with index and displacement	d(PC,Xn)	The value is at the address that is the sum of the address stored in the program counter, the 8-bit displacement d, and the index register Xn.
Immediate	#n	The value n.

The following sections describe the addressing modes listed in Table 3-1 in greater detail. You should read these sections to familiarize yourself with the way these addressing modes are used in sample MOVE instructions. You may find Table 3-1 useful when you're reading through disassembled code. You can also use it to see patterns in the addressing modes. For instance, five different addressing modes use "address register indirect" as all or part of the method for finding the operand. Once you understand address register indirect, you have an excellent start in understanding the rest of the addressing modes.

Absolute addressing

The absolute addressing mode is one of the simplest addressing modes. Here's an example:

```
MOVE.L $21F0,$21E4
```

This instruction copies the long word in memory location $21F0 into memory location $21E4. The number previously located in memory location $21E4 is overwritten. Note that this instruction doesn't change the number at memory location $21F0; it merely copies that number into location $21E4, as shown in Figure 3-3.

■ **Figure 3-3** Absolute addressing

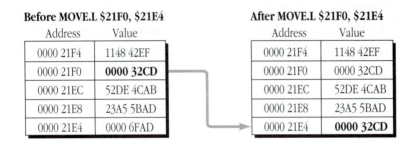

In this case, both operands use absolute addressing. It is also possible to have one of the operands use a different addressing mode. For example, the instruction

```
MOVE.L $21F0,D1
```

uses the absolute addressing mode and the data direct addressing mode, described next. The instruction

```
MOVE.L D1,$21F0
```

uses the data direct addressing mode and then the absolute addressing mode.

The ~~direct~~ *ABSOLUTE* addressing mode is most often used to access low-memory global variables, which are always stored at fixed addresses. Other than that it is not seen very often because of the architecture of the Macintosh Operating System.

Data and address register direct addressing

The data register direct or address register direct addressing mode has, as its operand, the value that is in the data or address register, respectively. The differences between these two modes are found in mnemonics (MOVEA for address registers, MOVE for data registers), the type of register (data or address register), the condition codes (bits in the status register) that are set, and the instructions for which the mode is valid.

Here's an example:

```
MOVE.L D0,A0
```

This instruction copies the long word in register D0 into register A0.

(In MacsBug, you would see Movea.l D0,A0. If the operands were reversed, however, the mnemonic would only be Move.l A0,D0 because the destination operand uses the data ~~address~~ *REGISTER* direct mode.)

◆ *Note:* Assemblers frequently accept the same mnemonic for the address register direct mode as for the data register direct. The Motorola manual, however, uses the data register direct mode mnemonic suffixed with an "a" for the same instruction when the address register direct is used for the destination operand; MacsBug follows this convention.

Address register indirect addressing

The address register indirect addressing mode is distinguished by a set of parentheses enclosing an address register. Thus the instruction

```
MOVE.L (A2),(A4)
```

takes the long word stored at the address in A2 and moves it to the address stored in register A4.

In Figure 3-4, register A2 contains the address 0000 21F4, so the microprocessor goes to that location to find the value, and moves it to the location contained in register A4, 0000 21E8.

■ **Figure 3-4** Indirect addressing

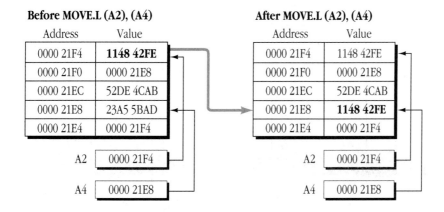

This MOVE.L instruction might be generated from the following C code:

```
main () {
pLocal1       *longint;
pLocal2       *longint;
*pLocal1 = *pLocal2
}
```

Chapter 3   An Assembly-Language Primer   **43**

The address register indirect addressing mode is the base of the next four addressing modes: address register indirect with predecrement, address register indirect with postincrement, address register indirect with displacement, and indexed indirect with displacement.

Address register indirect with predecrement addressing, and address register indirect with postincrement addressing

You will frequently see these two addressing modes (address register indirect with predecrement, and address register indirect with postincrement) used just before a routine call, and at the beginning and end of a routine. When a routine is called, the calling routine passes parameters onto a dynamic data structure known as the stack. Often, at the beginning of a routine, values in some registers are saved on the stack, and at the end of the routine, the register values are returned to their respective registers. The first two of these operations use the predecrement form; the last uses the postincrement form. In addition, the postincrement form is also used to perform repetitive operations on arrays with elements that are either 1, 2, or 4 bytes.

Like the address register indirect addressing mode, these two addressing modes use the value in the address register to find the operand. In addition, the value in the address register is adjusted. If the predecrement form is used, the value is decremented first, and the resulting value is used to find the operand. If the postincrement form is used, the value is first used to find the operand, then incremented. The amount by which the value in the address register is increased or decreased is either 1, 2, or 4, depending upon whether the size of the instruction is byte, word, or long, respectively.

The architecture of the 68000 family of microprocessors has register A7 permanently assigned as the stack pointer, sometimes called the SP. Stacks grow downward in memory, from numerically higher addresses to lower addresses. The stack pointer points to the last item that was stored, or "pushed," onto the stack. When a piece of data is pushed onto the stack, the address in A7 is decremented and the source operand is moved to the resulting address (the value now stored in A7); for instance,

```
MOVE.L #$2,-(A7)
```

pushes the number 2 onto the stack, as shown in Figure 3-5.

- **Figure 3-5** Predecrement register indirect addressing

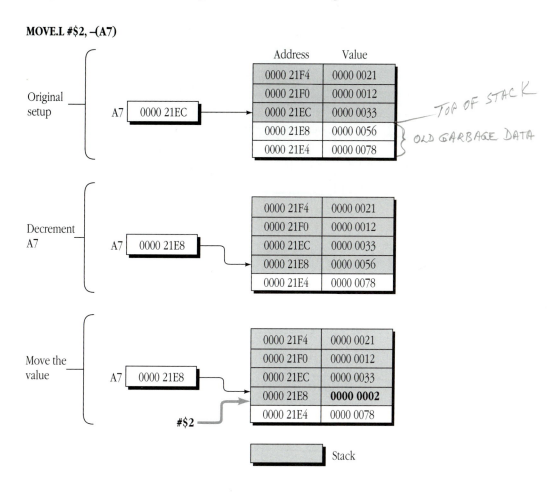

The register indirect with postincrement addressing (shown in Figure 3-6) is used to retrieve, or "pop" a value off the stack, like this:

MOVE.L (A7)+,D0

Before this instruction is executed, register A7 points to the last value pushed onto the stack. The instruction causes the value to be moved into the address stored in register D0 and then shrinks the stack by adding 4 (the size of the instruction) to the value in A7. (If you push 1 byte onto the stack, the stack pointer will be decremented by 2 because the value in the stack pointer must be even.)

For additional information, see the section "Life on the Stack" in Chapter 4.

■ **Figure 3-6** Postincrement register indirect addressing

MOVE.L (A7)+, $21E0

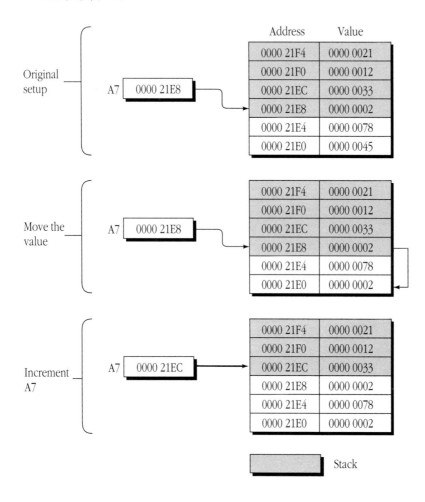

Address register indirect with displacement addressing

When you see an address register in parentheses with a number prefix, you are looking at the address register indirect with displacement addressing mode. The prefix is a 16-bit displacement, and, when used, will be sign-extended. To determine where the operand is, calculate the effective address, that is, the address that results when you take the value in the address register and add it to the sign-extended displacement. For example, the instruction

```
MOVE.L 4(A0),8(A0)
```

adds $4 to the address stored in register A0, uses the result as the address of the value to move, and moves that value to the address found by adding $8 to the address stored in register A0, as shown in Figure 3-7.

- **Figure 3-7** Address register indirect addressing with displacement

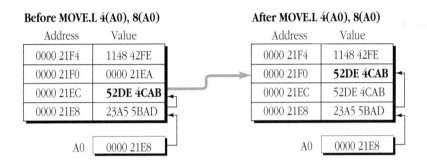

This addressing mode is most commonly used to reference your application's global variables, which are stored at addresses that are at a fixed distance from the address stored in register A5, and to reference your routines' parameters, local variables, return result, and return address, which are stored at addresses that are at a fixed distance from the address stored in register A6. For additional information, see the sections "Allocating Space for Global Variables" and "Stack Frames" in Chapter 4.

Indexed indirect addressing with displacement

The indexed indirect with displacement addressing mode looks very similar to the indirect with displacement addressing mode, except that the operand is composed of two addresses separated by a comma. When the microprocessor encounters the instruction

```
MOVE.L $-4(A0,D0.W),$4(A0,D0.W)
```

it takes the address in register A0, adds the low word in register D0, adds $-4 to that, and uses the result as the address of the value to move. It moves that value to the address found by adding register A0 plus the low word in register D0 plus $4, as shown in Figure 3-8.

This addressing mode is not often used. It comes in handy when the program has a table of addresses so that given

displacement (A*n* 1, X*n* 2)

the microprocessor can compute the effective address by using A*n* 1 + *displacement* to compute the starting address of the table and X*n* 2 as an index into the table.

■ **Figure 3-8** Indexed indirect addressing with displacement

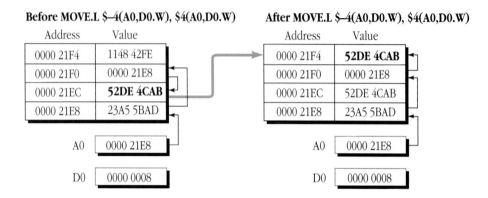

Program counter (PC) relative addressing modes

PC-relative addressing modes, which include PC-relative with displacement and PC-relative with index and displacement, are used to compute addresses relative to the address currently stored in the program counter. This mode of addressing is especially useful on the Macintosh because code resides in resources that are loaded as relocatable blocks. Thus if the code has to use a JSR instruction to jump to a location within the same segment, it must express the address of that location relative to the address stored in the program counter. PC-relative with displacement addressing makes this possible.

For example, the instruction

```
JSR $104(PC)
```

tells the microprocessor to execute the instruction stored 104 bytes from the address stored in the program counter.

The PC-relative with index and displacement addressing mode is used to switch control when the address to jump to must be calculated with reference to a table, as would be the case with Pascal CASE or C switch statements. Given the instruction

```
JSR $104(PC,A1.W)
```

the microprocessor computes the address to jump to by adding 104 to the address stored in the program counter and then adding the low word stored in register A1 (the index value) to the result.

The program counter is represented either by the initials PC or by an asterisk in disassembled code.

These two PC-relative addressing modes are very similar to the address register indirect with displacement and the indexed address register indirect with displacement addressing modes. The only difference is that the value in the program counter is used instead of the value in an address register.

Immediate addressing

The immediate addressing mode indicates a constant value rather than the contents of a memory location. A "#" sign before the first operand distinguishes this mode from the others. The instruction

```
MOVE.L #$2,$21E4
```

moves the number $2 (not the value at memory address $2) into memory location $21E4, as shown in Figure 3-9.

- **Figure 3-9** Immediate addressing

Before MOVE.L #$2, $21E4

Address	Value
0000 21F4	1148 42FE
0000 21F0	0000 32CD
0000 21EC	52DE 4CAB
0000 21E8	23A5 5BAD
0000 21E4	**0000 6FAD**

After MOVE.L #$2, $21E4

Address	Value
0000 21F4	1148 42FE
0000 21F0	0000 32CD
0000 21EC	52DE 4CAB
0000 21E8	23A5 5BAD
0000 21E4	**0000 0002**

Similarly, the instruction

```
MOVE.L #$2,A0
```

moves the number $2 into register A0.

Implied addressing

The effective mode used by some instructions is implied by the instruction itself. For example, the RTS (Return From Subroutine) instruction takes no operands; it takes the address stored in A7 (top of the stack), adds 4 bytes to that value, and then moves the result into the program counter. Program execution resumes at that address. To figure out the values used by instructions that use one operand or no operands, look up the description of the instruction in the Motorola manual for your microprocessor.

Assembly-language instructions

Now that you are familiar with the syntax of assembly-language instructions and operands, you can begin to look at the instructions you are most likely to encounter in reading your disassembled code. This section presents some of the most common instructions in three categories: integer arithmetic, program control, and stack frame instructions. If you want more detailed information about these instructions or others that are not covered in this section, please consult the Motorola manual for your microprocessor.

Before you begin learning specific instructions, you need to know something about the way negative numbers are represented in disassembled listings. The section that follows, "The Representation of Negative Numbers," provides a summary.

The representation of negative numbers

All numbers displayed by MacsBug are shown in hexadecimal notation unless they are preceded by a pound sign like this: #2110, which indicates a decimal value. It is important to note that many hexadecimal numbers shown by MacsBug appear to be positive; in fact they can be either positive or negative.

The microprocessor uses a mathematical scheme called two's complement arithmetic to represent negative numbers. Using this method, the microprocessor uses the highest bit of the value represented to specify its sign: 1 indicates a negative number; 0 indicates a positive number.

If the value is positive, the lower bits represent the value. If the value is negative, the remaining bit pattern (after the high-order bit) represents the two's complement of the value. The microprocessor must then calculate the two's complement of this pattern, or, as we think of it, the negative number. How the microprocessor does this is not important for debugging purposes. But you do need to remember two points about the microprocessor's handling and representation of negative numbers.

First, since all numbers look positive, you need to know which number is supposed to be negative, so that you can use MacsBug's command-line arithmetic to display its signed decimal value. For example, suppose you're testing register D0 on exit from a trap; this register normally holds the error number, which is negative, so you're definitely interested in what that number is. Second, since it is the highest bit of the number that determines its sign, it is very important to specify the size of the value you want converted. So, if you are testing the value of D0 and you enter

`D0`

MacsBug shows you that value as a hexadecimal number, an unsigned decimal number, and a signed decimal number.

```
D0 = $4080F2A8    #1082192552    #1082192552    '@•••'
```

In this case, MacsBug assumes you want the long word stored in D0. But most operating system errors are defined as integers, which are one word long. If you enter

`D0.W`

MacsBug shows you the value of the low word stored in D0; for example:

```
D0.W = $FFFFF2A8    #4294963880    #-3416    '••••'
```

If you enter

`D0.B`

MacsBug shows you the value of the low byte stored in D0; for example:

```
D0.B = $FFFFFFA8    #4294967208    #-88    '••••'
```

Notice that MacsBug has produced three different signed decimal values for data stored starting at the same memory location. The size of data you're converting matters. In summary:

- MacsBug displays all numbers as positive hexadecimal numbers, unless they are prefixed by a # sign, in which case they are decimal numbers. (The most common exception to this rule is that MacsBug displays negative displacements to an address register as negative numbers.)

- To have MacsBug display the signed decimal value of a hexadecimal number, just type the value you want converted (including its size) on the command line and press Return.

- You must know what the assembly-language instructions are doing and how these correspond to your source code in order to understand which numbers might be negative; you must also know the size of the data you are converting since this affects the result of the conversion.

Integer arithmetic instructions

The compiler produces integer arithmetic instructions whenever your source code statements perform some kind of integer arithmetic. Here are some examples of instructions that perform standard arithmetic operations with hexadecimal numbers:

```
ADD.W D0,D1
```

adds the low word stored in D0 to the low word stored in D1, and stores the result in D1. The high word is unchanged.

The following instructions perform signed and unsigned multiplication, respectively, of the value in D1 by $4:

```
MULS.W #$4,D1
```

```
MULU.W #$4,D1
```

The following instructions perform signed and unsigned division, respectively:

```
DIVS.W #$4,D1
```

```
DIVU.W #$4,D1
```

Table 3-2 provides a summary of integer arithmetic instructions. Remember that the size of the data being manipulated is represented by a size suffix appended to the operator. If no size is specified, a word size is used by default.

- **Table 3-2** Arithmetic integer instructions

Instruction	Action
ADD	Add operands and place result in destination operand.
CLR	Clear operand bits.
CMP	Compare operands and set condition codes.
DIVS	Signed: divide destination by source; place result in destination.
DIVU	Unsigned: divide destination by source; place result in destination.
EXT	Convert smaller size value to larger size value: byte to word, word to long.
MULS	Signed: multiply operands; place result in destination.
MULU	Unsigned: multiply operands; place result in destination.
NEG	Negate operand.
SUB	Subtract source from destination; place result in destination operand.
TST	Compare operand with 0 and set condition codes.

You might want to review the description of multiply and divide instructions in your Motorola manual to gain a better understanding of how the destination operand is used.

Program control instructions

Assembly-language instructions are stored as machine code. To the human eye this consists of a series of random-looking bytes located somewhere in memory. A special register called the program counter (PC) informs the microprocessor which bytes of code to execute and in what order.

The PC always contains the address of the next instruction to execute. After an instruction finishes executing, the PC automatically increments to point to the instruction that follows. Program control statements, which are compiled into program control instructions, allow programmers to direct the flow of a program along many possible paths. The instructions used to change the order of execution manipulate the address stored in the PC so that execution can shift to another location.

Nonconditional branching is implemented by JSR, BSR, JMP, and BRA instructions. For example, the JSR (Jump to Subroutine) instruction

```
JSR xxx
```

calls a subroutine, where *xxx* is the address of the subroutine. Usually this instruction looks like this:

```
JSR MYPROC
```

where MYPROC is the routine you want to call. The assembler replaces MYPROC with the actual address to jump to.

On the Macintosh, JSR instructions usually use some form of address register indirect addressing or PC-relative addressing. Generally, if the destination address is in the same code segment, PC-relative addressing is used. If the destination address is in another code segment, the JSR instruction will use the address register indirect with displacement addressing mode and go through the jump table. See the section "Intersegment Calls and the Jump Table" later in this chapter for additional information.

The BSR (Branch to Subroutine) instruction, for example,

```
BSR xxx
```

also calls a subroutine, but *xxx* is a PC-relative address—that is, *xxx* is added to the address of the current instruction (BSR) to get the address of the subroutine. Whether you use the JSR or BSR instruction to call a subroutine, you use the RTS (Return From Subroutine) instruction to return from the subroutine.

Another instruction that changes the flow of program control is JMP (Jump). For example,

```
JMP xxx
```

jumps to the instruction at address *xxx*. This is not a subroutine call, and it does not allow you to return using an RTS instruction. It resembles a GOTO statement in BASIC. The PC-relative version of the JMP instruction is the BRA (Branch) instruction; this instruction jumps to the instruction at *xxx*, where *xxx* is a PC-relative address.

To implement conditional branching, the compiler uses an instruction that performs a test, usually a CMP (Compare) or TST (Test) instruction, followed by an instruction that branches depending on the results of that test. The microprocessor sets bits in the status register (SR) to reflect the results of the test.

When you execute most instructions, the SR is modified to reflect certain aspects of the action that just took place. The SR contains five flag bits for condition codes, and their state (0 or 1) depends on the result of the last operation that occurred. For example, if the operation produces a 0, a flag called the Z(ero) flag is set to 1; or, if the result is negative, a negative flag is set. When flags are set in the SR, the letters that represent the respective flags are capitalized. (The contents of the status register are displayed on the MacsBug screen, in the middle of the status region.)

The instruction

```
CMP.L D0,D1
```

compares the values in registers D0 and D1. This command sets some flags in the SR, which can be checked by the next instruction to determine whether to branch. The instruction

```
BEQ xxx
```

will branch to *xxx* if D0 and D1 are equal. *xxx* is PC-relative. Conversely, the BNE (Branch if Not Equal) instruction will cause a branch if the values stored in D0 and D1 are not equal.

If you are about to execute a conditional branch instruction, MacsBug will tell you, in the upper-right corner of the PC region, whether you will branch or not. Figure 3-10 shows the PC region of the MacsBug display. The next instruction to be executed is the BNE instruction. Since MacsBug already knows the result of the previous CMP instruction, it can tell you whether the branch will occur.

■ **Figure 3-10** Conditional branching indicator

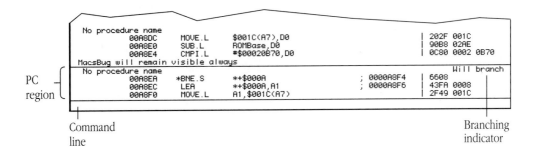

Table 3-3 provides a summary of the branch instructions.

■ **Table 3-3** Branching instructions

Instruction	Action
BCC	Branch if C flag is clear (no carry from previous operation).
BCS	Branch if C flag is set.
BEQ	Branch if Z flag is set; the operands compared by previous instruction are equal.
BGE	Branch if (in previous instruction) destination operand is greater than or equal to source.
BGT	Branch if (in previous instruction) destination operand is greater than source.
BHI	Branch if high (C and Z flags are clear).
BLE	Branch if (in previous instruction) destination operand is less than or equal to source.
BLS	Branch if low or same (C or Z flag set).
BLT	Branch if (in previous instruction) destination operand is less than source.
BMI	Branch if negative (N flag set).
BNE	Branch if operands of previous instruction are not equal (Z flag clear).
BPL	Branch if positive (N flag clear).
BVC	Branch if overflow is clear (V flag clear).
BVS	Branch on overflow (V flag set).

Note that the Z(ero) flag plays a part in determining whether two values are equal because, if they are, the difference between them is 0; if they are not, it is not 0.

Chapter 3   An Assembly-Language Primer

Intersegment calls and the jump table

Code for Macintosh applications is stored in resources of type 'CODE'. A 'CODE' resource is generally limited to 32K. Because applications are usually larger than 32K, they must be split up into multiple code segments, named 'CODE' 0, 'CODE' 1, 'CODE' 2, and so forth. Resource 'CODE' 1 usually contains the main entry point of your compiled program, that is, the first routine run.

When you compile and link a program, the linker places your program's routines into code segments, usually in the order in which they are fed into the linker. The Macintosh uses a table called the **jump table** to track the location of these multiple resources. Resource 'CODE' 0 is always the jump table.

The jump table is stored above the stack, next to the application parameters. Like the application parameters, the jump table is generated and used by the compiler, linker, and operating system without the programmer's direct knowledge.

'CODE' resources, like all other resources, are loaded in relocatable, purgeable heap blocks. These are locked while in use, but unlocked by the UnloadSeg routine that most applications call from their main event loop. This means that a routine in one segment can call a routine in another segment that has been unlocked and that the Memory Manager might have moved or even purged. The jump table keeps track of the location of each 'CODE' resource and the offset of each routine inside each segment.

If one routine needs to call another routine in a different segment, it must go through the jump table to determine the address where the other routine starts. If a routine calls another routine in its own segment, it does not need the jump table. Although 'CODE' resources move in the heap, their contents are constant, so the routines always keep a constant distance apart and can be accessed using a self-relative (PC-relative) branch. The section "Program Counter (PC)-Relative Addressing Modes" earlier in this chapter describes how routines are addressed by an intrasegment call.

Figure 3-11 shows how the jump table and a self-relative branch work. When Procedure A calls Procedure B, Procedure A must go through the jump table, since the procedures are in different segments. But Procedure C can call Procedure B without going through the jump table, since the procedures are in the same segment.

- **Figure 3-11** The jump table and self-relative branching

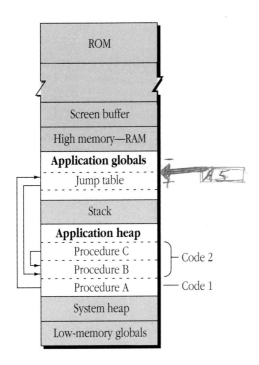

The Segment Loader loads a 'CODE' resource from disk when any routine inside that resource is called. The Segment Loader also locks the resource after it is loaded so that it won't move while it is running. Since the system cannot tell which segments you are actually using, it never unlocks them. The application itself unlocks the segments with the UnloadSeg call. This call makes a specific 'CODE' resource unlocked and purgeable and updates the jump table. You would normally want to include the UnloadSeg call for your application's segments in the main event loop.

The next time a routine in the same segment is called, the jump table checks to see whether the segment is still loaded. If the segment is still in RAM, the jump table locks the segment again. But if the segment has been purged, the jump table loads the segment from disk again.

If you are ever tracing through code and see an instruction like

```
JSR    60(A5)
```

you are looking at a call to a routine in another code segment—that is, a call that will go through the jump table. Remember that A5 points to the application's global variables and the jump table. Negative offsets from A5 reference global variables, while positive offsets (greater than 32) get you into the jump table.

If you step once using the S (Step) command, you will enter the jump table. If the segment is already loaded, the jump table will contain a single instruction, JMP, which will take you into the routine in the correct segment. But if the segment is not loaded, you will see something like this:

```
MOVE.W  #$0001, -(SP)
_LoadSeg
```

You can step through the MOVE instruction, but if you try to step over the LoadSeg trap with the SO command, you will not be successful. The LoadSeg trap does not return in the standard way, so the SO command never realizes the trap is over. The GS macro is designed to step over a LoadSeg trap, so you should use it instead. After executing the GS macro, you will end up at the first instruction of the routine in the code segment that was loaded.

Stack frame instructions

The section "Stack Frames" in Chapter 4 explains how the calling program and the called program work together to set up stack frames. The compiler uses stack frames as a way of referencing everything your routines need to do their work (parameters, local variables, return result, return address) relative to one register, usually register A6. The compiler uses two special instructions, LINK and UNLK, to set up and dismantle stack frames. This section describes these two instructions.

For example, the instruction

```
LINK A6,#$FFFE
```

sets up half of a stack frame. This instruction pushes the current value of register A6 onto the stack, and then sets A6 equal to the stack pointer (A7). It then allocates 2 bytes of space on the stack by adding –2 to A7 ($FFFE is –2 as determined by two's complement arithmetic). The 2 bytes of stack space is all the space the routine needs for its local variables. The LINK instruction could allocate more space, if required by the number and size of the routine's local variables.

When the routine has finished executing, the compiler will have appended one last instruction, the instruction UNLK, to the instructions that make up the routine; for example, the instruction

```
UNLK A6
```

removes everything that LINK put on the stack and restores register A6 to its previous value.

A simple assembly-language program

This section uses a simple program to demonstrate the basic building blocks of assembly language. The program just clears a specified section of memory, setting each byte to 0. The number of bytes it clears is determined by the value stored in register D1; the address at which it starts to clear memory is stored in register A0.

Figure 3-12 shows the assembly-language source code for the program; Figure 3-13 shows the disassembled version as you would see it from MacsBug. As you can see, the instructions are identical in each version, but there are some notable differences in formats.

- **Figure 3-12** Source code for an assembly-language routine

```
      MOVE.L    #$1000,A0      ; A0 is the address that will be cleared
      MOVE.W    #$10,D1        ; D1 is the number of bytes to clear
      MOVE.W    #$0,D0         ; D0 is the loop variable
@1    CLR.L     $0(A0,D0.W)    ; clear 4 bytes at A0+D0
      ADD.W     #$4,D0         ; increment loop variable by 4
      CMP.W     D1,D0          ; is the loop over yet?
      BLT       @1             ; if not, branch back and continue
```

The symbol "@1" is a statement label. It lets the programmer write the BLT (Branch if Less Than) instruction without having to compute how many bytes long the branch is. That is figured out by the assembler. Anything that appears after a semicolon is a comment.

Figure 3-13 shows the disassembled version of the program. Each instruction begins at a specific memory address, shown to the left of the instruction. Notice also that the assembler has resolved the statement label to a specific address and that the comments have been removed. MacsBug has inserted a comment of its own, to tell you the actual address that the branch instruction will go to.

■ **Figure 3-13** Assembly-language program: disassembled code

```
0001AB00        MOVE.L          #$1000, A0
0001AB04        MOVE.W          #$10, D1
0001AB08        MOVE.W          #$0, D0
0001AB0C        CLR.L           $0(A0, D0.W)
0001AB10        ADD.W           #$4, D0
0001AB14        CMP.W           D1, D0
0001AB18        BLT             *-$C                    ;0001AB0C
```

If you already understand how the program works, you can skip this next part. If not, work through the instructions one line at a time and use the charts in Figure 3-14 to record changes in registers and related changes in memory.

■ **Figure 3-14** Registers and memory for sample program

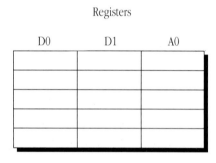

Begin with the first three instructions.

```
MOVE.L #$1000,A0        ; A0 is the address that will be cleared
MOVE.W #$10,D1          ; D1 is the number of bytes to clear
MOVE.W #$0,D0           ; D0 is the loop variable
```

60   MacsBug Reference and Debugging Guide

The first instruction puts the value $1000 into register A0. The next instruction puts $10 in register D1. The third instruction moves $0 into D0. After the first three instructions have been executed, your first row of registers should look like this:

D0	D1	A0
0	10	1000

Now that the registers have been set up, you're at the beginning of the loop. The next instruction,

```
CLR.L $0(A0,D0.W)      ; clear 4 bytes at A0+D0
```

clears memory (sets it to 0) at the address A0+D0+$0. Notice that this instruction uses an indexed indirect addressing with displacement mode. Since it operates on a long word (the operator has an ".L" suffix), it actually clears 4 bytes, starting at A0+D0+$0 and going for 3 more bytes. Compute the value of A0+D0+$0. You should get $1000. In the Memory portion of Figure 3-14, write 0 in the bytes $1000, $1001, $1002, and $1003.

Now you're ready to increment the loop variable. The next instruction,

```
ADD.W #$4,D0           ; increment loop variable by 4
```

adds $4 to register D0. The second row of your registers table now looks like this:

D0	D1	A0
4	10	1000

Next, you need to find out whether the loop is over yet. The next instruction,

```
CMP.W D1,D0            ; is the loop over yet?
```

compares the values in registers D0 and D1 to determine whether the loop is finished. This causes certain flags in your status register to be set; these flags are checked by the next instruction. If D0 is less than D1, the branch instruction executes, taking you back to the clear instruction. If D0 is not less than D1, you simply fall through to the next instruction.

The next instruction,

```
BLT @1                 ; if not, branch back and continue
```

goes back to the clear instruction,

```
CLR.L $0(A0,D0)        ; clear 4 bytes at A0+D0
```

Chapter 3 An Assembly-Language Primer

Once again, you must clear the memory in the 4 bytes starting at address A0+D0+$0. A0+D0+$0 should equal $1004. In the Memory portion of Figure 3-14, write 0 in the bytes $1004, $1005, $1006, and $1007.

Now you must increment the loop variable again using the ADD.W instruction:

```
ADD.W  #$4,D0          ; increment loop variable by 4
```

Write the result in the appropriate place on the Registers chart. Continue through the rest of the program on your own. Remember that $8 + $4 = $C, and $C + $4 = $10.

Comparing assembly-language code to source code

If you are debugging a program that you originally wrote in a high-level language, you need to learn not only how to navigate through the disassembled code using MacsBug commands, but also how to map this code back onto your source code.

This mapping is not necessarily straightforward. As explained at the beginning of this chapter, the compiler uses a great deal of discretion in compiling your code. In addition, disassembled object code looks very different from the equivalent source code: the compiler replaces your symbol names with address or register references, and it must often use many instructions to implement one high-level language statement. Compiler optimization can cloud things further. All these differences make the job of mapping the disassembled code back onto your source code a bit of a puzzle.

Although there is no set formula for matching your source code to the assembly code, here are a few hints.

- Aways have a complete, up-to-date printout of your source code next to you as you debug. This may sound obvious, but people often don't do it, and it makes debugging a lot harder. (If you wrote your original program in assembly language, your comments and variable names will be missing from the disassembled version, so it is still a good idea to keep an up-to-date hard copy of your source code handy.)

- If you are using certain control structures over and over, try compiling a dummy structure, just to see what its bare bones look like in assembly language. Having these disassembled structure "templates" around can help you locate these same structures in your real programs.

- Make sure you start debugging at a known place in your program. The easiest way to do this is to put a Debugger call in your program right before the statements you want to debug. The Debugger call drops you into MacsBug immediately after executing the Debugger trap, thus guaranteeing that you know where you're starting from. If you use the DebugStr trap, you can even include a string that MacsBug displays when it displays the debugging screen; for example:

  ```
  The IF clause starts here
  ```

For more information about the Debugger and DebugStr routines, see "Invoking MacsBug From Your Source Program" in Chapter 2.

After this, you have to use your wits. Walk through the assembly code, watching what each line does. When the assembly-language instruction(s) have done everything described by one line of Pascal or C source code, you know you're starting the next line of source code. This works well for simple instructions, like assignments or conditional branches. But some source instructions, like loops and case statements, are scattered across several other statements when translated into assembly language, and don't look anything like what you might expect.

For example, the compiler often moves the condition check in a loop to the bottom of the loop, regardless of whether the source code had it at the top or the bottom. Also, case statements are often implemented using a look-up table placed directly in the code. The disassembler doesn't realize that the table isn't code, and disassembles it into gobbledegook. You must read the code carefully to realize that the table is accessed as data and is never executed. Finally, some compilers optimize the code, which makes the assembly code look even less like the original source code.

If you have trouble figuring out what the assembly code is doing, write down each register and memory location in a chart, as described in the section "A Simple Assembly-Language Program" earlier in this chapter. If you run into an instruction or addressing mode that's unfamiliar, you might have to look it up.

The sections that follow walk you through some Pascal statements and the assembly-language instructions that might be generated by a compiler to implement them. Remember that every compiler will generate different assembly code for the same Pascal code. The assembly-language equivalents presented here are only examples.

Assignment statements

This section describes the way a Pascal compiler might translate assignment statements. The Pascal code

```
PROCEDURE David;
VAR
        X: integer;
BEGIN
        X := 12;
END;
```

has only one executable line, that is, a line that actually causes assembly language to be generated by the compiler—the line X := 12;. All the other lines simply set up the context. The line X := 12; generates the following line of assembly language when compiled:

```
MOVE.W #$C,-$2(A6)
```

This instruction simply moves the value 12 ($C) into the memory location where X is stored. Notice that X is stored at a negative offset from register A6.

If X were a parameter instead of a local variable, it would be stored at a positive offset from register A6. The Pascal code

```
PROCEDURE Stephen (X : integer);
BEGIN
        X := 12;
END;
```

would generate this line of assembly code when compiled:

```
MOVE.W #$C,$8(A6)
```

If X were a global variable, it would be referenced from register A5. The Pascal code

```
VAR
        X: integer;
PROCEDURE Graham;
BEGIN
        X := 12;
END;
```

would generate this line of assembly code when compiled:

```
MOVE.W #$C,-$8(A5)
```

For additional information about how variables are specified in disassembled listings, see "Life on the Stack" in Chapter 4.

A procedure call

The Pascal line

```
MyProc (X, 10);
```

calls the procedure MyProc with two parameters. It generates this assembly code:

```
MOVE.W   -$4(A6),-(A7)
MOVE.W   #$A,-(A7)
JSR      MYPROC
```

The first line pushes the variable X onto the stack. What kind of variable is X in this case? It has to be a local variable because it's referenced by a negative offset from register A6. The next line pushes the number 10 ($A) onto the stack. The third line calls MyProc. MyProc will remove the parameters from the stack before it returns.

A loop

Here's the Pascal code for a loop:

```
VAR
        X, J: integer;
FOR J := 1 TO 10 DO
BEGIN
        X := J;
END;
```

Here's the equivalent assembly code:

```
0000AB00        MOVEQ           #$1,D6
0000AB04        BRA.S           *+$C                    ;0000AB10
0000AB08        MOVE.W          D6,-$4(A6)
0000AB0C        ADDQ.W          #$1,D6
0000AB10        MOVEQ           #$A,D0
0000AB14        CMP.W           D6,D0
0000AB18        BGE.S           *-$10                   ;0000AB08
```

The remainder of this section steps through this code one line at a time.

```
0000AB00        MOVEQ           #$1,D6
```

The first line puts the value $1 into register D6. It got the $1 from the FOR statement. But why is it putting it into D6 instead of J? The compiler is doing a little optimization here. Even though J is a local variable, and thus is normally on the stack, the compiler has put it in a register, because it makes the code faster and smaller. Accessing registers is faster than accessing memory, and the machine code to do it is several bytes smaller.

```
0000AB04        BRA.S           *+$C                    ;0000AB10
```

The next instruction is a branch, which jumps down to the second MOVE instruction. But the FOR statement isn't finished yet! The test to see whether J is greater than 10 is located at the bottom of the loop in assembly language. In Pascal or C, you can put the test to see whether you should exit at either the top or the bottom of the loop. In compiled code, the test is usually put at the bottom of the loop, no matter where it was in the source code. If the test was at the top of the loop in the source code, a branch is put in above the loop contents that branches to the test. If the test was at the bottom of the loop in the source code, the branch is not put in. This is easier for the compiler to generate, and semantically the same.

```
0000AB10      MOVEQ       #$A,D0
0000AB14      CMP.W       D6,D0
0000AB18      BGE.S       *-$10                    ;0000AB08
```

The MOVE instruction puts 10 ($A) into D0, so that the next instruction can compare the loop variable and check whether it's greater than 10. The compare instruction compares the loop variable, which is in register D6, against 10, which is in register D0. Then the branch instruction goes back to the top of the loop if the loop variable has not hit 10 yet. Notice that it is doing the compare backward—that is, it is not checking whether the loop variable is less than or equal to 10; it is checking whether 10 is greater than the loop variable. Compilers often do things like this.

The next line,

```
0000AB08      MOVE.W D6,-$4(A6)
```

executes the statement inside the loop: X := J.

Finally, the instruction

```
0000AB0C      ADDQ.W  #$1,D6
```

adds 1 to J, the loop variable. You're back at the test to see whether you should exit the loop.

MacsBug's disassembly commands

MacsBug provides four commands that you can use to display disassembled code starting at an address you specify. The syntax of the dissassembly commands is

command name [*address*]

You can use a procedure name for the address. If you do not specify an address, MacsBug uses the address stored in the program counter (PC register).

Table 3-4 provides a summary of the disassembly commands. Each command is described in detail in Chapter 9, "MacsBug Commands."

- **Table 3-4** MacsBug's disassembly commands

Command	Action
ID [*addr*]	Disassembles and displays one line starting at *addr*.
IL [*addr*[*n*]]	Disassembles and displays *n* number of lines starting at *addr*.
IP [*addr*]	Disassembles and displays a half page (64 bytes) centered around *addr*.
IR [*addr*]	Disassembles and displays code from *addr* to the end of the procedure containing the instruction at *addr*.

The address you specify for a disassembly command must actually be the starting address of an instruction. MacsBug will disassemble code even if you give it an address that occurs in midinstruction—but the code will not make much sense. The section "Determining Where to Start Disassembling" at the end of this chapter provides additional information about selecting a valid and useful starting address for disassembly.

Reading the disassembly display

The format used to display disassembled code is exactly the same for all the disassembly commands. Figure 3-15 shows the meaning of each field in the display.

If MacsBug knows the name of the routine that contains the disassembled code, it displays the name and the offset of the instruction within the routine in the first (leftmost) column. If MacsBug does not know the procedure name, but the address is in a known resource, MacsBug displays the type of the resource, the number of the resource, the file in which the resource is stored, the name of the resource, and the offset within the resource where the instruction is found; for example:

```
'CODE 0007 0294 Init'+0A3C
```

The next column specifies the absolute address of the instruction. The two columns after that display the operator and operand(s) that make up the instruction. To the extreme right of the display, MacsBug shows you the same instruction in machine language.

■ **Figure 3-15** Reading the disassembly display

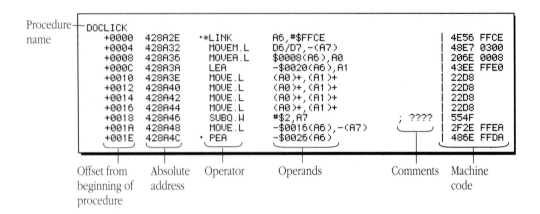

MacsBug uses several markers to provide additional information about your code:

- An asterisk preceding the operator indicates the next instruction to be executed (whose address is currently stored in the PC).
- A dot preceding the operator indicates that a breakpoint has been set on that instruction.
- A semicolon after the instruction indicates a comment, or, in the case of a branch instruction, it indicates that the object code specifies the address to jump to.

Determining where to start disassembling

If you crash into MacsBug, you'll probably want to disassemble around the program counter to see where you are and where you came from.

If you want to disassemble code that belongs to a specific routine, you can find the address of the routine you're interested in by using the Symbol Display command. You execute the command by pressing Command-: (or Command-D). MacsBug displays a pop-up window in which it lists all the routine names in the currently selected heap. You can then use the Up Arrow and Down Arrow keys to select the routine name you want to use. When you press Return, the procedure name will be inserted in the command line at the point you pressed Command-:.

If you want to restrict the names displayed in the pop-up window, type the first few letters that you want the names to include. If you've qualified the list and want to move back to the previous level of qualification, press the Delete key. To remove the menu without making a selection, press the Esc key.

Remember that the symbol display (also known as the symbol dump) only shows routines in the currently selected heap. If the routines you want aren't appearing in the symbol dump, stop and think about whether they're in another heap. (See the descriptions of the HZ and HX commands in Chapter 9 for more information about displaying and switching heaps.)

Sometimes the symbol dump won't display the routine name you want no matter what you do, but when you disassemble the code, it puts in the correct routine names. This can happen even when you have the correct heap set. If you know you have the correct heap set, the missing symbols are a sign that your code is not in a resource that MacsBug expects to contain code. For example, your resource may have been detached, or you may have made up your own custom code resource type. In both these cases, MacsBug will not show the routine names in the symbol dump.

When asked to perform a symbol dump, MacsBug goes through the selected heap and checks the relocatable blocks that contain resources of types that usually contain code. These include 'CODE', 'INIT', 'FKEY', 'WDEF', and dozens more. But the list is finite. When disassembling code, however, MacsBug gets the symbol names from the code itself, which is why it can sometimes find the correct names during disassembly even though it can't find them with a symbol dump.

Chapter 4 Macintosh Memory Organization

When you write a program in a high-level language, you manipulate local variables, global variables, resources, and files that you refer to by name. By the time this information is translated into a language the microprocessor can understand, however, the names are gone; they are replaced by addresses in memory. Although MacsBug can display procedure and trap names, you must use addresses to refer to your program's variables, and to determine the value of a variable you must understand how these values are stored in memory.

MacsBug provides commands that allow you to look at every memory location, but before you can put these commands to effective use, you need to understand where the information you're interested in is likely to be stored; that is, you need to understand how memory on the Macintosh is organized and how the contents of memory change as your program executes.

This chapter describes the kinds of memory used by the Macintosh, how to examine the different regions of memory using MacsBug commands, and how to interpret the information that MacsBug displays about these regions.

Although memory management remains the same across all Macintosh platforms, memory organization and memory addressing depend on two major factors:

- Whether you are running an application in a single-application environment (system software earlier than version 7.0, with MultiFinder turned off) or a multiple-application environment (system software version 7.0, or system software version 5.0 or 6.0 with MultiFinder turned on).
- Whether your code is 32-bit clean.

This chapter also discusses how these factors affect the information displayed by MacsBug.

An overview of Macintosh memory space

In the broadest sense, memory is simply a place where you store information. The Macintosh uses four different kinds of memory, which are distinguished from each other according to two criteria: whether memory is volatile or nonvolatile, and whether it is directly addressable by the microprocessor. As shown in Figure 4-1, the four kinds of memory are RAM, ROM, registers, and disk. For the purposes of this discussion, "disk" includes floppy and hard disks, tape drives, CD-ROM, optical disks, and other forms of mass storage.

- **Figure 4-1** Types of Macintosh memory

	Volatile	Nonvolatile
In address space	RAM	ROM
Not in address space	Registers	Disk

The memory in RAM and registers is volatile: the information it contains disappears every time you turn off your computer's power supply. The memory in ROM and on disks is nonvolatile: the information it contains remains intact whether or not the computer is turned on.

A computer's **address space** consists of the total amount of memory the microprocessor is capable of addressing. Every byte of memory in the address space has a unique address. RAM and ROM have addresses, and thus are in the address space. Registers and disks do not have addresses, and therefore are not in the address space.

Before you can manipulate information stored on disk, the information must first be loaded into RAM. To manipulate information stored in registers, you simply use the register name.

How much address space is available to your application depends upon the Macintosh on which it runs. The Macintosh Classic and the Macintosh SE, which use the 68000 microprocessor, have an address space of 16 megabytes (MB). Of this total space, anywhere up to 4 MB is assigned to RAM. The Macintosh II computers, which use the 68020 or 68030 processor, can address up to 4 gigabytes (GB) of address space. Of this total space, anywhere up to 128 MB can be assigned to RAM. As you can see, the amount of memory available varies widely. The *Macintosh Family Hardware Reference* describes in fine detail the amount and configuration of memory available on different Macintosh computers.

Fortunately, you do not need to know fine details about the hardware to debug your program because no matter how large the memory space, it is organized into regions whose starting addresses are stored in global variables that you can refer to by name and that are found at the same address in every Macintosh. The next section, "The Memory Map," describes the different regions of memory and explains what information is stored in each. The remainder of this chapter examines these regions in greater detail.

The memory map

The arrangement of information within the address space is represented by a memory map. Just as a road map can show you where to find a particular place in a large city, the memory map shows you where to find individual bytes of memory within your computer's address space. Every byte of memory has an address that you can identify and to which you can refer. In order to read a memory map, you need to understand the units of memory and how these are arranged in memory.

The next section, "Memory Units and Their Representation," discusses the conventions used to represent memory. The sections that follow explain how address space is used on the Macintosh by taking an increasingly detailed look at the Macintosh memory map.

Memory units and their representation

Whatever the upper limit of addressable memory is, it is referred to as **high memory.** The lowest limit is referred to as **low memory.** Figure 4-2 shows the typical figure used to represent memory, a rectangle. The base of the rectangle represents the lowest memory location, and the top of the rectangle represents the highest memory location.

■ **Figure 4-2** High and low memory

Locations on a Macintosh memory map start at 0 and go up to either $00FF FFFF or $FFFF FFFF, depending on whether the machine is using the 68000 or 68020/30 processor.

The units of memory are the nibble, the byte, the word, and the long word. Table 4-1 describes them.

■ **Table 4-1** Units of memory

Term	Size	Bits	Example
Nibble	Half a byte	4	C
Byte	1 byte	8	2C
Word	2 bytes	16	E22C
Long word	4 bytes	32	002C E22C

As mentioned earlier, only 1 byte of memory is stored at each address. If all the information you're using is cut up in byte-size chunks, then there's one piece of information stored at each address; but, if you need to store information in larger size units, you must use successive addresses to store one chunk of information. For example, suppose you need to store an address. An address is always a long word, 4 bytes long; for the sake of this example, assume the address is 1234 5678. Figure 4-3 shows how a long word is stored at four successive addresses.

■ **Figure 4-3** Storing a long word

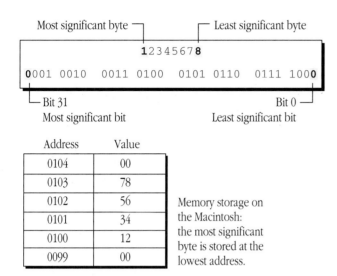

MacsBug displays all numbers, including addresses, in hexadecimal notation. As shown in Figure 4-3, the leftmost byte of a word or long word is referred to as the most significant byte, and the rightmost byte as the least significant byte. Similarly, when you translate a byte, word, or long word into bits, you determine the most significant and least significant bits in the same fashion.

The only additional terms that that you need to know are **low-order word, high-order word, low-order byte,** and **high-order byte.** The definitions are best furnished by examples.

■ In the long word 56E5 12FF, the high-order word is 56E5, and the low-order word is 12FF.

■ In the word 56E5, the high-order byte is 56, and the low-order byte is E5.

In accordance with the storage convention described in Figure 4-3, the high-order word or byte is stored at a lower memory location than the low-order word or byte.

Using MacsBug commands to display and set memory

The preceding section described the way data is stored in memory and the convention used to represent memory in this manual as well as throughout *Inside Macintosh*. This section describes how MacsBug displays memory. Table 4-2 summarizes the MacsBug commands that you can use to display information that is stored in memory and to change that information if you wish.

■ **Table 4-2** Commands that display and set memory

Command	Action
DM	Displays 16 bytes of memory starting at the specified address.
DP	Displays 128 bytes of memory starting from the specified address.
DB	Displays the byte at the specified address.
DW	Displays the word at the specified address.
DL	Displays the long word at the specified address.
SM	Assigns a value to memory starting at the specified address.
SB	Assigns a value to a byte starting at the specified address.
SW	Assigns a value to a word starting at the specified address.
SL	Assigns a value to a long word starting at the specified address.

Each of these commands is described in greater detail in Chapter 9, "MacsBug Commands."

To see an example of the way MacsBug displays memory, enter the command

```
DM 910
```

—that is, "display the information stored beginning at address 910." MacsBug displays the following information:

```
Displaying memory from 910
 00000910   0E4D 6963 726F 736F  6674 2057 6F72 6400   •Microsoft Word•
```

The DM (Display Memory) command displays memory in hexadecimal notation and also displays, at the extreme right, its ASCII representation. Also, although you specify only one address, the DM command shows you the byte at that address and 15 more bytes. The subsequent bytes, in accordance with the memory storage convention described in the previous section, are stored at increasingly higher memory locations. Figure 4-4 shows a graphic representation of the output to the DM command shown above.

Of course, not even the hardiest programmer can make much sense out of a string of hexadecimal numbers. Fortunately, MacsBug allows you to use templates to display memory so that you can immediately see what the stored values are about. The section "Using Templates to Display Memory," later in this chapter, explains how you can define templates that MacsBug can use to display memory intelligibly.

■ **Figure 4-4** Graphic representation of DM output

Address	Value
925	00
924	64
923	72
922	6F
921	57
920	20
919	74
918	66
917	6F
916	73
915	6F
914	72
913	63
912	69
911	4D
910	0E

Memory map regions

The DM command described in the last section displayed memory beginning at address 910. The hexadecimal dump didn't reveal much, but the ASCII representation of the same portion of memory gave the name of the current application. How would you know to look at that particular address for that piece of information? The answer to this is that specific locations in memory have special and consistent meanings for all Macintosh computers. Some of these locations hold pointers to other locations where certain information is stored (low-memory global variables); others are entire regions dedicated to some specific structure in memory that the system or your program uses to do its work (such as the stack, the heap, or the jump table).

Macintosh computers that use the 68000 microprocessor divide the available address space into four sections of 4 MB each, as shown in Figure 4-5. (On the 68020 and 68030, RAM gets 8 MB in 24-bit mode.) The first 4 MB is set aside for RAM, the next 4 MB for ROM, and the last 8 MB for memory-mapped I/O, meaning special chips like the disk drive controller. Chips that control I/O devices can access mass storage outside of the address space through a special 1-byte "window." Thus, most of the memory-mapped I/O section is empty, with 1-byte islands here and there.

Although not all of the available address space is used on every machine, every machine with the same microprocessor divides up the address space the same way.

- **Figure 4-5** Address space for the 68000 microprocessor

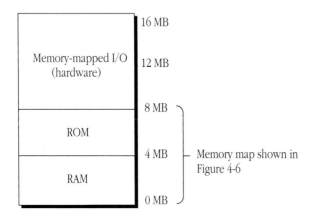

Figure 4-6 shows the area of memory that you'll be working with most of the time in debugging. Figure 4-6 assumes that your program is running in a single-application environment (system software earlier than version 7.0, with MultiFinder turned off). The principal difference between memory organization in a single-application environment and in a multiple-application environment concerns the application heap region. (See the section "Heap Management in a Multiple-Application Environment" later in this chapter for additional information.) Note that Figure 4-6 is not drawn to scale. Although the order of the regions is correct, their relative sizes are not. In reality the application heap is much larger than any of the other regions.

■ **Figure 4-6** A simple Macintosh memory map

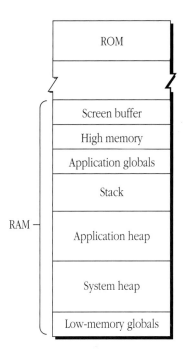

As Figure 4-6 shows, most of the regions of memory that are important for debugging purposes are part of RAM. The size of each region differs on different types of Macintosh computers, but the regions remain in the same order. If you add RAM to your system, the size of each region expands, but the order remains the same.

Since the size, and thus the starting point, of each region can change, you need a way to find each starting point. It is not possible to draw dividing lines in memory as shown in Figure 4-6, but it is possible to store the address where each region begins at specific addresses that we can count on not to change. This is accomplished by means of pointers to each region that are stored in low memory. (The low-memory region always starts at 0, so that the pointers in low memory are always in the same place on all Macintosh computers.)

Knowing how the memory you're working with is organized is important because debugging requires that you decide whether a piece of data—which might be an address—makes sense. Table 4-3 describes how each memory region illustrated in Figure 4-6 is used.

■ **Table 4-3** Memory regions

Region	Description
Low-memory globals	Contains single numbers or pointers used mainly by the operating system, rarely by applications.
System heap	Contains system information such as lists of the disks mounted, open files, and so on. Items in the system heap are not single numbers but larger data structures used mainly by the system, and rarely by applications.
Application heap	Used by applications to store application code, windows, dialog boxes, alert boxes, data, menus, icons, and so on.
Stack	Used by an application's routines to store function results, local variables, and return addresses of calling routines and to pass routines' parameters.
High memory	Used by resident programs such as debuggers. Note that the term *high memory* is used to refer both to high memory in RAM as well as to high memory in the total address space.
Application globals	Used by the application to store its global variables. QuickDraw™ and the operating system also place some information here.
Screen buffer	Read by the Macintosh hardware, which reads the screen buffer and displays its contents directly on the screen. This is called memory-mapped video. If you change the memory in the screen buffer, you will see the changes on the screen. On Macintosh computers that make use of the NuBus architecture, such as the Macintosh IIci, the screen buffer is actually above the ROM, not below it.
ROM	Located above RAM on the memory map, but not necessarily contiguous with RAM. The ROM contains system code and data (in the form of resources).

The next section, "Using Low-Memory Global Variables to Draw a Memory Map," explains how you can use the pointers to these regions to produce an exact map for the computer you're developing on.

Using low-memory global variables to draw a memory map

The Macintosh has hundreds of low-memory global variables. Most of these contain single values or pointers to other places in memory. *How to Write Macintosh Software* by Scott Knaster has the best publicly available list of low-memory global variables, although it is not complete or totally accurate. It is a very bad idea to write to low-memory global variables or even to read them except by using the routines for this purpose that are documented in *Inside Macintosh,* but you can make effective use of some low-memory global variables in debugging. This section describes how to use low-memory global variables to make a map that accurately describes the memory configuration of the machine you're developing on. "Exercise: Getting Started With MacsBug" in Chapter 2 provides an exercise that accomplishes the same thing.

As mentioned earlier in this chapter, the various regions of the memory map start at different addresses, depending on available RAM and the model of the Macintosh you have. Some of the most useful low-memory global variables are pointers to the beginning of each region, because they point to the correct location regardless of the characteristics of the particular machine being used.

To make low-memory globals easier to remember, every low-memory global variable has a name as well as an address, both of which MacsBug knows. If you identify a low-memory global variable by name, MacsBug automatically computes its address. (See the section "Standard Macros" in Chapter 8 if you would like to know how MacsBug translates low-memory global variable names to addresses.) Figure 4-7 shows the locations pointed to by low-memory global variables (and register A7).

■ **Figure 4-7** Memory regions and low-memory global variables

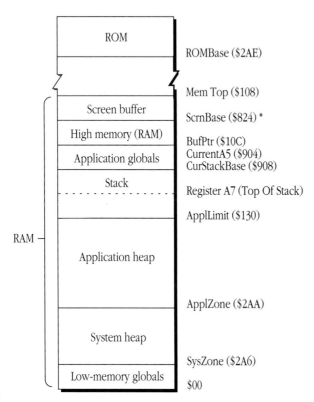

* On Macintosh II computers, the screen buffer is above the ROM, but ScrnBase still points to the correct location.

To find out the exact starting address for each memory region on your machine, you have only to dereference the low-memory global variable's pointer. For example, if you enter

`SysZone^`

MacsBug displays the address that is stored at the address 02A6 (SysZone):

`02A6^ = $00001E00    #7680    #7680    '••••'`

The starting address of the system heap is 1E00.

If you dereference every low-memory global variable that is used to store the address of a region in memory, you will obtain output like the following. You can use this data as a memory reference map for your machine.

```
02A6^  = $00001E00   #7680        #7680        '••••'
02AA^  = $0019713C   #1667388     #1667388     '••q<'
0130^  = $00294752   #2705234     #2705234     '•)GR'
A7     = $0029AE94   #2731668     #2731668     '•)••'
0908^  = $0029AF14   #2731796     #2731796     '•)••'
0904^  = $0029B114   #2732308     #2732308     '•)••'
010C^  = $003C06F0   #3933936     #3933936     '•<••'
0824^  = $FAA00020   #4204789792  #-90177504   '•†• '
0108^  = $00141350   #1315664     #1315664     '•••P'
02AE^  = $40800000   #1082130432  #1082130432  '@•••'
```

Table 4-4 describes the memory location to which each low-memory global variable points.

- **Table 4-4** Memory regions and low-memory global variables

Name	Address	Description
SysZone	$2A6	Points to the beginning of the system heap.
ApplZone	$2AA	Points to the beginning of the application heap.
ApplLimit	$130	Points between the application heap and the stack.
Register A7	—	Points to the top of the stack.
CurStackBase	$908	Points to the base of the stack.
CurrentA5	$904	Points to the application global variables.
BufPtr	$10C	Points to the bottom of high memory.
ScrnBase	$824	Points to the bottom of screen memory.
MemTop	$108	Points to the top of RAM. Used to determine the amount of RAM installed on the machine. Accurate only in a single-application environment.
ROMBase	$2AE	Points to the beginning of ROM.

Chapter 4 Macintosh Memory Organization

Memory management under system software version 7.0

System software version 7.0 introduces two features that affect memory management:

- 32-bit addressing, which allows software running on machines with 32-bit clean ROMs (for example, the Macintosh IIci and the Macintosh IIfx) to access up to 4 GB of address space.
- Virtual memory, which allows software running on 68030- and 68020-based machines (with a 68851 PMMU) to increase the amount of logical address space available to an application.

This section describes how these features affect your code's ability to run under system software version 7.0. For a complete and detailed description of memory management under system software version 7.0, see the "Memory Management" chapter in *Inside Macintosh*, Volume VI.

32-bit addressing

The 68000 microprocessor has 24 address lines and has an address space of 2^{24} bytes, or 16 MB. The 68020 and 68030 microprocessors used in the Macintosh II product line have 32 address lines, and thus have a total address space of 2^{32} bytes, or 4 GB (4000 MB). However, Macintosh computers that use the 68020 and 68030 usually run in 24-bit mode, and use only the low 24 address lines. The effective total address space for these computers is 16 MB, like that of the 68000-based computers. Starting with system software version 7.0, Macintosh computers with a 68020 (equipped with a PMMU) or 68030 microprocessor will be able to run in 32-bit mode, which means that programs can access the full 4-GB address space. (Note that the 68000 microprocessor has only 24 address lines, and thus cannot run in 32-bit mode.)

Programs will not work properly in 32-bit mode unless they strictly follow the Macintosh programming guidelines contained in *Inside Macintosh* and the Macintosh Technical Notes. Because the high 8 bits of each 32-bit address have not been used until now, the Macintosh Operating System has stored flags in the high byte. Some programmers have manipulated these flags directly instead of using the supplied system calls. For example, programmers occasionally set the bits that lock and unlock relocatable blocks directly instead of using the HLock and HUnlock calls. These bits are currently stored in the high byte of master pointers. Under systems that run in 32-bit mode, they are stored someplace else. The HLock and HUnlock calls will do the right thing regardless of which system a program is running under. However, if your program directly sets a bit in the high byte of a master pointer under a system that runs in 32-bit mode, you will end up changing the address stored in the master pointer rather than locking or unlocking the relocatable block.

Programs that follow the Macintosh programming guidelines and do not make use of this type of shortcut are described as **32-bit clean.** If your program is not 32-bit clean, you need either to change the program or to set a flag in your program's 'SIZE' resource that indicates you want to run in 24-bit mode. Programs must be 32-bit clean in order to run under A/UX.

For more information about keeping your code 32-bit clean and associated issues, see Macintosh Technical Note #212, *The Joy of Being 32-Bit Clean,* and the chapters "Compatibility Guidelines" and "Memory Management" in *Inside Macintosh,* Volume VI.

Virtual memory

Logical address space is the address space that the microprocessor can address. The amount of logical address space is determined by the number of address lines. If your processor has 24 address lines, it can address 16 MB of memory; if your processor has 32 address lines, it can address 4 GB of memory.

Physical address space is the address space that actually exists. Physical address space is limited in principle by the amount of logical memory that your processor can address and is determined in reality by the amount of memory shipped with your computer and any memory that you add by installing additional memory.

Until system software version 7.0, the only way you could increase physical memory was by installing additional memory. System software version 7.0 includes software that implements a virtual memory scheme. **Virtual memory** is a way of expanding available memory by using software rather than by installing additional hardware.

A program running under virtual memory can access the entire logical memory of the computer as if it were RAM, except for blocks of memory reserved for the system heap, ROM, NuBus cards, and a resident debugger. The operating system makes this possible by writing everything an application does not currently need to disk, and swapping it in as needed. In sum, expanding the memory available to your application by using virtual memory is cheaper but slower than buying additional physical memory.

Figure 4-8 illustrates how virtual memory affects memory allocation in 24-bit mode.

■ **Figure 4-8** Virtual memory in 24-bit mode

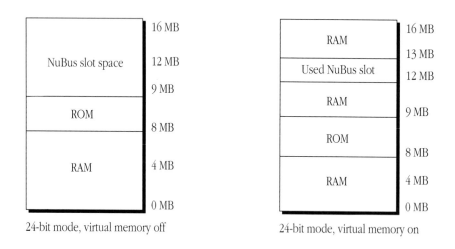

The use of virtual memory in 24-bit mode creates more than 8 MB of logical memory. NuBus slots that don't have cards in them are made available as RAM. If you designate the Process Manager (MultiFinder) heap as the target heap and use the HD command to display information about that heap, assigned NuBus slots, the resident debugger (if any), ROM, and the system heap will be represented as unrelocatable blocks. Thus, even though virtual memory increases the total amount of RAM available to your application, this amount does not represent contiguous free space in memory.

Figure 4-9 illustrates how virtual memory affects memory allocation in 32-bit mode.

■ **Figure 4-9** Virtual memory in 32-bit mode

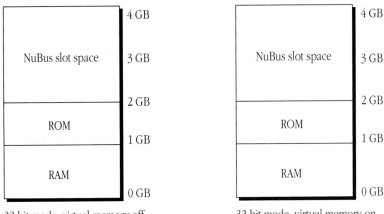

As you can see, the basic difference between virtual memory in 32-bit mode and virtual memory in 24-bit mode is that in 24-bit mode, it is possible for RAM locations to be at higher addresses than ROM. In 32-bit mode, ROM starts at $40800000 rather than at $800000 (24-bit mode); otherwise the allocation of memory above ROM is the same whether virtual memory is on or not. In other words, using virtual memory with a 32-bit configuration increases the amount of memory you can address, but does not affect the memory map. This is because the 1 GB set aside for RAM currently exceeds the capacity of any disk. If disks become available that can hold, say, 3 GB of information, the memory map in 32-bit mode with virtual memory on (shown on the right in Figure 4-9) would have to be altered.

MacsBug provides two markers in the status region of its display to indicate whether the machine is operating in 24-bit or 32-bit mode, whether virtual memory is installed, and, if so, whether you can access pages that are currently swapped out. For additional information, see "The Status Region" in Chapter 2.

The operation of virtual memory should be transparent to most applications. You need to be concerned about the swapping process if one or more of the following is true:

■ Your application calls the SCSI Manager directly.
■ You are writing a SCSI driver.
■ You are writing code that runs on a NuBus card and accesses the main memory.
■ You are writing code that runs at interrupt time.
■ You are writing a debugger that is meant to run under virtual memory.
■ You are writing an application that has critical timing needs.

The operating system provides routines that allow you to hold or lock portions of memory. Holding memory means that a portion of memory cannot be swapped out but can be relocated in RAM; locking memory means that a portion of memory can be neither swapped out nor moved. If you are writing a driver, or a sound or animation application with critical timing requirements, you might need to hold memory using the HoldMemory function. You should also use the HoldMemory function to prevent buffers or code used by code that runs at interrupt time from having to be paged in. This is to prevent a possible double-page fault, which can occur if the code that runs at interrupt time needs to swap in pages while the operating system is in the process of swapping pages in or out.

You can lock memory using the LockMemory function; this function is used by drivers and other code when hardware other than the Macintosh CPU is transferring data to or from user buffers, such as any NuBus master peripheral card or DMA hardware.

For additional information about holding and locking memory and how to avoid situations that can cause double-page faults, see the "Memory Management" chapter in *Inside Macintosh,* Volume VI.

Registers

In addition to memory that can be addressed and that is external to the microprocessor, the 68000, 68020, and 68030 microprocessors can also access a total of 70 bytes of memory in their own registers. These include the address registers A0 to A7, the data registers D0 to D7, the status register (SR), and the program counter (PC). Each register is 4 bytes long and holds a single value at a time (with the exception of the status register, which is 2 bytes long).

Registers are not shown on the memory map; when you refer to them using MacsBug commands, you use their names. For example, the command

```
DM A7
```

means "display the value stored in register A7."

The registers are the microprocessor's working space. When you cook a meal or work on a car, you need a working area that can hold the tools and ingredients that you need to complete the job at hand. You could fetch each item as you needed it from the store or from storage, but this would be inefficient. The microprocessor works the same way; it stores the instructions and data it's about to use in registers in order to do its work more quickly.

As their names indicate, registers have specialized functions:

- The **address registers,** A0–A7, hold addresses. Two of these, A6 and A7, are used to refer to addresses on the stack. See "Life on the Stack" later in this chapter for additional information. Register A5 contains an address relative to which the application's global variables, parameters, and jump table information can be accessed. See the sections "Allocating Space for Global Variables" and "Application Parameters and the Jump Table" later in this chapter for additional information.

- The **data registers,** D0–D7, hold data. Operating system routines, which are register-based, use some of these registers to pass data to or receive data from the calling program.

- The **PC register** holds the address of the next instruction to be executed by the processor. For additional information about this register see Chapter 2, "Getting Started."

- The **status** or **condition code register** holds information about the operation that has just taken place. For additional information, see the Motorola manual that describes your microprocessor.

The 68020 and 68030 microprocessors contain some additional special-purpose registers. It is not necessary to know about these extra registers for normal debugging purposes.

The values stored in the address registers, data registers, PC register, and status register are normally shown in the MacsBug display every time MacsBug is invoked. For information about interpreting MacsBug's display, see Chapter 2, "Getting Started." Table 4-5 lists the MacsBug commands that allow you to display the contents of other registers or to change the normal MacsBug display of register information. Each of the commands in Table 4-5 is described in greater detail in Chapter 9, "MacsBug Commands."

- **Table 4-5** MacsBug register commands

Name	Action
RAD	Allows you to choose between two register-naming conventions.
SHOW	Allows you to change the display format used in the status area of the MacsBug display. Allows you to show the contents of other registers or other memory regions in the status area.
TD	Displays the contents of all CPU registers.
TF	Displays the contents of the 68881 floating-point registers.
TM	Displays the contents of the 68851 MMU registers.

You can change the value of a register by using a command in this form:

RegisterName := *expression* or *RegisterName* = *expression*

Using templates to display memory

This section describes the TMP command, which lists the templates installed in your system, and explains how to create your own templates. This section also includes a brief exercise that you can work through to create a template that displays the mouse position.

Templates allow you to control the way MacsBug displays memory. When you use the DM (Display Memory) command to display memory, you have the option of specifying a basic type or a template name in order to make the display more intelligible. The syntax of the command is

DM *address template-name*

This means "display memory starting at the specified address using the specified template."

For example, you know that the mouse position is stored at address 830, so you execute the command DM 830 and MacsBug displays the following information:

```
Displaying memory from 0830
  00000830   0009 000F 0000 0000   01E0 0280 0008 0000   ················
```

You don't work with screen coordinates in hexadecimal form, however, so you would like MacsBug to display the same information in decimal notation. You know that the word at 830 contains the vertical position and that the word at 832 contains the horizontal position of the mouse. By using the basic type SignedWord as a template (see Table 4-6), you can get MacsBug to display the same information in a more useful way. For example, if you type the command

DM 830 signedword; DM 832 signedword

MacsBug displays the following:

```
Displaying signedword
  00000830     #438
  00000832     #402
```

You can use basic types to display memory on the run, but if you would also like to display information about what the values refer to, in this case vertical and horizontal points, or if you want to display information for larger data structures, you might need a more customized and permanent template.

You can use the names of templates defined by the 'mxwt' resource to display data structures created and maintained by User Interface Toolbox or operating system managers. For example, the 'mxwt' resource provides templates that you can use to display window records, grafPorts, heap zones, event records, and so forth. You can also create your own templates to display data structures created by your application or data structures created by the system that are not defined by the standard 'mxwt' resources.

Standard templates

The Debugger Prefs file contains 'mxwt' resources that define standard templates. To display the names of templates that are loaded when you install the Debugger Prefs file, use the TMP command. If you enter TMP without parameters, MacsBug displays a list of all available templates. You can use these names with the DM command; for example

DM   000234C4 EventRecord

or

DM @WindowList WindowRecord

MacsBug will then display memory in new and enlightening ways; for example, in response to the last command, MacsBug displays the following information:

```
Displaying WindowRecord at 002BEF10
    002BEF20   portRect           #0 #0 #429 #506
    002BEF28   visRgn             002BF024 -> 002D560C
    002BEF2C   clipRgn            002BF038 -> 002D8A6C
    002BEF7C   windowKind         0008
    002BEF7E   visible            TRUE
    002BEF7F   hilited            TRUE
    002BEF80   goAwayFlag         TRUE
    002BEF81   spareFlag          TRUE
    002BEF82   strucRgn           0025F9D4 -> 002D7ACC
    002BEF86   contRgn            0025F9C0 -> 002D7AE0
    002BEF8A   updateRgn          0025F9C8 -> 002D7760
    002BEF8E   windowDefProc      080020D4 -> 20832A5C
    002BEF92   dataHandle         0025F9A8 -> 002D8150
    002BEF96   titleHandle        0025F9CC -> 002D813C
    002BEF9A   titleWidth         0040
    002BEF9C   controlList        002BF1DC -> 002D5528
    002BEFA0   nextWindow         NIL
    002BEFA4   windowPic          NIL
    002BEFA8   refCon             00000003
```

Try the command without using the template, DM @WindowList, and you'll notice a significant difference.

Using basic and template types to define template fields

You can create your own templates using ResEdit, or you can build your own resource using the file Templates.r as a model and then use the Rez tool to add it to the Debugger Prefs file. The section "Exercise: Creating Your Own Templates," later in this chapter provides a hands-on exercise that shows you how to use ResEdit to create a template. Whichever method you use, you need to give MacsBug three pieces of information: a field name, type name, and count for each line that you want MacsBug to display.

Figure 4-10 shows how the use of field name, type name, and count determines the information displayed by MacsBug for the portRect field of a window record.

■ **Figure 4-10** Template fields

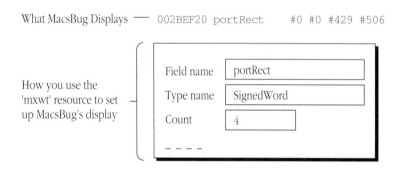

MacsBug uses the string you enter into the Field name field of the resource as a label to describe the information that follows. It's up to you to name the field.

MacsBug uses the Type name field of the resource to figure out how many bytes to display and in what format. The Type name SignedWord, in this example, tells MacsBug that you want 2 bytes displayed as a signed decimal number. You can use the types described in Table 4-6 and Table 4-7 to specify a Type name.

MacsBug uses the Count field of the resource to figure out the number of times items of the specified type should be displayed on one line. In this case, it will display 4 words as signed decimal numbers.

MacsBug figures out the address of the field by taking the address at which you specify memory display should start and then adding however many bytes you have specified for previous fields. This means that you must specify the correct starting address for the data structure and that you must correctly specify the size of all the fields in the structure, even the ones for which you do not want information displayed (see Table 4-7).

Table 4-6 lists the basic type names that you can use to specify the size of data you want MacsBug to display and how to display it.

■ **Table 4-6** Basic types

Type	Display
Byte	Display byte in hexadecimal.
Word	Display word in hexadecimal.
Long	Display long word in hexadecimal.
SignedByte	Display byte in decimal.
SignedWord	Display word in decimal.
SignedLong	Display long word in decimal.
UnsignedByte	Display byte in decimal.
UnsignedWord	Display word in decimal.
UnsignedLong	Display long word in decimal.
Boolean	Display byte as TRUE (nonzero) or FALSE (0).
pString	Display a Pascal string. If you specify this for the type name, the value you specify for count indicates the maximum string size and is used to compute the next field address. If the string is only as long as the actual number of characters, specify 0 for count; MacsBug uses the length byte to determine the end of the string.
cString	Display a C string (0-terminated).

In addition to these basic types, which can be used individually with the DM command, you can also use the type names listed in Table 4-7 to describe the display of data. You can only use these type names in templates.

■ **Table 4-7** Template type names

Name	Display/action
Text	Display a text string for the number of bytes specified in the Count field. (For example, you can display resource types with the Text type and a count of 4.)
Skip	Do not display the next *n* bytes. (Use the count field to specify *n*; leave the field name blank.)
Align	Align to a word boundary. (Use this as the type name for the field following a C or Pascal string. Leave the Field name and Count value blank.)
Handle	Dereference the next long word twice and display the address of the master pointer and then the address that the master pointer points to. (If you want to display what is stored at the address that the master pointer points to, use the ^^*BasicType* type name described below.)
^*BasicType*	Dereference the next long word and display the contents stored at that address using the specified *BasicType*.
^^*BasicType*	Dereference the next long word twice and display the contents of the address the master pointer points to using the specified *BasicType*. (For example, you can display a window title by specifying ^^pString as a type name for the titleHandle field.)

Constructing linked lists using the 'mxwt' resource

If a template named Temp contains a field type of ^Temp or ^^Temp, MacsBug assumes the field is a link to another data structure of the same type. Thus, MacsBug can display linked lists if you specify the appropriate type name in your 'mxwt' resource.

Figure 4-11 shows the entry for the nextWindow field for the WindowRecord template.

■ **Figure 4-11** Linked list field entry in 'mxwt' resource

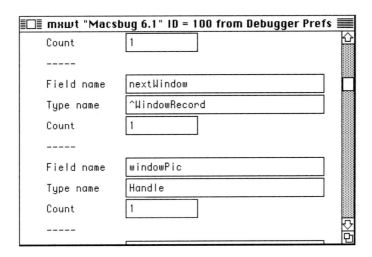

If you use the DM (Display Memory) command from MacsBug to show you a window record, for example,

DM @WindowList WindowRecord

and the application you're debugging has several windows open, MacsBug displays information similar to the following:

```
Displaying WindowRecord at 003E94CC
  003E94DC  portRect            #0 #0 #429 #516
  003E94E4  visRgn              003E7D0C -> 003E9570
  003E94E8  clipRgn             003E7D08 -> 003E9584
  003E9538  windowKind          0008
  003E953A  visible             TRUE
  003E953B  hilited             FALSE
  003E953C  goAwayFlag          TRUE
  003E953D  spareFlag           TRUE
  003E953E  strucRgn            003E7CB4 -> 003FF734
  003E9542  contRgn             003E7CB0 -> 003BCFA0
  003E9546  updateRgn           003E7CAC -> 003EC5E4
  003E954A  windowDefProc       080020D4 -> 20832A5C
  003E954E  dataHandle          003E7CA0 -> 003EC630
  003E9552  titleHandle         003E7CA8 -> 003FF24C   Untitled1
  003E9556  titleWidth          003C
  003E9558  controlList         003E7C94 -> 003FD6DC
  003E955C  nextWindow          003E7A50
  003E9560  windowPic           NIL
  003E9564  refCon              00000004
```

Chapter 4 Macintosh Memory Organization   95

If you press Return, MacsBug displays information about the next window in WindowList, whose address (003E7A50) is given in the nextWindow field.

```
Displaying WindowRecord at 003E7A50
  003E7A60    portRect               #0 #0 #429 #506
  003E7A68    visRgn                 003884B0 -> 003E7AF4
  003E7A6C    clipRgn                003884B4 -> 003F8DEC
  003E7ABC    windowKind             0008
  003E7ABE    visible                TRUE
  003E7ABF    hilited                FALSE
  003E7AC0    goAwayFlag             TRUE
  003E7AC1    spareFlag              TRUE
  003E7AC2    strucRgn               003E7B5C -> 003F8D68
  003E7AC6    contRgn                003E7B58 -> 003F8D7C
  003E7ACA    updateRgn              003E7B54 -> 003F88E8
  003E7ACE    windowDefProc          080020D4 -> 20832A5C
  003E7AD2    dataHandle             003E7B48 -> 003F8938
  003E7AD6    titleHandle            003E7B50 -> 003FD814 -> mbreleasenotes
  003E7ADA    titleWidth             006A
  003E7ADC    controlList            003E7B3C -> 003F8B5C
  003E7AE0    nextWindow             NIL
  003E7AE4    windowPic              NIL
  003E7AE8    refCon                 00000003
```

(The underlined portions of these listings are for your benefit; they are not underlined in the MacsBug display.)

When the nextWindow field has a value of NIL and you ask MacsBug to show you the next window record, it displays the message "End of linked list." Linked lists are 0-terminated. If a template contains more than one field specifying a link, MacsBug uses the last field found.

Exercise: Creating your own template

This exercise demonstrates how to create a template named MouseCoords, which will allow you to display the position of the cursor in an intelligible and useful way. The exercise assumes that you are using ResEdit 2.1.

1. **Place the cursor in the upper-left corner of the screen and use the interrupt switch to invoke MacsBug.**

2. **Type `DM Mouse` and press Return.**

    This command asks MacsBug to display memory at address 830, also known to MacsBug by the system global variable name, mouse. MacsBug displays information similar to the following:

    ```
    Displaying memory from 0830
      00000830  0009 000F 0000 0000  01E0 0280 0008 0000   ................
    ```

3. **Type `G`, press Return, and move the cursor to the lower-right corner of the screen.**

4. **Press the interrupt switch to invoke MacsBug.**

5. **Type `DM Mouse` again and press Return.**

    MacsBug displays something like the following:

    ```
    Displaying memory from 0830
      00000830  0017 0228 0000 0000  01E0 0280 0016 0220   ...(........
    ```

    Notice that the coordinates of the cursor have changed. Now you'll create a template that you can use to get a more useful display.

6. **Type `G` and press Return.**

7. **Double-click the Debugger Prefs file in your System Folder to launch ResEdit.**

8. **Open the 'mxwt' resource.**

9. **Choose Create New Resource from the Resource menu.**

10. **Click the five asterisks (*****). Choose Insert New Field(s) from the Resource menu.**

    ResEdit displays a template similar to the one shown in Figure 4-12.

■ **Figure 4-12** The 'mxwt' template

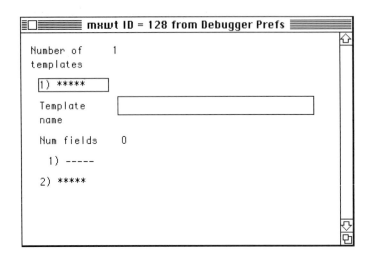

11. Type `MouseCoords` in the Template name field.

12. Click the dashed lines and choose Insert New Field(s) from the Resource menu.

13. Type `Vertical` in the Field name, `SignedWord` in the Type name, and `1` in the Count field.

14. Click the dashed line below the Count field. Choose Insert New Field(s) from the Resource menu.

15. Type `Horizontal` in the Field name, `SignedWord` in the Type name, and `1` in the Count field.

    Your template should look like the one shown in Figure 4-13.

16. Choose Save and then Quit from the File menu, then restart your Macintosh.

    You must restart because MacsBug only loads the template resources during system startup. Now you can use the new template.

17. **Place the cursor in the upper-left corner of the screen. Press the interrupt switch to invoke MacsBug. Type** `DM Mouse MouseCoords` **and press Return.**

    MacsBug should display something like the following:

    ```
    Displaying MouseCoords at 00000830
        00000830  Vertical            0002
        00000832  Horizontal          0001
    ```

18. **Type** `TMP` **to display template names.**

    You'll see MouseCoords at the bottom of the list.

19. **Type** `G` **to leave MacsBug.**

- **Figure 4-13** MouseCoords template

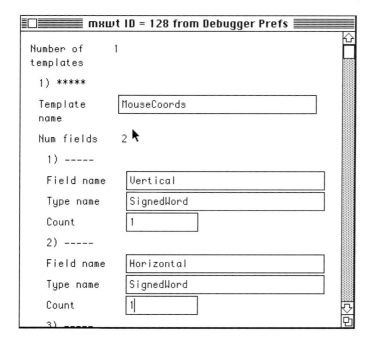

Chapter 4 Macintosh Memory Organization   99

Application space

Your application can store information in three places in memory: in local variables, in global variables, and in the heap.

- You use global variables to store information (or pointers to information) that needs to be accessed by different procedures in your program. The section "Allocating Space for Global Variables" in this chapter describes how global variables are stored in this area and how they are addressed with reference to register A5.

- Your routines' local variables, parameters, and return result (if any) are stored on the stack. The section "Life on the Stack" later in this chapter explains how this region of memory is used both by your application and by the system to execute routines and A-traps.

- The resources and data structures created by your application are stored in your application's heap. You allocate and deallocate space on the heap for the information you want to store there through calls to the Memory Manager. The next section, "The Heap," describes how this region of memory is organized.

MacsBug provides commands and standard macros that you can use to display information stored in these three areas. But in order to use these commands, you must understand the characteristics of each of these regions of memory.

The shaded area of Figure 4-14 shows the region of memory that belongs to your application if it's running in a single-application environment. The section "Heap Management in a Multiple-Application Environment," later in this chapter, provides additional information that you need to know if your application is running in a multiple-application environment. However, as the basic structure of the heap and the units (blocks) that make it up is the same in both environments, you need to read about the heap first before proceeding to that section.

Your application is not normally concerned with the system heap and low-memory global variables. You can use low-memory global variables for debugging; otherwise, you should access information stored in this area only by using system calls. The system heap stores data structures and resources it needs to do its work; in a multiple-application environment, it also stores resources that are shared by concurrently running applications. The Memory Manager uses the same scheme to manage the system heap as it does to manage the application heap.

■ **Figure 4-14** Application space in a single-application environment

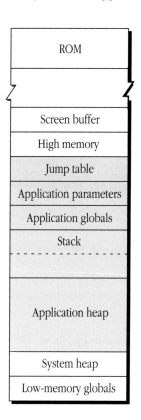

The heap

A **heap** or **heap zone** is a large piece of memory that is broken up into units called **blocks**. The current application heap's starting address is stored in the low-memory global variable ApplZone and ends at the address stored in the low-memory global variable HeapEnd, though it is possible to grow the zone up to the address stored in the low-memory global variable ApplLimit. The Memory Management chapters in *Inside Macintosh,* Volumes II, IV, and VI, describe how you use Memory Manager routines to allocate, resize, and deallocate blocks in the heap and how to grow the heap if necessary. This section summarizes some of this information in order to better describe the MacsBug commands that you use to examine the contents of the heap; however, it is no substitute for the detailed presentation in *Inside Macintosh*.

Chapter 4   Macintosh Memory Organization   **101**

The number of heaps varies depending on whether you are running in a single-application or multiple-application environment:

- In a single-application environment, there are two heaps: the system heap and the application heap, as shown in Figure 4-14. The system heap is used by the operating system to store system data, while the application heap is used by the application to store the application's code, data, resources, and anything else the application keeps in memory (except its variables).

- In a multiple-application environment, the number of heaps varies according to the number of applications that are launched. In addition to the system heap, all applications are launched within a larger heap managed by the Process Manager (or MultiFinder in system software versions previous to 7.0). Each open application has its own separate heap. For additional information, see the section "Heap Management in a Multiple-Application Environment," later in this chapter.

Whether the Memory Manager manages a heap in a single-application or multiple-application environment, the elements that make up the heap, the format of the heap, and the strategy used by the Memory Manager to allow your application to use space as efficiently as possible do not change.

Figure 4-15 shows the format of a heap zone. The important things to note are the zone header and the zone trailer. The placement of blocks within the heap varies for each heap, though they always occupy the content area of the heap. The arrangement of blocks in Figure 4-15 is just an example; the blocks would not have to be allocated in that order or in those specific locations.

■ **Figure 4-15** Heap zone format

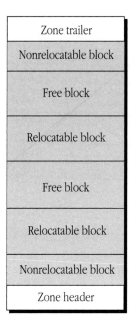

The Memory Manager uses a set number of bytes at the start of a heap zone to store information that it uses to manage the heap. This includes the address of the first byte of the contents of the zone, the address of the beginning of the zone trailer, and other data. The "Memory Manager" chapter of *Inside Macintosh,* Volume II, provides complete information about the contents of the zone header.

The Memory Manager is responsible for creating a heap zone in memory and for allocating and deallocating space within it. Your application does not manipulate any part of the heap directly. You need to understand, however, that if you happen to write over information contained in the zone header, the Memory Manager can no longer reliably find blocks it has allocated or allocate new ones, and this may cause your system to crash. The MacsBug HC (Heap Check) command tells you if the selected heap zone header or any block headers in that heap have been damaged.

MacsBug provides two commands that return information about heap zones.

The HZ (Heap Zone) command lists all the heaps. In a single-application environment, if you enter HZ, MacsBug returns the starting address of the current heap zones. For example:

```
Heap zones
 00001E00  SysZone
 0002D528  ApplZone  TheZone  TargetZone
```

Chapter 4   Macintosh Memory Organization   **103**

The HX (Heap Exchange) command selects the target heap for other heap commands. In a single-application environment, entering HX toggles between the system heap zone and the application heap zone.

The HZ and HX commands are described in greater detail in Chapter 9, "MacsBug Commands." For information about how these commands work in a multiple-application environment, see "Heap Management in a Multiple-Application Environment" later in this chapter.

Heap blocks

All heaps are made up of blocks. Your application does not create or delete heap blocks directly. The Memory Manager provides routines that you use to request the kind of block you need. You use other routines to give the Memory Manager additional information about how to handle these blocks and still others to resize the blocks or to dispose of the blocks when you no longer need them.

All blocks in the heap have the format shown in Figure 4-16. Blocks have two parts: the header area and the contents area.

■ **Figure 4-16** The format of a heap block

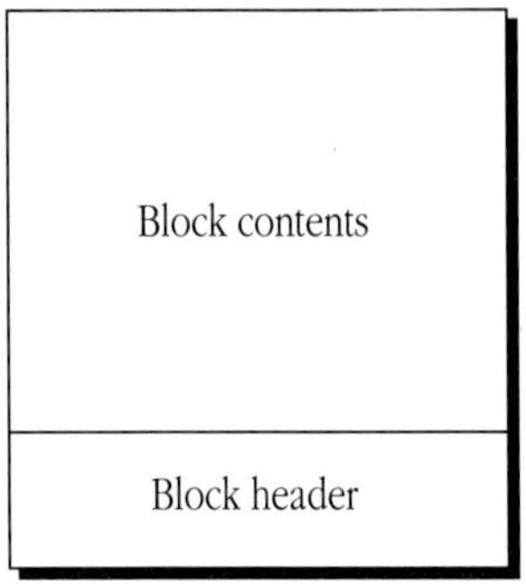

The Memory Manager uses the information kept in the block header to manage the heap. Although the Memory Manager is responsible for creating and managing blocks, you need to be aware of three things:

- The logical size of a block is the amount of space you specify with the size parameter when you call NewPtr or NewHandle. The physical size of the block includes the header region as well as whatever padding the Memory Manager adds to the block. The number of bytes added for padding is stored in the size correction field of the block header and is displayed in the output for the MacsBug HD (Heap Display) command.

- The starting address of the block, displayed by the MacsBug HD command, is the starting address of the block's content area.

- If you allocate a block that is 100 bytes in size and then write 120 bytes into it, you will write past the end of your heap block and over the beginning of the next block. Worst of all, you'll be writing over the block header of the next block, and, whatever kind of block that is, even if it's free, you will destroy the information stored in that header. The Memory Manager needs most of the information stored in the block header to manage the heap. If you write over this information, the next time you call the Memory Manager, it will crash. Fortunately, MacsBug provides a special command, HC (Heap Check), that you can use to check the heap and find the cause of such crashes.

There are three kinds of heap blocks: nonrelocatable, relocatable, and free:

- **Nonrelocatable blocks** never move. You request space for these blocks by using a NewPtr call or by calling another routine that calls NewPtr, such as NewWindow. The Memory Manager allocates these kinds of blocks as near to the bottom of the heap as it can. After it has allocated space in the heap for a nonrelocatable block, it returns a pointer to the block; the pointer contains the address of the start of the block. When you no longer need the block, you can call the DisposePtr routine to deallocate the space in the heap.

    Using too many nonrelocatable blocks can cause the heap to become fragmented, because when you deallocate them, you leave gaps in the heap that the Memory Manager can only fill with nonrelocatable or relocatable blocks that are that size or smaller.

- **Relocatable blocks** can be moved by the Memory Manager at certain well-defined times. You request space for these blocks by using a NewHandle routine or by calling another routine that calls NewHandle. The Memory Manager allocates space for these blocks right above the nonrelocatable blocks. After it has allocated space in the heap for a relocatable block, it stores the starting address of the block in a master pointer and then returns the address of the master pointer to you. Whenever you need to access the contents of the block, you use that pointer to the master pointer, or handle for short. When you no longer need the block, you call the DisposHandle routine to get rid of it.

Figure 4-17 shows the relationship between a relocatable block, the master pointer, and a handle. Whenever the Memory Manager moves the block, it also updates the address stored in the master pointer. In the example shown, the master pointer, at address 00022B40, stores the starting address of the relocatable block, 00091C2C. The handle, at address 0009BCE6, stores the address of the master pointer, 00022B40.

- **Figure 4-17** Handles and master pointers

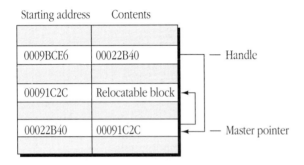

- **Free blocks** are chunks of space that have not yet been allocated. Although their name would suggest that they are bits of blank space, this is not the case. Each free block has a header that contains information which the Memory Manager uses to keep track of the contents of the block and of the structure of the heap. Overwriting the header of a free block has the same dire consequences as overwriting the header of any other block: a corrupt heap and a nontrivial bug.

Relocatable blocks have three properties not associated with other types of blocks:

- They can be locked or unlocked. Locking a relocatable block prevents it from being moved. While locked, a relocatable block acts like a nonrelocatable block and fragments the heap. The HLock and HUnlock calls lock and unlock relocatable blocks. Unecessarily locking relocatable blocks or neglecting to unlock them as soon as you can also causes heap fragmentation.
- They can be purgeable or unpurgeable. Making a block purgeable allows the Memory Manager to deallocate it, if necessary, to make room for another block. The HPurge and HNoPurge calls make relocatable blocks purgeable and nonpurgeable.
- They can contain resources.

If a block is marked as both locked and purgeable, the locked marking takes precedence over the purgeable marking.

Purgeable blocks are useful for data stored on disk that must be read in and used periodically, because they allow you to take full advantage of the memory available on any given machine. When you are finished with a block of data for the time being, but you might need to use it again, you can mark it as purgeable. As long as there's enough memory, the Memory Manager will leave a purgeable block sitting around in the heap after it has been used. This means that the next time your program needs that particular block, it will be available without having to be read into memory again from disk. But if memory is tight, the Memory Manager purges the block (deallocates it) to make room for something else. When you need the original data again, you have to read it in again from disk.

Using purgeable blocks thus allows your program to run faster on computers with lots of RAM. Your program doesn't need to keep track of whether memory is tight or not—the Memory Manager does that for you, and adjusts your program's memory usage accordingly.

Displaying information about heap blocks

MacsBug provides two commands that display information about heap blocks: the HT (Heap Totals) command and the HD (Heap Display) command. Before you use either of these commands, you must use the HX command to select the heap to which the blocks belong. If you are running in a multiple-application environment, use the HZ (Heap Zone) command to list the beginning address of all heap zones. You can then select the heap you're interested in by specifying its starting address as a parameter to the HX command.

The HT command displays information about the total number of each kind of block in the heap. Its output looks like this:

```
Totaling the Application heap at 00279FB8
                              Total Blocks      Total of Block Sizes
     Free                      0D1B   #3355      00040954   #264532
     Nonrelocatable            000E   #14        00037924   #227620
     Relocatable               00D8   #216       00085368   #545640
       Locked                  0003   #3         0006B73C   #440124
       Purgeable and not locked 000C  #12        00002D24   #11556
     Heap size                 0E01   #3585      000FD5E0   #1037792
```

The HT display can be slightly misleading if you're trying to figure out how much room you've got left in the heap. The amount it shows you is a total of all free blocks in the heap; if the heap is fragmented, you have nowhere near that amount of contiguous free space. To get a more exact picture of the heap, use the HD command. This command displays information about each block in the heap, including its starting address, its length, its type, the address of its master pointer and whether it's purgeable (if it's a relocatable block), its resource attributes (if it's a resource), and the file reference number and name (if it's a resource block).

The output of the HD command is similar to the following:

```
Displaying the Application heap
      Start    Length       Tag   Mstr Ptr Lock Prg  Type   ID    File    Name
•   0031CFE8 00000100+00     N
•   0031D0F0 00000018+00     R    0031D0E4   L
•   0031D110 00000032+02     N
•   0031D14C 0001CD36+02     N
    00339E8C 0000BDFC+00     F
•   0035232C 00000A60+00     N
•   00352D94 00029800+00     R    0031D070   L
•   0037C59C 00000006+02     N
    0037C5AC 0000009C+00     F
•   0037C650 0000000C+00     N
    0037C664 0000000C+00     F
    0037C678 00000010+00     F
•   0037C690 00000100+08     N
```

Each line of the display provides information about one heap block. Heap blocks are listed in order from the lowest address to the highest address. You can use the HD command to obtain information about one particular block or about all the blocks in a heap. (The description of the HD command in Chapter 9 describes the syntax and output of the command in greater detail.) Because the HD command lists information about blocks in the order in which blocks are stored in the heap, it literally gives you a picture of the heap.

If the starting address of a block is preceded by a dot, this indicates that the block cannot be moved, either because it's a nonrelocatable block or because it is a locked relocatable block. A look at the output of the HD command will quickly reveal whether your heap is fragmented. There's some serious fragmentation in the example just shown.

Although the Memory Manager is responsible for allocating blocks and letting you know where they are, it is your responsibility to request space in ways that allow you to make long-term efficient use of memory. The Memory Manager uses two methods to avoid heap fragmentation: memory reservation and memory compaction. It compacts the heap to create space for new relocatable blocks, and it reserves space on the heap for new nonrelocatable blocks. Volume I, Issue 2, of *Develop* magazine contains an excellent article by Richard Clark, "The Secret Life of the Memory Manager," that explains exactly how the Memory Manager manages the heap and what you can do to help it. The optimal arrangement of blocks on the heap is shown in Figure 4-18.

If the "picture" of your heap provided by the HD command looks very different from that shown in Figure 4-18, take a look at "The Secret Life of the Memory Manager" in *Develop* to find out what you can do about it.

- **Figure 4-18** Optimal arrangement of blocks in the heap

| Locked relocatable |
| Locked relocatable |
| Locked relocatable |
| Free blocks |
| Relocatable blocks |
| Nonrelocatable blocks |

Corrupting the heap

A heap becomes corrupt when the information that is stored in the heap zone header or the header of any block stored in the heap is overwritten. As with any form of corruption, the more damage occurs, the more difficult it is to find its source. That's why the best cure for heap corruption is to prevent it from occurring in the first place or, if it does occur, to set things up in such a way that it is easy to find the cause. This section provides a brief summary of the things that can corrupt the heap and describes two MacsBug commands that can help you anticipate problems and keep damage to a minimum.

The one thing you can do that will corrupt the heap every time is to write over the heap zone header or the header of a block in the heap. There are several ways to accomplish this:

- Writing beyond the end of the block you should be writing to and into the beginning of the next block. Even if the next block is free, the Memory Manager needs the information in its header to keep track of all the blocks, and, if that information is not valid, it can no longer manage the heap.

- NIL or dangling pointers and handles. If the address they point to happens to be in a heap header or block header, the heap will become corrupted the first time you write to that address. The next section, "Lost in the Heap," describes the most common causes of NIL or dangling pointers and handles.

The MacsBug HC (Heap Check) command allows you to check whether the information in block headers and the heap header is intact. If you suspect that your application is crashing because of a corrupt heap, you can narrow down the cause of your troubles by executing the HD (Heap Display) command. If a block header, rather than the heap header, is damaged, you'll get a listing of all the blocks that are OK. You should be able to extrapolate the beginning address of the block that's not OK by looking at this listing. If the heap header contains bad information, this won't work, but then at least you'll know that.

To find what instruction is causing the damage, turn A-trap recording on using the ATR (A-trap Record) command. Then, start by checking the heap every time you call an A-trap from your application by re-running your program using the ATHCA (A-trap Heap Check) command. Once the ATHCA command returns an error message, you'll know that either the previous A-trap call or any instruction following that call (but before the A-trap pointed to by the PC) has caused the problem. Use the ATP (A-trap Playback) command to display the last traps executed; from this listing you'll be able to figure out what the previous A-trap call was. If the range of instructions that you get using this procedure is small enough, you can step through the instructions, checking the heap after each instruction with the HC command to discover the offending instruction. If the range is too large to do this, you can take some educated guesses and then step through the smaller range of instructions.

Alternately, you can narrow down the source of heap corruption by using the DebugStr trap with an argument of ';HC;G'. For example, inserting the following call at key points in your program will cause MacsBug to be invoked every time the microprocessor encounters the DebugStr trap:

```
DebugStr ';HC; G'
```

The HC; G commands direct MacsBug to check the heap and continue executing if everything is OK. Otherwise, the HC command displays an error.

Lost in the heap

As mentioned in the last section, NIL or dangling pointers or handles can corrupt your heap—if you're lucky. If you're not lucky, they'll just corrupt your data and be that much more difficult to find. The sections "Catch NIL Pointers and Handles Instantly" and "Nasty Pointers" in Chapter 7 offer detailed suggestions on how to prevent and deal with these problems.

A **NIL** pointer or handle is what the Memory Manager returns to you when it can't allocate the space you ask for. When this happens, the Memory Manager stores an error code in the low-memory global variable MemErr that provides some additional information about why space could not be allocated. If, before using the pointer or handle, you test for the possibility of its being NIL, you'll be OK. Otherwise, if the Memory Manager can't find the space you need, your pointer will contain whatever value is stored at address 0; your handle will contain whatever value is stored at the address pointed to by the value stored at address 0. When you write to or read from the location your pointer or handle points to, you'll be corrupting the heap or the system data. Not checking for NIL handles and pointers is one of the most common causes of system crashes.

Dangling pointers and handles are pointers and handles that you think refer to the starting address of a block in memory, but that, for one of the following reasons, do not in fact refer to the block you're interested in:

- You deallocate space using a DisposePtr or DisposHandle routine, forget all about it, and use the pointer or handle to write or read to that block again.
- For greater run-time efficiency, you sometimes dereference the handle—that is, make a copy of the block's master pointer, and then use that pointer to access the block by single indirection. However, if the Memory Manager moves the relocatable block after you got the value stored in the master pointer (the address of the block), and you access the data in the block, you will read or write to the wrong place in memory. That is, you will write to where the data was, not to where it is now.

If you must make a copy of the master pointer, remember that your copy may be invalidated when you make a system call, because the Memory Manager may move the relocatable block to which the master pointer points. Appendix B of *Inside Macintosh* contains a list of system calls that can cause the Memory Manager to move heap blocks. If you must make one of the system calls listed, you can do one of two things to make sure that the data the handle is pointing to remains valid:

- You can use the MoveHHi call to move the block as high in memory as possible and then lock the relocatable block so it will not move. Unlock it again as soon as possible—a locked relocatable block fragments the heap just as a nonrelocatable block does.

- You can store the data in a temporary variable and use that variable any time that you think a block might move.

There are many subtle ways in which your program can crash because of dangling pointers. For example, suppose you need to make the system call GetNextEvent. GetNextEvent returns information in an EventRecord—so, being a good programmer who doesn't want to fragment the heap, you allocate a relocatable block for an EventRecord called MyEventHandle. You call GetNextEvent like this:

```
result := GetNextEvent (everyEvent, MyEventHandle^^):
```

When you call GetNextEvent, the address of MyEventHandle is passed to GetNextEvent. But GetNextEvent can cause heap blocks to move, thus invalidating the address passed in. However, GetNextEvent has no way of knowing that the event record was in a relocatable block. It therefore writes to the address that was passed in and trashes your heap.

There are two easy solutions to this problem. One is to lock the handle before the GetNextEvent call (remember to unlock it afterward). Alternatively, don't use a relocatable block to store your EventRecord. Store it somewhere else, for example, in a local or global variable.

As previously noted, a dangling pointer or handle, depending what address it's *really* pointing to, can cause you to corrupt the heap (if it points into a block or heap header) or to corrupt the data in the heap if it points into a block's contents. The HC (Heap Check) command, described in the previous section, "Corrupting the Heap," can help you find the trouble; but if you're trashing a block's contents, you'll get symptoms that are much harder to pin down.

The MacsBug HS (Heap Scramble) command is a very useful tool for finding dangling pointers and handles. Normally, the Memory Manager only moves blocks around when it has to; if you're developing a program and you've got lots of RAM to play with, the Memory Manager might not have to move blocks very often. In this case, you might not discover that you have a dangling handle because the block it's pointing to is never moved. This is where the HS command comes in; it makes the Memory Manager move relocatable blocks around whenever the move is legitimate—that is, during every A-trap call that can allocate memory directly or indirectly. This process also simulates running your program on a Macintosh with very little memory.

The HS command is described in greater detail in Chapter 9, "MacsBug Commands." It's mentioned here to emphasize the fact that it is a great aid in development and testing. If by moving blocks around the HS command only causes you to trash the contents of your blocks, you won't get any error messages (aside from possible bus errors), you'll just get some weird and inconsistent behavior on the part of your application. But chances are that the HS command will get your application to damage some block headers, in which case you'll corrupt the heap and be able to use the HC command to find the trouble.

If you run your program with heap scrambling turned on, you are likely to find a lot more bugs than if you leave it off. But these bugs are not *created* by the HS command; they are created by your program, and the earlier you find them, the easier they'll be to fix. A program with no bugs will run perfectly with heap scrambling turned on.

Heap management in a multiple-application environment

The section "Application Space" earlier in this chapter described how application space was organized in a single-application environment. As shown in Figure 4-19, the memory map in a multiple-application environment looks different from the memory map in a single-application environment (see Figure 4-14).

In a multiple-application environment, the Process Manager (MultiFinder in system software version 5.0 or 6.0) manages a heap within which it allocates a locked relocatable block, called a **partition,** for each open application. An open application or **process** is the Finder, any application launched by the user, or any application that runs only in the background. The partition for each open application is structured like the application space in a single-application environment: it contains the application's heap, stack, A5 world, and jump table. When you create an application, you specify the amount of memory you want the Process Manager to allocate for your application's partition using the application's 'SIZE' resource. (The Process Manager allocates a locked relocatable block for each open application, because each application can allocate nonrelocatable blocks in its heap; if the Process Manager moved an application's partition around within its heap, the application's nonrelocatable blocks would also move, which is not allowed.)

■ **Figure 4-19** Application space in a multiple-application environment

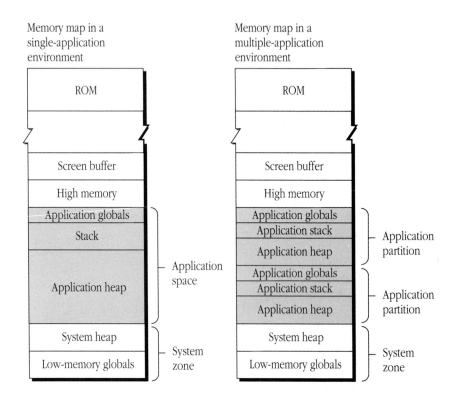

When you launch an application, the Process Manager places the application's partition as high as possible in its heap. Because the Process Manager cannot move the partition, it is possible to fragment the Process Manager's heap, as illustrated in Figure 4-20.

Since the Finder is automatically launched at startup, its heap is always the highest (unless you have background printing on, in which case that heap is the highest, and the Finder is next). If you launch MacPaint®, MacPaint's heap will be right below the Finder's. If you then launch MacWrite®, MacWrite's heap will be next. The left half of Figure 4-20 shows the situation at this point, with 500K still available in the Process Manager's heap. You want to launch FullWrite Professional, but you need 1000K for FullWrite. So you quit MacPaint. Can you launch FullWrite now? No—even though you have 1000K free, it is fragmented, as shown in the right half of Figure 4-20. If you were to quit MacWrite and relaunch it, it would be launched as high as possible (in MacPaint's old spot), the heap would be unfragmented, and you could then launch FullWrite.

■ **Figure 4-20** Fragmenting the Process Manager's heap

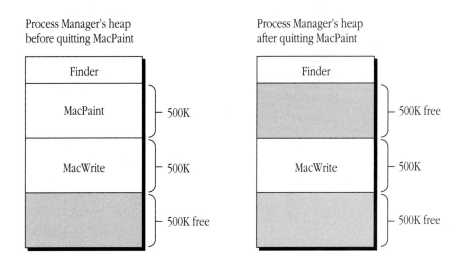

The Process Manager places application partitions as high as possible for a good reason. In a single-application environment, when an application needs a system resource, such as a printer driver, the resource is loaded into the application's heap. But in a multiple-application environment, it would be a waste of memory for each application to get its own copy of every system resource. So these resources are automatically loaded into the system heap, allowing every application that's open to share the same copy.

This means the system heap will contain much more in a multiple-application environment than it would in a single-application environment. Originally, the system heap was designed to be small, hold a few system resources, and remain pretty much static once it was loaded. It had just enough space to hold the basics, and very little extra free space. In a multiple-application environment, the system heap might have to accept all kinds of system resources dynamically. To allow it to do this, the Process Manager expands the system heap as needed by shrinking the bottom of its own heap. But it's important that the Process Manager's heap not have any nonrelocatable blocks at its base, or this strategy won't work.

For additional information about the Process Manager, see the "Process Management" chapter in *Inside Macintosh,* Volume VI.

Displaying heaps in a multiple-application environment

When you drop into MacsBug in a multiple-application environment, MacsBug behaves as though you were running a single application. MacsBug sees two heaps: the system heap and the heap of the currently running application, which is usually the frontmost application. The name of the current application is shown in the status region of the MacsBug display. It's a good idea to check this item in case the application that caused MacsBug to be invoked was a background application that was running at the time of the crash.

If you enter the HZ (Heap Zone) command, MacsBug displays a list of addresses that indicate the start and end of each heap. The current application has its heap labeled as ApplZone. The addresses of the Process Manager's heap and of the other application heaps are listed but not labeled. The HZ command also tells you, in the leftmost column of the display, whether the heap is 24-bit or 32-bit. For example,

```
Heap zones
    24      00001E00 to 0006B41F  SysZone^
    24         00001FB8 to 0000248B
    24      0006B420 to 004C40DB
    24         004092C4 to 00482A53  ApplZone^  TheZone^  TargetZone
    24         0048A2CC to 004AEFF3
    24         004B62D4 to 004B7BB7
```

The HZ display identifies embedded heaps by indenting them. In the output just shown, the heap zone from 00001FB8 to 0000248B is embedded in the system heap; the heap zones from 004092C4 to 00482A53, from 0048A2CC to 004AEFF3, and from 004B62D4 to 004B7BB7 are all embedded in the Process Manager's heap zone, which starts at 0006B420 and ends at 004C40DB. All heap zones in this example are 24-bit.

The HZ command uses three low-memory global variables and one MacsBug variable to describe some of the heaps:

- ApplZone (low-memory global variable) points to the start of the current application heap.

- TheZone (low-memory global variable) points to the zone currently set by the SetZone routine.

- TargetZone (MacsBug variable) points to the zone currently set by the MacsBug HX command.

- SysZone (low-memory global variable) points to the start of the system heap.

The other heaps are identifiable only by their addresses and by your knowledge of the fact that the earlier the application was launched, the higher its address. See the description of the HZ command in Chapter 9, "MacsBug Commands," for additional information.

Switching heaps in a multiple-application environment

You can use the HX (Heap Exchange) command to switch among the various heaps that are currently in RAM. If you simply type HX, MacsBug switches between the system heap and the current application heap. If you type HX and the address of a heap, MacsBug will switch to that specific heap. If you do specify an address for the HX command, MacsBug identifies that heap in the display as "UserZone" just to remind you that this was the last heap you were specifically interested in.

Remember that all MacsBug heap commands (except for the HS command) work on the heap you selected with HX. The beginning address of this heap is stored in the MacsBug variable TargetZone. When you start MacsBug, it defaults to the frontmost application heap.

The HX command does not do anything else except to select a heap as the implied target for most heap commands. It does not make the selected heap the frontmost application, for example. This can affect the information that's displayed about heaps if the selected application is not frontmost. For example, if you use HX to select a heap belonging to a background application, MacsBug displays resource blocks in that heap, but identifies them only as relocatable blocks and displays the message "Resource not found" in the space where it would normally display resource information.

This happens because the Process Manager disconnects the resource chains of applications when they are not running. This prevents the foreground application from accidentally loading a resource from another application. It also means that when you switch to another application's heap in MacsBug, resources in the heap won't be identified as such if that application is not running in the foreground. The HD command will only display resource information for resource blocks in the currently running application.

Life on the stack

As mentioned in the beginning of this chapter, the compiler does not know variable names, but only their addresses. Since your program can be loaded at different locations in memory, the compiler needs to use some scheme of relative addressing that allows it to manipulate variables (addresses) and what's stored in them independently of where your program is loaded. The compiler does this by using a data structure called the **stack** and three address registers, A5, A6, and A7, that the compiler can use to reference the global variables, local variables, parameters, and context information that your program needs to use as it's running.

This section explains how registers A5, A6, and A7 are used to reference data placed on the stack. It describes the units of the stack, called **stack frames.** It also describes the different conventions used by Pascal and C compilers in implementing routines, and what C programmers must do when calling A-traps, which use Pascal calling conventions. Finally, it discusses how you can use the MacsBug command MR (Magic Return) to step out of a procedure, and the commands SC (Stack Crawl) or SC7 (Stack Crawl [A7]) to obtain information about the current calling chain.

Looking at the stack

It's unfortunate that Microsoft Word can't display the title of this section upside down, just to imprint in your mind the first thing about stacks: they grow *down,* toward low memory.

The left side of Figure 4-21 shows a picture of the stack in memory; the right side shows the picture of the stack that MacsBug shows you by default in the status region of the display.

As you can see from the picture on the left of Figure 4-21, the stack grows down. The "top of the stack" is a euphemism; it is literally at the bottom of the stack. The address of the base of the stack, which remains fixed, is stored in the low-memory global variable CurStackBase. To display its location, enter

`DM CurStackBase`

or

`CurStackBase^`

The address of the top of the stack is always stored in register A7. Displaying the value of A7 displays the address; dereferencing A7, by entering A7^, displays what is stored at that address.

The MacsBug display of the stack, which takes up the upper half of the status region, is slightly misleading because it turns the stack upside down, so that the top of the stack is at the top of the display.

■ **Figure 4-21** Representations of the stack

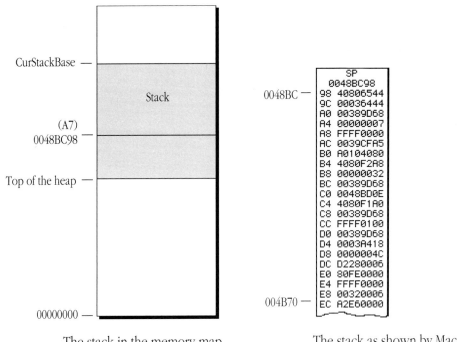

The stack in the memory map   The stack as shown by MacsBug

The stack display begins with SP (for stack pointer) and the address that it points to right underneath. (If you look in the register area of the status region, you'll notice that this same address is stored in register A7.) The next line of the stack display shows the least significant byte of this address and 4 bytes of memory starting at that address. The display then shows 4 bytes of memory for every line of the display, preceded by the least significant byte of the address. The address is not shown in its entirety to save space and because, for the range that can be shown in the display, the upper 3 bytes are not likely to change. You can figure out the upper 3 bytes by looking at the SP address at the top of the display. Figure 4-22 shows how the top two lines of the MacsBug stack display (shown in Figure 4-21) translate into memory storage at consecutive addresses.

Chapter 4   Macintosh Memory Organization   119

■ **Figure 4-22** Stack display and storage in memory

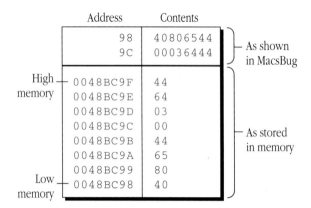

After you compile your program, the instructions that are generated to allocate space for your global variables and for implementing routines do their work by allocating space on the stack, and representing all values as offsets from key addresses on the stack, which are stored in registers A5, A6, and A7. The following sections explain how.

Before proceeding, though, make sure you're familiar with these three aspects of the stack:

- Space on the stack is always allocated and released in last-in, first-out (LIFO) order; the last item allocated is always the first to be released. In this respect, the stack is like a pile of papers in a basket: you can put papers on the top or take them off the top, but you can't put things into or take things from the middle of the pile without first dealing with the stuff on top.

- To push something means to put it on the stack; to pop something means to take it off the stack. The stack pointer is used in assembly language to push individual items onto the stack or to pop them off. See "Stack Frame Instructions" in Chapter 3 for additional information.

- The size of each item on the stack varies, just as a pile of papers in a basket might include magazines and reports as well as smaller clipped or stapled groups of papers. Although MacsBug's default display of the stack might suggest that all items on the stack take up exactly 4 bytes, this is a characteristic of the display, not of the stack. Furthermore, there are no boundaries between items on the stack (as there are block headers to mark heap units off from each other). Rather, the compiler (or the assembly-language programmer) allocates the right amount of space on the stack for each item that is pushed on. The section "Stack Frames," later in this chapter, explains how.

Allocating space for global variables

Although it can be argued that global variables are not part of the stack at all, learning how space is allocated for global variables provides a good introduction to the way the compiler allocates space for your routines' results, parameters, and local variables, which is described in the next section.

When your program begins to execute, there is nothing on the stack. The first thing that the compiler allocates space for on the stack is your global variables. Before it does this, however, it must record a point of origin, relative to which it can find the beginning address of every global variable. The way the compiler does this is to take the address the stack pointer is pointing to and put it in register A5. Then, as it allocates space for each global variable, it decrements the address in A5 by exactly the number of bytes that the global variable is going to take up. If the global variable is an integer, the compiler decrements the address by 2 bytes; if the global variable is an address, the compiler decrements the address by 4 bytes; and so forth.

Why does the compiler *decrement* the address stored in A5? Because the stack grows toward low memory. What happens to the stack pointer (the address stored in A7)? It is also decremented as space is allocated on the stack and the stack grows; it always points to the address where items can be pushed onto or popped off the stack.

Figure 4-23 shows the correspondence between the space allocated for global variables and your high-level language declarations.

- **Figure 4-23** Allocating space for global variables

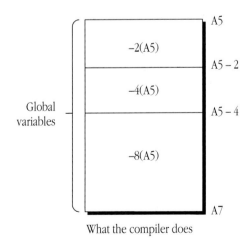

Notice how the addresses where the variables are stored are computed in Figure 4-23. If you want to display the value of one of your global variables, you use the command

```
DM (A5 - 2)
Displaying memory from (A5-2)
 003BFFD6  0000 0027 DDBA 6DB6  DB6D 0000 0000 0000   •••'••m••m••••••
```

or just

```
(A5 - 2)^
 (a5 -2)^ = $00000027    #39     #39     '•••''
```

Also, notice how the compiler has "renamed'" your variables. What is *age* to you is –2(A5) to the compiler. The compiler reads –2(A5) as follows: "Take the address stored in register A5, subtract 2 from it, and dereference the resulting address."

All the compiler has done so far is to allocate space on the stack for your variable. The space that is allocated is not necessarily blank, nor does it magically hold the value that you want *age* to be. To put a useful value in the space that the compiler has conscientiously reserved, you have to initialize your variable. To find out whether the variable contains the correct value, you can display memory at the address you are interested in by using the DM command as shown in the example just provided.

Finally, after allocating space for your variables, the compiler will forever refer to the value of these variables as they are shown on the left side of Figure 4-23. Thus, if you ever see an expression of the form –*X*(A5) in the code generated by the compiler, you will know that it is referring to a global variable.

Stack frames

In addition to storing global variables, the compiler also uses the stack to reserve space for your routines' return result, local variables, parameters, and other information needed to restore the context that was current when your main program called a routine or one routine called another. Because there are so many kinds of information to allocate space for and to find, the compiler needs a systematic way to place that information on the stack so that it is readily identifiable and accessible. The way it accomplishes this is through the use of stack frames.

The compiler uses a stack frame to allocate the information a routine needs to execute and to return to the right place after it's finished. Just as the compiler uses register A5 to store an address relative to which it can reference all global variables, it uses register A6 to store an address relative to which it can reference everything in the stack frame. Figure 4-24 shows a complete stack frame.

■ **Figure 4-24** A stack frame

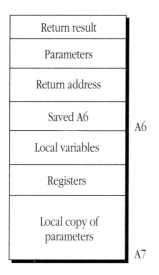

This section describes each step involved in building a stack frame. Since system routines follow Pascal's conventions for using the stack, the description focuses on those conventions. If you are a C programmer, you'll need to consult the documentation for your own compiler and the section "Pascal and C Calling Conventions" later in this chapter for additional information.

Every routine is called either by the main program or by another routine. Because a stack frame is partly built by the calling routine and partly by the called routine, it is easiest to understand its structure by understanding what information the calling routine has and what information the called routine has.

What does the calling routine (be it the main program or another routine) know about the called routine when it's about to call it? At that point the program counter is pointing to either a BSR or a JSR instruction, so one of the things it knows is that when the routine is finished executing and control is returned to the calling routine, the calling routine has to resume execution at the instruction following the JSR or BSR instruction. In short, by adding 4 bytes to the address stored in the PC register, it knows the return address.

The calling routine also knows whether the called routine is a function or a procedure; that is, it knows whether the routine will return a result or not. If the called routine returns a result, the calling routine knows the size of the result. The calling routine also knows how many parameters (if any) are passed to the called routine, their order, their size, and their value.

With this information, the calling routine is ready to build the first half of the stack frame, which it does in a predetermined order: first it makes room for the routine's result, then for the routine's parameters, and then for the return address. Finally, the compiler knows that after the calling routine has finished building its part of the stack, the first thing the called routine will do is to save the current value of A6 on the stack and then set A6 equal to A7. Thus everything that the calling routine puts on the stack can be referenced relative to the address in A6. Figure 4-25 shows an example of the part of the stack frame that is built by a calling routine.

- **Figure 4-25** Part of stack frame built by calling routine

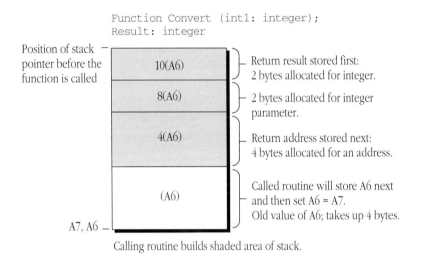

As you can see, everything the calling routine puts on the stack is referenced as a positive offset from A6. When the PC points to the JSR instruction, the compiler will have already allocated space on the stack for the return value (if any) and the parameter(s). When the JSR instruction executes, the compiler will have allocated 4 more bytes for the return address and stored it. The first instruction of the called routine is a LINK instruction; this instruction saves the current value in A6 on the stack and stores the current value of A7 in A6. Every item the called routine now allocates on the stack will be referenced as a negative offset from A6.

Pascal uses the following conventions when it puts values for your routine's parameters on the stack:

- The compiler pushes a pointer onto the stack for any parameter that's passed by reference (VAR parameters).

- The compiler pushes a pointer onto the stack for any parameter that is larger than 4 bytes.
- The compiler pushes a pointer onto the stack for any Pascal string, even if it's smaller than 4 bytes.
- The compiler pushes a pointer onto the stack for any SANE® (Standard Apple Numerics Environment) variable: Real, Single, Double, Extended, or Comp.

This means that the addresses of such parameters, not their values, are stored on the stack.

What does the called routine know after it executes the LINK instruction? It knows the sizes and order of its local variables, but it does not know their value until the instructions that assign each value are executed, and these can be anywhere in the procedure. It also knows the current values of all the registers, and it is required to save the values of some of these registers on the stack (D3–D7 and A2–A6). The routine might need to save the values of all registers it expects to use. Then, when the routine has finished executing, it can restore the original values so that these are available to the calling routine.

Depending on the values of the parameters, the called routine might also add a copy of a parameter that is passed by reference in the first half of the stack frame because it is too large. Why does the compiler store a copy on the stack now if the parameter was deemed too large to be placed on the stack in the first place? Because when the rule was made, stacks were very tiny; when stacks got larger, additional room existed to make an actual copy of the parameter, though the rule was still observed about how it should be stored in the first half of the stack frame.

Figure 4-26 illustrates the order in which the called routine adds pieces to the stack frame.

- **Figure 4-26** Part of stack built by called routine

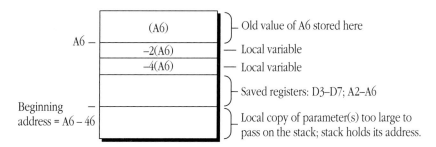

Figure assumes that the called routine allocates space for two local variables that take up 2 bytes each, and that the routine saves the standard set of registers.

Chapter 4 Macintosh Memory Organization **125**

When the procedure starts to execute—to initialize variables, to compute and store new values in these variables, or to use values passed to it in parameters—it can access all these variables as offsets from A6. If you understand how the compiler sets up a stack frame, you can display memory at various addresses on the stack to see the values of your variables, parameters, and so forth. Figure 4-27 shows a complete picture of the stack frame.

- **Figure 4-27** The stack frame

Return result
Parameters
Return address
Saved A6 — A6
Local variables
Registers
Local copy of parameters — A7

What happens when the called routine finishes executing? Basically, everyone cleans up their own mess:

- The called routine executes an UNLK instruction, which moves the stack pointer back to the address stored in A6, moves the saved value of A6 into A6, and then increments the stack pointer by 4 bytes so that it is now pointing at the return address. All that is left of the stack now is what the calling routine has put there.

- The calling routine pops the return address off the stack and saves it in register A0, increments the stack pointer by the amount allocated for the parameters, and then jumps to the address stored in A0. You'll notice that if the routine is a function, this leaves the function result sitting neatly on top of the stack, where the instruction that has been jumped to conveniently finds it.

MacsBug allows you to do several useful things that depend on stack frames. These are described in the next sections, "Stepping Out of a Procedure," "Displaying a Function's Result," and "Using Stack Frames to Establish a Calling Chain."

Stepping out of a procedure

The MR (Magic Return) command allows you to step out of a procedure that you've accidentally stepped into. That is, the MR command executes the rest of the procedure and invokes MacsBug when the PC points to the return address. MR lets you do this by setting up a breakpoint at the return address on the stack, but you have to help the MR command figure out where that value is stored on the stack. The syntax of the MR command is

MR [*param*]

The value you specify for *param* gives the MR command the information it needs. The value you choose depends on how far you've stepped into the procedure:

- If the program counter points to the LINK instruction, enter MR with no parameters. In this case the return address is assumed to be stored on the top of the stack.

- If the program counter points after the first instruction, you should specify A6 as the parameter to the MR command, like this:

    `MR A6`

    If you do, the MR command looks for the return address at A6 + 4.

The MR command is described in greater detail in Chapter 9, "MacsBug Commands."

Displaying a function's result

Another useful thing you can do using the MR command and your knowledge of stack frames is to define a breakpoint so that every time a certain function is called, MacsBug is invoked and displays the function result. For example, if you enter the following commands:

`BR` *functionname* `' ; MR ; DW  SP '`

whenever the breakpoint is reached, MacsBug executes the MR command and displays the top word on the stack (the function result). For functions that return long words, use the command

`BR` *functionname* `' ; MR ; DL  SP '`

For functions that return pointers, dereference the pointer and display the structure using a template; for example:

`BR` *functionname* `' ; MR ; DM SP^` *templatename* `'`

Using stack frames to establish a calling chain

What does the stack look like when one procedure calls another? Figure 4-28 shows what the stack looks like in the case of procedure A calling procedure B, which calls procedure C.

■ **Figure 4-28** Multiple stack frames

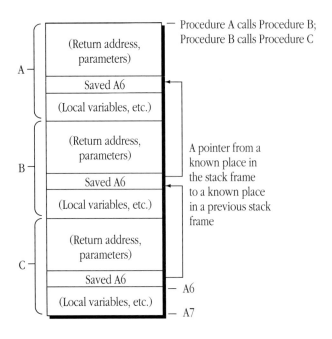

Each stack frame in Figure 4-28 has been stripped of most of its detail to emphasize the way in which the frames are linked together through the use of register A6 as a stack frame pointer.

When procedure C executes, it locates everything it needs to do its work relative to the value stored in register A6. When it has finished and it executes the UNLK instruction, it cleans up after itself (as explained earlier) and moves the saved value of A6 from the stack into register A6. Now procedure B (the calling procedure at this point) can clean up its part of the stack and resume execution.

Since A6 now points to the right place in B's stack frame, B can do all its work with reference to that value. When it is finished, B executes an UNLK instruction, and puts the value of A6 it has saved in its stack frame into register A6. Procedure A can now clean up its part of B's stack frame and resume execution using the current value of A6 as a way of referencing everything it needs to work with.

As noted earlier in this chapter, the use of stack frames allows the compiler to generate instructions that reference everything a routine creates and manipulates relative to one address, stored in register A6. The use of stack frames also allows MacsBug to determine the calling chain when one procedure calls another. This can be very helpful when you're hunting for bugs.

How does MacsBug use stack frames to determine the calling chain? The return address, which is always an address in the calling procedure, is always stored 4 bytes off A6. The stack frame makes the address easy to find; once MacsBug has the address, it can figure out what procedure it's in. To display the calling chain, use the SC (Stack Crawl) command. MacsBug displays information like the following:

```
Calling chain using A6 links
 A6 Frame    Caller
 0027BB5C    00218DC6 CONVERSI+0016
 0027BB54    00218D2A DOMAINEV+003A
 0027BB0A    00218B72 DOCLICK+0038
 0027BAC4    00218AB6 DOMENUDI+002C
 0027BA98    003B418A
 0027B93C    0080F19E _GetMouse+0070
```

The first row describes the oldest stack frame (procedure); the last row describes the newest stack frame (procedure). This listing can be interpreted as follows:

1. At address 00218DC6 the procedure CONVERSI stored an instruction (JSR or BSR) that called the DOMAINEV procedure.

2. At address 00218D2A the procedure DOMAINEV stored an instruction that called the DOCLICK procedure.

3. At address 00218AB6 the procedure DOMENUDI stored an instruction that called an unnamed procedure.

4. At address 003B418A an unnamed procedure stored an instruction that called the GetMouse trap.

The value of A6 when each of the calling procedures is current is listed in the first column.

If MacsBug does not know the procedure name, but the address is in a known resource, it displays the type of the resource, the number of the resource, the file in which the resource is stored, the name of the resource, and the offset within the resource where the instruction is found; for example:

```
'CODE 0007 0294 Init'+0A3C
```

Pascal and C calling conventions

The conventions described so far for setting up stack frames are the conventions used by Pascal compilers. C compilers use different conventions. Since A-trap routines expect to be called according to Pascal conventions, you have nothing to worry about if you're writing a Pascal program. Setting up a stack frame for a system routine is just like setting one up for a routine you've written yourself. The parameters are placed on the stack in the same order (left to right); large parameters, string parameters, and VAR parameters are passed by reference. The calling routine sets up and cleans up its part of the stack; the A-trap sets up and cleans up its part of the stack.

If you're writing a C program and call an A-trap, you need to use the Pascal compiler directive before the A-trap declarations (this is done in the C include header file); this directive will take care of most of the differences, but not all. Keep the following points in mind:

- In Pascal, return results are passed back onto the stack. In C, they are passed back in register D0. Using the *pascal* keyword with a C compiler for the Macintosh will take care of this.

- In Pascal, parameters are pushed in left to right order. In C, they are pushed in right to left order. Using the *pascal* keyword with a C compiler for the Macintosh will take care of this.

- The calling function always puts the parameters on the stack. In Pascal, the *called* function removes the parameters from the stack. In C, the *calling* function removes the parameters from the stack. Using the *pascal* keyword with a C compiler for the Macintosh will take care of this.

- In Pascal, any parameter that is 4 bytes or smaller is passed by value. In other words, the value of the parameter is simply pushed onto the stack. Any parameter larger than 4 bytes is passed by reference. This means that the *address* of the parameter is pushed onto the stack. VAR parameters are always passed by reference, no matter what their size. In C, scalar parameters (such as char, int, or long) are passed by value. Structures (similar to records in Pascal) are passed by value. Arrays are passed by reference. Using the *pascal* keyword with a C compiler for the Macintosh *will not* take care of this. The programmer must take care of this explicitly.

In other words, if your C program calls an A-trap routine that requires you to pass a pointer, you must pass a pointer even though you would not have to if this were a C routine. This does not involve extra work; it only means that you must pass parameters to A-trap calls exactly as described in *Inside Macintosh*.

Application parameters and the jump table

The remaining two regions of memory that belong to the application's memory space are reserved for the application parameters and the jump table. Figure 4-29 shows these regions.

- **Figure 4-29** Application parameters and jump table

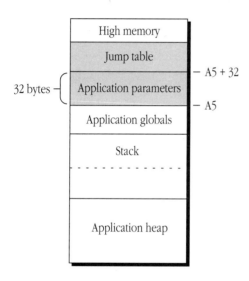

The allocation of space for your program's global variables is discussed in the section "Allocating Space for Global Variables" earlier in this chapter. The chief thing to remember is that anything the compiler translates into the form –X(A5) is a global variable.

The application parameters reside above the global variables. Register A5 points to the first byte of the application parameters. The system accesses the application parameters using positive offsets from A5, while the application accesses the application global variables using negative offsets from A5.

Application parameters contain information about the program. However, the system, and not the application, sets up and uses this information. The most important application parameter is at the address stored at 0(A5); it points to the first QuickDraw global variable. QuickDraw global variables are stored in your program's global variables region, just after the space reserved for your program's global variables.

The jump table is discussed in greater detail in the section "Intersegment Calls and the Jump Table" in Chapter 3. The main points to remember are that the jump table resides above the application parameters, and that it contains pointers to the routines in each code segment. Routines in one code segment use the jump table to find routines in another code segment.

Since the application parameters are always exactly 32 bytes long, the application gets to the jump table by adding 32 to the value in A5. The jump table is set up by the linker and used automatically by your application; you don't usually need to worry about it.

Operating system or User Interface Toolbox routines sometimes save the value in A5 so they can use it as another register. When this happens, the routine always restores the value of A5 before returning. The low-memory global variable CurrentA5 ($904) contains the proper A5 value for the currently executing application. This is useful if you find yourself in a ROM routine in which A5 is used to store other information. CurrentA5 is not valid during the Process Manager's context switches.

Chapter 5 The Macintosh Operating System

From the point of view of your application, Macintosh system software consists of a set of external routines grouped under a specific manager according to their functions. These routines are divided into User Interface Toolbox routines and operating system routines. This chapter describes how these routines are implemented by means of exception processing and how they are modified and extended using patches and glue.

Understanding how system routines work allows you to make better use of MacsBug. In particular, this chapter explains how you can use MacsBug to monitor the execution of these routines: how to invoke MacsBug when a routine is called, how to record and play back the sequence in which these routines are executed, and how to perform heap checks when a routine is called. It includes a hands-on exercise that you can use to watch how a system routine is implemented.

Many system routines typically operate upon one or more data structures that are maintained by the managers. Managers use various means of maintaining and keeping track of these data structures. Although a detailed description of how each manager does this lies beyond the scope of this manual, this chapter includes descriptions of three standard dcmds, vol, file, and drvr, that allow you to look at the information maintained by the File Manager for mounted volumes and files, and by the Device Manager for installed drivers and desk accessories. This chapter also describes the vbl dcmd, which lists all VBL tasks currently scheduled to run.

To understand this chapter, you should be familiar with the way the compiler uses the stack to implement procedures and functions. If you are not, please read the relevant sections in Chapter 4, "Macintosh Memory Organization."

If you are thoroughly familiar with Macintosh programming, you do not need to read the entire chapter, but you might want to review the descriptions of the vbl, vol, file, and drvr dcmds.

Exception processing

The microprocessor is always in one of three states: normal, exception, or halted. The normal state means that the microprocessor can understand and knows how to process every instruction it encounters. In the halted state, a catastrophic system failure has occurred; only an external reset can restart a halted processor. Exception processing lies somewhere between these two extremes: something has happened that the microprocessor cannot understand or handle directly, but it knows that there is a routine designed to take care of the "exceptional" condition; its job is to find that routine and transfer control to it.

Exception processing refers to the means used by the microprocessor to handle unusual conditions caused by the hardware or by the software that must be addressed before normal processing resumes.

During exception processing, the microprocessor must save sufficient information about its current state (PC and register values) to be able to restore that state after the exception has been processed. As just mentioned, the microprocessor itself does not know the details of how to handle the various kinds of exceptions, but it is responsible for figuring out the address of a routine that does and for transferring control to that routine by putting the routine's address into the program counter. Processing then resumes at that address.

Exception processing can be generated by the hardware, in which case it's called an **interrupt,** or it can be generated by the software, in which case it's called an **exception.**

- If the exception is generated by the hardware, the routine that handles the exception is called an **interrupt handler.** The section "Interrupts" later in this chapter explains how the processor handles interrupts and the guidelines you must follow when writing code that runs at interrupt time.

- If the exception is generated by the software and is due to an error condition (division by zero, illegal instruction, bus error, or address error), the routine that handles the exception is called an error handler. Chapter 1, "MacsBug and Low-Level Debugging," describes error handling and how MacsBug functions as an error handler.

- If the exception is generated by the microprocessor as a result of encountering an unimplemented instruction, the routine that handles the exception is called the trap dispatcher. To the microprocessor, all A-trap calls in your application are unimplemented instructions that cause it to begin exception processing. The first half of this chapter describes how A-traps are processed.

How does the microprocessor know where to transfer control? Motorola has provided for the possibility that 256 different kinds of exceptions can occur; a vector table in low memory assigns a number to every kind of exception. When an exception occurs, the microprocessor determines the number (also called the vector number) that identifies that particular kind of exception. For an interrupt, the microprocessor obtains the number from an internal location; for a software-generated exception, internal logic provides the number. The microprocessor then uses this number to calculate the address of the routine that can handle the exception. This address is also called an **exception vector.**

A-trap exceptions

When the compiler generates code for any call you make to the User Interface Toolbox or the operating system, it substitutes a 2-byte instruction, which always begins with the hexadecimal digit A, for the function or procedure name in your source code. (These instructions are not implemented in the microprocessor; the microprocessor calls the trap dispatcher to handle them.) This is why system routines are generically known as A-traps. For instance, the A-trap A913 is NewWindow, and A92D is CloseWindow. Appendix C of *Inside Macintosh* contains a complete list of A-traps sorted both by name and by number. (Note that each volume of *Inside Macintosh* has a different Appendix C, each with a different list.) MacsBug knows the name, number, and address of every A-trap.

A-traps are also referred to as ROM calls, but, as we shall shortly see, this name is inaccurate, because the code such instructions cause to be run is not always in ROM. This manual refers to User Interface Toolbox and operating system routines as system routines, distinguishing between them when necessary.

To the microprocessor, any instruction that causes a system routine to execute is an unimplemented instruction: that is, an instruction that was not defined by Motorola. Unimplemented instructions are a kind of exception, and the microprocessor has to determine the address of the routine that knows what to do with them and transfer control to that routine.

The following section explains what happens when an application calls an A-trap instruction: how control is transferred to the trap dispatcher, how the trap dispatcher executes the right routine, and how control is handed back to your program.

How the operating system handles an A-trap

Figure 5-1 demonstrates how the operating system handles an A-trap instruction. The right part of the figure shows the flow of control. The remainder of this section describes the process in detail.

- **Figure 5-1** How the operating system handles an A-trap

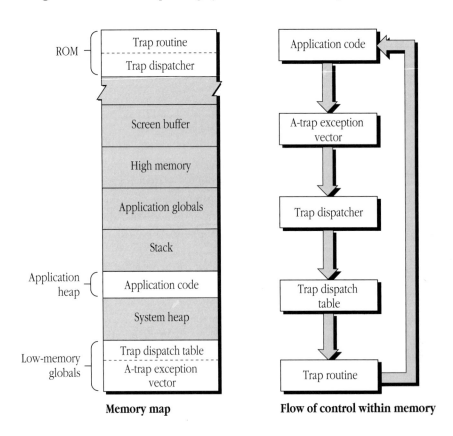

Suppose the microprocessor is running an application and encounters an A-trap. Because an A-trap is not a defined instruction, it causes an exception. The microprocessor handles the exception by following these steps:

1. The microprocessor fetches the vector number for the exception and calculates the address of the exception handler.

2. Every A-trap uses the same exception vector, which always points to the same exception handler, the trap dispatcher. The microprocessor turns control over to the trap dispatcher.

3. The trap dispatcher looks up the address of the A-trap in the **trap dispatch table** in RAM. The trap dispatch table is simply a table listing the address of every A-trap routine. (The trap dispatcher also sets things up so that the A-trap routine can terminate with an RTS instruction and return to the instruction following the A-trap call when the A-trap routine is finished.)

4. The trap dispatcher then jumps to the code at the address it got from the dispatch table. This code is usually the actual ROM routine (although it could just as easily be in RAM) that does whatever your application wants done, such as opening a window.

5. When the trap is done executing, it returns control to your application.

Why such a roundabout procedure? Why have the trap dispatcher in ROM and the trap dispatch table in RAM? The answer has to do with the ongoing evolution of software. If a routine in ROM needs to be fixed, improved, or extended or if new routines are added, a trap dispatch table in RAM provides a very easy way to implement such changes: simply change the address of the routine in the table to the new address of the changed routine, place the routine in the system file in RAM, replace the old system file with the new system file, and everything will work just right. The code that changes the address of an A-trap is called a **patch.** The next section describes this process in greater detail.

Patches and glue

There are two cases in which a system routine is not located in ROM:

- In the first case, the code for an existing routine in ROM has been modified and the trap dispatch table has been patched so that it now points to an address in RAM where the modified code resides. This process, called patching, is used to modify existing routines or to add new routines.

- In the second case, the code that constitutes the system routine is so simple that, rather than going through the multiple instructions that are needed to process an exception, the compiler or the linker inserts the code that makes up the routine directly into your program. This process is called inserting **glue.**

The sections that follow describe these two situations and discuss the consequences for debugging.

Patching an A-trap

Installing a patch changes the address of the A-trap entry in the A-trap dispatch table so the table points to the patch (in RAM) rather than to the original routine in ROM, as shown in Figure 5-2. Apple uses patches to fix bugs in system software or to add features to a system routine.

■ **Figure 5-2** Patching an A-trap

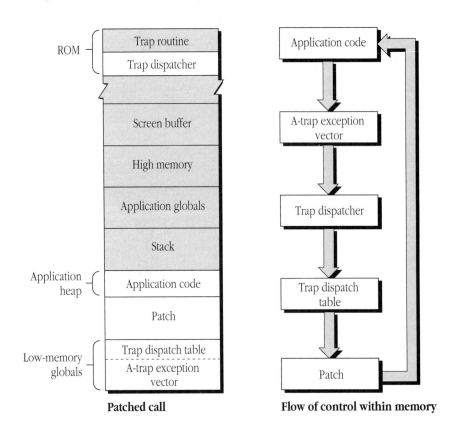

Figure 5-2 shows how control goes from the application to the patched A-trap and back to the application in the case of an A-trap that is patched so that it entirely replaces the old trap. Note that in the case where a patch is designed to completely replace a ROM routine, control returns to the calling application from the patch itself. Only Apple should install these kinds of patches.

Developers can also use patches to customize A-traps. Figure 5-3 shows how control should flow in the case of a trap that you are patching yourself.

■ **Figure 5-3** Prepatched A-trap

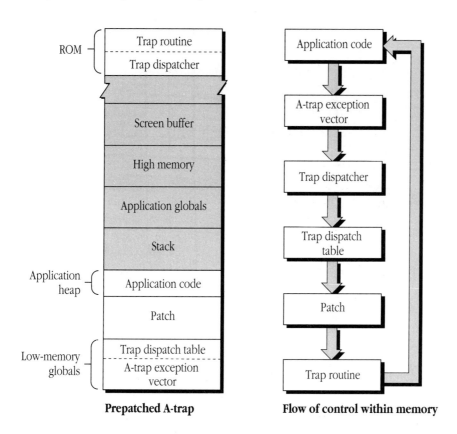

In general, it is a bad idea to patch an A-trap unless there is absolutely no other way to do what you want. If you need to patch an A-trap, however, you should follow the procedure described here. For example, suppose that you are writing a resident program that needs to install its menu in the menu bar of whatever application is currently frontmost. One way to achieve this is by prepatching the DrawMenuBar routine.

The system routine GetTrapAddress returns the address of an A-trap, and the system routine SetTrapAddress puts a new address into the trap dispatch table. To prepatch the DrawMenuBar routine, follow these steps:

1. Use the GetTrapAddress routine to obtain the address of the A-trap and save this value. In this case, you would save the address of the DrawMenuBar routine.

2. Use the SetTrapAddress routine to insert the address of the code you want to execute into the trap dispatch table. In this case, your code would consist of a call to the InsertMenu routine to add the menu of your program to the menu bar right before calling the DrawMenuBar routine.

Chapter 5   The Macintosh Operating System   **139**

3. After your patch does its stuff, it must use a JMP instruction to the saved address of the original A-trap. Note that if at this point the patch simply makes an A-trap call, it will wind up at its own address again. Because you must use a JMP instruction, you must write your patch in assembly language, not C or Pascal.

4. When your application exits, you must use SetTrapAddress again to restore the old A-trap in the trap dispatch table. If a trap dispatch table entry still points to an old patch that has been cleared, the next application will crash when it calls that A-trap.

   INITs cannot remove their own patches because someone might have patched behind them.

In general, you can install multiple layers of patches as long as each patch, when complete, calls the original A-trap. Finally, if there is any chance that your patch can be called from an interrupt, you must observe the guidelines for any code that runs at interrupt time. These are described in the section "Code That Runs at Interrupt Time" later in this chapter. In general, you should assume that your trap will be called at interrupt time and take the proper precautions.

It is illegal for a patch to do any of the following:

- Modify the stack or register values and not restore them when it is finished.
- Call the original A-trap as a subroutine, and then perform its function after the original A-trap runs. It must call the original A-trap as described above.
- Perform its function and return control to the program, ignoring the original A-trap.

Determining whether a trap has been patched

There are two ways of determining whether a trap has been patched.

From MacsBug, you can use the WH (Where) command to find out whether a trap is patched. Given a trap name, this command returns information about the location of the trap. For example, the command

WH menuselect

tells you that the MenuSelect routine is in RAM:

```
Trap number A93D (_MenuSelect) starts at 003C02A2 in RAM
It is 0019F732 bytes into this heap block:
    Start    Length      Tag  Mstr Ptr Lock Prg  Type   ID   File       Name
    00220B70 00054FF0+00  F
```

If you need to find out whether a trap is patched from within your application program, you can use the GetTrapAddress routine to find out its address and then compare that value to the value stored in the low-memory global variable ROMBase. If the address is greater than ROMBase, the routine is not patched. (Note that if your program runs under virtual memory, some portion of RAM could be above the ROM in the memory map, so that a patch could be stored at an address that is higher than ROMBase; however, this is highly unlikely.)

Using in-line glue to implement a system routine

Some system routines are so simple that the compiler or linker puts the code, called **glue,** needed to perform the routine directly into your program. For example, when you execute the function GetDateTime, the glue simply loads the value from a low-memory global variable, because the load takes only one instruction. If you run through the A-trap dispatcher, more than ten instructions are required. Figure 5-4 shows how glue is inserted into your application's code. Compare this figure with Figure 5-1.

Obviously, the glue can load a single value faster than you can call an A-trap. However, using glue presents a problem. If the glue contains an error, that error remains in the program until the program is recompiled with new glue. But if an A-trap contains an error, Apple can fix the error with a patch in the next release of system software. The patch allows Apple to fix the error without altering any applications.

Glue routines do not have A-trap numbers and are not known to MacsBug. As a result, you cannot use the MacsBug A-trap commands to define any action for an A-trap that is implemented in this way. In addition, if you are looking at disassembled code using MacsBug, you will see one or more assembly-language instructions instead of the usual _trapname_ entry. If you are stepping through your code in MacsBug and find yourself looking at code you're sure you didn't write, you may be looking at glue.

Operating system routines can also use glue code that is stored in libraries. For additional information, see "Operating System Routines" later in this chapter.

■ **Figure 5-4** Using in-line glue to implement an A-trap

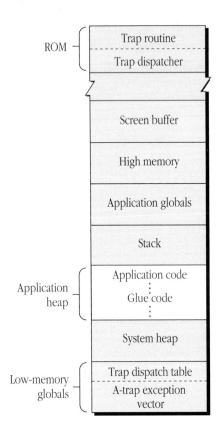

Using the stack to implement A-traps

The previous section described the method by which the microprocessor transfers control to a User Interface Toolbox or operating system routine—that is, how the microprocessor actually finds the first instruction of the routine. But when the routine begins to execute, like any routine that you have written yourself, it expects to find the parameters it needs on the stack, and, if the routine is a function, it expects to find space on the stack for the return result. The compiler generates instructions that allocate the necessary amount of space on the stack with the help of interface files that are included with your development system. These files contain public declarations of every A-trap routine. In MPW Pascal, the declaration takes the following form:

PROCEDURE trapname (param1: type; [param2: type]...); Inline $trapword

When the compiler encounters an A-trap, it allocates space on the stack for the specified parameters and then inserts the word specified by *trapword* directly in the code. For example, let's suppose that your code includes the following function call:

```
WPtr: = GetNewWindow(WindowID,WRec,WindowPtr(-1));
```

The compiler needs to make space on the stack for the function result and also allocate space for three parameters. The code generated looks something like this:

```
CLR.L          -(A7)                ;make space on stack for result
MOVE.W         #$012C,-(A7)         ;push WindowID
PEA            -$01E8(A5)           ;push WRec address
PEA            $FFFF                ;push -1
_GetNewWindow                       ;call GetNewWindow
MOVEA.L        (A7)+,A0             ;pop return result from stack
MOVE.L         A0,-$01EC(A5)        ;save it in a variable
```

Although setting all this up is the compiler's business, it is important to understand how this work is reflected in the disassembled code. You can use this information if you need to check that you are passing the right values to the function or if you need to check the function's return result. To watch an A-trap being called from inside a Pascal program, work through "Exercise: Watching an A-trap Call," later in this chapter.

Operating system routines

The use of the stack to implement A-trap routines becomes slightly more complicated in the case of operating system routines. If you are writing a program in a high-level language, the compiler generates code that resolves the problem for you, but again, it's useful to understand what the compiler is doing when you're reading through disassembled code.

User Interface Toolbox routines pass their parameters and return the result on the stack as described in the previous section. Parameters are always passed in Pascal sequence, whether the application is written in Pascal or not. (Some managers introduced in system software version 7.0 pass parameters in C format.) Operating system A-traps pass their parameters and return the result in registers. Register A0 often holds the input parameter or the pointer to the parameter. Register D0 usually holds the return result, which is often an operating system error code (a code of zero means that no error resulted).

The previous section described how the compiler allocates space on the stack for a routine's return result (if any) and parameters. In the case of an operating system routine, two extra steps are needed. In the first step, the parameters must be moved from the stack, where the compiler puts them, into the registers where the routine expects them. In the second step, after the routine returns, the return result must be moved from the register where the routine has left it back onto the stack where the compiler expects it.

The extra code that does this work for you is also called glue and can be implemented as in-line glue, in which case you'll see the actual instructions in your disassembled code, or as library glue, in which case you'll see a JSR instruction to the procedure that moves the values from the stack into the registers, calls the trap, and, when the trap is finished, moves the values from the registers back onto the stack.

There are two complications that can arise, from a debugging standpoint, if the glue resides in a library.

- If you crash in the ROM while an operating system trap is executing and you need to find your way back to the point in your program where you called the trap, you'll need to do a stack crawl to find out where the library routine that called the trap was called from.

- If you set an A-trap break on an operating system call when MacsBug is invoked, you'll find yourself in the library routine right before the trap call is made. In this case you'll need to disassemble around the PC to find out the return address. Usually, the first instruction in the glue is something like MOVE.L (A7)+, A1; that is, save the return address in register A1. The address stored in register A1 should tell you where in your program you've made the A-trap call.

Exercise: Watching an A-trap call

This exercise uses disassembly and step commands to walk through a program. It uses a User Interface Toolbox function as an example of how the stack is used to implement a system routine.

This is the Pascal code for this example:

```
CONST
        WindowID = 300;
VAR
        WPtr:   WindowPtr;
        WRec:   WindowRecord;
BEGIN
        WPtr: = GetNewWindow (WindowID, WRec, WindowPtr(-1));
END;
```

Note that there is only one line of executable code, that is, a line for which the compiler generates machine code:

```
WPtr: = GetNewWindow (WindowID, WRec, WindowPtr(-1));
```

The other lines simply set up the variables and the constant required to execute this one line. The function GetNewWindow is an A-trap routine and is listed in *Inside Macintosh*. As you might guess, it creates a new window and returns its address in WPtr.

This is the assembly code generated from the Pascal code:

```
CLR.L         -(A7)                 ;make space on stack for result
MOVE.W        #$012C,-(A7)          ;push WindowID
PEA           -$01E8(A5)            ;push WRec address
PEA           $FFFF                 ;push -1
_GetNewWindow                       ;call GetNewWindow
MOVEA.L       (A7)+,A0              ;pop return result from stack
MOVE.L        A0,-$01EC(A5)         ;save it in a variable
```

Throughout this exercise, "entering" a command means to type the specified command and then to press Return.

1. **Launch the "A-Trap Demo" application on the MacsBug disk and choose the Watch GetNewWindow A-trap item from the Debug menu.**

   This invokes MacsBug. The figure that follows shows the bottom of the MacsBug display. The commands you enter will be displayed in the command line area. The PC region shows the next command to be executed. Depending on how you have configured MacsBug, the PC region might display more than one line. If it does, the line preceded by an asterisk (*) is the next instruction to be executed.

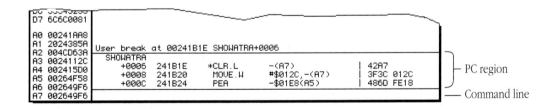

Chapter 5 The Macintosh Operating System   **145**

2. **Enter `IR PC`**

   The MacsBug IR command disassembles code from the address you specify until the end of the procedure containing the instruction at the specified address. MacsBug displays the following information:

   ```
   Disassembling from pc
   ShowATrap
       +0006  00216DCE  *CLR.L      -(A7)                           | 42A7
       +0008  00216DD0  MOVE.W      #$012C,-(A7)                    | 3F3C 012C
       +000C  00216DD4  PEA         -$01E8(A5)                      | 486D FE18
       +0010  00216DD8  PEA         $FFFF                           | 4878 FFFF
       +0014  00216DDC  _GetNewWindow               ; A9BD          | A9BD
       +0016  00216DDE  MOVEA.L     (A7)+,A0                        | 205F
       +0018  00216DE0  MOVE.L      A0,-$01EC(A5)                   | 2B48 FE14
       +001C  00216DE4  UNLK        A6                              | 4E5E
       +001E  00216DE6  RTS
   ```

   The call to GetNewWindow is implemented by the seven instructions starting with `CLR.L -(A7)` and ending with `MOVE.L A0,-$01EC(A5)`. These are the instructions you'll be stepping through in this exercise. The asterisk shows the next instruction to be executed. Note that this instruction is the same as that shown in the PC region.

   MacsBug does not update the disassembled code shown in the output area of the display. To see an updated display, you would need to enter an IL command each time you step through an instruction. But it is more convenient to look at the PC region, which is updated, to see the next instruction to be executed.

In the remainder of this exercise, you'll be stepping through the first four lines of the assembly code, which set up the first part of the stack frame for the routine. Then you'll step over the code that makes up the routine itself. Finally, you'll step through the last two instructions, which retrieve the return result and save it in a variable.

3. **Look at the stack at the top of the status region in the MacsBug display.**

   The top of the stack is at the top of the display, and the stack pointer's value is shown right above that. The stack pointer's value is also stored in register A7. Look at the value of register A7; the two values are identical.

For the remainder of the exercise, you will be concerned only with what gets put on the stack, not what's already on it. Because the stack is updated, you'll be using the DM command to display memory starting with the top of the stack so that you can compare the old values with the updated values.

4. **Enter DM A7**

   MacsBug displays memory starting with the address stored in A7, which always holds the address of the stack pointer. MacsBug displays something like the following:

   ```
   Displaying memory from A7
     0048BA16  0048 BB2A 0046 8ADC  4080 6544 0046 8130   •H•*•F••@•eD•F•0
   ```

   This display shows you 16 bytes starting at the address in A7. In this case the address is 0048BA16.

   The first assembly-language instruction makes space on the stack to hold the return result from the GetNewWindow routine. The S (Step) command executes one instruction and then invokes MacsBug.

5. **Enter S**

   The screen flashes as MacsBug allows the application to run for one instruction, and then returns. Notice that the PC region now displays the next instruction to be executed, MOVE.W.

   ```
   A0 00346A7C  | Step (into)
   A1 2034883E  | SHOWATRA
   A2 004CD5FE  |   +0006  346AF2  CLR.L    -(A7)           | 42A7
   A3 003460FC  | SHOWATRA
   A4 003465A4  |   +0008  346AF4  *MOVE.W  #$012C,-(A7)    | 3F3C 012C
   A5 00369F2C  |   +000C  346AF8  PEA      -$01E8(A5)      | 486D FE18
   A6 003699CA  |   +0010  346AFC  PEA      $FFFF           | 4878 FFFF
   A7 003699C6  |
   ```

6. **Enter DM A7 to display memory starting with the top of the stack.**

   MacsBug displays two lines similar to the following:

   ```
   Displaying memory from A7
     0048BA12  0000 0000 0048 BB2A  0046 8ADC 4080 6544   •••••H•*•F••@•eD
   ```

   Compare the output of this command with that of the DM A7 command you entered in step 4. The address of the stack pointer has been decreased by 4 bytes (remember, the stack grows toward low memory), and a long word of zero has been pushed onto it. This is not the value of the return result; it simply holds the place where the return result will be placed later.

Now that space for the return result has been reserved, you can execute the next three instructions, which push the three parameters onto the stack. In Pascal, the parameters are pushed from left to right. So WindowID will be first, then WRec, and finally –1.

The first parameter, WindowID, is a word equal to 300 ($12C).

7. **Enter s to execute the next instruction.**

    Again, the PC region is updated.

    ```
                  Step (into)
                    SHOWATRA
    A0 003C6A7C     +0006    3C6AF2    CLR.L      -(A7)                    | 42A7
    A1 203C883E     +0008    3C6AF4    MOVE.W     #$012C,-(A7)             | 3F3C 012C
    A2 004CD5FE   SHOWATRA
    A3 003C60FC     +000C    3C6AF8   *PEA        -$01E8(A5)               | 486D FE18
    A4 003C65A4     +0010    3C6AFC    PEA        $FFFF                    | 4878 FFFF
    A5 003E9F2C     +0014    3C6B00    _GetNewWindow              ; A9BD   | A9BD
    A6 003E99CA
    A7 003E99C4
    ```

8. **Enter DM A7 to look at the stack again.**

    MacsBug displays something like this:

    ```
    Displaying memory from A7
      0048BA10   012C 0000 0000 0048  BB2A 0046 8ADC 4080   •,•••••H•*•F••@•
    ```

    Compare the memory display with that of the DM A7 command you entered in step 6. The stack pointer address has been decreased by 2 bytes, and the first parameter, 12C, has been pushed onto the stack.

The next parameter you'll be pushing onto the stack is WRec, which is a pointer to a window record. A window record is a pretty big data structure. But the assembly code simply pushes its address. This is because Pascal has a rule that any data structure larger than 4 bytes has its address pushed, instead of the data structure itself.

The PEA (Push Effective Address) instruction simply pushes the address it's given. The operand is the address of the window record, and that address is pushed onto the stack. Addresses are always 4 bytes. Note that in this example the address of the window record is stored in a global variable. You can tell it's a global variable, not a local variable or parameter, because it's expressed as a negative offset from register A5.

9. **Enter s to execute the first PEA instruction.**

    MacsBug executes the instruction and updates the PC region.

    ```
    D7 2E140081   Step (into)
                    SHOWATRA
                    +0006    3C6AF2    CLR.L      -(A7)                    | 42A7
    A0 003C6A7C     +0008    3C6AF4    MOVE.W     #$012C,-(A7)             | 3F3C 012C
    A1 203C883E     +000C    3C6AF8    PEA        -$01E8(A5)               | 486D FE18
    A2 004CD5FE   SHOWATRA
    A3 003C60FC     +0010    3C6AFC   *PEA        $FFFF                    | 4878 FFFF
    A4 003C65A4     +0014    3C6B00    _GetNewWindow              ; A9BD   | A9BD
    A5 003E9F2C     +0016    3C6B02    MOVEA.L    (A7)+,A0                 | 205F
    A6 003E99CA
    A7 003E99C0
    ```

148   MacsBug Reference and Debugging Guide

10. **Enter DM A7 to look at the stack.**

    MacsBug displays something like this:

    ```
    Displaying memory from A7
     0048BA0C  0048 BD90 012C 0000  0000 0048 BB2A 0046   •H•••,•••••H•*•F
    ```

    Compare this output with the output of the DM A7 command you entered in step 8. The stack pointer has been decreased by 4 bytes, and the address of the window record is now on top of the stack.

Next you'll push the last parameter, which is –1. In two's complement arithmetic, –1 is $FFFFFFFF. The last parameter is also a pointer, so it's 4 bytes. The instruction PEA $FFFF is a fancy way of pushing –1 onto the stack. Even though $FFFF is only a word, it is automatically expanded to be a long word, because PEA deals with addresses, and addresses are always long words.

11. **Enter S to execute the instruction.**

    MacsBug displays the following information:

    ```
    D5 00000000 | Step (into)
    D6 53545253 |   SHOWATRA
    D7 00030081 |     +0006  3C6AF2    CLR.L    -(A7)                  | 42A7
                |     +0008  3C6AF4    MOVE.W   #$012C,-(A7)           | 3F3C 012C
    A0 003C6A7C |     +000C  3C6AF8    PEA      -$01E8(A5)             | 486D FE18
    A1 203C883E |     +0010  3C6AFC    PEA      $FFFF                  | 4878 FFFF
    A2 004CD5FE |   SHOWATRA
    A3 003C60FC |     +0014  3C6B00   *_GetNewWindow          ; A9BD   | A9BD
    A4 003C65A4 |     +0016  3C6B02    MOVEA.L  (A7)+,A0               | 205F
    A5 003E9F2C |     +0018  3C6B04    MOVE.L   A0,-$01EC(A5)          | 2B48 FE14
    A6 003E99CA |
    A7 003E99BC |
    ```

12. **Enter DM A7 to look at the values on the stack.**

    MacsBug displays something like this:

    ```
    Displaying memory from A7
     0048BA08  FFFF FFFF 0048 BD90  012C 0000 0000 0048   •••••H•••,•••••H
    ```

You have now pushed all the parameters onto the stack, which is just what the calling routine should have accomplished. The next instruction is the call to GetNewWindow. When the routine begins to execute, it will expect to find all the information you've put on the stack. The called routine takes the parameters off the stack and fills in the return result. When GetNewWindow returns, you'll take another look at the stack.

If you executed another S command, you would be executing the first instruction of the GetNewWindow routine. It will be more useful at this point to use the SO (Step Over) command to execute all the instructions in the A-trap call; this will bring you to the next instruction in the code, MOVEA.L (A7)+, A0.

Chapter 5   The Macintosh Operating System   **149**

13. **Enter so**

    MacsBug executes the A-trap and updates the PC region as shown:

    ```
    A0 004EBAC2  Step (over)
    A1 8004D5E8  SHOWATRA
    A2 004CD5FE    +0014  3C6B00   _GetNewWindow              ; A9BD | A9BD
    A3 003C60FC  SHOWATRA
    A4 003C65A4    +0016  3C6B02  *MOVEA.L  (A7)+,A0                | 205F
    A5 003E9F2C    +0018  3C6B04   MOVE.L   A0,-$01EC(A5)           | 2B48 FE14
    A6 003E99CA    +001C  3C6B08   MOVE.L   -$01EC(A5),-(A7)        | 2F2D FE14
    A7 003E99C6
    ```

14. **Enter DM A7 to look at the stack again.**

    MacsBug shows you something like this:

    ```
    Displaying memory from A7
     0048BA12  0048 BD90 0048 BB2A  0046 8ADC 4080 6544   •H•••H•*•F••@•eD
    ```

    The stack has shrunk back. The return result, 0048 BD90—the address of the nonrelocatable block where the window has been stored—is stored at the top of the stack.

    Now you're ready to step through the code that takes the return result off the stack and puts it in the variable WPtr. First you need to take the return result off the stack.

15. **Enter s to execute the next instruction.**

    Macsbug updates the PC region as shown:

    ```
    A0 003E9D44  Step (into)
    A1 8004D5E8  SHOWATRA
    A2 004CD5FE    +0016  3C6B02   MOVEA.L  (A7)+,A0                         | 205F
    A3 003C60FC  SHOWATRA
    A4 003C65A4    +0018  3C6B04  *MOVE.L   A0,-$01EC(A5)                    | 2B48 FE14
    A5 003E9F2C    +001C  3C6B08   MOVE.L   -$01EC(A5),-(A7)                 | 2F2D FE14
    A6 003E99CA    +0020  3C6B0C   JSR      STAGGERW          ; 003C6DF2 | 4EBA 02E4
    A7 003E99CA
    ```

16. **Enter DM A7 to look at the stack.**

    MacsBug displays information like the following:

    ```
    Displaying memory from A7
     0048BA16  0048 BB2A 0046 8ADC  4080 6544 0046 8130   •H•*•F••@•eD•F•0
    ```

    The return result was popped from the stack and placed in A0. The stack is now the same as it was before you put anything on it. The next instruction moves the return result from A0 into the variable WPtr.

150   MacsBug Reference and Debugging Guide

17. **Enter s to step through the next instruction.**

```
D7 2E140081  Step (into)
             SHOWATRA
A0 003E9D44       +0016   3C6B02   MOVEA.L   (A7)+,A0                    | 205F
A1 8004D5E8       +0018   3C6B04   MOVE.L    A0,-$01EC(A5)               | 2B48 FE14
A2 004CD5FE  SHOWATRA
A3 003C60FC       +001C   3C6B08  *MOVE.L    -$01EC(A5),-(A7)            | 2F2D FE14
A4 003C65A4       +0020   3C6B0C   JSR       STAGGERW         ; 003C6DF2 | 4EBA 02E4
A5 003E9F2C       +0024   3C6B10   ADDQ.L    #$4,A7                      | 588F
A6 003E99CA
A7 003E99CA
```

The return result was placed into the variable WPtr. Is the window up?

18. **Press the tilde (~) key to look at the A-Trap Demo application.**

    The screen is empty. The GetNewWindow routine simply allocates a block of memory for the window and adds the window to the window list. To position the window and make it visible, you would also need to execute the ShowWindow routine.

19. **Press the tilde (~) key again to return to MacsBug.**

    Now you've executed one line of Pascal code. As you can tell, stepping through code can be a slow process. It can also be hard to tell which disassembled lines correspond to a particular line of Pascal, but it gets easier with practice.

20. **Enter G to return to the A-Trap Demo application.**

    The window is now visible, because the G command has executed the rest of the code, which includes the A-trap call that positions the window and makes it visible.

Interrupts

As mentioned in the beginning of this chapter, exception processing can also be generated by the hardware, in which case it is called an interrupt. The hardware sends the microprocessor a signal that tells it to stop what it's doing and do something else.

The microprocessor uses exception processing to handle an interrupt: it saves the current context, determines the address of the routine or interrupt handler that knows what to do in response to that interrupt, and sets the PC equal to the address of the first instruction in the interrupt handler. When the interrupt handler returns, the microprocessor restores the context that was current when the interrupt occurred using the information it has saved. The interrupted program should not be aware that it has been interrupted. This places some restriction on the code that runs at interrupt time.

The procedure used by the microprocessor to handle interrupts is similar to that used to handle A-traps. A clean context switch is needed in both situations. However, in the case of interrupt handling, the microprocessor recognizes seven **interrupt priority levels,** numbered from 1 to 7. The system prioritizes the handling of interrupts by defining an interrupt mask, which it can set (or which your application can set) at a level from 0 to 7. The incoming interrupt must have a level higher than the current interrupt mask, or the interrupt is ignored. A program cannot mask out the highest interrupt, level 7. The level 7 interrupt is processed without regard to the interrupt mask setting. The highest-level interrupt is called a nonmaskable interrupt (NMI).

When you invoke MacsBug, you generate a level 7 interrupt, which means that all interrupts are disabled while MacsBug is running. The interrupt mask set by the operating system before you entered MacsBug is shown just to the right of the status register. In the following example of the status register display, the interrupt mask is set to 0:

```
SR Smxnzvc 0
```

AppleShare uses interrupt routines to keep continuous communication going between a file server and a workstation. If you are logged on to a file server, and you enter MacsBug for more than 2.5 minutes, the file server will assume your application has died and you will lose your server connection.

Macintosh interrupts

Interrupts are used for several purposes on the Macintosh. Here are some examples:

- The interrupt switch. The interrupt switch generates a level 7 interrupt. MacsBug is the interrupt handler for level 7. This level of interrupt cannot be masked out. (On a Macintosh Plus, the interrupt switch generates a level 4 interrupt.)

- Mouse movement. Every time you move the mouse on a Macintosh Plus, you generate an interrupt. The interrupt handler for this interrupt updates the mouse's location.

- The disk driver. Floppy disk drives generate interrupts to permit asynchronous access to information on the disk.

- Serial ports. The serial ports can generate interrupts for incoming data such as AppleTalk packets.

- Programmable timer, implemented by the Time Manager. Applications can use a millisecond timer that generates an interrupt when it goes off and runs a specified interrupt task.

- Screen refresh. This is also referred to as vertical blanking, or VBL. A VBL interrupt occurs every time the CRT electron beam (not the software) redraws the screen, that is, about 60 times per second.

The VBL Manager maintains a list of interrupt tasks that it performs at each VBL interrupt. For example, during each VBL interrupt, the system runs the stack sniffer to check whether the stack has overflowed into the heap, checks for inserted disks, and looks for mouse clicks. Your application can add its own routines to the VBL Manager's list. The vbl dcmd, which is shipped with MacsBug, lists all the VBL tasks currently installed. The next two sections provide information about writing code that runs at interrupt time and using the vbl dcmd.

Code that runs at interrupt time

The code that recognizes an interrupt and gives control to the appropriate routine is called the interrupt handler. If you are writing code designed to run at interrupt time, you must take account of certain restrictions: you can't use any handles to unlocked relocatable blocks, and you can't make any system calls that might move or allocate memory.

Because interrupts can occur at any time, an interrupt routine might be running while the heap is being compacted. As a result, a handle might be invalid, because the data it points to might have been moved and the Memory Manager might not yet have updated the master pointer. So using a handle at interrupt time is taboo unless the relocatable block to which the handle points is locked before the interrupt routine starts to run.

It's also possible that the current application may be calling the Memory Manager when the interrupt occurs. The Memory Manager is not reentrant—that is, it cannot accept a call while one or more previous calls to it are pending. So you can't use the Memory Manager during an interrupt. But lots of A-traps call the Memory Manager indirectly, so you can't call any of those either. A-traps that move memory are listed in Appendix B of *Inside Macintosh*. (Note that each volume of *Inside Macintosh* contains a different Appendix B, each with a different list of calls.)

In addition to these two restrictions, if your code uses global variables, you need to set up register A5 before using them and to restore it when you're finished. You need to make sure A5 points to the right global variables for the following reasons:

- In an environment where multiple applications are running at once, any one of these applications might be using A5 when your code is called.

- An interrupt can occur right after the application has called a ROM routine. ROM routines sometimes save register A5 (the global variable pointer) and use it as just another register in which to store data. Before the ROM exits, it restores A5, so the application is not messed up. However, if an interrupt routine were to run after a ROM routine had changed A5 but before it had restored it, the interrupt routine would not be able to access the application's global variables, since they are addressed relative to the address stored in register A5.

Chapter 5   The Macintosh Operating System   **153**

For additional information, see the section "Using Application Global Variables in Tasks" in the "Time Manager" chapter of *Inside Macintosh,* Volume VI.

Displaying information about VBL tasks

A VBL task, which always runs at interrupt time, is described by a VBLTask record that the Vertical Retrace Manager maintains in a linked queue. The vbl dcmd uses the information in this queue to display information about all currently installed VBL tasks. If you are writing interrupt routines that are handled by the Vertical Retrace Manager, you can use the vbl dcmd to list information about all currently installed VBL tasks. For example:

```
vbl
Displaying VBL tasks
   Addr    Count  Phase    VBL at
   82e23e  0006   0000     002e98
   82f3fe  0011   0009     003008
   004b7c  003f   0000     005518
   00317e  0001   0000     003170
   3cbbb6  7f95   0000     3b5852
#5 VBL tasks
```

Table 5-1 describes the meaning of the information displayed by the vbl dcmd.

- **Table 5-1** vbl dcmd information

Field	Description
Addr	Address where code for VBL task starts.
Count	Ticks between successive invocations of task.
Phase	Integer (smaller than Count), used to stagger execution times slightly for VBL tasks that are started at the same time and have equal count values.
VBL at	The address of the VBLTask record; the address is a queue element.

MacsBug's A-trap commands

MacsBug includes eight commands that are entirely concerned with the execution of A-traps. Table 5-2 provides a brief summary of these commands. Note that only the A-trap command name is listed in the table; the complete syntax of each command is shown under the description of that command in Chapter 9, "MacsBug Commands."

■ **Table 5-2** A-trap commands

Command	Action
ATB	Invokes MacsBug whenever the microprocessor encounters the specified A-trap. You can display the state of the microprocessor and memory just before the A-trap is executed.
ATC	Clears actions set using the ATB, ATT, ATHC, and ATSS commands.
ATD	Displays information about all actions currently set with the ATB, ATT, ATHC, and ATSS commands.
ATHC	Checks the heap before executing the specified A-trap.
ATP	Displays information saved while trap recording is on.
ATR	Turns trap recording on and off.
ATSS	Invokes MacsBug if the value for a memory location or range has changed before an A-trap is executed.
ATT	Writes information to the MacsBug output buffer without stopping the current program whenever the microprocessor encounters the specified A-trap.

These eight MacsBug commands are specifically dedicated to monitoring the execution of A-traps in your program. They are necessary because of the different kind of processing that is involved in executing system routines. The main difference between these commands and other MacsBug commands that perform similar functions can be illustrated by the difference between the BR command and the ATB command. The BR command invokes MacsBug when the program counter reaches an address you specify; the ATB command invokes MacsBug every time a specified A-trap is encountered.

You can take advantage of A-trap processing to focus in on bugs. For example, you can use the ATSS command to checksum a range of memory before the execution of every A-trap. When the ATSS command invokes MacsBug, you know that the A-trap that is about to execute is not responsible for the change in value. You also know that the instruction you are looking for is either the previous A-trap or any instruction executed between the previous A-trap and the current call. You can now use the SS command within the suspect range to find that instruction. Having trap recording turned on while using the ATSS command allows you to determine the previous A-trap call. You can also disassemble backward from the current PC until you find the previous A-trap.

The A-trap action table

When MacsBug is installed and an A-trap exception occurs, MacsBug prepatches the trap dispatcher. That is, MacsBug becomes the all-purpose exception handler, and the microprocessor hands the trap word to MacsBug.

MacsBug keeps an internal table in which it records the A-trap actions you have defined using one of the commands in Table 5-2. When the PC points to an A-trap, the microprocessor starts exception processing. The microprocessor passes control to MacsBug. MacsBug first checks the internal table to see whether there's any action that has been associated with that A-trap. Next, because the A-trap commands allow you to specify further conditions that have to be met before any action is taken, MacsBug checks to see whether these conditions are satisfied. If an action for that A-trap has been entered in the table and the conditions are satisfied, MacsBug displays the debugging screen and halts the program when the PC points to the A-trap call. If there is no entry for the A-trap in the internal table or if the other conditions you specified are not satisfied, then MacsBug passes the information to the trap disptacher, which in turn locates the routine and jumps to the first instruction of that routine.

You use the ATD command to display the contents of the A-trap table. For example:

```
ATD
A-Trap actions from System or Application
  Trap Range         Action  Cur/Max or Expression      Commands
  _MenuSelect        Check   00000000 / 00000003
  _WaitNextEvent     Break   every time
  _WaitNextEvent     Break   every time                 ;hc
  _GetPort           Break   D0 = 6
  _Pack0             Break   SP^.W=#68
```

You use the ATC command to remove one or more entries from the table.

Using A-trap commands

This section presents information that applies to using any of MacsBug's A-trap commands.

Specifying an A-trap name

Every A-trap has both a number and a name. You use the name in your source code. The trap dispatch table is organized by number. MacsBug knows both the name and the number of every A-trap. Thus, you can use either the name or the number of a trap in a MacsBug command.

When you look through your disassembled code, the A-trap call is usually listed as follows:

_A-TrapName

for example:

```
_WaitNextEvent
```

There are two situations in which the name listed in the disassembled listing or in the A-trap action table will not match the name you specified in your source program:

- If the trap belongs to a package, the package name and number will be displayed rather than the A-trap name. See the section "A-traps in Packages" later in this chapter for additional information.
- Because assembler names must be unique to eight characters, special macro names must be used for Pascal routines whose names aren't unique to seven characters (the underscore counts as one character). In the case where the first seven characters of a trap macro name would duplicate another name, the spelling of the macro name will differ from the name of the Pascal routine itself. This is noted in the documentation for the particular routine in *Inside Macintosh*.

There are about 700 A-traps defined, and they are listed in Appendix C of *Inside Macintosh*. (Note that each volume of *Inside Macintosh* has a different Appendix C, each with a different list.)

Setting an A-trap action on a range of traps

All A-trap commands that take a trap name as a parameter also allow you to specify a range of traps. Basically, this allows you to set some action on all traps belonging to a particular manager. The numerical listing of A-traps in Appendix C of *Inside Macintosh* should help you determine the range for the manager you're interested in.

Restricting A-trap actions to your application

Most A-trap commands give you the option of setting an action on an A-trap only if that A-trap is being called from your application. A-traps often call other A-traps. If you want to focus on the calls that are made from your application's heap rather than from ROM or the system heap, you should use this option.

You tell MacsBug to take action only on traps called from your application's heap by appending the letter A to the A-trap command. For example, the command

```
ATBA GetNewWindow
```

tells MacsBug to break on all calls to GetNewWindow that are made from the application heap. Note that there is no space between the command name and the "A" option.

A-traps in packages

Some A-trap routines are stored in packages; these are stored either as resources of type 'PACK' in the system file, or they are stored in ROM. There are two reasons for placing routines in packages. The first reason is that at one time there were more routines than there was room in ROM, so that some nonessential routines were moved into the system file, from where they could be loaded in as needed.

The second reason is that as the number of routines exceeded the number of A-traps available, it was necessary to find a way to access several routines using one A-trap number. The solution to the space problem was to include all traps belonging to one manager in a package and to put the package in a resource that could be loaded as needed from the system file. When ROM got bigger, this problem was eliminated, but the second problem (too few numbers for A-traps) remained, and the package solution was used, though packages could now reside in ROM.

A **package** is simply a group of related calls. Each package contains the code for several related routines, which are listed separately in *Inside Macintosh*. There is only one A-trap number for all the routines in a given package. Packages are transparent to the high-level programmer. Glue automatically calls the correct routine. But you must understand how the system uses packages to debug them with MacsBug.

Because each package includes multiple routines, each routine has an index number that locates it within the package. When a program calls a routine in the package, the routine's parameters are pushed onto the stack first, and then the routine's index number. This index number is called a routine selector. The Package Manager reads the index number and jumps to the correct routine inside the package.

Thus, the same package A-trap can be called with different parameters, depending on the routine for which the A-trap is indexed. Since MacsBug does not know which routine in the package is being called, it just disassembles it as a 'PACK' A-trap. You can see which routine the A-trap is destined for by looking at the routine selector on the stack. (Some routine selectors are put in registers.)

Because all of the routines in a package are implemented by one A-trap number, you can't place an A-trap break on a single routine as you normally would using the ATB command. What you must do instead is break on the package and then test for the routine selector on top of the stack or in a register to make sure that the routine you're interested in is executing.

MacsBug is shipped with several sets of macros that allow you to place A-trap breaks on individual routines inside a package. The macros actually place an A-trap break on the whole package, with a condition that checks the index selector to see if it's the routine you wanted. The description of the ATB command in Chapter 9, "MacsBug Commands," includes a detailed description of how to place a break on a routine inside a package.

Macintosh managers

As mentioned at the beginning of this chapter, each system manager is responsible for creating and maintaining data structures that you manipulate using system routines. For example, the Event Manager creates and tracks event records, the Window Manager maintains window records, and so forth. The following two sections provide an overview of how the File Manager and the Device Manager keep track of the data structures and tasks they are responsible for. These sections also explain how you can use low-memory global variables to locate these structures in memory and how you can use standard dcmds to display information about open files, mounted volumes, and installed drivers.

Although detailed descriptions of every Macintosh manager lie outside the scope of this manual, these two sections will give you an idea of the "pieces" you need to simplify the debugging of routines belonging to a particular manager:

- Learn what data structures are characteristic of that manager and how the manager maintains and tracks these structures. Does it queue records in a linked list? Does it put the information in a buffer?
- How does the manager use low-memory global variables to locate the items it needs?
- Using this information, you can write your own dcmds to locate the information you need, and you can create your own templates to display that information. This takes a bit of work but makes debugging a lot easier. See Chapter 4, "Macintosh Memory Organization," for information on creating templates for system and private data structures, and Chapter 8, "Introduction to MacsBug Commands," for information on writing your own dcmds.

The file system

This section gives an overview of the lower levels of the Macintosh File System. It does not discuss the normal way to read or write a file from an application.

To read from a file, an application calls the File Manager (HFS), which knows where each file resides on the disk volume. The File Manager, in turn, calls the Device Manager, which knows which device driver runs that disk. Then the Device Manager calls the appropriate driver for the device:

- If it's a floppy disk, the driver talks directly to the floppy disk drive hardware.
- If it's a SCSI disk, the SCSI driver calls the SCSI Manager, which talks to the hardware (the SCSI chip).
- If it's a file server, the AppleShare driver calls the serial driver, which talks to the serial port hardware.

Figure 5-5 shows the calling chain for these three types of drivers.

■ **Figure 5-5** Calling chain for reading from or writing to a disk

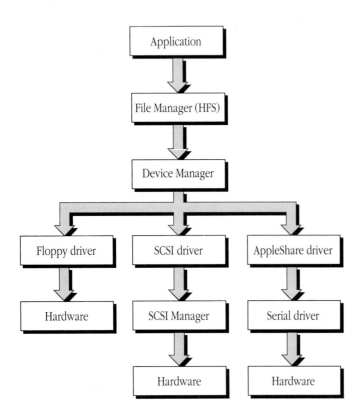

The File Manager stores internal information about its current state in queues in the system heap. The Queue Manager (an operating system utility) manages these queues. The following sections describe these queues and how you can use low-memory global variables to access the first element in a list.

Drive queue

The drive queue is a linked list of all drives connected to a Macintosh. The list includes one entry, or queue element, for each connected drive.

The low-memory global variable DrvQHdr contains a pointer to the first element in the list. This global variable is useful when you are looking at the drive queue from MacsBug. You can use the system call GetDrvQHdr from a program to get the pointer to the first element in the list.

Finding and displaying information about mounted volumes

The volume queue is a linked list of all volumes mounted on a Macintosh. The list includes one entry, or queue element, for each volume, SCSI driver, and file server. Not every entry in the drive queue has a corresponding entry in the volume queue: a floppy drive without a disk is in the drive queue but not the volume queue. A floppy disk that has been ejected and appears dimmed on the desktop is in the volume queue but not the drive queue.

The low-memory global variable VCBQHdr contains a pointer to the first element in the list. This global variable is useful when you are looking at the volume queue from MacsBug. The system call GetVCBQHdr can be called from a program to get the pointer to the first element in the list. You can use the MacsBug template VCB to look at volume queue entries.

You can also use the standard dcmd vol to display information about mounted volumes. For example:

```
vol
Displaying Volume Control Blocks
  vRef Vol          Flg dRef Drive FSID #Blk  BlkSiz #Files  #Dirs Blsd Dir VCB at
  ffff Neuromanc... Dsh ffdf 0008  0000 a46a  000400 0003ac  0000d3   000018 00bf24
  fffe Descartes    dsh ffdb 0009  0000 cb72  000600 000a13  00016a   000000 003fbc
  fffd Backpack     dsh fffb 0001  0000 063a  000200 000011  000001   000000 01fce8
#3 VCBs
```

Table 5-3 describes the fields of the vol display.

- **Table 5-3** vol display fields

Field	Description
vRef	Volume reference number.
Vol	The name of the volume.
Flg	D/d:Uppercase = Dirty; S/s:Uppercase = Software locked; H/h:Uppercase = Hardware locked.
dRef	Driver reference number.
Drive	Drive number.
FSID	File system ID. Zero means Macintosh File System.
#Blk	Number of allocation blocks on volume.
BlkSiz	Size in bytes of an allocation block.
#Files	Number of files on the volume.
#Dirs	Number of directories on the volume.
Blsd Dir	Directory ID of the System Folder.
VCB at	Address of the volume control block.

File control blocks (FCBs)

A buffer in the system heap contains space for a number of file control blocks, or FCBs. Each FCB contains information on one currently open file. This buffer is not a queue. When the buffer is full, you must close a file to obtain room to open another. The low-memory global variable FCBSPtr points to the buffer. The system call PBGetFCBInfo can be called from a program to get the FCB for any open file.

The standard file dcmd displays information about all open files. For example:

```
file
Displaying File Control Blocks
fRef File            Vol        Type Fl Fork      LEof    Mark   FlNum  Parent FCB at
0002 System          Neuroma... ZSYS dW rsrc    #393111 #70829  001b86 000018 005aa6
0060                 Neuroma... •••• dw data    #336896 #0      000003 000000 005b04
00be                 Neuroma... •••• dw data    #673792 #0      000004 000000 005b62
011c OnBase          Neuroma... POP2 dw data    #255833 #534    001245 000018 005bc0
017a Suitcase• II    Neuroma... INIT dW rsrc    #39954  #28649  002433 000018 005c1e
01d8 Apple Fonts     Neuroma... FFIL dW rsrc    #103077 #64716  002441 00243a 005c7c
0236 Laser Fonts     Neuroma... FFIL dW rsrc    #302184 #7590   002442 00243a 005cda
0294 Debugger Fk...  Neuroma... FKEY dW rsrc    #351    #351    00243e 002439 005d38
```

Note that some files don't have names. In the listing above there are two files without names. These are the two B*tree files stored on each HFS volume, which contain the directory information.

Table 5-4 describes the fields of the file display.

■ **Table 5-4** file display fields

Field	Description
fRef	The file's reference number.
File	The name of the file.
Vol	The volume the file is on.
Type	The file's type.
Fl	D/d:Uppercase = Dirty; W/w:Uppercase = Writable.
Fork	Which fork is open, resource or data.
LEof	Logical end-of-file in bytes.
Mark	Current file mark position in bytes.
FlNum	File number.
Parent	File's parent directory ID.
FCB at	Address of the file's file control block.

File I/O queue

The file I/O queue is a linked list of all pending asynchronous I/O requests. The list includes one entry, or queue element, for each request.

The low-memory global variable FSQHdr contains a pointer to the first element in the list. This global variable is useful when you are looking at the file I/O queue from MacsBug. You can call GetFSQHdr from a program to get the pointer to the first element in the list.

Debugging low-level file system calls

The low-level file system calls are easy to debug in MacsBug. (The high-level calls are all implemented with glue, which ends up calling the low-level calls.) The low-level HFS calls all pass a pointer to their parameter block in register A0.

Some HFS calls use packaged traps, which means they are dispatched by means of a single A-trap number. Macros shipped with MacsBug allow you to set A-trap breaks on the particular A-trap you want.

First use the ATBA command to set a break on the HFS call you are interested in. (If you wrote the program in C or Pascal, the HFS call will be in glue. The glue takes the parameter block pointer off the stack, where the compiler put it, and puts it in A0.) Then type

```
DM A0 IOPB
```

and MacsBug will display the parameter block using the IOPB template, which is the most common parameter block template. All the information for a File Manager call is in this parameter block.

You can step over (using the SO command) the HFS trap, and then enter DM A0 IOPB again to examine what the trap returned. You can easily make your own templates for the more esoteric parameter blocks; see Chapter 4, "Macintosh Memory Organization," for information about making templates.

The Device Manager works just like the File Manager; it passes a pointer to a parameter block in A0, and the parameter block contains all the relevant information for the call. Use DM A0 IOPB as described above to examine the parameter block.

Synchronous and asynchronous I/O

Synchronous I/O refers to an I/O operation in which the calling process does not resume until the operation is finished. **Asynchronous I/O** refers to an I/O operation in which the calling process can continue to run at the same time that the I/O operation is being performed.

With synchronous I/O, your program tells the File Manager to read from a file. The File Manager in turn makes calls all the way down the line to the driver. The driver then makes the call to read the file. The driver retains control until the call has been processed and then returns control to the application. While the call is in progress, no other actions occur.

With asynchronous I/O, your program tells the File Manager to read from a file. The File Manager in turn makes a call to the Device Manager and returns control to the application while the call is being processed. This allows the application to keep running while the I/O operation is still being performed.

The driver gets slices of time to process the call periodically through an interrupt. When the driver completes the call, it sets a variable in the parameter block. The application needs to check the variable periodically to determine when the call has been processed. The driver also calls a completion routine that the application designates to be run when the call is complete.

Asynchronous I/O improves program speed by allowing the application to process during disk access. This time is otherwise wasted waiting for a disk drive head to get into position.

Currently, the only driver that can execute asynchronously is the floppy disk driver. If you call a driver asynchronously that can't support that mode, it simply runs synchronously.

For additional information about the File Manager, see the "File Manager" chapters in *Inside Macintosh,* Volumes IV and VI. (Note that the File Manager chapter in Volume II is obsolete.)

Drivers

Drivers are programs that connect applications to hardware devices. (A desk accessory is a special kind of driver.) The driver's job is to present a uniform software interface to an application no matter which of several similar hardware devices the application is using. For example, the ImageWriter and LaserWriter drivers present the same interface to the application, so the application doesn't need to take account of which printer the user chooses. The application simply sends data to the current print driver. The two drivers are responsible for dealing with the very different ImageWriter and LaserWriter hardware. Drivers can run at the same time that an application is running.

A driver does not contain a main entry point as does a normal application, but consists of a set of five independent routines:

- Open: opens a driver.
- Close: closes a driver.
- Prime: handles read and write operations.
- Status: returns the status of the driver.
- Control: handles all other driver operations, such as ejecting a disk from a floppy disk drive.

Only the Open and Close routines are required for a driver.

Most drivers are stored in resources of type 'DRVR'. The Resource Manager automatically loads them into memory when they are needed and disposes of them when they are closed. Every driver includes a header that lists its name, critical information, and the location of all its routines. The routines follow the header.

Applications use system calls to call the Device Manager rather than calling drivers directly. The Device Manager then directs the request to the proper driver. Applications can request either synchronous or asynchronous driver service. See "The File System," earlier in this chapter, for more information about synchronous and asynchronous I/O.

Device control entry (DCE)

The first time a driver is opened, information about it is read into a relocatable block in memory (usually in the system heap) called a device control entry, or DCE. The DCE includes a handle or pointer to the driver and other information that it copies from the driver (see the detailed view of the DCE in Figure 5-6). The block allocated for the DCE is locked when the driver it points to is open and unlocked when the driver is closed. Figure 5-6 shows the relationship of the DCE to the driver. (If the driver serves a device that is plugged into a NuBus slot, five additional entries are appended to the DCE shown in Figure 5-6. The "Device Manager" chapter in *Inside Macintosh,* Volume V, describes the fields added to the DCE for such drivers.)

If the driver is in ROM, the DCE has a pointer to it. If the driver is in RAM, the DCE has a handle to it. The DCE also contains a flag that tells you whether the driver is RAM-based or ROM-based. SCSI drivers are the only exception to this scheme. Although they are always in RAM, the flag can be set either way, and the DCE usually contains a pointer to the appropriate driver. The flag should therefore be ignored for SCSI drivers.

■ **Figure 5-6** Device control entry

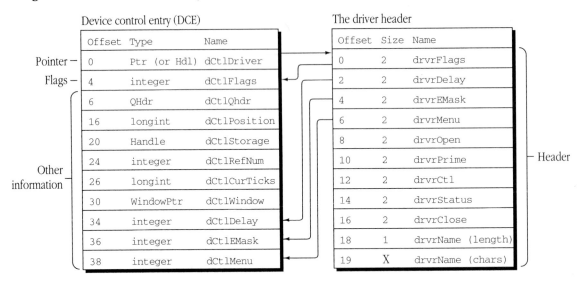

Figure 5-7 shows the word labeled dCtlFlags (see Figure 5-6). The high-order byte of this word is copied from the driver into the DCE; the low-order byte is only set up in the DCE. The bits of the low-order byte are subsequently changed as necessary by the operating system.

■ **Figure 5-7** Flag bits in the dCtlFlags word

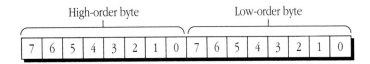

Table 5-5 describes the meanings of the high-order dCtlFlags flag bits in both the driver and the DCE.

■ **Table 5-5** High-order dCtlFlags flag bits

Bit	Name	Meaning
0	dReadEnable	Driver can respond to Read calls.
1	dWritEnable	Driver can respond to Write calls.
2	dCtlEnable	Driver can respond to Control calls.
3	dStatEnable	Driver can respond to Status calls.
4	dNeedGoodBye	Tell driver before application quits.
5	dNeedTime	Driver needs to be called periodically.
6	dNeedLock	Driver needs to be locked in memory.

Table 5-6 describes the meanings of the low-order dCtlFlags flag bits (in the DCE only).

■ **Table 5-6** Low-order dCtlFlags flag bits

Bit	Meaning
5	Driver is open.
6	Driver is RAM-based.
7	Driver is currently executing.

The unit table

The location of each device control entry is maintained in a list called the unit table. The unit table is an array of handles and is located in the system heap. It is divided into sections, as shown in Figure 5-8. Each section of the unit table is devoted to one type of driver and is divided into units with one unit per driver. In some sections, such as those for system drivers and SCSI drivers, each unit is reserved for one particular driver. In the other sections, any unit can be taken by any driver, as long as the driver belongs to the group of drivers assigned to that section. The reserved section mostly contains various network drivers.

Each unit contains a handle to the device control entry for that driver, or contains the value 0 if no driver is installed. The unit table has from 32 to 128 units, depending upon what type of Macintosh you have. The low-memory global variable UTableBase ($11C) contains a pointer to the unit table. Figure 5-8 shows a simplified view of the Unit Table and the way it relates to the DCE.

- **Figure 5-8** A simplified view of the unit table

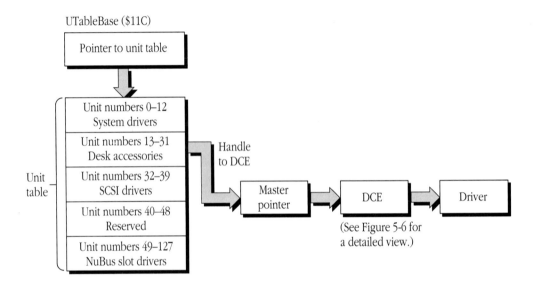

Figure 5-9 shows a more detailed view of the unit table.

- **Figure 5-9** Detailed view of the unit table

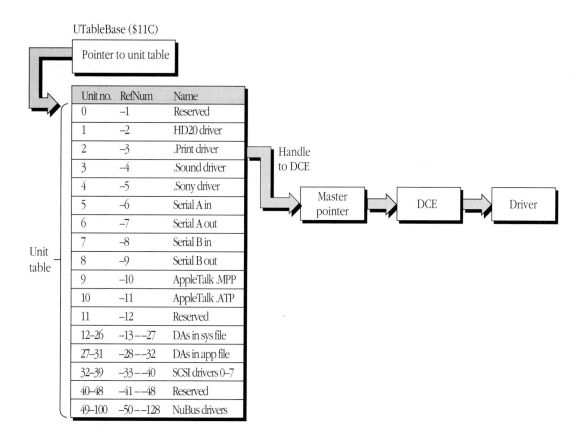

Desk accessories

Desk accessories (DAs) are a special type of Macintosh driver. Hardware drivers don't have user interfaces or interact with the user directly at all. Desk accessories can have menus and/or windows. Each desk accessory contains fields in its DCE to store pointers to a menu and a window that the DA uses. These fields are left blank by hardware drivers.

Since hardware drivers and desk accessories are both resources of type 'DRVR' and all 'DRVR' resources are required to have names, the system has a simple way to tell them apart. Hardware driver names begin with a period, like ".Sony" or ".Sound." Desk accessory driver names begin with a null character (a 0 that is a nonprinting ASCII character), like "Calculator" or "Alarm Clock." Nonprinting characters are displayed as boxes in some fonts. The system looks through all the 'DRVR' resources in the system file at startup time and lists the ones that don't start with a period under the Apple menu.

Desk accessories usually implement different calls from hardware drivers. In addition to Open and Close routines, desk accessories are required to implement the Control call. They usually don't implement the Prime or Status call used by many hardware drivers. Applications interact with desk accessories through the Desk Manager, which makes all of the appropriate Device Manager calls. The drvr dcmd, described in the next section, displays information about desk accessories as well as hardware drivers.

Displaying information about installed drivers

The standard drvr dcmd lists all the drivers currently installed, along with information about each driver and its device control entry. For example:

```
drvr
 Displaying Driver Control Entries
   dRef dNum Driver       FlgVer qHead   Storage Window Dely  Drvr at  DCE at
   fffd 0002 .Print       bHO #27 000000  000000  000000 0000 a0026838 8001b82c
   fffc 0003 .Sound       bPO #0  000000  000000  000000 0000 82f010   80002fcc
   fffb 0004 .Sony        bPO #1  000000  000000  000000 0000 82d72c   80002e58
   fffa 0005 .AIn         bPC #3  000000  000000  000000 0000 a082ab92 8000322c
   fff9 0006 .AOut        bPC #3  000000  000000  000000 0000 a082abaa 80003268
   fff8 0007 .BIn         bPC #3  000000  000000  000000 0000 a082abc2 800032ac
   fff7 0008 .BOut        bPC #3  000000  000000  000000 0000 a082abda 800032e8
   ffdf 0020 .SCSI00      bPO #0  000000  0058bc  000000 0000 0041a6   800054bc
   ffdb 0024 .SCSI00      bPO #0  000000  0058bc  000000 0000 0041a6   8001ba04
   ffcf 0030 .Display_V…  bHO #0  000000  001f28  000000 0000 c001bb5c 80003020
   #64 Unit Table entries, #12 in use, #52 free
```

Table 5-7 describes the fields of the drvr display.

- **Table 5-7** drvr display fields

Field	Description
dRef	The driver reference number, in two's complement arithmetic.
dNum	The driver's unit number.
Driver	The name of the driver.
Flg	B/b: Uppercase = Busy; H/P: driver is stored in a Handle or a Pointer; O/C: Open/Closed.
Ver	The driver's version number.
qHead	The head of the driver's request queue.
Storage	Pointer or handle to the driver's private storage.
Window	Pointer to a window that belongs to the driver.
Dely	How often the driver would like to be called, in ticks.
Drvr at	The address of the driver itself.
DCE at	The address of the driver's device control entry.

Chapter 6 **Discipline**

Discipline is a set of routines that a debugger calls to test the validity of parameters passed to a User Interface Toolbox or operating system routine and to test the validity of parameters passed back to your application by that routine. This chapter describes how you install Discipline, how you determine which tests Discipline should use to test parameters, and how you work with Discipline during application development.

Discipline is not a stand-alone tool; it must always be used with a resident debugger. This chapter assumes that the debugger is MacsBug.

For additional information about the way Discipline interfaces with MacsBug, see Appendix E, "MacsBug Internals and Discipline Interface."

How Discipline works

If Discipline is installed and your application makes a system call, MacsBug passes the call to Discipline instead of passing the call to the trap dispatcher. Discipline is responsible for performing two series of tests: it runs the first series before the call executes and the second series after the call executes.

Discipline selects the tests it's going to use depending on the call being tested and on the configuration file you selected when you installed Discipline. Thus Discipline might test the order in which you have specified the parameters for a call, test the validity of pointers, or check valid ranges for some or all of the parameters.

If the system call fails its initial (pre-execution) test, MacsBug saves the results in a history buffer and drops into MacsBug where you can examine the information it returns. If the call passes its initial test and you have set no actions on that trap (using ATB, ATHC, ATSS), MacsBug hands it off to the trap dispatcher, which finds the location of the call in ROM or RAM and executes the call.

After the call executes, Discipline again tests the values returned by the call. If it finds that the values are invalid or less than optimal, it drops into MacsBug and displays a diagnostic message. If the returned values pass Discipline's tests, the next instruction is executed.

Installing Discipline

You can install Discipline either as an INIT file or as an application, depending on your memory requirements and on whether you plan to run it in a single-application environment (system software version earlier than 7.0 with MultiFinder turned off) or a multiple-application environment (system software version 7.0, or system software version 5.0 or 6.0 with MultiFinder turned on).

Installing Discipline as an INIT file

If you are working in a single-application environment, you should install Discipline as an INIT file. In this case, Discipline remains installed until you shut down your Macintosh. To install Discipline, follow these steps:

1. Insert and open the Discipline disk.

2. Move the Discipline file into your System Folder.
3. Open the Configuration folder on the Discipline disk.
4. Open either the Lenient or the Strict configuration folder. Select the Discipline Startup file and move it into your System Folder.

   You indicate which tests you want Discipline to apply by selecting one of two configuration files: Lenient or Strict. Each of these files contains different tests that Discipline uses to test the parameters of each system call. The difference between these configurations is implied by their names: it will be easier for the parameters you supply to satisfy the lenient tests than to satisfy the strict tests.

5. Restart your Macintosh.

The message shown in Figure 6-1 is displayed to let you know that the installation was successful.

- **Figure 6-1** Discipline installation message

> DISCIPLINE needs a minute to load the Startup file.

You can prevent Discipline from loading when you start up your machine either by taking Discipline out of your System Folder and restarting, or by holding the Option key down while your Macintosh is starting up.

Discipline is turned off initially. It does not check trap calls until you turn it on. The command syntax you use to turn Discipline on and off and to select Discipline options depends on the debugger with which Discipline is running. The section "Using Discipline During Application Development" later in this chapter describes how you use Discipline from MacsBug.

Installing Discipline as an application

If you are working in a multiple-application environment, you will probably want to install Discipline as an application. In this case, Discipline remains installed until you turn it off from the debugger or press Command-Q to quit the Discipline application.

To install Discipline as an application, follow these steps:

1. Insert and open the Discipline disk.

2. Move the Discipline file into any folder you wish. It does not have to be the System Folder.

3. Open the Configuration folder on the Discipline disk.

4. Open either the Lenient or Strict configuration folder and move the Discipline Startup file into the folder containing Discipline.

    You indicate which tests you want Discipline to apply by selecting one of two configuration files: Lenient or Strict. Each of these files contains different tests that Discipline uses to test the parameters of each system call. The difference between these configurations is implied by their names: it will be easier for the parameters you supply to satisfy the lenient tests than to satisfy the strict tests.

5. To install and launch Discipline, hold the Option and Command keys down while double-clicking the Discipline file.

When Discipline is installed, the message shown in Figure 6-1 is displayed. When Discipline is launched, its icon will be displayed in the space where the active application's icon is normally displayed, and the rest of the menu bar will be completely blank; even the Apple menu will be gone. This is just as it should be. You can get back to the Finder by clicking the Discipline icon or the desktop.

When you return to the Finder, you can see Discipline listed as an active application in the Apple menu. Also, Discipline is turned on and you are very likely to find yourself in MacsBug or the resident debugger because Discipline seldom approves of the way in which the Finder accesses system calls. This would be a good time either to turn Discipline off or to leave it on only for applications.

If MacsBug is the resident debugger, you can turn Discipline off by entering

`DSC OFF`

on the command line or by typing Command-Q. When you are ready to use Discipline to test an application, you can turn it back on.

To leave Discipline on but arrange things so Discipline doesn't have to worry about the Finder's manners, enter

`DSCA`

from MacsBug.

If you are working in a multiple-application environment, you can install Discipline either as an INIT file or as an application. In this case, it is your need for memory that might dictate which way you install it. If you install it as an INIT file, Discipline will take up space in the system heap until you shut down your computer. If you install it as an application, Discipline will only take up space in the system heap when it is turned on.

Reading Discipline output

Reading Discipline's output is fairly straightforward. Figure 6-2 shows two messages from Discipline in the output region of the MacsBug display. Each message was created by Discipline when a system routine failed one of Discipline's tests.

- **Figure 6-2** Sample Discipline output

```
 Welcome to Discipline!
MACSBUG REPORTS DISCIPLINE BREAK:

 Before:   BeginUpdate
 Located:  004AF95A
 PC:       004AF95A

 Parameters:
    theWindow      before      004B6B9A

 TEST:
  | 00  Test {before Parameter theWindow} as a WindowPtr.

 FAILURE:
    Invalid structRgn.
MacsBug will remain visible always
MACSBUG REPORTS DISCIPLINE BREAK:

 Before:   EndUpdate
 Located:  004AF980
 PC:       004AF980

 Parameters:
    theWindow      before      004B6B9A

 TEST:
  | 00  Test {before Parameter theWindow} as a WindowPtr.

 FAILURE:
    Invalid structRgn.
```

The first three entries in the Discipline output tell you when Discipline performed the test, the address of the instruction being tested, and the value of the program counter. Discipline performed this test before executing the BeginUpdate call. It tells you this in the beginning of its message:

`Before:   BeginUpdate`

But you can also tell because the value of the program counter (PC) and the address of the instruction being tested are the same.

The next field, Parameters, lists the parameters to the call. The BeginUpdate call takes one parameter, a window pointer.

The next field, Test, lists the test(s) used to evaluate the parameter.

The next field, Failure, further narrows the cause for the break. In this case, it pinpoints one of the fields of the window record, structRgn. The display gives you all the information you need to check the value of this field. The following MacsBug command displays memory starting at 004B6B9A using the template windowRecord to make sense of the bits:

```
dm  004B6B9A  windowRecord
```

Using Discipline during application development

This section describes how you call Discipline from MacsBug. It also suggests ways you can use Discipline during various stages of application development and explains how to use Discipline to test system routines made from code that runs during system startup and from code that executes within another application's partition.

This is the syntax of the DSC command:

DSC[A][X] [ON | OFF]

    A
specifies that Discipline only checks toolbox calls made from your application.

    ON
turns Discipline on.

    OFF
turns Discipline off.

    X
directs MacsBug to keep the Discipline error report internally and continue execution rather than stopping before and after every A-trap call to display Discipline messages.

Using Discipline to test applications

The way you use Discipline depends largely on how confident you are in your code. You might want to define three stages: module development, initial application testing, and final application testing.

Whenever you add a piece of new code, use the strict Discipline configuration. Use the DSCA command to turn Discipline on at the start of the new module. You can use the DebugStr command in the source code to do this. You could include the following command at the beginning of the piece of code you are adding:

```
DebugStr "Activating Discipline; DSCA ON; G"
```

Turn Discipline off at the end of the module in the same way:

```
DebugStr "Turning Discipline off; DSCA OFF; G"
```

You should also turn Discipline on (DSCA ON) using the lenient configuration every time you run your application during development. Using the DSCA option will speed up Discipline's performance, but you should use the DSC command—to test for every system call—during final testing.

The DSCX option, which allows Discipline to log test results internally while continuing to execute your program, is something to save for last, when you're sure that your code won't crash. Although the DSCX option keeps Discipline from complaining, it might also prevent you from seeing a message that would have warned you of an impending crash. If the Macintosh crashes, the log file that Discipline has used to record test results will be useless.

Using Discipline to test INITs and other startup code

If you want to use Discipline to test INITs or other code resources that run during the startup sequence, you must make sure that Discipline is loaded before your INIT. You can do this by placing a Debugger call at the start of your INIT to drop into MacsBug and then turn Discipline on yourself. Or you can use the DebugStr command to turn Discipline on and continue execution. For example:

```
DebugStr "Turn Discipline ON; DSCA ON; G"
```

When the INIT completes, turn Discipline off. It is recommended that you use the strict configuration every time to test an INIT.

Using Discipline to test DAs and XCMDs

If you are writing desk accessories, XCMDs, or other code resources that execute within an application's partition (in a multiple-application environment, desk accessories have their own partitions), you need to be careful when you are using the DSCA command. DSCA simply looks at the local HeapZone where the PC points, whether it be a nested zone or the application zone. It confines Discipline's actions to that zone. You must therefore make sure that you are in the right application partition.

This is relatively easy to do with MacsBug 6.2, since it displays the name of the current application in the status region of its display. Check the name of the current application before you enter DSCA.

Restrictions on Discipline

You must observe the following restrictions when using Discipline.

If you are using MacsBug:

- A command line containing a DSC command cannot contain macros.
- You cannot log MacsBug output if DSC is on.
- If Discipline crashes, you must turn it off using the DSC OFF or DSCA OFF command before you use the ES (Exit to Shell) command.

If you are using any debugger (including MacsBug) and the Finder is the current application, do not turn Discipline on or you will be inundated with complaints. This does not mean that there is anything wrong with the Finder, and it does not mean that there is anything wrong with Discipline. It just means that you should keep the Finder away from Discipline.

Chapter 7 Debugging Strategies

If there were a formula for writing programs, there would also be a formula for debugging them. Unfortunately, there are no formulas; only experience, patience, and intelligence can help you in either case. Error handling on the Macintosh is especially tricky because of the extensive interplay between your code and the system code. You have to understand what your code is doing, how the disassembled code that MacsBug shows you relates to your source code, and how the system implements User Interface Toolbox and operating system routines and manages memory in order to find and fix bugs.

This chapter describes some strategies that can make your work in developing, testing, and debugging programs easier:

- It describes how you can take advantage of compiler options and system error-handling routines to catch bugs before they happen.
- It describes common bugs and their causes and cures.
- It explains how you can use MacsBug commands to focus on potential sources of bugs and to test your program.

For additional information about Macintosh debugging, see Scott Knaster's *How to Write Macintosh Software*. The information presented in this chapter relies heavily on this work.

Before the crash

The best way to cure bugs is not to let them happen in the first place. The next best way is to observe them when they happen rather than hunting for them after your program has crashed. This section describes some of the things you can do during development that can prevent bugs from happening or make them easy to find when they do happen.

Use the compiler's directives

Most compilers include directives that can help you catch errors resulting from range violations, integer overflow, uninitialized variables, and unsafe use of handles. You can selectively turn these options on and off in your source program to catch potential bugs while keeping compilation times to a minimum.

If you anticipate having to do some low-level debugging, use the compiler directive that allows debugging symbols to be placed in object code. If this directive is not turned on, MacsBug will not be able to display routine names in its disassembly commands. This will make it difficult for you to determine where you are in your program when it crashes and equally difficult to find your way around when you're working with MacsBug.

Turn trap recording on

The MacsBug ATR (A-trap Record) command copies information about each system call that executes into an internal buffer. If your program crashes or behaves erratically, you can use the ATP (A-trap Playback) command to display information stored in that buffer. (By default, the buffer contains information about the last 24 traps encountered.) The information includes the value of the program counter at the time the trap was executed as well as the contents of any registers on entry (for an operating system routine) or the 12 bytes on top of the stack (for a User Interface Toolbox routine).

You can use this information to get a quick history of what code was executing right before the crash; you can also check the information saved about the stack or the registers to see if there were any suspect values recently passed to a system routine.

Trap recording slows execution down just a little bit, but can give you valuable information when you need it most. For additional information about the information returned and the number of traps saved, see the description of the ATR and ATP commands in Chapter 9, "MacsBug Commands."

Check operating system errors whenever possible

Operating system (OS) errors are available for the program to inspect but should never be shown to the user. Some managers, such as the File Manager, provide a return result from every call. Others, such as the Memory Manager, return zero to indicate than an error occurred, and you must call a special function (MemError for the Memory Manager) to get the actual error number.

There are hundreds of OS error codes. They are very specific and often tell you exactly what went wrong. OS errors are usually (but not always) negative numbers. Zero always means that there was no error. (For more information about the way the microprocessor stores negative numbers, see "The Representation of Negative Numbers" in Chapter 3.)

Make sure you validate every system return value when you're programming. Most programmers don't check them all, yet this is the easiest way to avoid a crash, since the operating system is telling you that something is wrong before the problem becomes serious and hard to track down.

OS errors are listed in Appendix C of this manual, as well as in Appendix A of each volume of *Inside Macintosh*. (Note that each volume of *Inside Macintosh* contains a different list of errors.) The System Errors desk accessory provides an on-line list of user alerts and system errors.

The OS error returned by the last call to certain managers is stored in some low-memory global variables. From a high-level language, you should call the routine that returns the error (see Table 7-1). If the Macintosh crashes, you can look at the low-memory global variables listed in Table 7-1 to try to determine the reason for the crash.

■ **Table 7-1** Low-memory global variables that store operating system errors

Name	Address	Format	Description	Routine to get error
DSErrCode	$AF0	Word	Current user alert error	
MemErr	$220	Word	Error from last call	MemError
ResErr	$A60	Word	Error from last call	ResError

Results from calls to the Resource Manager are not reported by individual calls but are stored in the low-memory global variable ResErr. The best way to check for resource errors is to use the ResErrProc low-memory global variable, which is a pointer to a resource error-handling procedure. You can use the error-handling procedure to invoke MacsBug. When MacsBug displays the debugging screen, use the DM command to display the contents of ResErr. Register A7 should contain the return address of the routine that called the Resource Manager. (If your error-handling procedure is set up using a stack frame, you'll find the return address at A6 + 4.) Using ResErrProc rather than testing ResError every time you make a Resource Manager call is more efficient and also allows you to catch resource errors that result from routines that make unanticipated calls to the Resource Manager.

The other low-memory global variable that is worthwhile testing in the debugging version of your code is MemErr. You can do this by setting a conditional breakpoint in your program from MacsBug; for example:

```
ATB memerr <> 0;G
```

To check the value stored in MemErr when MacsBug is invoked, enter

```
DW MemErr
```

MacsBug displays something like the following:

```
word at 00000220 = $FF94  #65428  #-108   '..'
```

The signed decimal value identifies the memory error.

Use signals and error handler routines

Signals are a form of intraprogram interrupt that allow you to do elegant (memory-inexpensive) error trapping in stack frame–intensive languages or when you are implementing deeply nested procedures. Using signals, your program can call the Signal procedure and immediately return to the last invocation of the CatchSignal function, which cleans up the stack frame up to the point where it is called. For complete details, see Macintosh Technical Note #88, *Signals*.

Use assertions in your source program

An assertion is a procedure that tests a condition and invokes MacsBug if the condition fails the test. You can use a compile-time variable to conditionally compile assertions for the debugging version of your program.

Here is an example of an assertion:

```
PROCEDURE Assert (condition: Boolean);
BEGIN
IF condition = FALSE then
      DebugStr ('assertion failed');
END;
```

You can then call the Assert routine from anywhere in your source program where you want to check a value. Notice that this gives you the flexibility of testing for any condition; for example:

```
X = GetNumber (0,1)
   .
   .
   .
Y = 10 * x
Assert ( Y > 0 AND Y < 10 )
```

If you're mixing assembly and high-level languages, you can use assertions to check stack balance after executing assembly code. One common problem arises when your assembly-language routine fails to return the stack pointer to its original location. This results in an unbalanced stack and bugs. The cure is to save the value of A7 (the stack pointer) when your assembly-language routine starts and then to compare its final value to the saved value. If the values don't match, it's time to drop into MacsBug and find out why.

Note that assertions are normally used only in beta versions of the software. In release versions, the Assert routine is replaced with a null routine. In C, Assert is usually a macro, and the macro is replaced with null, so the release application doesn't even have the call stubs to Assert. In Pascal, conditional compiles are used to remove assertions in the final version. The standard C library includes an Assert routine.

Test code on all machines

There are many reasons for testing code on all machines; this section lists just a few.

The 68000, 68020, and 68030 microprocessors use slightly different instruction sets. If your compiler is translating your source code using an instruction that the 68030 recognizes but the 68000 does not, your program will crash when run on the 68000 with an illegal instruction error.

The 68000 microprocessor will generate an address error if you attempt to move a word or long word to an odd address; the 68020/30 microprocessors will not generate an error but will run more slowly. Testing your code on a 68000 allows you to find out if you're doing this and thereby allows you to get better performance on the 68020/30 when you've fixed the bug.

Because the 68000 does not allow you to write words or long words to an odd address, it also gives you a good chance to catch invalid pointers or handles. For example, if you've failed to initialize a handle or pointer, when you dereference it, the microprocessor will use whatever value is stored at that location as the address to write to; if the value is odd, you'll get an instant crash. Thus testing code on the 68000 allows you to find invalid handles and pointers at the time they happen rather than after they've done a lot of damage and you have to track down the cause.

The 68020 and 68030 processors report invalid addresses (addresses not in ROM, RAM, or memory-mapped I/O) as bus errors. The Macintosh Plus hardware does not generate this error but puts in a bogus value. So, if your program crashes on the 68020 or 68030 with a bus error, but not on a 68000, you're trying to access an invalid address.

Catch NIL pointers and handles instantly

A NIL pointer or handle is what the Memory Manager returns when it can't allocate the space you ask for. If you fail to test for this, you'll wind up writing either to memory location 0 or to the address equal to the value stored there. Writing to $0 can have dire consequences because all the system's low-memory global variables are stored in that vicinity, as well as the exception vectors that send the microprocessor to the right address when an error happens or a system call is made. This means you might not be able to get into MacsBug except by pressing the interrupt switch.

To catch a NIL pointer, you need to test the value returned by the Memory Manager when you allocate space for a nonrelocatable block.

To catch a NIL handle, you need to declare a procedure that sets memory location $0 to $50FFC003 and to call the procedure from your main event loop. You should only use this procedure in the debugging version of your program.

- If you're working in Pascal, you can declare the following procedure in the main segment of your program:

  ```
  PROCEDURE SetZero(); INLINE $21FC, $50FF, $C003, $0000;
  ```

  and then call SetZero from your main event loop.

- If you're working in C, you can declare the following procedure in the main segment of your program:

  ```
  pascal void SetZero(void) = {0x21FC, 0x50FF, 0xC003, 0x0000};
  ```

  and then call SetZero from your main event loop.

Once you do this, any attempt to use a NIL handle will result in an instant crash that won't hurt anything and that will allow you to find the cause quickly. For additional information, see "Nasty Pointers" later in this chapter.

Use SetPort correctly

Any drawing done by QuickDraw, directly or indirectly, is done to the current GrafPort. There is only one current GrafPort, and its address is stored in the global variable thePort; register A5 contains the address of a pointer to thePort. The function GetPort returns the current value of thePort; the function SetPort changes the value. It's obviously important to write to the right current port. One technique that used to be recommended for making sure of the right GrafPort was the use of GetPort to find the current port and then the use of SetPort to change it if it was not the port you wanted. Unfortunately, this did not prove to be a good solution because system calls intervening between SetPort and the first use of the port sometimes resulted in the port being changed.

A better solution is to call SetPort as close as possible to writing to the current port, and not to rely on the GetPort/SetPort technique as a guarantee that you are writing to the right port.

After the crash

Finding the cause and cure for a bug that catches you by surprise is, of course, much more difficult than fixing one that you've forced in order to catch it before it has covered its trail.

When your program crashes, what MacsBug or the bomb box tells you is not the cause of the bug but the symptom. For example, an illegal instruction error can be caused by an instruction your processor does not recognize (see "Test Code on All Machines" earlier in this chapter) or by your having inadvertently written to the location on the stack where the return address of an instruction was stored. Once the symptom manifests itself, through a crash or through your program's erratic behavior, debugging is the process of finding the cause. The symptom is only the last clue on the bug's trail.

The same bug might give rise to different symptoms. For example, an invalid pointer that results in your writing to the wrong address might produce a crash if you wind up writing over a block header in the heap; it might produce odd sounds if you wind up writing to the sound buffer; it might put blotches on your screen if you wind up writing to the screen buffer; it might simply corrupt data and never let you know anything is wrong if you wind up writing to the contents of a heap block. For this reason, you should not assume that you can make the same bug happen again by rerunning your application. When a crash occurs, gather as much information as you can. If you can force the same bug, the information won't hurt you; if you can't, it will be very helpful.

The sections that follow describe a few ways you can gather information after your program crashes. These methods by no means exhaust the possible ways of finding and curing bugs.

Where am I?

Debugging begins with gathering information, and the first piece of information you'll need is what part of your code was executing when the crash occurred. First, get visual information. Use the tilde or Esc key to take a look at what the screen looked like just before the crash. Next, use the MacsBug WH (Where) command. The command takes an address as a parameter; a good address to use is that stored in the current program counter. Since the WH command uses that address by default, entering

```
WH
```

will display information about the location of the instruction pointed to by the PC register. If the instruction is in ROM, the WH command will display the address of the instruction as an offset from the start of the trap. If the instruction is in RAM, the WH command will tell you which heap block the instruction is stored in, the name of the routine containing the instruction, and the offset of the instruction from the start of the routine.

Remember, the instruction pointed to by the PC is not likely to be the one that caused the crash. The next step is finding that instruction.

Who done it?

If the microprocessor executed only one instruction at a time, finding the instruction that caused the crash would be easy; it would always be the instruction just preceding the instruction stored in the program counter. Unfortunately, the microprocessor is doing several things at once (pipelining), and it is often the case that the instruction you're looking for is a few bytes ahead of or behind the PC. Where the instruction is depends on the kind of error that caused the crash:

- For an illegal instruction error, it is very likely that the instruction currently pointed to by the PC did cause the error.
- For a bus error, the PC might point one or two instructions ahead of or behind the bad instruction.
- For an illegal address, the PC might point one or two instructions ahead of or behind the bad instruction.

These are the most common errors you are likely to get. The situation is often similar for other errors. Don't just examine the instruction pointed to by the PC. Look around. The MacsBug command that lets you do this is the IP (Disassemble Around Address) command. This command takes an address as a parameter; if you don't specify one, it uses the address stored in the program counter by default. If you enter

```
IP
```

MacsBug displays 64 bytes centered around the PC. Use the information displayed by the break message to figure out which instruction caused the error. For example, if you get a division-by-0 error, you'll want to look for a DIVS or DIVU instruction; if you get an address error, look for a MOVE.W or MOVE.L instruction with an odd operand or for the PC to have an odd address; if you get a bus error, look for an instruction with an operand that refers to an invalid address.

After you have found the instruction that caused the crash, the next step is to figure out how that instruction came to be executed.

Why did it happen?

You've found the offending instruction, but you trust that the compiler has been faithfully and accurately translating your source code. Where, then, did it get the bad value? This is the point where it is important to be able to relate the disassembled code to your source code and to check the values that you think are being referenced against the values that are actually being referenced.

Check the source code

Most crashes are the direct result of a bad line in the source code. To locate the offending source-code statement, use this procedure following a crash:

- Execute an SC (Stack Crawl) command. If the output to the SC command looks reasonable—that is, you can recognize routine names—look at the last address on the stack (most recent call) by disassembling around the last address shown. Use the command

    IP *xxxxxxxx*

    where *xxxxxxxx* is the last address shown.

- If you can see a routine name in the disassembled output, figure out which source-statement line was executing. (Major clues include JSR instructions, which are subroutine calls, and A-traps.)

- If you can't recognize the subroutine indicated by the last address on the stack, try disassembling around the next-to-last address. Keep going until you're either on familiar territory or until you run out of addresses. (For additional information about using Stack Crawl commands and interpreting the information they display, see the descriptions of the SC and SC7 commands in Chapter 9 and the section "Life on the Stack" in Chapter 4.)

- If you run out of addresses, switch tactics. Place SysBeep or DebugStr commands throughout the code, and count or watch the number of times they are executed.

- When the program crashes, go to the approximate area indicated by the number of beeps or debugger breaks. Remove the old SysBeep or DebugStr calls and place new ones only within the suspect portion of code. Keep running and refining until you discover the offending line.

Other suspects

If looking at the source code does not help you find the cause of the bug, you need to check for more subtle causes. The usual suspects include uninitialized variables, invalid pointers or handles, or fragmented memory.

If you are working with MPW Pascal, use the –u option, which sets all variables to a special uninitialized pattern when they are allocated. This helps catch subtle bugs that might have slipped by otherwise, and makes spotting an uninitialized variable much easier.

To check for bad pointers and handles, use the MacsBug HC (Heap Check) command. This command tells you if the information in the heap zone header or any of the block headers in the current heap has been corrupted. There are two ways that this information becomes corrupted. If you are writing to an address pointed to by a dangling pointer or handle, you are likely to be writing anywhere in memory, including a heap block or heap zone header. In the second case, you might be writing to a valid address, but writing more data than you think, thus writing over the header of the next block. Note that it is possible that a bad pointer or handle can cause you to write to the contents of a block, in which case the HC command will not return an error message. You can, however, force bad pointers to show themselves by using the HS (Heap Scramble) command to turn heap scrambling on when you run your program. This command forces the Memory Manager to move relocatable or unlocked blocks during every A-trap call that can allocate memory directly or indirectly. This vastly increases the chance that a bad pointer will write over a block or zone header and corrupt the heap. If the heap becomes corrupted, MacsBug is invoked and displays an error message.

To check for fragmented memory, which can prevent the Resource Manager from loading the resources your program needs to execute, use the HD (Heap Display) command. The HD command displays information about all the blocks in the current heap, listed from the lowest address to the highest address. A dot in the first column of the display indicates that the block cannot move. Ideally, blocks that cannot move should be located either at the bottom or at the top of the heap. If the HD command shows that nonrelocatable and locked blocks (neither of which can be moved) are interspersed throughout your heap, this means that memory is fragmented.

Common problems

This section describes the symptoms and possible causes of common problems caused by bugs.

The deep freeze

Some crashes don't give you a chance to use MacsBug. If you've been programming the Macintosh long, you've probably had this experience: your program locks up. You hit the interrupt switch, but nothing happens.

Pointers in low memory called exception vectors point to MacsBug. These vectors allow the system to transfer control to MacsBug when a crash happens. If your program wipes out low memory, you can't get into MacsBug.

Unfortunately, there is a fairly common error that can cause low memory to be wiped out. When you ask the Memory Manager for a block of memory, it gives you a pointer to that block. If it can't allocate the memory you asked for (perhaps memory is full), it returns 0. If you neglect to check the result, your program might start writing to the address the Memory Manager apparently returned—which is 0. All the important MacsBug vectors are in the first 256 bytes of memory, so they tend to get wiped out quickly. Nothing but the reset button on the programmer's switch will get you out of this one. Moral: *always* check what the Memory Manager returns to see if it's 0.

The restart surprise

In this situation, the Macintosh simply up and restarts somewhere in the middle of your program.

This is usually caused by two bus errors in a row. Bus errors are handled by a bus error handler. If, in the course of crashing, your program damages the bus error handler and then generates a bus error, and the damaged bus error handler generates a second bus error before the microprocessor can finish processing the first bus error, you've got a problem. Whenever the microprocessor gets a bus error before it's finished processing another bus error, it gives up and restarts. This is called a double bus fault.

Nasty pointers

Invalid pointers or handles are a common cause of any number of symptoms, depending on where the pointer or handle actually points to. Symptoms include bus errors, address errors, illegal instruction errors, corrupted heap, corrupted data, trashed stack, odd sounds and flashing screen, and many others.

To win the battle against nasty pointers, you need to do one or more of the following:

- Become familiar with the situations in which the Memory Manager will move memory and use a temporary local or global variable to store a duplicate of the relocatable block. The article "The Secret Life of the Memory Manager," in Volume I, Issue 2, of *Develop*, contains invaluable information about memory management on the Macintosh and gotchas not previously documented that can result in bad pointers. The first thing to read, however, is the "Memory Manager" chapter in *Inside Macintosh*, Volume II.

- Set memory location 0 to $50FFC003. This will produce an instant crash when you access a NIL handle.

- If you suspect that a relocatable block is being moved out from under you, use the MacsBug ATSS (A-trap Step Spy) command to checksum memory at the location of the block's master pointer. The ATSS command will invoke MacsBug when memory changes at that location—that is, right after a system call that causes your block to be moved. This is a less expensive way of guarding yourself against unanticipated moves than to lock every handle in your program. Handles only need to be locked if they are going to be dereferenced and if a call will be made that can cause relocation.

- Use the HS (Heap Scramble) command to force invalid pointers and handles to show themselves. This command moves all relocatable blocks whenever they might be moved—in other words, whenever the NewPtr, NewHandle, ReallocHandle, SetPtrSize, or SetHandleSize trap or any trap that calls these traps is called. (With SetPtrSize and SetHandleSize, the heap is scrambled only if the block size is being increased.)

No room to maneuver

You can run out of space in the heap even if you check for memory allocation. For example, when you call MenuSelect, the Menu Manager temporarily saves the part of the screen that's going to be covered up by the menu; if there's no space available, the program crashes. Use the HD command to check for heap fragmentation. Try to preserve as much contiguous free space in the heap as possible.

Another common cause of an out-of-memory condition is when an instruction writes over the start of a block's header. If you're allocating blocks of different sizes, you need to be especially careful about writing only within the confines of each block. (Arrays in C are especially bad this way.)

You can also run out of space on the stack. If your program uses the MaxApplZone routine to expand its heap, it has 8K of stack space left (24K on 68020/68030). If you are using large local variables, passing large variables by value, or nesting procedures too deeply (especially recursive procedures), you can get a stack overflow error or, if the stack sniffer fails to catch the overflow, a corrupted heap. (The stack sniffer is a routine that checks to see that the stack pointer does not point into the space allocated for the heap; it does not check after every instruction, so that it is possible to corrupt the heap without being caught.)

Mind-reading problems

Crashes in the ROM are common. This does not mean the ROM has bugs in it; it means that you probably passed bad parameters to the system routine.

If you make a system call specifying a parameter that refers to an object that exists and whose type matches that of the formal parameter required by the routine, the system will do exactly what you ask. For example, if you ask the Window Manager to dispose of a window and pass it a window pointer, whatever the window pointer points to will be disposed of. It's your responsibility to make sure that you are referring to the right objects. The system can't read your mind.

Using MacsBug to control program execution

Certain MacsBug commands allow you to control the execution of your program; these include breakpoint commands and flow control commands. Table 7-2 provides a summary of these commands.

■ **Table 7-2** Commands that control program execution

Command	A-trap command	Effect
BR	ATB	BR sets a breakpoint at a specified address. ATB sets a breakpoint before the specified A-trap(s) execute.
BRC	ATC	Clears specified breakpoints.
BRD	ATD	Displays current breakpoints or other actions (set with A-trap commands).
BRM		Sets breakpoints using partial name matching.
S		Executes the specified instruction(s) or executes instructions until a specified condition has been met.
SO		Like the S command except that SO steps over A-traps, JSRs, and BSRs, treating them like single instructions.
SS	ATSS	Both SS and ATSS check a specified range of memory as they step through code.
G		Resumes program execution beginning with the instruction stored in the PC.
GT		Resumes execution (like G), but breaks at the specified address.

The syntax and effect of each of these commands are described in detail in Chapter 9, "MacsBug Commands."

As you can see from Table 7-2, in some cases MacsBug provides two sets of program control commands: one set depends upon the execution of the instructions that make up your source code, and the other set depends upon the execution of A-traps. The way A-traps are implemented makes this distinction necessary even though the effect of the two sets of related commands is similar. This distinction can be used to advantage in debugging.

Every Macintosh application consists of A-trap calls interspersed with implemented instructions (the object code into which the compiler translates your source code). There are normally many more implemented instructions than A-trap calls, especially if you restrict the examination of A-traps to those being called from the application heap. This situation creates two levels of granularity in your program: the level on which A-traps are called, which is the coarser, and the level on which implemented instructions are executed, which is the finer. You can take advantage of this situation to focus in on bugs in two steps: in the first step, you use an A-trap command to invoke MacsBug when a certain condition is met; in the second step, you focus on the range of instructions that lie between the A-trap that is about to execute and the last A-trap executed to determine which specific instruction is causing the trouble. You can use the following pairs of commands in this way: ATB/BR; ATHC/HC; ATSS/SS. See the section "MacsBug's A-trap Commands" in Chapter 5 as well as the description of the ATB, BR, ATHC, HC, ATSS, and SS commands in Chapter 9 for additional information.

Controlling program execution

Two commands let you execute instructions one at a time. The S (Step) command executes a single instruction, stops at the next instruction, and returns to MacsBug. The contents of the program counter—in other words, the next instruction to be executed—are disassembled and displayed. You can also step through a specified number of instructions, or until a condition is met (for instance, until a register contains a particular value).

When the S command reaches a subroutine or an A-trap call, it steps right in. Particularly with ROM routines, which are often very long and typically not of interest, you'll probably want to use the SO (Step Over) command instead. The SO command works exactly like the S command except that it treats A-trap calls and subroutines as a single instruction, stopping at the first instruction after the A-trap or subroutine returns. (With traps that have the auto-pop bit set, MacsBug returns to the address on the top of the stack at the time of the trap call.)

While stepping through code, MacsBug decodes conditional statements (DBcc, Bcc, and Scc instructions) to determine whether branches will be taken or will fall through. This information is shown to the right of the PC information.

If you've stepped into a procedure with the S command and want to get out, you can use the MR (Magic Return) command to move to the end of the procedure. The MR command needs to know where the return address is; for this reason, it's a good idea to use the LINK A6 prologue for your procedures.

If you're stepping through your program and find you want to move past some code, you can use the GT (Go Till) command to resume execution until a specified address is reached.

Setting breakpoints

Once you've narrowed down the location of a bug, you might want to invoke MacsBug when a particular point in your program is reached. There are several ways of doing this.

The ATB (A-trap Break) command lets you specify a break when A-traps are encountered. You can specify individual traps or a range of traps, as well as conditions that must be met. For instance, you could specify a break when the HFSDispatch trap is encountered and the value of register D0 is 6 (which is the routine selector for the DirCreate routine). You can also specify commands to be executed once MacsBug has been invoked.

Another way to stop program execution is to set a breakpoint at a specified address using the BR command. You can specify the address as an actual address or as an offset from a procedure name. This information will have been found by disassembling or stepping through your code. The BR command also lets you specify commands to be executed when the breakpoint is reached. You can specify multiple breakpoints; MacsBug stores this information in a table, which you can see at any time with the BRD command. Breakpoints remain set until you clear them with the BRC command.

You can also set breakpoints by using partial name matching with the BRM command. You pass BRM a sequence of characters; it sets breakpoints on all names that contain those characters. The BRM command is especially useful with C++ and object Pascal debugging; you might, for instance, wish to break on all methods of a given class.

The BR command can be useful in working with A-traps as well as with your own code. With some ROM routines, the actual trap is often preceded by glue code that sets up the parameters. Whereas the ATB command stops right before the trap is made, the BR command can be used to stop at the point where your program calls the routine, letting you examine what goes on with the glue code.

An advantage of using breakpoints is that they don't require changes to your source code and can be used after the application has been built. However, breakpoints cannot be set in a procedure until the segment containing that procedure is loaded and the address determined. One way around this problem is to specify a break from within your procedure by using the traps Debugger ($A9FF) and DebugStr ($ABFF). Debugger is a system trap that invokes MacsBug and displays the message "User break at *address.*" DebugStr also lets you supply a custom message for display, as well as MacsBug commands for execution. The section "Invoking MacsBug From Your Source Program" in Chapter 2 provides additional information.

The DebugStr trap pushes a pointer to a Pascal string onto the stack and then invokes MacsBug. You can take advantage of the fact that DebugStr takes a string parameter to display the value of a variable at a specific point in your program. You do this by calling the NumToString trap, which converts an integer into a string that represents its decimal value, and then calling DebugStr to display the string. For example:

```
Begin
        thisnumber := 666;
        NumToString (thisnumber; mynumber);
        DebugStr (mynumber);
        newnumber := thisnumber
End
```

If the value of the number is negative, the string is preceded by a minus sign.

To display the value of a non-integer variable, convert its address to a string and send the string to MacsBug. For example:

```
Begin
        thisnumber := 666.66;
        NumToString (@thisnumber; mynumber);
        DebugStr (mynumber);
        newnumber := thisnumber
End
```

When MacsBug is invoked, it will display the variable's address. Remember, however, that the address is expressed in base ten. When you use the DM command to display the value stored at that address, remember to prefix the address with a pound (#) sign.

DebugStr only accepts Pascal strings. If you are writing in C, be sure to pass a Pascal string.

The DX (Debugger Exchange) command lets you disable breaks from the Debugger and DebugStr traps without having to go in and remove them from your program.

Watching for memory to change

Several commands let you determine when and where a particular area of memory is being changed. One common problem occurs when a program inadvertently changes the contents of a memory location. You can detect when a range of memory changes by using the SS (Step Spy) command. This command checksums a given range and then executes instructions one at a time until the checksum changes. The SS command can slow down a program considerably, so MacsBug treats a long word as a special case and optimizes for speed. If you suspect a certain range of memory is being altered, you usually don't need to check the whole range but can check just a long word within the range. If you must check a long range, you'll probably want to use a hardware emulator.

You can also use the SS command as a way of slowing down certain routines—those that draw to the screen, for instance—so you can actually watch how they work. The best way to do this is to use the command

```
SS   @Rombase
```

This command simply slows your program down, since ROM never changes.

A variation on the SS command, the ATSS (A-trap Step Spy) command, lets you checksum a memory range before specified A-traps are executed. ATSS is much faster than SS.

The CS (Checksum) command lets you monitor whether a range of memory has changed. The first time you execute the CS command, you specify a range and MacsBug computes a checksum. Subsequent CS commands compute the checksum and compare it with the previous value.

Make it easy on yourself

If you associate low-level debugging with excessive grinding of teeth, please remember that MacsBug provides several tools that can make your work easier. These include the following

- Templates, which allow you to display memory in intelligible names and values rather than bits and bytes. The section "Using Templates to Display Memory" in Chapter 4 describes the standard templates defined by the 'mxwt' resource to display data structures used by the system and explains how you can use ResEdit to create additional 'mxwt' resources to display data structures that are specific to your program.

- Macros, which allow you to use names instead of addresses or command sequences that you need to enter often. The section "Using Macros" in Chapter 8 explains how to create temporary and permanent macros.
- dcmds, which allow you to extend MacsBug's command set. The section "Using dcmds" in Chapter 8 describes the standard dcmds shipped with MacsBug and provides detailed instructions on how to write your own dcmds.

In addition, several desk accessories provide instant references to system calls and system errors. Find the ones you like and use them.

Chapter 8 Introduction to MacsBug Commands

This chapter and Chapter 9, "MacsBug Commands," provide a complete reference to MacsBug commands and the rules for their use. While Chapter 9 explains the syntax and use of each MacsBug command, this chapter describes methods that work with any of the commands you can use in MacsBug. It explains how to:

- Use the command line to enter commands.
- Use the command line to perform calculations.
- Specify command parameters.
- Use expressions to define conditions or addresses.
- Edit the command line and use the command line buffer to simplify your work.
- Get help while you're working with MacsBug.

This chapter also describes two other kinds of commands you can use in MacsBug: macros and dcmds.

Macros are names that you can substitute for addresses, expressions, or groups of commands that you are likely to use many times. The section "Using Macros" in this chapter explains how you define temporary and permanent macros and describes the standard macros that are shipped with MacsBug.

dcmds allow you to add commands to MacsBug. The section "Using dcmds" in this chapter describes the dcmds that are shipped with MacsBug and explains how you write 'dcmd' resources to define your own dcmds.

[Handwritten note: MACSBUG COMMANDS USUALLY TAKE UP ONLY ONE COMMAND LINE, ALTHOUGH MULTIPLE COMMANDS MAY BE MADE ON ONE LINE, THE NUMBER IS LIMITED BY THE LENGTH OF THE COMMAND LINE.]

[Handwritten note: MACROS ALLOW A SERIES OF COMMANDS LONGER THAN THE COMMAND LINE.]

[Handwritten note: SEE BOTTOM OF PG 207]

The MacsBug command line

When you invoke MacsBug, you can't use the mouse or the menus, the normal channels of communication provided by the human interface. You communicate with MacsBug using the MacsBug command line, the line at the bottom of the MacsBug display.

Figure 8-1 shows the position of the MacsBug command line relative to the PC region and the MacsBug output region. For additional information about the MacsBug display, see Chapter 2, "Getting Started." Although you can reconfigure other areas of the MacsBug display using the 'mxbi' resource and the SHOW command, you cannot change the size or capacity of the command line.

- **Figure 8-1** MacsBug command line

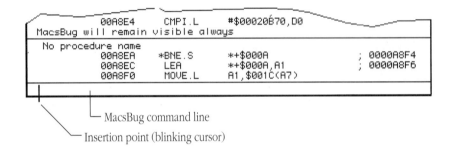

You can use the command line to communicate with MacsBug by entering commands, or you can use the command line as a calculator to perform base conversions or to evaluate arithmetic expressions.

As you can see from Figure 8-1, your input to MacsBug and MacsBug output use two physically separate areas of the display. Since this separation cannot be conveniently represented in the description of sample commands and their output, input to MacsBug is represented by bold Courier text, and MacsBug output is represented by normal Courier text. For example, in the following two lines, BRC is what you enter on the command line, and "All breakpoints cleared" is what MacsBug displays in the output region of the display.

BRC
  All breakpoints cleared

This convention is used throughout this manual.

Using the command line to enter commands

You can use the command line to enter one or more MacsBug commands. The blinking cursor shows you the current insertion point. To enter a command, type the command and its parameters on the command line. When you press the Return key, MacsBug executes the command or commands on the command line. If you press Return without entering a command, MacsBug executes the last command you entered.

Some MacsBug commands, such as HD (Heap Display), generate a lot of output. While such commands are executing, you can press the Return key or the Space bar to pause and resume execution. To cancel execution of a command, press any other key. For information about editing the command line, see the section "Command Line Editing Commands" later in this chapter.

The basic format of command line entries is

command [*parameters*] [; *command* [*parameters*]]...

command specifies the name of a MacsBug command, macro, or dcmd. The *parameters* of a command, macro, or dcmd are defined in the description of the command, macro, or dcmd. For additional information about command parameters, see "Specifying Command Parameters" later in this chapter.

Table 8-1 describes the conventions used to describe the syntax of MacsBug commands. Developers who write help messages for dcmds should use these conventions.

■ **Table 8-1** Command syntax conventions

Convention	Meaning
italics	Italics indicate a parameter that you must replace with specific information. Possible parameter types are described in the next section, "Specifying Command Parameters."
[optional]	Brackets indicate that the enclosed elements are optional. Omit the brackets when you enter the command.
...	Ellipses (...) indicate that you can repeat the preceding item as needed.
|	A vertical bar indicates a choice. For example, *n* | *expr* means that you can specify either a number *n* or an expression *expr* as a parameter.

Specifying command parameters

MacsBug assumes that any number you specify is hexadecimal. To indicate a decimal number, prefix the number with a pound (#) sign—for example, #256.

MacsBug commands use a limited set of parameters. The basic types are described in Table 8-2.

- **Table 8-2** Parameter types for MacsBug commands

Type	Description
addr	An expression that resolves to an address.
cmd	A MacsBug command or dcmd.
expr	A numeric, Boolean, or string expression.
n	A number. All numbers are assumed to be hexadecimal.
str	A string expression.
trap	A trap number in the range A000 to ABFF, or a trap name.

Specifying an address

Most MacsBug operations—setting breakpoints, displaying memory, disassembling code—need an actual address to work with. An address can be a hexadecimal or decimal number, a trap name or number, a register name, or the name of a procedure.

The following command uses a hexadecimal number to specify an address:

```
DM 002191C8
```

The following command uses a trap name to specify an address:

```
BR FindWindow
```

The following command uses a register to specify an address:

```
DM A7
```

Using procedure names

Whenever possible, MacsBug accepts and returns symbols in place of addresses. Procedure names are the most common example of this. Most compilers for the Macintosh have the option of embedding character names after the code generated for each procedure or function. (If you are writing a compiler, consult Appendix D, "Procedure Names," for details on procedure name definition.) If your compiler uses this option, you can specify a procedure name and offset to specify an address. Conversely, MacsBug returns addresses as offsets from procedures whenever it can. For instance, if the instruction shown in the PC region is part of a valid procedure, the name and offset of that instruction are displayed in the PC region. The following command uses an offset within a procedure to specify an address:

```
BR MouseDwn + 18
```

If you enter Command-:, MacsBug displays a menu that lists all the procedure names in the current application. Typing the first few letters in the name restricts the list to procedures that begin with the letters you type. You can use the arrow keys to move up and down the list. When the name of the procedure you want is highlighted, press Return to insert the selected name into the command line at the insertion point. If you've qualified the list and want to move back to the previous level of qualification, press the Delete key. To remove the menu without making a selection, press the Esc key.

If your keyboard does not allow you to type Command-:, type Command-D (an alias for Command-:) instead.

The dot address and the colon address

Because entering addresses is the most tedious and fault-prone part of entering MacsBug commands, MacsBug defines two additional variables that you can use to specify addresses: the dot address and the colon address.

- The **dot address** is a MacsBug variable that contains the last address used by certain commands. The period character (.) refers to this address; you can use it in any command that expects an address, for example:

```
DM .
```

The dot address is set by MacsBug commands in anticipation of your next move. For example, if you use the WH command to find a trap address, the WH command stores the address it returns in the dot address, since the next thing you might want to do is to disassemble around or starting from that address. The description of each MacsBug command in Chapter 9, "MacsBug Commands," indicates whether that command sets the dot address. To display the current value of the dot address, type a period and press Return.

- The **colon address** is a MacsBug variable that contains the starting address of the procedure shown in the PC. The colon character (:) refers to this address; you can use it in any command that expects an address. In the following example, the IP command disassembles a half page around the instruction beginning 18 bytes into the current procedure:

    `IP : + 18`

    To display the current value of the colon address, type a colon and press Return. If the current procedure does not have a name, the colon address does not contain a valid value.

You can also use an expression to specify an address.

Using expressions in MacsBug commands

The general form of an expression is

value1 [*operator value2*]

   value
   is a hexadecimal number, the name of a register, a trap name or number, or a procedure name. MMU 64-bit registers and floating-point registers are not allowed in expressions.

   operator
   is one of the following:

Arithmetic	+ – * / MOD
Boolean	AND or & OR or | NOT or ! XOR
Equality	= or == <> or != < > <= >=
Indirection	@ (prefix) or ^ (postfix)

You can use parentheses to control the order of evaluation. Otherwise, the expression is evaluated from left to right.

Expressions always evaluate to a 32-bit value unless you append one of the following prefixes to *value* to specify otherwise: .W specifies a 16-bit value; .B specifies an 8-bit value.

Expressions evaluate to either a numeric or a Boolean value depending on the operators used. The actions of some commands change based on this result. For instance,

`BR` *addr expr*

breaks at the specified address after *n* times if *expr* evaluates to a numeric value, or it breaks when *expr* is true if *expr* evaluates to a Boolean value.

You can use an expression to tell MacsBug to take some action when a certain value is stored on the stack. For example, the following command specifies that MacsBug should be invoked when the GetResource routine is about to get a 'DLOG' resource:

```
ATB GetResource (A7 + 2)^ = 'DLOG'
```

This command specifies that MacsBug should be invoked when the LNew routine is about to be executed; the LNew routine is implemented as a package, and the expression checks to see whether its index number (#68) is stored at the top of the stack:

```
ATB Pack0 SP^.W = #68
```

Resolving conflicting name references

There are two situations in which name references might be ambiguous: a trap that has the same name as a procedure or a numeric value that is identical to a register name.

If a trap name conflicts with a procedure name, attach the symbol † to the trap name to distinguish it from the name of the procedure—for example, †GetMouse. (To obtain the † symbol, press Option-T.)

If a numeric value conflicts with a reference to a register, you have three choices. Either use the $ prefix with the number—for example,

```
DM D0 + $D0
```

or use the RAD command to change the register-naming convention and specify

```
DM RD0 + D0
```

or use a 0 prefix in front of the number—for example,

```
DM D0 + 0D0
```

For additional information, see the description of the RAD command in Chapter 9, "MacsBug Commands."

Extending the command line

MacsBug provides no continuation character or any other way to extend the command line. If you find that a command or commands you want to enter exceeds the capacity of the command line, you can define one or more macros that will expand to the desired command or commands and fit within the existing boundaries.

The command line as calculator

By stripping you of menus, MacsBug makes it impossible for you to get to desk accessories. But MacsBug does provide some of the functions you need while you're in MacsBug: you can use the command line to convert numbers from one base to another and to perform arithmetic calculations.

Base conversion

To convert from hexadecimal to decimal values while you are running MacsBug, type the hexadecimal number and press Return. MacsBug displays the value you entered in hexadecimal, signed and unsigned decimal, and ASCII formats, as shown in Figure 8-2. It's up to you to determine which formats are relevant and which are not.

■ **Figure 8-2** Base conversion using the command line

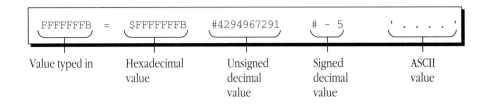

The dots in the ASCII section indicate there is no equivalent ASCII character for the value typed in.

To convert from decimal to hexadecimal values, type a "#" followed by the decimal number.

In the text of this manual, numbers preceded by a dollar sign (like this: $21E8) are in hexadecimal, and all other numbers are in decimal. In any MacsBug display, all numbers are in hexadecimal unless they are preceded by a pound sign (like this: #2148).

Command line arithmetic

You can do simple arithmetic on the command line in hexadecimal and decimal format. MacsBug recognizes the arithmetic operators shown in Table 8-3.

You can use @ (prefix) or ^ (postfix) to cause *indirection* (also called *dereferencing*), which gives you the value a pointer points to rather than the value of the pointer itself. Wherever you can enter a number in a calculation, you can also enter a register or an expression made up of numbers and registers.

■ **Table 8-3** Arithmetic operators

Operator	Operation
+	Addition
–	Subtraction
*	Multiplication
/	Division
MOD	Modulus

If you enter

`A0+20`

MacsBug adds $20 to register A0 and displays the result. If you enter

`A0+#20`

MacsBug adds 20 (decimal) to register A0 and displays the result. If you enter

`$A0+20`

MacsBug adds 20 to the number $A0 (not register A0) and displays the result.

Finally, if you enter

`20^ or @20`

MacsBug treats $20 as a pointer and displays the value it points to. This method of indicating indirection is valid even in more complex expressions; for example, the expression

`((D0*4)+(A2/#42))/@A4`

is valid.

Getting help

The Help command displays help about MacsBug commands, macros, dcmds, and other likely topics that you might need help with when you're working with MacsBug.

To display a list of topics that Help knows about, simply type Help and press Return. MacsBug displays the following information:

```
Editing
Selecting procedure names
Expressions
Values
Operators
Flow control
Breakpoints
A-Traps
Disassembly
Heaps
Symbols
Stack
Memory
Registers
Macros
Miscellaneous
dcmds
```

To display information about any of these topics, enter HELP followed by the topic name. To display information about an individual command, enter HELP and the command name; for example:

HELP BR
```
BR addr [n | expr] [';cmds']
    Break at addr after n times or when expr is true and optionally
    execute one or more commands. If no n or expr then break always.
    The addr can be in ROM but will be much slower.
```

For additional information, see the description of the Help command in Chapter 9, "MacsBug Commands."

Command line editing commands

Using MacsBug often involves having to type complicated expressions on the command line. MacsBug provides a set of editing commands that allow you move the cursor left and right across the command line. Figure 8-3 shows the command line editing commands.

- **Figure 8-3** Command line editing commands

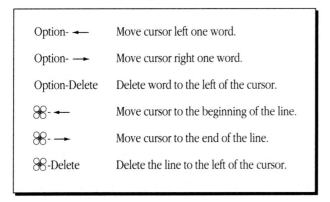

◆ *Note:* If you have worked with previous versions of MacsBug, please note that the command line editing commands have been redefined in version 6.2 to work as described above. This was done to make command line editing in MacsBug more like command line editing in MPW.

The command line buffer

In addition to providing commands that edit the current command line, MacsBug also provides commands that you can use to copy command lines that you have previously entered to the current command line; you can then edit these lines and press Return to execute them, or you can execute them as they are.

MacsBug places each command you execute in a circular buffer. Typing Command-V scrolls the buffer down, copying the previous command to the current command line. Typing Command-B scrolls the buffer up. Figure 8-4 shows the effects of Command-V and Command-B. (In this example, the greater the command line number, the more recent the command.)

■ **Figure 8-4** Effect of Command-B and Command-V

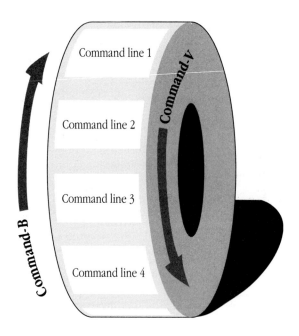

For example, suppose you have just entered the following commands:

```
vol
ip main
hd code
? sc
ip pc
```

After executing the last command, the command line is blank. If you now press Command-V, MacsBug copies the command `ip pc` from its internal buffer to the command line. If you press Command-V again, MacsBug copies the command `? sc` to the command line. If you press Command-B, MacsBug copies the command `ip pc` to the command line. You can scroll through the buffer using these two Command-key combinations. When you have copied the command you're interested in, you can press Return to execute the command, or you can edit the command and then execute it.

212   MacsBug Reference and Debugging Guide

Using macros

Using macros simplifies your work in MacsBug. A macro allows you to substitute one string for another. If you anticipate having to type in the same command, expression, or address over and over again, you can use the MC (Macro Create) command to assign the command a macro name, which you can then use instead of the more complicated entry.

For example, the command

`DM @windowlist windowrecord`

displays data about the frontmost window. But it takes a while to type and it's likely you'll have to type it repeatedly. A word like "Topwind" is easier to remember and type. To make "Topwind" a macro for the above command, use the MC command to specify first the macro name and then its expanded form, the form in which you would have to type it in for MacsBug to understand it:

`MC Topwind 'DM @windowlist windowrecord'`

From this point on (until you restart), whenever you type Topwind, MacsBug executes the command DM @windowlist windowrecord.

Macro commands

MacsBug contains three commands that help you work with macros:

- MC: The Macro Create command defines macros that you can use until you restart.
- MCD: The Macro Display command displays currently installed macros; this includes macros defined with the MC command as well as macros defined using the 'mxbm' resource. The MCD command displays the name of the macro in the first column and its expanded form in the second column; for example:

  `RTS                     PC = SP^;SP = SP + 4`

  This standard macro demonstrates how you can use a macro to emulate an instruction.
- MCC: The Macro Clear command clears all macros from memory. Macros defined in the Debugger Prefs file are always available. You load them into memory when MacsBug loads at startup time.

These commands are described in greater detail in Chapter 9, "MacsBug Commands."

▲ **Warning** Be careful not to use the name of an existing MacsBug command as a macro name. If you do, you will no longer be able to use the name to execute the command. If you want to make sure a name isn't already assigned, execute the Help command followed by the name. If MacsBug displays the message "Unable to find help for this topic," the name is available for use. Note that the macro names FirstTime and EveryTime are also reserved. ▲

Using 'mxbm' resources to define permanent macros

When you use the MC command to create a macro, you can use the macro until you shut down the Macintosh. When you restart, you have to recreate that macro if you want to use it again. To make a macro permanent, you must define it using a resource of type 'mxbm'.

This section explains how you use MacsBug macro resources to define and store macros permanently, and describes most of the predefined macros that ship with MacsBug.

Standard macros

MacsBug includes 'mxbm' resources that define standard macros that are generally helpful in debugging: some are used to define useful command lines or expressions and others to provide a means of translating low-memory global variable names (macro names) into the appropriate addresses (macro expansion), giving you the convenience of using names rather than addresses. These 'mxbm' resources are part of the Debugger Prefs file and are loaded when you start the system.

Table 8-4 describes the macros defined by the 'mxbm' resource.

■ **Table 8-4** Macros defined by the 'mxbm' resource

Macro	Expansion and purpose
GG	BRC;ATC;G The GG macro clears all breakpoints and A-trap breaks and resumes execution.
GS	SB 12D 1;G;T 2;SB 12D 0 The GS macro allows you to step over the LoadSeg trap. After you execute the GS macro, the PC will point to the first instruction of the routine in the code segment that was loaded. See the section "Intersegment Calls and the Jump Table" in Chapter 3 for additional information.
RTS	PC = SP^;SP = SP + 4 After executing a JSR or BSR, but before the LINK instruction is executed, the RTS macro allows you to abort the current procedure and return to the return address. In order for the RTS macro to do the right thing, the return address must be at the top of the stack. The RTS macro is an example of how you can use a macro to emulate an instruction.
GTO	GT :+ The GTO macro allows you to specify an address as an offset from the start of the current procedure. Thus GTO 12 means Go till the instruction stored at the twelfth byte from the start of the current procedure. For additional information, see the description of the GT command in Chapter 9.
BRO	BR :+ The BRO macro allows you to set a breakpoint and specify the breakpoint address as an offset within the current procedure. Thus BRO 12 means set a breakpoint at the instruction stored at the twelfth byte from the start of the current procedure. For additional information, see the description of the BR command in Chapter 9.
thePort	DM RA5^^ GrafPort The macro thePort displays the data defining the current GrafPort.
theWindow	DM RA5^^ WindowRecord The macro theWindow displays the data defining the frontmost window.
theCPort	DM RA5^^ CGrafPort The macro theCPort displays the data defining the current color GrafPort.

(continued)

■ **Table 8-4** Macros defined by the 'mxbm' resource (continued)

Macro	Expansion and purpose
IJ	IL (.+2)^
	If you're tracing into a jump table entry that contains a JMP to an absolute address instruction, the IJ macro allows you to disassemble as many lines as you like starting with the instruction that is being jumped to. Thus IJ 12 disassembles 12 lines.
DevList	DM @@DeviceList GDevice
	The DevList macro displays the GDevice record for each currently installed video device. If you press Return, MacsBug displays the record for the next device. MacsBug displays the message "End of linked list" when it has displayed information about the last device in the list.
VcbList	DM @(VCBQHdr+2) VCB
	The VcbList macro displays a volume control block record for each mounted volume. If you press Return, the volume control block record for the next volume is displayed. See Chapter 5, "The Macintosh Operating System," for additional information.
WindList	DM @WindowList WindowRecord
	The WindList macro displays the window record for the frontmost window of the current application. If you press Return, MacsBug displays the window record for the next window. MacsBug displays the message "End of linked list" when it has shown you information about all the windows that are open in the current application.
AP	DM CurApName pString
	The AP macro displays the name of the current application.
VBLTasks	DM @(VBLQueue+2) VBLTask
	The VBLTasks macro displays information about each VBL task that is currently installed. To display information about the next VBL task, press Return. MacsBug displays the message "End of linked list" when it has shown you information about all currently installed VBL tasks.
RamF – RamFP	You use these macros to define RAM as the range for the Find command. See the description of the Find command in Chapter 9 for additional information.
SysF – SysFP	You use these macros to define the system heap as the range for the Find command. See the description of the Find command in Chapter 9 for additional information.

(continued)

■ **Table 8-4** Macros defined by the 'mxbm' resource (continued)

Macro	Expansion and purpose
ApF – APFP	You use these macros to define the current application heap as the range for the Find command. See the description of the Find command in Chapter 9 for additional information.
ZF – ZFP	You use these macros to define the current TargetZone (heap zone set with the HX command) as the range of the Find command. See the description of the Find command in Chapter 9 for additional information.

Creating permanent macros

You can create your own 'mxbm' resources in two ways. First, you can use ResEdit; the Debugger Prefs file contains templates for creating and editing 'mxbm' resources. Or, you can use the file Macros.r (included on the MacsBug disk) as a model for building your own resource. Be sure to give your resource a unique ID, and then use the Rez tool to add it to the Debugger Prefs file.

This section includes step-by-step instructions that you can follow to create your own 'mxbm' resource using ResEdit version 2.0 or later.

Follow these steps to create a permanent macro called *Topwind* for the command

```
DM @WindowList WindowRecord
```

1. **Open the System Folder and double-click the Debugger Prefs file.**

    This launches ResEdit.

2. **From ResEdit, open the Debugger Prefs file in the System Folder of your startup volume.**

3. **Open the 'mxbm' file.**

4. **Choose Create New Resource from the Resource menu.**

    ResEdit opens a new 'mxbm' resource.

5. **Click the * * * * ***

6. **Choose Insert New Field(s) from the Resource menu.**

    ResEdit displays a template like the one shown in Figure 8-5.

■ **Figure 8-5** New 'mxbm' template

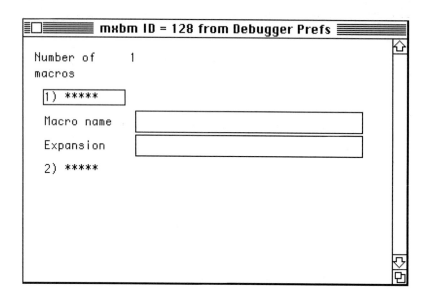

7. **Use the Tab key to position the insertion point in the Macro name field.**

   This field contains the name of the macro.

8. **Type** `Topwind`

9. **Use the Tab key to position the insertion point in the Expansion field.**

   This field contains the command or commands you want MacsBug to execute when you enter the macro name.

10. **Type** `DM @WindowList WindowRecord`

    At this point, if you wanted to use this resource to define more macros, you would click the bottom row of * * * * * and repeat steps 6 through 8.

11. **Choose Save and then Quit from the File menu. Restart your Macintosh to load the macro.**

12. **Invoke MacsBug and type** `Topwind`

    MacsBug should display the window record that describes the frontmost window.

The FirstTime and EveryTime macros

Two macro names have been predefined by MacsBug to allow you to customize your debugging environment:

- **FirstTime** is a special initialization macro that loads and executes automatically when MacsBug loads during system startup. You can use the FirstTime macro to set up certain options, specify default values, or execute certain commands every time you start or restart your Macintosh. For example, you can use the FirstTime macro to turn on A-trap recording.

  To have the startup process continue automatically, end the FirstTime macro with the G command. Be aware that on a Macintosh Plus, the G command is required. Because the keyboard is initialized after MacsBug, you won't be able to type G to continue.

  You need to use the 'mxbm' resource to define a FirstTime macro.

- **EveryTime** is a macro that is executed every time except the first time MacsBug is invoked. For example, you could define HC as an EveryTime macro. If you create an EveryTime macro, be aware that the last command executed by that macro is set as the default command; this command will be repeated if you press Return.

  Do not end an EveryTime macro with the G command or you will never be able to invoke MacsBug.

  You can use either an 'mxbm' resource or the MC command to define this macro.

Using dcmds

No matter how many features and commands are build into new versions of MacsBug, developers who use it keep thinking of refinements that would make their own work easier. If you need to extend or modify MacsBug's command set, you can use dcmds. A dcmd is a piece of code that you write and compile to provide the additional functions you need in your work.

dcmds are code resources of type 'dcmd'. MacsBug is shipped with standard dcmds that are loaded into the system heap when you install the Debugger Prefs file. You can use ResEdit to install the dcmds you write yourself in the Debugger Prefs file. MacsBug loads all the dcmds from this file during system startup, so, after adding a dcmd, you must restart your Macintosh in order to use it. Each dcmd is a separate resource; you can assign it any resource number that has not been used before for a 'dcmd' resource. MacsBug identifies dcmds by their resource names.

[Handwritten note: IF YOU CHANGE A dcmd RESOURCE NAME FOR CLARIFICATION WHILE IN ResEdit, MACSBUG MAY NOT RECOGNIZE THE RESOURCE.]

Because dcmds reside in a separate file, there's no complicated installation process to follow when MacsBug is updated. You just move the 'dcmd' resources from the old Debugger Prefs file to the new Debugger Prefs file, renumbering them if necessary. Because they are not tied to MacsBug, dcmds can potentially be shared with other debuggers.

The following section, "Standard dcmds," describes the standard dcmds that are included in the Debugger Prefs file.

"Creating Your Own dcmds" later in this chapter describes in detail how to write code defining a dcmd and how to link and build the dcmd.

Standard dcmds

Table 8-5 lists the dcmds included in the Debugger Prefs file 'dcmd' resource.

■ **Table 8-5** Standard dcmds

dcmd	Description
drvr [*refnum*	*num*]	Lists all the currently installed drivers or lists information for the specified driver. See Chapter 5 for an explanation of this display.
file [*fRefNum*	"*filename*"]	Lists all open files or information about the specified file. See Chapter 5 for an explanation of this display.
vol [*vRefNum*	*drvNum*	"*volumeName*"]	Lists all the volumes on line or displays volume information for the specified volume. See Chapter 5 for an explanation of this display.
vbl	Lists all the VBL tasks currently installed. See Chapter 5 for an explanation of this display.
printf "*format*" arg...	Displays the arguments according to the format. See the description of this command in the next section.

The printf dcmd

The printf dcmd is a formatted output command that behaves very much like the C programming language printf command. This section describes how you use the printf command if you are unfamiliar with C, and gives several examples of how you can use it in debugging. To avoid confusion, please interpret any reference to the printf command in this section as a reference to the MacsBug printf dcmd, *not* the C printf command.

The syntax of the printf command is

printf "*string*" *arg* [*arg*] ...

"*string*"
is a combination of literals and conversion specifications.

arg
is an expression that is evaluated and converted according to the conversion specification to which it corresponds.

A conversion specification consists of the percent symbol (%), which introduces the specification; an optional digit specifying the field width of the converted argument; and a conversion character specifying how the argument is to be represented.

Table 8-6 shows how MacsBug interprets the conversion characters you use in the printf dcmd.

■ **Table 8-6** Conversion characters for the printf dcmd

Conversion character	Meaning	Example
d	Decimal integer	93
o	Octal integer	77
x	Hexadecimal integer	2F
u	Unsigned decimal integer	99
c	Single character	q
s	String	application

In the sample printf command below, %d and %s are the conversion specifications, and 1990 and Wednesday are the arguments.

```
printf "Data for %d will be available on %s" 1990, Wednesday
```

The command produces the following output:

```
Data for 1990 will be available on Wednesday
```

If you're logging the output of a MacsBug session, you can use the printf dcmd to make MacsBug output more intelligible. The command

`printf "this application is %s" curapname`

produces this output:

`this application is Finder`

If you are using the DebugStr inline call to invoke MacsBug from within your source program, you can use the printf command to have MacsBug output key values during program execution.

This printf command:

`printf "Register A7 (%8x) points to word %x (= #%d)." RA7 RA7^.W RA7^.W`

produces this output:

`Register A7 (  4b7026) points to word 4080 (= #16512).`

Note the use of 8 in the first specification (%8x) to specify the field width of the converted argument.

Listing available dcmds

To find out what dcmds are installed, drop into MacsBug and enter

`HELP dcmd`

MacsBug will list all the dcmds that are available, along with a brief description of what each one does and its parameters, if any. To get help on a specific dcmd, type HELP and the name of a specific dcmd; for example:

`HELP vbl`

MacsBug displays the same help message in both circumstances; using the more specific help request just saves space in the output region of the MacsBug display.

Creating your own dcmds

The MacsBug distribution disk includes a dcmd folder that contains sample dcmds, written in both C and Pascal, interface files, and a glue file to be linked with the compiled dcmd when you build the dcmd. The dcmd folder also includes an application you can use to debug your dcmd, TestDcmd, and an MPW tool, BuildDcmd, that translates an application into a 'dcmd' resource and copies it into the Debugger Prefs file. This section explains how you use all these pieces to write your own dcmd.

Writing dcmds is very similar to writing HyperCard® 'XCMD' resources. A 'dcmd' resource begins with a 4-byte segment header, followed immediately by the program code. Since dcmds are limited to a single segment, the segment header is used to specify a dcmd version number and the amount of space MacsBug needs to allocate for the dcmd's global variables. The segment header is written by the BuildDcmd tool; you don't need to be concerned with it.

All calls to a dcmd are made through the entry point defined as the fifth byte of the resource. MacsBug calls a dcmd as a Pascal procedure taking a single parameter, a pointer to a parameter block. The procedure declaration is

```
PROCEDURE CommandEntry (paramPtr: dcmdBlockPtr);
```

This is a public declaration for the dcmdGlue file and must be included in every dcmd. You cannot change the procedure name. See Figure 8-6 for a skeleton dcmd.

Passing information to the dcmd

The parameter block passed to the CommandEntry procedure is a record that is used to store information the procedure needs. It is defined as follows:

```
TYPE dcmdBlockPtr = ^dcmdBlock
     dcmdBlock    = RECORD
            registerFile: RegFilePtr;
            request:      INTEGER;
            aborted:      BOOLEAN;
      END;
```

The registerFile field is a pointer to an array containing the contents of the registers. MacsBug copies the contents of the registers into this array when you execute the dcmd. This allows you to use constant names for identifying the registers in your dcmd; for example:

Data registers:	D0Register–D7Register
Address registers:	A0Register–A7Register
Program counter:	PCRegister
Status register:	SRRegister (value stored in high word)

The request field contains one of the following request numbers, which the debugger passes to the dcmd:

```
dcmdInit = 0;
dcmdDoIt = 1;
dcmdHelp = 2;
```

The first call MacsBug makes to a dcmd is an initialize request (dcmdInit). This happens when MacsBug is installed and requires no user action. In response to this request, the dcmd can do nothing, or it can initialize global variables or gather system information.

The two other calls MacsBug can make to a dcmd are the dcmdHelp call, if the user asks for help for a dcmd, and the dcmdDoIt call, if the user executes a dcmd.

The aborted field is used to inform the dcmd when the user has terminated the command; it's set to TRUE when the user presses a key (other than Return or the Space bar) while scrolling.

Figure 8-6 shows the format of the source code for a dcmd. A dcmd can contain more than one procedure; however, the main procedure must be called CommandEntry.

You can write source code for a dcmd using Pascal, C, or assembly language. You can also use callback routines to parse the MacsBug command line, display information, and so on. These routines are defined in the interface files. It is not a good idea to include system calls in your dcmd. For additional information, see the section "Restrictions on dcmds," later in this chapter.

If you are using assembly language to write the source code, please be aware that a dcmd uses Pascal calling conventions: the dcmd is responsible for popping the parameters off the stack. The dcmd must also preserve registers D3 through D7 and A2 through A6.

■ **Figure 8-6** Skeleton dcmd

```
UNIT dcmdname;
{$R-}
INTERFACE
        USES MemTypes, dcmd;
        PROCEDURE CommandEntry (paramPtr: dcmdBlockPtr);
VAR     {declare global variables if any}
IMPLEMENTATION
PROCEDURE CommandEntry (paramPtr: DCmdBlockPtr);
VAR     {declare local variables if any}

BEGIN
  IF paramPtr^.request = dcmdInit THEN
        BEGIN { The dcmd gets called once when loaded to init itself }
        END    {this can be an empty statement}
  ELSE
  IF paramPtr^.request = dcmdDoIt THEN
        BEGIN { Do the command's normal function }
        END
  ELSE
  IF paramPtr^.request = dcmdHelp THEN
          BEGIN { Display the command's help information }
                dcmdDrawLine ('dcmdname syntax');
                dcmdDrawLine ('    helpmessage');
                dcmdDrawLine ('    helpmessage--continued');
          END;
  END;
END
```

Table 8-7 provides a summary of the callback routines that you can use in writing dcmds. In addition to the routines listed in Table 8-7, MacsBug also includes a dcmdSwapWorlds routine and a dcmdForAllHeapBlocks routine. For information about these two routines and for more detailed information about the rest of the routines, please refer to the dcmd interface file.

■ **Table 8-7** dcmd callback routines

Name	Description
dcmdDrawLine(*mystr*)	Draws the text in *mystr* as one or more lines separated by CRs.
dcmdDrawString(*mystr*)	Draws the text in *mystr* as a continuation of current line.
dcmdDrawText(*strptr, n*)	Draws *n* characters starting from *strptr*, as a continuation of current line.
dcmdScroll	Scrolls the output region up one line; leaves a blank line at the bottom.
dcmdDrawPrompt(*mystr*)	Displays *mystr* in the command line area and waits for key to be pressed. Returns TRUE if user presses CR; returns FALSE for other keys.
dcmdGetPosition	Returns an integer for the current command line position.
dcmdSetPosition(*pos*)	Sets *pos*, which should be a value returned by dcmdGetPosition.
dcmdGetNextChar	Returns the next character or CR if entire line has been scanned.
dcmdPeekAtNextChar	Returns next character or CR if entire line has been scanned; does not change current command line position.
dcmdGetNextParameter(*mystr*)	Copies all characters from the command line to *mystr* until a delimiter or CR is reached. Strings with matching quotes are allowed.
dcmdGetNextExpression(*value, ok*)	Parses command line for next expression; evaluates expression and returns in *value*. *ok* is TRUE if line was parsed successfully. Returns delimiter.
dcmdGetBreakMessage(*mystr*)	Copies break message last displayed by MacsBug into *mystr*.
dcmdGetNameAndOffset(*addr, mystr*)	Returns offset within procedure for *addr*, in *mystr*.
dcmdGetTrapName(*number, name*)	Returns the trap name in *name* for the trap *number*.
dcmdGetMacroName(*value*)	Returns pointer to macro name for *value*.
dcmdSwapScreens	Toggles between user and debugger displays.

Responding to a dcmdHelp request

When the user enters help and the dcmd name, MacsBug will call the appropriate dcmd with a dcmdHelp request. In response, your dcmd code can use one of the callback routines that display text to display the help message for the dcmd. Figure 8-7 shows how the Where dcmd responds to the dcmdHelp request.

- **Figure 8-7** Responding to the dcmdHelp request

```
IF paramPtr^.request = dcmdHelp THEN
        BEGIN {Display the command's help information.}
                dcmdDrawLine ('WHERE [addr | trap]');
                dcmdDrawLine ('   Display information about address or trap');
                dcmdDrawLine ('   If no parameter then use PC as the address');
        END;
```

If possible, your dcmd help messages should use the same format as that used to provide help for MacsBug commands: the command syntax should be displayed first, followed by an explanatory message. The syntax conventions used to describe MacsBug commands are described near the beginning of this chapter.

Responding to a dcmdDoIt request

When the user executes a dcmd, MacsBug calls the dcmd with a dcmdDoIt request. Figure 8-8 shows how the Where dcmd responds to the dcmdDoIt request.

The code uses the dcmdPeekAtNextChar routine and the dcmdGetNextExpression routine to parse the command line. If the user presses Return following the dcmd name, the routine returns the value of the program counter. If the user specifies a trap address, the routine returns the name of the trap using the dcmdGetTrapName routine. If the user specifies an address that's an offset in a procedure, the routine uses the dcmdGetNameAndOffset routine to return the name of the procedure and the offset of the instruction within the procedure.

■ **Figure 8-8** Responding to the dcmdDoIt request

```
IF paramPtr^.request = dcmdDoIt THEN
      BEGIN {Do the command's normal function.}
            IF dcmdPeekAtNextChar = CHR(CR) THEN
              address := paramPtr^.registerFile^[PCRegister]
            ELSE
              BEGIN
              ch := dcmdGetNextExpression (address, ok);
                  IF NOT ok THEN
                    BEGIN
                    dcmdDrawLine ('Syntax error');
                    Exit (CommandEntry);
                    END;
              END;
            IF (address >= $0000A000) AND (address <= $0000ABFF) THEN
              BEGIN
              dcmdGetTrapName (address,name);
              dcmdDrawLine (name);
              END
            ELSE
              BEGIN
                  dcmdGetNameAndOffset (address,name);
                  IF Length (name) > 0
                    THEN dcmdDrawLine (name)
                    ELSE dcmdDrawLine ('No procedure name found');
              END;
      END
```

Restrictions on dcmds

The restrictions that you should observe in writing a dcmd are a result of the circumstances under which you are likely to use the command: debugging code following a system crash.

■ Because the system might be in an unstable state, making a system call is generally a bad idea.

■ Never allocate memory on a heap or make a system call that allocates memory; remember, you could have entered MacsBug at interrupt time.

- A dcmd has about a 1K stack available to it; if you need more memory than this, allocate it in global variables.
- Although you can write dcmds that override existing MacsBug commands, it is recommended that you do not override flow control commands like G, S, ATB, and so on.

Building a dcmd

To build a dcmd in MPW 3.1, enter the following commands. (You need to specify your own information for the italicized fields.)

```
Pascal dcmdname.p
Link dcmdGlue.a.o dcmdname.p.o {Libraries}Runtime.o -o dcmdname
BuildDcmd dcmdname resource_number
```

It is important that the dcmdGlue.a.o file be the first file you link with. The BuildDcmd builds a 'dcmd' resource with the name and number you specify.

The source code provided for dcmds requires MPW 3.1 to build the dcmds. It does not currently build with MPW 3.2. This does not affect the execution of the dcmds included in the file Debugger Prefs.

Debugging dcmds

Debugging dcmds can be difficult, since they function within MacsBug. A special application called TestDCMD, which ships with MacsBug, is designed to help you debug your own dcmds. TestDCMD is a shell that calls the dcmd and provides the normal support the dcmd expects from MacsBug. But since the dcmd is running within the TestDCMD application, you can debug it using MacsBug.

You do not have to load the dcmd by restarting your system to test it. The TestDCMD tool will execute the dcmd as if it had already been loaded and display information to let you know if it's not working.

Chapter 9 MacsBug Commands

This chapter describes most MacsBug commands except for dcmds and macros, which are described in Chapter 8, "Introduction to MacsBug Commands." The commands in this chapter are listed in alphabetical order. In addition to these commands, MacsBug provides two others that are not included in this chapter:

- The dot command displays the current value of the dot address.
- The procedure display command, Command-D or Command-:, displays a menu of procedure names for the current application.

    For additional information about these commands, please see "The Dot Address and the Colon Address" in Chapter 8.

Chapter 8 provides a complete introduction to the use of MacsBug commands. This chapter assumes that you are familiar with the material covered in Chapter 8.

ATB — A-trap Break

Description The A-trap Break command invokes MacsBug whenever the microprocessor encounters the specified A-trap.

Syntax ATB[A] [*trap* [*trap*]] [*n* | *expr*] [';*cmd* [;*cmd*]...']

A
specifies that MacsBug should only be invoked when the A-trap is called from the application heap.

trap
is a trap name or number specifying the trap. Specifying two traps indicates a range of traps. If you omit this parameter, MacsBug is invoked every time an A-trap is called.

n
is a hexadecimal number specifying that MacsBug should be invoked every *n*th time that the trap is encountered.

expr
specifies that MacsBug should be invoked when the trap is encountered and *expr* is TRUE.

cmd
specifies a command for MacsBug to execute after it is invoked.

See also ATC, ATD

Considerations

A-trap breaks are not associated with a specific instance of an A-trap call. Rather, MacsBug is invoked any time the specified A-trap is called and the other conditions you specify using the ATB command are met.

When you set one or more breakpoints using the ATB command, MacsBug records the number in a table. Whenever the microprocessor encounters an A-trap, MacsBug compares the A-trap with the entries in the table. If it finds a match (and if whatever other conditions you have specified using the ATB command are met), MacsBug displays the debugging screen and shows you the state of the microprocessor and memory just before the A-trap is executed. The program counter is set to the address of the instruction that invoked the A-trap.

Use the ATD command to display current trap actions; use the ATC command to clear A-trap breaks.

Breaking on related A-traps

Because A-traps belonging to the same manager are grouped together by number, specifying a range is another way of telling MacsBug to break on every A-trap belonging to a particular manager. If you want to exclude some A-traps belonging to a particular manager, you can use the ATC (A-trap Clear) command. For additional information, see the description of the ATC command.

Breaking on A-traps called from the application heap

The A option restricts MacsBug to breaking only when the specified A-trap is called from the application heap. MacsBug does this by checking that the value of the program counter lies within the application heap range. Note that if you set a breakpoint in one application and you do not clear it, the breakpoint remains valid so that if you quit the application and run another application, the same A-trap call will invoke MacsBug.

Breaking on A-traps in a package

If the A-trap that you want to break on is part of a package, you need to follow a slightly different procedure. All of the routines in a package are implemented by one A-trap number. Each routine within a package is identified by an index number. When a program calls a routine in the package, the routine's parameters are pushed onto the stack first, and then the routine's index number. This index number is called a routine selector. Sometimes the routine selector is placed in a register. To determine where the routine selector is placed, consult the description of the package to which it belongs in *Inside Macintosh*.

This means that in order to break on an individual routine in a package, you need to supply the package number as the routine name and then check the value on the stack to see if it matches the index value for the routine you're interested in. For example, to place a break on the routine LNew, a List Manager routine, you would use the ATB command

```
ATB Pack0 SP^.W = #68
```

That is, break whenever the A-trap Pack0 is called and the word stored on top of the stack equals 68. Note that your specification of the routine selector is just part of the normal ATB syntax; the specification is the *expr* that is an option for the command. This means that if you want to impose additional conditions, you would have to use AND to connect them with the condition that looks for the routine selector; for example:

```
ATB Pack0 SP^.W = #68 AND PC < ApplZone
```

MacsBug is shipped with several sets of macros that allow you to place A-trap breaks on individual routines inside a package. The macros actually place an A-trap break on the whole package, with a condition that checks the index selector to see if it's the routine you want—just as in the previous example. This saves you the work of looking up an individual routine and finding out what its index selector is and whether it is placed on top of the stack or in a register. For example, you can just enter

```
ATB LNew
```

and MacsBug expands the macro to

```
ATB Pack0 SP^W = #68
```

You need to remember, however, that the macro name includes an expression. This means that you can't use the *n* option and that, if you want to impose an additional condition, you have to put an AND in front of it; for example:

```
ATB LNew AND PC < ApplZone
```

Creating a custom A-trap trace

You can create a custom A-trap trace by executing the ATB command with an associated action. For example, if you enter

```
ATBA ';TD;G'
```

MacsBug displays all registers when the breakpoint is reached. The ATT command only shows information for selected registers. If you do this, you might want to log the output in case you exhaust the limits of MacsBug's output buffer.

For additional information about A-traps, see Chapter 5, "The Macintosh Operating System."

Examples

The following examples show some uses of the ATB command.

Break on every A-trap:

```
ATB
```
A-Trap Break at A000 (_Open) thru ABFF (_DebugStr) every time

Break on every call to MenuSelect:

```
ATB    MenuSelect
```
A-Trap Break at A93D (_MenuSelect) every time

Break on every call to MenuSelect made from within the application heap:

```
ATBA   MenuSelect
```
A-Trap Break at A93D (_MenuSelect) every time

Break on every A-trap between A010 and A020, inclusive:

```
ATB a010 a020
```
A-Trap Break at A010 (_Allocate) thru A020 (_SetPtrSize) every time

Break on MenuSelect calls when register D0 equals $6:

```
A-Trap Break at A93D (_MenuSelect) when d0 = 6
```

Break on every third MenuSelect call:

```
ATB    MenuSelect 3
```
A-Trap Break at A93D (_MenuSelect) every #3 times

Break on every MenuSelect call, and execute the commands HC and DM910:

```
ATB MenuSelect ';HC;DM 910'
```
A-Trap Break at A93D (_MenuSelect) every time and execute ;hc;dm 910

ATC — A-trap Clear

Description The A-trap Clear command clears actions set on all the specified A-traps with the ATB, ATT, ATHC, and ATSS commands.

Syntax ATC [*trap* [*trap*]]

trap
is a trap name or number specifying the trap. Specifying two traps indicates a range of traps. If you omit this parameter, MacsBug clears all A-trap actions.

See also ATB, ATD, ATHC, ATSS, ATT

Considerations

You can use the ATC command following an ATB, ATT, ATHC, or ATSS command to exclude A-traps from the range specified for these commands. For example, if you set the range for the ATHC command to be all A-traps,

`ATHC`

MacsBug displays the message

`A-Trap Check at A000 (_Open) thru ABFF (_DebugStr) every time`

If you then use the ATC command to exclude the StripAddress command

`ATC StripAddress`

MacsBug displays the message

`A-Trap Check at A000 (_Open) thru ABFF (_DebugStr) split into two ranges`

Since the ATC command does not execute conditionally, it is not possible to clear an A-trap belonging to a package. However, if you don't mind excluding all the A-traps in a package, you can clear the package as a whole.

When you use the ATC command to exclude an A-trap from the action you define for a range, what you are actually doing is setting two ranges. The ATC command saves you the trouble of setting two ranges by doing the work itself. This means that, even though you are ostensibly clearing a trap action, you are actually creating an additional entry in the A-trap table and could receive the error message "Entry will not fit in the table."

Examples

Clear all A-trap actions:

ATC

```
All A-Traps actions cleared
```

Clear actions on WaitNextEvent; leave actions on other A-traps unchanged:

ATC WaitNextEvent

```
A-trap Break at A860 (_WaitNextEvent) cleared
```

ATD — A-trap Display

Description   The A-trap Display command displays information about all actions currently set with the ATB, ATT, ATHC, and ATSS commands.

Syntax   ATD

See also   ATB, ATC, ATHC, ATSS, ATT, WH

Example

Assume you have entered the following commands:

```
ATHC MenuSelect  3
ATB  WaitNextEvent  ';hc'
ATB  GetPort  D0=6
ATB  LNew
```

If you then enter the ATD command, MacsBug displays the following information:

```
A-Trap actions from System or Application
   Trap Range       Action   Cur/Max or Expression    Commands
   _MenuSelect      Check    00000000 / 00000003
   _WaitNextEvent   Break    every time
   _WaitNextEvent   Break    every time              ;hc
   _GetPort         Break    D0 = 6
   _Pack0           Break    SP^.W=#68
```

MacsBug lists the name of the trap or the trap range in the first column. It lists the action set on the trap in the second column.

The value displayed in the third column depends on whether you use the *n* or *expr* option with the ATB command. If you specify that the trap action should occur every *n*th time the trap executes, MacsBug displays the current value (Cur) and the value you have specified (Max) at which the action should occur. If you specify that the trap action should occur when *expr* is true, MacsBug displays the expression it is evaluating in the third column.

If the A-trap belongs to a package and you use a macro to specify the individual trap, MacsBug expands the macro and displays the expression that tests for the routine's index value in the third column. See the description of the ATB command for additional information.

MacsBug uses the fourth column to display any commands that you specify should be executed when the action on the A-trap takes place.

ATHC — A-trap Heap Check

Description The A-trap Heap Check command checks the heap before executing the specified A-trap. If the heap is bad, MacsBug displays the debugging screen and an error message. See the description of the HC command later in this chapter for a list of possible errors.

Syntax ATHC[A] [*trap* [*trap*]] [*n* | *expr*]

A
specifies that MacsBug should only check the heap when the A-trap is called from the application heap.

trap
is a name or number specifying the trap. Specifying two traps indicates a range of traps. If you omit this parameter, MacsBug checks the heap every time an A-trap is called.

n
is a hexadecimal number specifying that MacsBug should check the heap every *n*th time that the trap is encountered.

expr
specifies that MacsBug should check the heap only when *trap* is encountered and *expr* is TRUE.

See also ATC, ATD, HC

Considerations

Because the ATHC command checks the heap before executing an A-trap, it is not the A-trap that the PC is currently pointing to that has corrupted the heap, but either the previous A-trap or an instruction belonging to your application. The ATHC command therefore allows you to narrow the range of statements that might be causing your problem.

The most common way to use the ATHC command is without parameters, thus checking the heap before every A-trap. If you use it in this way, you need to note that the Memory Manager makes trap calls while moving heap blocks around. In such cases, the ATHC command will return an error message because the heap is inconsistent, albeit temporarily. You can eliminate these error messages by using the ATHCA command to check the heap only when traps are called by your application.

You can specify an A-trap belonging to a package for the *trap* parameter to the ATHC command; see "Breaking on A-traps in a Package," under the description of the ATB command earlier in this chapter, for additional details.

For additional information about A-traps, see Chapter 5, "The Macintosh Operating System"; for additional information about heaps, see Chapter 4, "Macintosh Memory Organization."

Example

The following commands direct MacsBug to check the heap before executing every A-trap except for StripAddress:

ATHC
```
A-Trap Check at A000 (_Open) thru ABFF (_DebugStr) every time
```
ATC StripAddress
```
A-Trap Check at A000 (_Open) thru ABFF (_DebugStr) split into two ranges
```

The following ATHC command checks the heap before every LNew routine. The LNew routine is a List Manager (Pack0) routine. In this example LNew is a macro; LNew expands to Pack0 SP^.W = #68.

ATHC LNew
```
A-Trap Check at A9E7 (_Pack0) when SP^.W=#68
```

ATP — A-trap Playback

Description The A-trap Playback command displays the information saved while trap recording is on. If trap recording is turned off, the ATP command displays information from the most recent ATR command.

Syntax ATP

See also ATR

Considerations

The ATP command returns the following information about each trap call:

- The trap number and trap name.
- The address from which the call was made; this is the PC value. If your compiler embeds procedure names, MacsBug also shows you the address of the PC as an offset from the beginning of the procedure from which the A-trap is called.
- If the trap is an operating system trap, the values of registers A0 and D0 and the 8 bytes stored at the address in A0.

  Operating system traps pass their parameters and return the result in registers. Register A0 often holds the input parameter or the pointer to the parameter. The ATP command displays information about these registers to allow you to check parameter values on entry to the routine.

- If the trap is a toolbox trap, the value of register A7 and the 12 bytes stored beginning at that address.

  Toolbox traps normally pass their parameters and return the result on the stack. Parameters are always passed in Pascal format. The ATP command shows you information about the top of the stack so that you can check parameter values and return results.

If you suspect that the call is getting bad parameters, you can set a breakpoint at the address specified by the PC and watch it more closely the next time you run the program.

For additional information about trap recording, see the description of the ATR command later in this chapter.

Example

The following command displays information recorded after A-trap recording was turned on with the ATR command:

ATP
```
Trap calls in the order in which they occurred
  A031 _GetOSEvent
    PC = 4080F21A  _GetMouse+00EC
    A0 = 004B67C4  0000 0000 0000 0003 D0 = 0000FFFF
  A9A0 _GetResource
    PC = 4080F278  _GetMouse+014A
    A7 = 004B65BC  0007 464B 4559 4080 F224 DB6D
  A03C _CmpString
    PC = 0002F69E
    A0 = 00000911  4669 6E64 6572 2020 D0 = 00060006
  A025 _GetHandleSize
    PC = 0002E5C8
    A0 = 00036050  2000 3CA4 0003 6060 D0 = 00000000
  A029 _HLock
    PC = 4080F29C  _GetMouse+016E
    A0 = 00036050  2000 3CA4 0003 6060 D0 = 20003CA4
```

ATR — A-trap Record

Description The A-trap Record command turns trap recording on and off.

Syntax ATR[A] [ON | OFF]

A
specifies that MacsBug should only record A-traps that are called from the application heap. If you don't specify ON or OFF, the ATR command toggles between modes.

See also ATP, ATT

Considerations

You use the ATP command to display the information recorded by the ATR command.

The number of lines saved by the ATR command depends on whether the 'mxbi' resource is installed and whether it has been modified.

- If the 'mxbi' resource is not installed, the ATR command records the last 16 A-traps encountered by the microprocessor.
- If the 'mxbi' resource is installed, the ATR command records the last 24 A-traps encountered by the microprocessor by default. You can change this value by opening the 'mxbi' resource from ResEdit and entering a new number for "# of traps recorded."

The information saved by the ATR command includes the trap name and the contents of the program counter. For operating system traps, the ATR command saves the values of registers A0 and D0 as well as the 8 bytes pointed to by register A0. For toolbox traps, the ATR command saves the value of register A7 and the 12 bytes to which it points. See the description of the ATP command earlier in this chapter for additional information about how you use these values in debugging.

The ATT command outputs the same information as the ATR command. However, the ATT command causes your program to execute much more slowly because MacsBug needs to copy information about each A-trap, convert it to text, and write it to the screen. The ATR command simply copies information about each A-trap to an internal buffer; in this case, it's the ATP command that converts the information from the internal buffer to text displayed on the screen.

If ATR is off, the ATP command will play back information from the most recent ATR.

Example

The following command turns trap recording on for A-trap calls made from the application heap:

```
ATRA
```

ATSS — A-trap Step Spy

Description The A-trap Step Spy command calculates a checksum for a specified memory range or for a word at a specified address before executing the specified traps. If the checksum value changes, the ATSS command invokes MacsBug and does not execute the A-traps.

Syntax ATSS[A] [trap [trap]] [n | expr], addr1 [addr2]

A
Specifies that MacsBug should calculate a checksum only before executing A-traps that are called from the application heap.

trap
is a trap name or number that specifies the trap to be executed. Specifying two traps indicates a range. If you omit this parameter, MacsBug calculates a checksum before executing every A-trap.

n
is a hexadecimal integer specifying that MacsBug should calculate a checksum after every *n*th time the specified A-trap(s) executes.

expr
specifies that MacsBug should calculate a checksum before the specified A-trap executes if *expr* is TRUE.

addr1
specifies that MacsBug should calculate a checksum for the long word at *addr1*. If you specify *addr2*, MacsBug calculates a checksum for the range of memory defined by *addr1* and *addr2*.

See also ATC, ATD, SS

Considerations

Checksumming is a technique used by the debugger to determine whether the contents of memory have changed. The debugger adds all the values in the specified memory range and saves the result. After one or more instructions are executed (depending on whether checksumming is implemented by the ATSS, CS, or SS command), the debugger recalculates a sum for the same memory range and compares the new result to the saved result. If the values differ, MacsBug is invoked.

The ATSS command works fastest when you are calculating a checksum for *addr1*.

The ATSS command is much faster than the SS (Step Spy) command because the ATSS command only checks memory before executing A-traps, whereas the SS command checks after each 68000 instruction. You can use the ATSS command to zero in on a range of instructions containing the instruction that is affecting the value that concerns you. When the ATSS command invokes MacsBug, you know that the A-trap that is about to execute is not responsible for the change in value. You also know that the instruction that you are looking for is either the previous A-trap or any instruction executed between the previous A-trap and the instruction pointed to by the PC. You can now use the SS command within the suspect range to find that instruction.

Having trap recording turned on while using the ATSS command allows you to determine the previous A-trap call. You can also disassemble backward from the current PC until you find the previous A-trap.

Use the ATC command to clear actions set with the ATSS command. Use the ATD command to display actions set with the ATSS command.

Example

The following command checksums the long word at $100 on every A-trap call:

```
ATSS 100
Checksumming from 00000100 to 00000103
  A-Trap Spy at A000 (_Open) thru ABFF (_DebugStr) every time
```

ATT — A-trap Trace

Description The A-trap Trace command writes information to the MacsBug output buffer whenever the microprocessor encounters the specified A-trap, without stopping the current program.

Syntax ATT[A] [*trap* [*trap*]] [*n* | *expr*]

A
specifies that only information about A-traps called from the application heap should be written to the output buffer.

trap
is a name or number specifying the trap. Specifying two traps indicates a range of traps. If you omit this parameter, MacsBug writes information about every A-trap called.

n
is a hexadecimal number specifying that MacsBug should write information every *n*th time the trap is encountered.

expr
specifies that MacsBug should write information when the trap is encountered and *expr* is TRUE.

See also ATC, ATD, ATR, SWAP

Considerations

The ATT command outputs the same information as the ATR command, only in more compact form.

The information saved by the ATT command includes the trap name and the contents of the program counter.

- For operating system traps, the ATT command saves the values of registers A0 and D0 as well as the 8 bytes pointed to by register A0.

  Operating system traps pass their parameters and return the result in registers. Register A0 often holds the input parameter or the pointer to the parameter. The ATP command displays information about register A0 to allow you to check parameter values on entry to the routine.

- For toolbox traps, the ATT command saves the value of register A7 and the 12 bytes to which it points.

    Toolbox traps normally pass their parameters and return the result on the stack. Parameters are always passed in Pascal format. The ATP command shows you information about the top of the stack so that you can check parameter values and return results.

If you suspect that the call is getting bad parameters, you can set a breakpoint at the address specified by the PC and watch it more closely the next time you run the program.

The ATT command allows you to record information about the state of the microprocessor right before an A-trap executes. Unlike the ATR command, it allows you to record information only when the conditions you have specified for the command are met.

The ATT command outputs the same information as the ATR command. However, the ATT command causes your program to execute much more slowly because MacsBug needs to copy information about each A-trap, convert it to text, and write it to the screen. The ATR command simply copies information about each A-trap to an internal buffer; in this case, it's the ATP command that converts the information from the internal buffer to text displayed on the screen.

Use the ATC command to clear the ATT command; use the ATD command to display actions set with the ATT command.

▲ **Warning**   Using the ATT command when you're working with a single monitor and you have swapping turned on can create problems. See the description of the SWAP command later in this chapter for additional information. ▲

Creating a custom A-trap trace

You can create a custom A-trap trace by executing the ATB command with an associated action. For example, if you enter

```
ATBA ';TD;G'
```

MacsBug displays all registers when the breakpoint is reached. The ATT command only shows information for selected registers. If you use a custom A-trap trace, you might want to log the output in case you exhaust the limits of MacsBug's output buffer.

Example

The following command records information about all A-traps:

```
ATT
A-Trap Trace at A000 (_Open) thru ABFF (_DebugStr) every time
  A02A _HUnlock         PC=4080F2A6 D0=00000000 A0=00020960 A1=0027DE84
  A972 _GetMouse        PC=4080F2E4 A7=0037FEA0 A7^=0000 09FA 0000 0001
  A871 _GlobalToLocal   PC=4080F13E A7=0037FE98 A7^=0000 09FA 4080 F2E6
  A8E2 _EmptyRgn        PC=003AF0EE A7=0037FE80 A7^=0038 5D00 EDA6 0000
  A8E2 _EmptyRgn        PC=003AF0EE A7=0037FE80 A7^=0038 5BA0 01A6 0000
  A8E2 _EmptyRgn        PC=003AF0EE A7=0037FE80 A7^=0038 5C54 01A6 0000
  A8E2 _EmptyRgn        PC=003AF672 A7=0037FEA0 A7^=003B 8B34 EDA6 0000
  A924 _FrontWindow     PC=003AF33E A7=0037FE6A A7^=4080 60AC 0000 0000
```

BR — Breakpoint

Description The Breakpoint command sets a breakpoint at the specified address. When the program counter is equal to the specified address, MacsBug displays the debugging screen and you can examine the state of the microprocessor right before the instruction executes.

Syntax BR *addr* [*n* | *expr*] [' ;*cmd* [;*cmd*] ...']

addr
specifies the address of the instruction where you want to set the breakpoint.

n
specifies that MacsBug break after reaching the instruction *n* times.

expr
specifies that MacsBug break when *addr* is reached and *expr* is TRUE.

cmd
specifies a command that you want MacsBug to execute after displaying the debugging screen.

See also BRC, BRD, BRM

Considerations

Entering BR without any parameters is the same as using the BRD (Breakpoint Display) command; MacsBug displays the breakpoint table.

After you set a breakpoint, type G. The microprocessor executes until it reaches the specified breakpoint.

Breakpoints remain in effect until you restart. When you no longer need the breakpoints, remove them with the BRC (Breakpoint Clear) command.

MacsBug stores information for breakpoints, step commands, and A-trap command actions in a single table. It adds new entries at the end of the table. If MacsBug displays the message "Entry will not fit in the table," you need to clear some of the other actions before you can add the breakpoints.

If you set a breakpoint in a relocatable block, MacsBug stores the breakpoint as a handle to the breakpoint address. This means that if the block moves, the Memory Manager automatically updates the breakpoint address.

Breakpoints are shown in disassembly displays by means of dots placed to the left of the instruction mnemonic. The disassembled code shown below shows two breakpoints: one set at the LINK instruction and one at the FindWindow routine.

```
MouseDwn
    +0000   373818    •*LINK       A6,#$FFF0                    | 4E56 FFF0
    +0004   37381C     MOVEA.L     $0008(A6),A0                 | 206E 0008
    +0008   373820     MOVE.L      $000A(A0),-$0008(A6)         | 2D68 000A FFF8
    +000E   373826     CLR.W       -(A7)                        | 4267
    +0010   373828     MOVE.L      -$0008(A6),-(A7)             | 2F2E FFF8
    +0014   37382C     PEA         -$0004(A6)                   | 486E FFFC
    +0018   373830    • _FindWindow                    ; A92C   | A92C
    +001A   373832     MOVE.W      (A7)+,D0                     | 301F
    +001C   373834     CMPI.W      #$0001,D0                    | 0C40 0001
```

How MacsBug implements breakpoints

When you use the BR command to break on an instruction, MacsBug replaces the instruction with a TRAP instruction and stores the instruction. When the microprocessor encounters the TRAP instruction, it generates a trap exception, which invokes MacsBug. MacsBug puts the original instruction back in its place and displays the debugging screen. You can use the S (Step) command to execute the instruction.

The only way you can go wrong in using the BR command is if you specify an address that points to the middle of an instruction. In this case, MacsBug follows its usual procedure of replacing the instruction with a TRAP instruction. However, because the TRAP instruction now begins in the middle of an instruction, the microprocessor might regard it as part of the instruction, which will probably cause an error.

Setting breakpoints in ROM

When you set a breakpoint at a ROM address, the debugger cannot substitute a TRAP instruction for your instruction because that would require that it write to ROM, which is impossible. Instead MacsBug zeroes in on the instruction by executing a loop in trace mode: it executes one instruction and checks the value of the PC. If the PC is equal to the specified address, it displays the debugger screen and shows the state of the microprocessor just before the instruction executes. If the PC is not equal to the specified address, MacsBug allows the instruction to execute and checks the next PC value.

This tracing process is excruciatingly slow, so you might want to use GT (Go Till) to get to the address of the instruction calling the A-trap, then set the breakpoint, and then use G (Go) until the microprocessor reaches the breakpoint. The output from the BRD (Breakpoint Display) command indicates whether the breakpoint implemented in trace (T) or step (S) mode.

Setting breakpoints within a procedure

If you are working within a procedure, the BRO standard macro allows you to specify the address of an instruction in that procedure as an offset from the beginning of the procedure. Thus the command

```
BRO 18
```

would set a breakpoint 18 bytes from the beginning of the current procedure and save you the trouble of entering an address. The BRO macro expands to BR :+.

Using the BR command to display function results

You can display the result of a function every time it's called by entering the command

BR *functionname* ' ; MR ; DW SP '

Whenever the breakpoint is reached, MacsBug executes the MR (Magic Return) command and displays the top word on the stack (the function result). Functions that return long words should use the command

BR *functionname* ' ; MR ; DL SP '

Functions that return pointers could dereference the pointer and display the structure using a template; for example:

BR *functionname* ' ; MR ; DM SP^ *templatename* '

Examples

The following command sets a breakpoint at the address where the first instruction of the MouseDwn procedure is stored:

```
BR MouseDwn
Break at (00373818 MouseDwn) every time
```

The next command macro, which expands to BR :+, sets a breakpoint 18 bytes into the current procedure. In this case the current procedure is MouseDwn.

BRO 18

```
Break at (00373830 MouseDwn+0018) every time
```

After you reach the first breakpoint, disassembling from the PC shows the following:

```
Disassembling from pc
MouseDwn
    +0000   373818    •*LINK      A6,#$FFF0                  | 4E56 FFF0
    +0004   37381C     MOVEA.L    $0008(A6),A0               | 206E 0008
    +0008   373820     MOVE.L     $000A(A0),-$0008(A6)       | 2D68 000A FFF8
    +000E   373826     CLR.W      -(A7)                      | 4267
    +0010   373828     MOVE.L     -$0008(A6),-(A7)           | 2F2E FFF8
    +0014   37382C     PEA        -$0004(A6)                 | 486E FFFC
    +0018   373830    • _FindWindow              ; A92C      | A92C
    +001A   373832     MOVE.W     (A7)+,D0                   | 301F
    +001C   373834     CMPI.W     #$0001,D0                  | 0C40 0001
```

BRC — Breakpoint Clear

Description   The Breakpoint Clear command clears the breakpoint at the specified address. If you do not specify an address, the command clears all breakpoints.

Syntax   BRC [*addr*]

addr
specifies the address where you want to clear the breakpoint. If you omit this parameter, MacsBug clears all breakpoints.

See also   BR, BRD, BRM

Considerations

Use the BR command to set breakpoints. Use the BRD (Breakpoint Display) command to display current breakpoint settings.

If you don't use the BRC command to clear breakpoints, they remain in effect until you restart.

Example

The following command clears all breakpoints:

```
BRC
All breakpoints cleared
```

BRD — Breakpoint Display

Description The Breakpoint Display command displays addresses where breakpoints are currently set.

Syntax BRD

See also BR, BRC, BRM

Considerations

MacsBug implements the GT (Go Till) command by setting a temporary breakpoint. If you enter MacsBug by some other means and execute the BRD command, this breakpoint remains set and you'll see an entry for it in the breakpoint table.

Use the BR command to set breakpoints; use the BRC command to clear breakpoints.

See the following example for an explanation of BRD output.

Example

MacsBug displays information like the following in response to the BRD command:

```
BRD
 Breakpoint table
    Address    Module name        Cur/Max or Expression   Commands
  t 0040E794 R AbleMenu           every time
  t 0040E778 R UseAppRes          every time
  t 0040E7D4 R ABSPoint           every time
  t 0040E800 R BubbleUp           every time
```

- The first column contains a marker that indicates whether the breakpoint is reached in Trace (T) or Step (S) mode.
- The Address column shows the address of the instruction where the breakpoint has been set. The column preceding the Module name column contains the letter R if the instruction is in a relocatable block.

- If you leave MacsBug, run your program, and then go back to examine the breakpoint table, do not be surprised if the addresses of instructions belonging to relocatable blocks have changed.
- The Module name column displays the name of the procedure in which the instruction belongs. (MacsBug cannot supply the name of the procedure if your compiler does not embed procedure names.)
- If you specified that MacsBug should be invoked every nth time the instruction executes, the Cur/Max or Expression column shows you the current value of the counter (Cur) and the value you specified for n (Max). If you specified that MacsBug implement the breakpoint when some condition is met, this column shows what that condition is.
- The Commands column lists the commands you specified should be executed following the breakpoint.

BRM — Multiple Breakpoints

Description The Multiple Breakpoints command allows you to set breakpoints using partial name matching.

Syntax BRM *name*

name
is a string. MacsBug sets a breakpoint at the beginning of all routines whose names contain *name*.

See also BR, BRC, BRD

Considerations

You can use this command for setting breakpoints on groups of related routines. This is useful for programs written in object-oriented languages, because you can use the name of an object to set breakpoints on all the object's methods.

Use the BRC command to clear breakpoints set with the BRM command; use the BRD command to display information about breakpoints set with the BRM command.

If you are debugging a C++ program and need to break on a name that is qualified using double colons, you must enclose the string in quotation marks, since the colon has another meaning in MacsBug. The following command breaks on all classes that contain a Draw method:

```
BRM '::Draw'
```

This command breaks on all methods in the class TParseNode:

```
BRM 'TParseNode::'
```

Example

The following listing shows the output to the BRM command:

```
BRM
  Break at 00411A14 (strcpy) every time
  Break at 00411A48 (strncpy) every time
  Break at 00411A86 (_SA_DeletePtr) every time
  Break at 00411AAE (operator new(unsigned int)) every time
  Break at 00411AF8 (operator delete(void *)) every time
  Break at 00411D04 (ostream::operator <<(const char *)) every time
  Break at 00412314 (ostream::operator <<(long)) every time
```

CS — Checksum

Description The Checksum command allows you to determine whether the contents at the specified address or within the specified memory range have changed.

Syntax CS [*addr* [*addr*]]

addr
If you specify a single address, MacsBug checksums the long word at that address; if you specify two addresses, MacsBug checksums the range of memory defined by the addresses.

See also SS, ATSS

Considerations

Checksumming is a technique used by the debugger to determine whether the contents of memory have changed. The debugger adds all the values in the specified memory range and saves the result. After one or more instructions are executed (depending on whether checksumming is implemented by the ATSS, CS, or SS commands), the debugger recalculates a sum for the same memory range and compares the new result to the saved result. If the values differ, MacsBug is invoked.

The Checksum command checksums a range of memory and stores the value. If you enter CS again without an address parameter, it checksums the same range of memory and compares the new value to the stored value. It then displays a message letting you know whether the value has changed.

Examples

The following examples checksum the long word at address 9D:

```
cs 9d6
```
Checksumming from 000009D6 to 000009D9

```
cs
```
Checksum is the same

DB — Display Byte

Description The Display Byte command displays the byte at the specified address.

Syntax DB [*addr*]

addr
specifies the address containing the byte to be displayed. If you omit this parameter, the DB command displays the byte at the dot address.

See also DL, DM, DP, DW

Considerations

If you press Return following a DB command, MacsBug displays the next byte. MacsBug then sets the dot address to the address of the byte displayed.

The DB command displays four values for the specified memory location. The first column shows the hexadecimal value, the second column shows the unsigned decimal value, the third column shows the signed decimal value, and the fourth column shows the ASCII value, as shown in the example that follows.

Example

The following example shows the output from the command DB 910, followed by the output from pressing Return seven times:

```
DB 910
  Byte at 00000910 = $07    #7      #7      '•'
  Byte at 00000911 = $63    #99     #99     'c'
  Byte at 00000912 = $69    #105    #105    'i'
  Byte at 00000913 = $72    #114    #114    'r'
  Byte at 00000914 = $63    #99     #99     'c'
  Byte at 00000915 = $6C    #108    #108    'l'
  Byte at 00000916 = $65    #101    #101    'e'
  Byte at 00000917 = $73    #115    #115    's'
```

DH — Disassemble Hexadecimal

Description The Disassemble Hexadecimal command converts one or more hexadecimal values to assembler mnemonics.

Syntax DH *expr* ...

expr
is an expression that evaluates to a hexadecimal value.

Considerations

For information about assembled and disassembled code, please see Chapter 3, "An Assembly-Language Primer."

Examples

The DH command displays the address of the internal buffer it uses to disassemble code in the first column—you need not be concerned about this value—then displays the disassembled opcode:

```
DH 0B30 0000
Disassembling hex value
     3DD494    BTST      D5,$00(A0,D0.W)               | 0B30 0000
DH 7E1E
Disassembling hex value
     3DD494    MOVEQ     #$1E,D7                       | 7E1E
```

DL — Display Long

Description The Display Long command displays the long word at the specified address.

Syntax DL [*addr*]

addr
specifies the address containing the long word to be displayed. If you omit this parameter, the DL command displays the long word at the dot address.

See also DB, DM, DP, DW

Considerations

If you press Return following a DL command, MacsBug displays the next long word. MacsBug then sets the dot address to the address of the (last) long word displayed.

The first column of the display shows the hexadecimal value of the long word; the second column shows the unsigned decimal value; the third column shows the signed decimal value; and the fourth column shows the ASCII value, as shown in the example that follows.

Examples

The following example shows the output from the command DL 970, followed by the output from pressing Return three times. After the last Return, the dot address is set at 97C.

```
DL 970
{Return}
{Return}
{Return}
Long at 00000970 = $0E436C69    #239299689    #239299689    '•Cli'
Long at 00000974 = $70626F61    #1885499233   #1885499233   'pboa'
Long at 00000978 = $72642046    #1919164486   #1919164486   'rd F'
Long at 0000097C = $696C6520    #1768711456   #1768711456   'ile '
```

DM — Display Memory

Description The Display Memory command displays memory starting from the specified address.

Syntax DM [*addr* [*nbytes* | *template* | *basic type*]]

addr
specifies the address from which to start displaying memory. If you omit this parameter, the DM command starts the display at the dot address.

nbytes
is a hexadecimal integer specifying the number of bytes to display. If you omit this parameter, the DM command displays 16 bytes.

template
specifies the name of a template to use in formatting the display.

basic type
specifies the name of a basic type to use in formatting the display.

See also DB, DL, DP, DW

Considerations

If you are displaying a low-memory global variable, you can type its name and MacsBug will expand the macro to the address. For example:

```
DM SysResName
Displaying memory from 0AD8
 00000AD8  0653 7973 7465 6D20  2020 2020 2020 2020   •System
```

The DM command displays the address at the left, followed by 16 bytes starting at that address. It displays the same 16 bytes in ASCII at the extreme right of the display.

Most people find it difficult to make heads or tails of straight hexadecimal code. Although ASCII helps, a lot of data isn't in ASCII code. To help you through the hexadecimal maze, MacsBug lets you display memory using predefined templates or basic types. Which you use depends on what you are displaying. The basic types are defined in Table 9-1.

■ **Table 9-1** Basic memory display types

Type	Display
Byte	Display in hexadecimal.
Word	Display in hexadecimal.
Long	Display in hexadecimal.
SignedByte	Display in decimal.
SignedWord	Display in decimal.
SignedLong	Display in decimal.
UnsignedByte	Display in decimal.
UnsignedWord	Display in decimal.
UnsignedLong	Display in decimal.
Boolean	Display byte as TRUE (nonzero) or FALSE (zero).
pString	Display a Pascal string.
cString	Display a C string (0-terminated).

Templates are composed of fields defined using the types shown above and other types that cannot be used with the DM command but are useful for building templates. You can use the basic types to display small chunks of memory, or you can use predefined templates to display larger structures.

The TMP command, described later in this chapter, lists the names of all the templates that are currently defined. For information about creating your own templates, see "Using Templates to Display Memory" in Chapter 4.

Example

The following example uses the DM command to display information about a window record whose address is stored in the WindowList global variable. WindowRecord is the name of the template that formats the display of memory starting at @WindowList.

```
DM  @WindowList  WindowRecord
Displaying WindowRecord at 002191C8
  002191D8  portRect        #0 #0 #300 #350
  002191E0  visRgn          002190EC -> 00222A20
  002191E4  clipRgn         002190B4 -> 00222A34
  00219234  windowKind      0008
  00219236  visible         TRUE
  00219237  hilited         TRUE
  00219238  goAwayFlag      TRUE
  00219239  spareFlag       TRUE
  0021923A  strucRgn        002190B0 -> 00222A48
  0021923E  contRgn         002190AC -> 002192A8
  00219242  updateRgn       002190A8 -> 002192BC
  00219246  windowDefProc   080020D4 -> 20832A5C
  0021924A  dataHandle      0021909C -> 002192F4
  0021924E  titleHandle     002190A4 -> 002192D0 -> circles
  00219252  titleWidth      002B
  00219254  controlList     00219090 -> 00220B28
  00219258  nextWindow      00219124 ->
  0021925C  windowPic       NIL
  00219260  refCon          00219088
```

DP — Display Page

Description The Display Page command displays a page (128 bytes) of memory starting from the specified address.

Syntax DP [*addr*]

addr
specifies the address containing the lowest 4 bytes of memory displayed. If you omit this parameter, the DP command displays memory starting at the dot address.

See also DB, DL, DM, DW

Considerations

After you execute the DP command, MacsBug sets the dot address to the address of the first byte displayed. If you press Return, the DP command displays the next 128 bytes and sets the dot address to the address of the first byte of the new range.

Example

The following example displays memory from address 100:

```
DP 100
 Displaying memory from 100
  00000100   FFFF 0048 0048 0080   0013 A878 003C 06F0   •••H•H•••••x•<••
  00000110   0037 9B10 0037 9758   0027 C144 0000 2CDC   •7•••7•X•'•D••,•
  00000120   F03E C45A FFFF FFFF   FFFF FFFF 0000 0003   •>•Z••••••••••••
  00000130   0037 975A 0000 2F20   FFFF FFFF FFFF 0000   •7•Z••/ ••••••••
  00000140   0000 0000 FFEF 0000   3964 0000 0000 0000   ••••••••9d••••••
  00000150   0000 0000 0013 0003   0BAC 0604 FFFF FFFF   ••••••••••••••••
  00000160   0000 0000 2F24 003A   AF46 0003 3C0A 0003   ••••/$•:•F••<•••
  00000170   0BAD 80FF 0000 0000   0000 0000 0000 0000   ••••••••••••••••
```

DSC — Discipline

Description The Discipline command turns the Discipline utility on and off. You use Discipline to check the validity of the parameters you pass to A-traps and the values returned to your applications by the A-traps.

Syntax DSC[A][X] [ON | OFF]

> A
> specifies that Discipline only checks A-trap calls made from your application.
>
> X
> directs MacsBug to keep the Discipline error report internally and continue execution rather than stopping before and after every trap call to display Discipline messages.
>
> ON
> turns Discipline on.
>
> OFF
> turns Discipline off.

Considerations

You must install Discipline before you can use the DSC command.

Discipline is an invaluable aid to debugging. The fact that it can report errors before they can affect other parts of your program and become difficult to find can save you time and energy. For information about how to install and use Discipline during program development, please see Chapter 6, "Discipline."

Example

The following command turns Discipline on and specifies that Discipline only check A-trap calls made from your application:

```
DSCA ON
```

DV — Display Version

Description   The Display Version command displays the version of MacsBug currently in use.

Syntax   DV

Example

```
DV
 MacsBug version 6.2
 Copyright Apple Computer, Inc. 1981-1991
   CODE  Leo Baschy, Michael Tibbott, scott douglass
   TEST  Leo Baschy, Keith Nemitz
   BOOK  Joanna Bujes, Bob Anders
   PMGR  Tom Chavez
```

DW — Display Word

Description The Display Word command displays the word at the specified address.

Syntax DW [*addr*]

addr
specifies the address of the word you want to display. If you omit this parameter, the DW command displays the word at the dot address.

See also DB, DL, DM, DP

Considerations

If you press Return, the DW command displays the next word.

The DW command displays the hexadecimal value at the specified address in the first column; it displays the unsigned decimal value in the second column, the signed decimal value in the third column, and the ASCII value in the fourth column.

The DW command sets the dot address to the address of the last word shown.

Example

The following example shows the output from the DW command, followed by the output from pressing Return twice. After the last Return, the dot address is set to 104.

```
DW
{Return}
{Return}
Word at 00000100 = $FFFF    #65535     #-1    '••'
Word at 00000102 = $0048    #72        #72    '•H'
Word at 00000104 = $0048    #72        #72    '•H'
```

DX — Debugger Exchange

Description The Debugger Exchange command disables user breaks.

Syntax DX [ON | OFF]

If you do not specify ON or OFF, the DX command toggles between the two modes.

Considerations

MacsBug defines two traps, Debugger ($A9FF) and DebugStr ($ABFF), that allow you to invoke MacsBug from within your program. The Debugger trap simply invokes MacsBug; the DebugStr trap invokes MacsBug, displays a message, and executes any commands you have specified. The DX command allows you to disable these user breaks. It saves you the work of having to remove the trap calls from your program, and it allows you to restore them easily whenever you need to.

This command is useful when you have so many user breaks in your program that you are continuously dropping into MacsBug. For example, if you have placed a user break in a loop and you wish you hadn't, you can disable it with the DX command without having to change and recompile your source program.

Even when user breaks are disabled, messages specified by DebugStr will still be displayed; however, MacsBug will ignore commands associated with DebugStr. The DX command does not affect breakpoints, exceptions, or other A-traps.

See "Invoking MacsBug From Your Source Program" in Chapter 2 for additional information about how to include user breaks in your program.

Example

The following command enables user breaks:

```
DX ON
User breaks enabled
```

EA — Exit to Application

Description The Exit to Application command restarts the application from which MacsBug was invoked.

Syntax EA

See also ES

Considerations

The EA command has the same effect as returning to the Finder and relaunching the application. If you want to return to the application at the point where you left it when MacsBug was invoked, use the G (Go) command.

MacsBug defines a number of commands that allow you to leave MacsBug: G, EA, ES, RS, and RB. For additional information about how to select the appropriate command, see Chapter 2, "Getting Started."

Example

EA

ES — Exit to Shell

Description   The Exit to Shell command returns you to the Finder.

Syntax   ES

See also   EA

Considerations

Use the ES command when you are in MacsBug because your application crashed, but you don't think the system as a whole is dead. If you use this command after a crash, you should restart soon after because the system might have been damaged.

The ES command might not work with applications that override system traps. The ES command executes the ExitToShell trap, which initializes the application heap, usually destroying any system patches located there.

MacsBug defines a number of commands that allow you to leave MacsBug: G, EA, ES, RS, and RB. For additional information about how to select the appropriate command, see Chapter 2, "Getting Started."

Example

ES

F — Find

Description The Find command searches for a specified pattern of bytes.

Syntax F[B | W | L | P] *addr nbytes expr*

or

F *addr nbytes expr* | *"string"*

B
specifies that the Find command should search for the byte value specified by *expr*.

W
specifies that the Find command should search for the word value specified by *expr*.

L
specifies that the Find command should search for the long word value specified by *expr*.

P
specifies that the Find command should search for the lower 3 bytes of *expr*.

addr
specifies the starting point of the range where MacsBug should begin the search. MacsBug uses the value of *addr* + *nbytes* –1 to determine the end point of the range. MacsBug provides a number of standard macros that make it easier to specify address ranges.

nbytes
specifies the range: MacsBug uses the value of *addr* + *nbytes* –1 to determine the end point of the range.

expr
specifies the value to search for.

"string"
specifies the string to search for.

Considerations

If you use the F command without indicating the length you are looking for (B, W, L, or P), MacsBug looks for the smallest unit (Byte, Word, or Long word) that will contain the value specified by *expr*.

When it has found the pattern you specify, the Find command displays the address of the pattern's first byte, 16 bytes starting at that address, and the same bytes in ASCII format.

To search for the next occurrence of *expr* or "*string*", press Return. Once the Find command finds the specified pattern, it adds the size of the pattern to the address where the pattern begins and sets the dot address to that address.

Using the Find command to locate references to a pointer

A specific Find command that looks for pointers (FP) is useful because in software releases prior to system software version 7.0, applications (and managers) sometimes used the high byte of the long word containing an address to pass data. For example, the Memory Manager used the high byte of the long word containing the address of a relocatable block to specify whether the block was purgeable, locked, or a resource. This means that you cannot use the FL command to find every reference to an address because the high byte of the address can change, though the same address is being referenced. The FP command allows you to work around this problem by looking only for the lower 3 bytes and returning a 4-byte address.

Macros for the Find command

MacsBug provides a number of standard macros that you can use to specify common address ranges for the Find command. Table 9-2 describes these macros.

The variable TargetZone used in the Z Find commands described in Table 9-2 is defined as the zone currently selected by the HX command. You can use it with other MacsBug commands to indicate a range.

■ **Table 9-2** Macros for the Find command

Macro	Description	Macro expansion
RamF	Defines RAM as the address range of the Find command.	F 0 BufPtr^
RamFW		FW 0 BufPtr^
RamFL		FL 0 BufPtr^
RamFP	Example: `RamF 'Main'`	FP 0 BufPtr^
SysF	Defines the system zone as the address range of the Find command.	F SysZone^ (SysZone^^–SysZone^)
SysFW		FW SysZone^ (SysZone^^–SysZone^)
SysFL		FL SysZone^ (SysZone^^–SysZone^)
SysFP	Example: `RamFW 1234`	FP SysZone^ (SysZone^^–SysZone^)
ApF	Defines the application zone as the address range of the Find command.	F ApplZone^ (ApplZone^^–ApplZone^)
ApFW		FW ApplZone^ (ApplZone^^–ApplZone^)
ApFL		FL ApplZone^ (ApplZone^^–ApplZone^)
ApFP	Example: `ApFP 0032e232`	FP ApplZone^ (ApplZone^^–ApplZone^)
ZF	Defines the zone selected by the last HX command as the address range of the Find command.	F TargetZone (TargetZone^–TargetZone)
ZFW		FW TargetZone (TargetZone^–TargetZone)
ZFL		FL TargetZone (TargetZone^–TargetZone)
ZFP		FP TargetZone (TargetZone^–TargetZone)
	Example: `ZFL 000A232B0`	

Examples

This example uses the FP command to search for references to the pointer 022B40 in RAM. Note that you could also enter `RamFP 022B40`.

```
FP 0 BufPtr^ 022B40
{Return}
{Return}
Searching for xx022B40 from 00000000 to 003C06EF
  0017D14E  7002 2B40 F442 7008  C06B 0012 670E 2F2B  p•+@•Bp••k••g•/+
Searching for xx022B40 from 0017D152 to 003C06EF
  0018081E  0202 2B40 E48A 70FF  2B40 E48E 558F 486D  ••+@••p•+@••U•Hm
```

This example uses the F command to search for the string "Chapter 9/Commands" in the application heap. Note that you could enter `ApF "Chapter 9/Commands"` instead.

`F ApplZone^ (ApplZone^^-ApplZone^) "Chapter 9/Commands"`
```
Searching for "Chapter 9/Commands" from 0027C144 to 00379757
 0027C295   4368 6170 7465 7220  392F 436F 6D6D 616E   Chapter 9/Comman
```

G — Go

Description   The Go command allows you to leave MacsBug and resume program execution.

Syntax   G [*addr*]

addr
specifies the address where you want to resume execution of your program. If you omit this parameter, MacsBug resumes execution at the current program counter.

See also   GT, MR

Considerations

If you have used any commands to execute your program after invoking MacsBug, the Go command (without an address specification) will resume execution of your program at the next instruction. If the value of the program counter has not changed since you invoked MacsBug, executing the Go command resumes execution at the exact point where MacsBug was invoked.

You can use Command-G as an alternate way of entering G. In this case, MacsBug ignores any commands in the current command line.

Example

G

GT — Go Till

Description The Go Till command executes your program until the program counter reaches the specified address.

Syntax GT addr [';cmd [;cmd] ...']

addr
specifies an address. When the program counter is equal to this address, the GT command invokes MacsBug.

cmd
specifies a command that MacsBug should execute when the breakpoint specified by *addr* has been reached.

See also BRD, G, MR

Considerations

The GT command sets a temporary breakpoint at the specified address and resumes execution of your program until the program counter reaches that address.

The breakpoint specified with the GT command has an entry in the breakpoint table. If you enter MacsBug by some other means, this breakpoint remains set and you can see an entry for it in the table. For example, if you use the command GT 00A602, invoke MacsBug before the instruction at that address is reached, and then use the BRD command to display information about break actions, MacsBug will show you the following information about the break set with the GT command:

```
Breakpoint table
    Address    Module name      Cur/Max or Expression   Commands
  t 0000A602 R NEWPROC                    once
```

See the description of the BRD command earlier in this chapter for an explanation of the display.

When the GT command invokes MacsBug, it also clears the entry in the table. You can use the BRC command if you want to remove the breakpoint before reaching the address.

Specifying an address in ROM will cause execution to be slow because MacsBug must trace through each instruction until it reaches the breakpoint address. See the description of the BR command earlier in this chapter for additional information.

Using the GT command within a procedure

If you want to use the GT command to Go till an instruction in the current procedure, you can use the GTO standard macro to save yourself some work. The GTO macro allows you to specify the address of an instruction in the current procedure as an offset from the beginning of the procedure. Thus the command

```
GTO 18
```

executes the current procedure until the program counter reaches the instruction that is 18 bytes from the current procedure and saves you the trouble of entering an address. The GTO macro expands to GT :+.

Example

The following command invokes MacsBug when the program counter reaches A602 and displays the long word to which A7 points:

```
GT A602 ';DL    A7^'
```

HC — Heap Check

Description The Heap Check command tells you whether the information in the heap zone header or in any of the block headers in the current heap has been corrupted. If it has, your application will crash.

Syntax HC

See also ATHC, HD

Considerations

A common cause of damaged block headers is writing past the end of a heap block and over the beginning of the next one. HC is a good command to try after any crash, before proceeding with more commands.

The HC command checks the consistency of the current heap—that is, the heap set with the HX command. You can use the HZ command to determine the current heap: the HZ command displays the starting address of all the heaps and labels the current heap as TargetZone. See the description of the HZ command later in this chapter for additional information.

If the HC command returns an error message, you should run your program with ATHC on the next time to narrow down the range of calls that might be corrupting your heap. See the descriptions of the ATHC command earlier in this chapter for additional information.

An alternate way of narrowing down the source of heap corruption is to use the DebugStr trap with an argument of ';HC;G'. Sprinkle the DebugStr ';HC;G' throughout your program. Each time the microprocessor encounters the DebugStr routine, MacsBug will do a heap check. If the heap is bad, it will break and report the error. If the heap is OK, your program will continue to execute.

HC error messages

The HC command performs consistency checks by comparing information stored in the heap zone header with information stored in the header of each relocatable and nonrelocatable block in the heap. The "Memory Manager" chapter in *Inside Macintosh*, Volume II, provides specific detail about the information that is stored in the zone and block headers.

The information in the heap zone header and the block header is created and maintained by the Memory Manager. But the Memory Manager has no way to prevent your writing over information maintained in the zone header or block header. This might happen either because of dangling pointers or handles that cause you to write to the wrong location or because you write beyond a block's boundary and into the next block. For example, if a block contains an array of n elements and you write to the $n+1$ element, you might be writing into the next block's header. Thus, although the HC command can return fairly specific information in its error messages about what header fields have been corrupted, the two most common causes for the inconsistencies it finds are the ones described above: bad handles/pointers and writing beyond a block's boundary and into the header of the next block.

Note that all the heap commands check the heap as they execute; if a heap error is detected, they cancel the operation and return one of the error messages shown below. For additional information about heap zones and heap blocks, see Chapter 4, "Macintosh Memory Organization."

The following list describes the HC error messages and the consistency checks that produce them:

- bkLim does not agree with heap length

    Walking through the heap block by block must terminate at the start of the trailer block, as defined by the bkLim field of the zone header.

- Block length is bad

    The block header address plus the block length must be less than or equal to the trailer block address. Also, the trailer block must be a fixed length.

- Free bytes in heap do not match zone header

    The zcbFree field in the zone header must match the total size of all the free blocks in the heap.

- Free master pointer list is bad

    Free master pointers in the heap are chained together, starting with the hFstFree field in the zone header and terminated by a NIL pointer.

- Master pointer does not point at a block

    The master pointer for a relocatable block must point at a block in the heap.

- Nonrelocatable block: pointer to zone is bad

  Block headers of nonrelocatable blocks must contain a pointer to the zone header.

- Relative handle is bad

  The relative handle in the header of a relocatable block must point to a master pointer.

- Zone pointer is bad

  The zone pointer for the current heap (SysZone, ApplZone, or user address) must be even and in RAM. In addition, the bkLim field of the header must be even and in RAM, and must point after the header.

To display the information maintained in the heap zone header, enter the command

```
DM ApplZone ^zone
```
```
Displaying Zone at 003879E0
    003879E0    bkLim           00484FF4 ->
    003879E4    purgePtr        00387A14 ->
    003879E8    hFstFree        003EC5F8 ->
    003879EC    zcbFree         0003A2C4
    003879F0    gzProc          004CD0DA ->
    003879F4    moreMast        0040
    003879F6    flags           0000
    003879FE    heapType        00
    00387A08    purgeProc       NIL
    00387A0C    sparePtr        4080EE4E ->
    00387A10    allocPtr        003BC418 ->
```

Example

```
HC
  The Application heap is ok
```

HD — Heap Display

Description The Heap Display command displays information about the blocks in the current heap.

Syntax HD [*qualifier*]

qualifier
specifies the kind of block that you want information to be displayed for. You can specify one of the following for *qualifier*:

F	Free blocks
N	Nonrelocatable blocks
R	Relocatable blocks
L	Locked blocks
P	Purgeable blocks
Q	Questionable blocks
RS	Resource blocks
type	Resource blocks of this type only

If you do not specify a qualifier, the HD command displays information about all blocks in the current heap.

See also HC

Considerations

To stop and restart a heap display listing, press Return. To cancel the listing, press the Backspace or Delete key.

Before displaying information about the heap blocks, the HD command tells you the name of the current heap. At the end of the heap display, the HD command displays a message that tells you the number of blocks listed, the total number of bytes used, how many of these bytes store data, and how many free or purgeable bytes are left in the current heap zone. Free bytes do not necessarily represent memory that can be allocated to any one block, since this free space is probably fragmented.

It is now possible to obtain a full heap dump display even if there is some partial damage to block headers. The HD display includes the following special symbols to indicate the problem:

- An exclamation point (!) is placed in the Mstr Ptr column for a nonrelocatable block if the part of the block header containing the pointer to the heap zone has been damaged.
- An exclamation point (!) is placed in front of a relocatable block's master pointer if the address of the master pointer is not in the heap.
- A question mark (?) is placed in front of a relocatable block's master pointer if the master pointer does not in fact point to the start of the block.

The HD command with Q as a parameter lists all blocks with partially damaged headers as just described. The error messages displayed by the HC command provide the same information.

If you request information about resource blocks of a particular resource type, it is not necessary to place quotation marks around the name unless you want MacsBug to distinguish between uppercase and lowercase characters.

If the HD command does not find the specified blocks, it displays the message "No blocks of this type found."

Interpreting the heap display

Each line of the heap display gives information about one heap block. Heap blocks are listed in order from the lowest address to the highest address. Table 9-3 describes the information provided by the columns of the display.

■ **Table 9-3** Interpreting the HD display

Column	Description
1	A dot specifies that the block cannot move. The block is either nonrelocatable or it is a locked relocatable block.
Start	Specifies the address of the first byte of the block's contents.
Length	Shows as the addition of two operands. The first operand is the block's logical size; the second operand is the padding added by the Memory Manager to meet other requirements. The sum of the operands is the block's physical size.
Tag	Indicates whether the block is free (F), nonrelocatable (N), or relocatable (R).

(continued)

■ **Table 9-3** Interpreting the HD display (continued)

Column	Description
Mstr Ptr	Specifies the address of the master pointer if the block is relocatable.
Lock	Specifies L for locked blocks.
Prg	Specifies P for purgeable blocks.
Type	Specifies the resource type name for a resource block.
ID	Specifies the resource ID number for a resource block.
File	Specifies the resource file reference number for a resource block.
Name	Specifies the resource name for a resource block if a name has been assigned.

If the block for which information is being displayed is in a resource, but MacsBug does not know the name of the resource, it displays the message "Resource not found." This might happen because the resource is detached or because the block for which you are displaying information is not in the current TargetZone.

For additional information about heaps and blocks, see Chapter 4, "Macintosh Memory Organization."

Example

In the following example, the HX command sets the system heap as the current heap, and the HD command displays information for 'FOND' resource blocks in the system heap:

```
HX
The target heap is the System heap
HD FOND
 Displaying the System heap at 00001E00
    Start    Length    Tag    Mstr Ptr  Lock Prg    Type    ID    File      Name
    00025C54 0000003C+00  R   00001E70                FOND   0000  0002      Chicago
    0002C630 00000924+00  R   00020AD4                FOND   009C  0002      Garamond
    00043944 00000060+00  R   00020AE0        P       FOND   0003  0002      Geneva
    00052848 00000902+02  R   00020A84        P       FOND   0016  0002      Courier
 #4 blocks listed, which use #4836 bytes, storing #4802 bytes
 There are #220624 free or purgeable bytes in this heap
```

HELP — Help

Description The Help command displays information about the given command or section.

Syntax HELP [*cmd* | *topic*]

cmd
is the name of a MacsBug command or dcmd.

topic
is one of the topics displayed when you just enter HELP.

Considerations

If you do not specify a command or a topic, the Help command displays a list of topics for which it can provide help. If you then press Return, the Help command displays information for each topic.

Examples

HELP SC
```
SC6 [addr [nbytes]]
   Show the calling chain based on A6 links. If no addr then the
   chain starts with A6. If addr then the chain starts at addr. If no
   nbytes then the stack base is CurStackBase. If nbytes then the
   stack base is addr+nbytes.
```

HELP LOG
```
LOG [pathname | Printer]
   Log all MacsBug output to a file or to an ImageWriter printer.
   LOG without parameters turns logging off.
```

HELP

Return shows sections sequentially. "HELP name" shows that section.
 Editing
 Selecting procedure names
 Expressions
 Values
 Operators
 Flow control
 Breakpoints
 A-Traps
 Disassembly
 Heaps
 Symbols
 Stack
 Memory
 Registers
 Macros
 Miscellaneous
 dcmds

HOW — Display Break Message

Description The Display Break Message command redisplays the break message that was displayed when you initially entered MacsBug.

Syntax HOW

Considerations

The HOW command is handy if the original text has scrolled out of sight or if you want to record the information to a log file.

If you want to log essential information following the break message, you might want to define the following macro and execute it right after MacsBug is invoked:

```
MC totalhow 'LOG breakinfo; HOW; TD; TF; DM SP 100'
```

Of course, you can specify your own name for the log file. This might even be a good EveryTime macro; for additional information, see "Using Macros" in Chapter 8.

The macro logs the user break message, the contents of all registers, and the first 100 bytes on the stack when MacsBug was invoked; the following listing shows the information MacsBug displays or logs in response to this macro.

Example

```
LOG breakinfo; HOW; TD; TF; DM SP 100
```
User break at A000A5E6
 68030 Registers
  D0 = 00000000   A0 = A000A5E4   USP = CD3F9E97
  D1 = 00000007   A1 = 0027DE84   MSP = E149F8FD
  D2 = FFFF457A   A2 = 0027DE84   ISP = 0037FE74
  D3 = 00000000   A3 = 0027DE84   VBR = 00000000
  D4 = 0027FFFF   A4 = 0027DA30   CACR = 00002101   SFC = 7
  D5 = 00280000   A5 = 003BFFD8   CAAR = EF9FDFF2   DFC = 7
  D6 = 003BFFD8   A6 = 0037FE84   PC   = A000A5E6
  D7 = 0027C2EC   A7 = 0037FE74   SR   = SmXnzvc   Int = 0
 68881/68882 FPU Registers
  FP0 = 4011 A1F74CA2 339C0EBF   3.31706394800000000e+5
  FP1 = 7FFF FFFFFFFF FFFFFFFF   NAN(255)
  FP2 = 7FFF FFFFFFFF FFFFFFFF   NAN(255)
  FP3 = 7FFF FFFFFFFF FFFFFFFF   NAN(255)
  FP4 = 7FFF FFFFFFFF FFFFFFFF   NAN(255)
  FP5 = 7FFF FFFFFFFF FFFFFFFF   NAN(255)
  FP6 = 7FFF FFFFFFFF FFFFFFFF   NAN(255)
  FP7 = 7FFF FFFFFFFF FFFFFFFF   NAN(255)
          EE MC   CC QT ES AE
  FPCR = 00 00   FPSR = 00 00 02 08   FPIAR = 00000000
 Displaying memory from sp
   0037FE74 4080 F2A4 0002 0944 0000 0001 4080 F18E   @•••••D••••@•••
   0037FE84 0028 3FE0 4080 F1A0 0027 DE84 FFFF 0100   •(?•@••†•'•••••
   0037FE94 0027 DE84 003B 4584 457A 0000 000F 0000   •'•••;E•Ez•••••
.
.   {display slightly abbreviated here to save space}
.
   0037FF04 43EF FFFC 2509 250E 4DEA FFFA 94FC 0010   C•••%•%•M•••••••
   0037FF14 4E90 A9F4 003C 0622 DB6D B6DB 6DB6 DB6D   N•••<•"•m••m••m
   0037FF24 B6DB 6DB6 DB6D B6DB 6DB6 DB6D B6DB 6DB6   ••m••m••m••m••m•
   0037FF34 DB6D B6DB 6DB6 DB6D B6DB 6DB6 DB6D B6DB   •m••m••m••m••m••
   0037FF44 6DB6 DB6D B6DB 6DB6 DB6D B6DB 6DB6 DB6D   m••m••m••m••m••m
   0037FF54 B6DB 6DB6 DB6D B6DB 6DB6 DB6D B6DB 6DB6   ••m••m••m••m••m•
   0037FF64 DB6D B6DB 6DB6 DB6D B6DB 6DB6 DB6D B6DB   •m••m••m••m••m••
   SP = $0037FE74   #3669620   #3669620   '•7•t'

HS — Heap Scramble

Description The Heap Scramble command turns heap scrambling on and off. When heap scrambling is on, the Memory Manager moves all unlocked relocatable blocks whenever the move is legitimate—that is, during every A-trap call that can allocate memory directly or indirectly.

Syntax HS [*addr*]

addr
specifies the starting address of the heap you want scrambled. If you omit this parameter, the HS command scrambles the application heap.

See also HC

Considerations

The HS command is very useful in allowing you to determine whether you have any dereferenced handles or to find problems that might occur when your program is running in very limited memory and the Memory Manager has to move blocks around a lot. It's simple to use; you turn HS on and run your program.

The Memory Manager will move unlocked relocatable blocks when it encounters one of the following calls: NewPtr, NewHandle, ReallocHandle, SetPtrSize, or SetHandleSize. With the latter two, the heap is scrambled only if the block size is being increased. The HS command checks the heap before scrambling. If it is corrupted, MacsBug breaks and reports the error. See the description of the HC command earlier in this chapter for a list of possible errors. MacsBug automatically turns heap scrambling off when it detects a bad heap.

Unlike the other heap commands, which take the zone currently set by the HX command as the target zone by default, the HS command works on the application heap by default. You can scramble the system heap if you specify SysZone for *addr*.

Example

```
HS
Scrambling heap at 0027C144
```

HT — Heap Totals

Description   The Heap Totals command displays information about the current heap.

Syntax   HT

See also   HD

Considerations

The HT command displays the following information for the current heap:

- The total number and size for each type of block (free, relocatable, and nonrelocatable)
- The number of locked, unlocked, and purgeable blocks
- Totals for the heap

The HT command displays hexadecimal as well as decimal values for all totals.

The total free space listed by the HT command does not represent all the contiguous free space available because the heap is probably fragmented. Most heaps are at least a bit fragmented. Use the HD command to determine the size of the largest available free block.

You can use the HT command to get an overall sense of the contents of your heap. Too many locked blocks and too few purgeable blocks might indicate that you need to put some time into managing your heap.

Example

```
HT
Totaling the Application heap at 00279FB8
                              Total Blocks      Total of Block Sizes
  Free                        0D1B    #3355     00040954    #264532
  Nonrelocatable              000E    #14       00037924    #227620
  Relocatable                 00D8    #216      00085368    #545640
    Locked                    0003    #3        0006B73C    #440124
    Purgeable and not locked  000C    #12       00002D24    #11556
  Heap size                   0E01    #3585     000FD5E0    #1037792
```

HX — Heap Exchange

Description The Heap Exchange command selects the current heap.

Syntax HX [*addr*]

addr
specifies the address of a heap zone. If you omit this parameter, the HX command switches from the application heap to the system heap (in a single-application environment) or cycles through the heaps (in a multiple-application environment).

See also HC, HD, HT, HZ

Considerations

All the heap commands (except Heap Scramble) work on the heap selected by the HX command. When you start MacsBug, the HX command sets the application heap as the current heap.

If you are running in a multiple-application environment, use the HZ command to determine the addresses of the other heaps. See the section "Heap Management in a Multiple-Application Environment" in Chapter 4 for additional information.

Example

The following HX command selects the system heap as the current heap. The subsequent HZ command labels the system heap as the TargetZone because it has been selected with the HX command.

```
HX
The target heap is the System heap
HZ
 Heap zones
  24   00001E00 to 0006B41F  SysZone^  TargetZone
  24    00001FB8 to 0000248B
  24   0006B420 to 004C40DB
  24    004092C4 to 00482A53  ApplZone^  TheZone^
  24    0048A2CC to 004AEFF3
  24    004B62D4 to 004B7BB7
```

Chapter 9   MacsBug Commands   **293**

HZ — Heap Zone

Description   The Heap Zone command lists all known heap zones.

Syntax   HZ [*addr*]

addr
is the starting address of a heap containing embedded heaps.

See also   HC, HD, HT, HX

Considerations

The Heap Zone command lists the addresses that indicate the starting and ending addresses of each heap. Note that the starting address is the address of the first byte in the heap zone header, and the ending address is the address of the last byte of the heap zone trailer. The HZ command also indicates whether each heap is a 24-bit or 32-bit heap in the leftmost column of its display.

The heap zone display differs depending on whether you are running in a single-application or multiple-application environment:

- If you are running in a single-application environment, the list includes the system heap and the application heap.

- If you are running in a multiple-application environment, the list displayed by the HZ command includes the system heap, a private heap within the system heap, the Process Manager heap, the current application heap, the Finder heap, and the heap of any application running in the background. This order might change with future software releases.

(The Process Manager allocates a locked relocatable block in its heap for each application that you launch. The HZ command identifies application heaps by doing a heap check on each block in the Process Manager's heap. If the block passes, it's assumed to be a heap.)

The HZ display identifies embedded heaps by indenting them. For example, in the following output,

```
Heap zones
  24   00001E00 to 0006B41F   SysZone^
  24    00001FB8 to 0000248B
  24   0006B420 to 004C40DB
  24     004092C4 to 00482A53   ApplZone^   TheZone^   TargetZone
  24     0048A2CC to 004AEFF3
  24     004B62D4 to 004B7BB7
```

the heap zone from 00001FB8 to 0000248B is embedded in the system heap; the heap zones from 004092C4 to 00482A53, from 0048A2CC to 004AEFF3, and from 004B62D4 to 004B7BB7 are all embedded in the Process Manager's heap zone, which starts at 0006B420 and ends at 004C40DB. All heap zones in this example are 24-bit.

You can use the *addr* parameter to the HZ command to display the heaps embedded in the heap starting at *addr*. For example:

HZ 000573B0
```
Heap zone 000573B0 and embedded heap zones
  24   000573B0 to 003B69C7
  24    00279FB8 to 003775D7   ApplZone^   TheZone^   TargetZone
  24    0037DFC0 to 003A2CAB
  24    003A9FC8 to 003AB8AF
```

The HZ command cannot display heap zones stored on the stack, nor does it list heap zones that don't start at the beginning of a heap block.

The HZ command uses two low-memory global variables and one MacsBug variable to describe the heaps:

- ApplZone (low-memory global variable) points to the beginning of the current application heap.
- TheZone (low-memory global variable) points to the zone currently set by the SetZone routine.
- TargetZone (MacsBug variable) points to the zone currently set by the MacsBug HX command.

The HZ command uses one additional MacsBug variable, UserZone, to indicate the heap whose address you last specified as a parameter to the HX command.

Chapter 9 MacsBug Commands

For example, given the zones

```
Heap zones
  24   00001E00 to 0006B41F  SysZone^   TargetZone
  24    00001FB8 to 0000248B
  24   0006B420 to 004C40DB
  24    004092C4 to 00482A53  ApplZone^  TheZone^
  24    0048A2CC to 004AEFF3
  24    004B62D4 to 004B7BB7
```

If you enter the command

HX 0048A2CC

MacsBug displays this message:

```
The target heap is the heap at 0048A2CC
```

If you now enter the HZ command once more, MacsBug displays the following information:

```
Heap zones
  24   00001E00 to 0006B41F  SysZone^
  24    00001FB8 to 0000248B
  24   0006B420 to 004C40DB
  24    004092C4 to 00482A53  ApplZone^  TheZone^
  24    0048A2CC to 004AEFF3  TargetZone  UserZone
  24    004B62D4 to 004B7BB7
```

The zone whose address you specified for the HX command is now also identified as UserZone. If you were to use the HX command without parameters to cycle through the heaps, the heap starting at 0048A2CC would still be identified as the UserZone, simply to remind you that this was the heap you were specifically interested in.

For additional information about heaps, see Chapter 4, "Macintosh Memory Organization."

Example

The following example shows the output of the HZ command in a single-application environment:

HZ

```
Heap zones
  24   00001E00   SysZone
  24   0002D528   ApplZone  TheZone  TargetZone
```

ID — Disassemble One Line

Description   The Disassemble One Line command disassembles one line, starting at the specified address.

Syntax   ID [*addr*]

addr
specifies the address containing the first byte to be disassembled. If you do not specify *addr*, the ID command uses the program counter for *addr*.

See also   IL, IP, IR

Considerations

If you press Return after executing an ID command, the next line is disassembled. The dot address is set to the last address used.

The ID command displays the procedure name (if any) and offset in the first column, followed by an address. If MacsBug does not know the procedure name, but the address is in a known resource, MacsBug displays the type of the resource, the number of the resource, the file in which the resource is stored, the name of the resource, and the offset within the resource where the instruction is found; for example:

```
'CODE 0007 0294 Init'+0A3C
```

The next two fields of the display contain the opcode and operand(s) that make up the instruction. An asterisk character (*) before the opcode indicates the instruction pointed to by the current program counter. A dot character (.) before the opcode indicates that a breakpoint is set at that instruction.

The comment field, the field preceded by the semicolon (;), gives the target of a JMP, JSR, or BSR instruction, the trap number of a trap, or the ASCII value of a DC statement. The last field shows the actual hexadecimal words of the instruction. If the instruction contains too many words, an ellipsis (...) is displayed. Note that you can only see this last field on larger screens. You can, however, always see the field by sending the output to a file or printer with the LOG command.

The IL, IP, and IR commands allow you to dissassemble larger chunks of code.

For additional information about reading disassembled code, see Chapter 3, "An Assembly-Language Primer."

Examples

ID PC
```
Disassembling from pc
 DOSCROLL
    +0000   2187F8    *LINK      A6,#$FFE4                  | 4E56 FFE4
```

ID DOSCROLL + 6
```
Disassembling from doscroll + 6
 DOSCROLL
    +0006   2187FE    MOVEA.L    $000A(A6),A0               | 206E 000A
```

IL — Disassemble From Address

Description The Disassemble From Address command disassembles as many lines as you like starting from an address you specify.

Syntax IL [addr[n]]

addr
specifies the address containing the first byte you want disassembled. If you do not specify *addr,* the IL command uses the value of the program counter.

n
is a hexadecimal integer specifying the number of lines you want disassembled. If you omit this parameter, the IL command disassembles a half page (64 bytes) of code.

See also ID, IP, IR

Considerations

Pressing Return disassembles the next *n* lines if you specify *n*. If you do not, the IL command disassembles the next half page (64 bytes) of code. The IL command sets the dot address to the last address used.

The IL command is the same as the IP command, except the disassembly starts at the address you enter, rather than being centered around that address.

The IL command displays the procedure name (if any) and offset in the first column, followed by an address. If MacsBug does not know the procedure name, but the address is in a known resource, MacsBug displays the type of the resource, the number of the resource, the file in which the resource is stored, the name of the resource, and the offset within the resource where the instruction is found; for example:

`'CODE 0007 0294 Init'+0A3C`

The next two fields of the display contain the opcode and operand(s) that make up the instruction. An asterisk character (*) before the opcode indicates the instruction pointed to by the current program counter. A dot character (.) before the opcode indicates that a breakpoint is set at that instruction.

The comment field, the field preceded by the semicolon (;), gives the target of a JMP, JSR, or BSR instruction, the trap number of a trap, or the ASCII value of a DC statement. The last field shows the actual hexadecimal words of the instruction. If the instruction contains too many words, an ellipsis (...) is displayed. Note that you can only see this last field on larger screens. You can, however, always see the field by sending the output to a file or printer with the LOG command.

For additional information about reading disassembled code, see Chapter 3, "An Assembly-Language Primer."

Example

The following IL command disassembles ten lines starting at the starting address of the DOSCROLL procedure:

```
IL   DOSCROLL 10
Disassembling from doscroll
  DOSCROLL
      +0000  2187F8   *LINK     A6,#$FFE4                        | 4E56 FFE4
      +0004  2187FC    MOVE.L   A4,-(A7)                         | 2F0C
      +0006  2187FE    MOVEA.L  $000A(A6),A0                     | 206E 000A
      +000A  218802    MOVE.L   A0,D0                            | 2008
      +000C  218804    BNE.S    DOSCROLL+0010      ; 00218808    | 6602
      +000E  218806    TRAP     #$0                              | 4E40
      +0010  218808    LEA      $0010(A0),A0                     | 41E8 0010
      +0014  21880C    LEA      -$001C(A6),A1                    | 43EE FFE4
      +0018  218810    MOVE.L   (A0)+,(A1)+                      | 22D8
      +001A  218812    MOVE.L   (A0)+,(A1)+                      | 22D8
      +001C  218814    MOVE.W   -$0016(A6),D0                    | 302E FFEA
      +0020  218818    ADDI.W   #$FFF1,D0                        | 0640 FFF1
      +0024  21881C    TRAPV                                     | 4E76
      +0026  21881E    MOVE.W   D0,-$0016(A6)                    | 3D40 FFEA
      +002A  218822    MOVE.W   -$0018(A6),D0                    | 302E FFE8
```

IP — Disassemble Around Address

Description The Disassemble Around Address command disassembles a half page (64 bytes) centered around the specified address.

Syntax IP [*addr*]

addr
specifies the address around which instructions should be disassembled. If you omit this parameter, the IP command uses the value of the program counter.

See also ID, IL, IR

Considerations

Pressing Return disassembles the next half page (64 bytes) of code. The dot address is set to the first address displayed.

The IP command displays the procedure name (if any) and offset in the first column, followed by an address. If MacsBug does not know the procedure name, but the address is in a known resource, MacsBug displays the type of the resource, the number of the resource, the file in which the resource is stored, the name of the resource, and the offset within the resource where the instruction is found; for example:

```
'CODE 0007 0294 Init'+0A3C
```

The next two fields of the display contain the opcode and operand(s) that make up the instruction. An asterisk character (*) before the opcode indicates the instruction pointed to by the current program counter. A dot character (.) before the opcode indicates that a breakpoint is set at that instruction.

The comment field, the field preceded by the semicolon (;), gives the target of a JMP, JSR, or BSR instruction, the trap number of a trap, or the ASCII value of a DC statement. The last field shows the actual hexadecimal words of the instruction. If the instruction contains too many words, an ellipsis (...) is displayed. Note that you can only see this last field on larger screens. You can, however, always see the field by sending the output to a file or printer with the LOG command.

For additional information about reading disassembled code, see Chapter 3, "An Assembly-Language Primer."

Example

In this example, the disassembly takes place around the instruction pointed to by the program counter: LINK A6, #$FFE4.

```
IP  PC
DOCIRCLE
    +00CA  2187DE      _StillDown                      ; A973        | A973
    +00CC  2187E0      TST.B       (A7)+                             | 4A1F
    +00CE  2187E2      BNE         DOCIRCLE+0014       ; 00218728    | 6600 FF44
    +00D2  2187E6      MOVEA.L     (A7)+,A4                          | 285F
    +00D4  2187E8      UNLK        A6                                | 4E5E
    +00D6  2187EA      MOVEA.L     (A7)+,A0                          | 205F
    +00D8  2187EC      ADDQ.W      #$8,A7                            | 504F
    +00DA  2187EE      JMP         (A0)                              | 4ED0
DOSCROLL
    +0000  2187F8     *LINK        A6,#$FFE4                         | 4E56 FFE4
    +0004  2187FC      MOVE.L      A4,-(A7)                          | 2F0C
    +0006  2187FE      MOVEA.L     $000A(A6),A0                      | 206E 000A
    +000A  218802      MOVE.L      A0,D0                             | 2008
    +000C  218804      BNE.S       DOSCROLL+0010       ; 00218808    | 6602
    +000E  218806      TRAP        #$0                               | 4E40
    +0010  218808      LEA         $0010(A0),A0                      | 41E8 0010
    +0014  21880C      LEA         -$001C(A6),A1                     | 43EE FFE4
    +0018  218810      MOVE.L      (A0)+,(A1)+                       | 22D8
    +001A  218812      MOVE.L      (A0)+,(A1)+                       | 22D8
    +001C  218814      MOVE.W      -$0016(A6),D0                     | 302E FFEA
```

IR — Disassemble Until End of Procedure

Description The Disassemble Until End of Procedure command disassembles code from the address you specify until the end of the procedure containing the instruction at the specified address.

Syntax IR [*addr*]

addr
specifies the address where you want disassembly to begin. If you omit this parameter, the IR command uses the value of the program counter.

See also ID, IL, IP

Considerations

The IR command assumes that the instruction beginning at the specified address is part of a procedure. The dot address is set to the specified address.

If the routine is longer than a full screen, MacsBug prompts you to press Return to display the next screen. The IR command is similar to the IL command, except that the IR command stops at the end of the routine.

The IR command displays the procedure name (if any) and offset in the first column, followed by an address. If MacsBug does not know the procedure name, but the address is in a known resource, MacsBug displays the type of the resource, the number of the resource, the file in which the resource is stored, the name of the resource, and the offset within the resource where the instruction is found; for example:

`'CODE 0007 0294 Init'+0A3C`

The next two fields of the display contain the opcode and operand(s) that make up the instruction. An asterisk character (*) before the opcode indicates the instruction pointed to by the current program counter. A dot character (.) before the opcode indicates that a breakpoint is set at that instruction.

The comment field, the field preceded by the semicolon (;), gives the target of a JMP, JSR, or BSR instruction, the trap number of a trap, or the ASCII value of a DC statement. The last field shows the actual hexadecimal words of the instruction. If the instruction contains too many words, an ellipsis (...) is displayed. Note that you can only see this last field on larger screens. You can, however, always see the field by sending the output to a file or printer with the LOG command.

For additional information about reading disassembled code, see Chapter 3, "An Assembly-Language Primer."

Example

In the following example, the IR command is used to disassemble a routine that sets up menus:

```
IR DOSETUPMENUS
DOSETUPM
    +0000  2186B2    LINK       A6,#$FFE0              | 4E56 FFE0
    +0004  2186B6    SUBQ.W     #$4,A7                 | 594F
    +0006  2186B8    MOVE.W     #$1389,-(A7)           | 3F3C 1389
    +000A  2186BC    _GetRMenu                ; A9BF   | A9BF
    +000C  2186BE    MOVE.L     (A7)+,-$0020(A6)       | 2D5F FFE0
    +0010  2186C2    SUBQ.W     #$4,A7                 | 594F
    +0012  2186C4    MOVE.W     #$138A,-(A7)           | 3F3C 138A

.   {part of output deleted to save space}
.
.
    +002E  2186E0    _GetRMenu                ; A9BF   | A9BF
    +0030  2186E2    MOVE.L     (A7)+,-$0014(A6)       | 2D5F FFEC
    +0034  2186E6    MOVE.L     -$0020(A6),-(A7)       | 2F2E FFE0
    +0038  2186EA    CLR.W      -(A7)                  | 4267
    +003A  2186EC    _InsertMenu              ; A935   | A935
    +003C  2186EE    MOVE.L     -$001C(A6),-(A7)       | 2F2E FFE4
    +0040  2186F2    CLR.W      -(A7)                  | 4267
    +0042  2186F4    _InsertMenu              ; A935   | A935
    +0044  2186F6    MOVE.L     -$0018(A6),-(A7)       | 2F2E FFE8
    +0048  2186FA    CLR.W      -(A7)                  | 4267
    +004A  2186FC    _InsertMenu              ; A935   | A935
    +004C  2186FE    MOVE.L     -$0014(A6),-(A7)       | 2F2E FFEC
    +0050  218702    CLR.W      -(A7)                  | 4267
    +0052  218704    _InsertMenu              ; A935   | A935
    +0054  218706    _DrawMenuBar             ; A937   | A937
    +0056  218708    UNLK       A6                     | 4E5E
    +0058  21870A    RTS                               | 4E75
```

LOG — Log to a Printer or File

Description The Log to a Printer or File command sends MacsBug output to the specified text file or to an ImageWriter via the serial port.

Syntax LOG [*pathname* | Printer]

pathname
specifies a partial pathname: *filename, diskname:filename,* or a full pathname: *diskname:foldername:filename*. If you specify *filename*, MacsBug opens the file in the current directory.

Printer
specifies that you want output to be sent to an ImageWriter. The LOG command does not work with the LaserWriter driver, so you can't send MacsBug output directly to a LaserWriter. Instead, you can send it to a file and then print it on a LaserWriter.

Considerations

You do not have to enclose *pathname* in quotation marks even though it includes colons, which normally specify the beginning of the current procedure in MacsBug. However, if you use the MC (Macro Create) command to use a macro name for a pathname, you must enclose the pathname in quotation marks. See the description of the MC command later in this chapter for additional information.

If the file you specify does not already exist, MacsBug creates the file as an MPW text file, which you can open from word-processing applications as well as from MPW. If the specified file already exists and is of type 'TEXT', the LOG command appends MacsBug output to the existing file.

If you log to a file while MPW Pascal is running, or while an application is running in a multiple-application environment, be aware that the log file will be closed when you leave MPW or quit the application. However, if you have not quit the application, you must close the file from MacsBug using the LOG command before you can open it and examine its contents.

You cannot log to more than one file. To turn logging off, enter LOG with no parameters.

MacsBug, by design, uses as little of the system as possible; the LOG command violates this design criterion. Logging may not work, depending on the state of the file system during your debugging session. In general, you should observe the following restrictions:

- Do not log to file server volumes.
- Because logging enables interrupts briefly while executing its low-level calls, if your program depends on interrupts being completely disabled, you should not use the LOG command.

You cannot log output to an ImageWriter if you are working with MacsBug under A/UX. However, you can still log to a file and then print the file.

Examples

```
LOG   ATHENA:MACSBUG:FIRSTLOG
```
Logging to ATHENA:MACSBUG:FIRSTLOG

```
LOG
```
Closing log

MC — Macro Create

Description The Macro Create command creates a new macro with the given name that expands to the expression you specify.

Syntax MC name 'expr' | expr

name
specifies the name of the macro. The names FirstTime and EveryTime are reserved as are the names of MacsBug commands and the standard macro names defined by the 'mxbm' resources 100, 101, and 102.

expr
specifies the expression that the macro expands to. If you specify *expr*, it is evaluated when you create the macro and that value is substituted for *name* every time you use the macro. If you specify '*expr*', it is evaluated every time you use the macro.

See also MCC, MCD

Considerations

A macro can contain anything you can type in a command line. You can use macros to contain command name aliases, reference global variables, and name common expressions.

This MC command defines a command name alias:

```
MC SelectHeap HX
```

This MC command names an expression:

```
MC ReturnAdrs A6 + 4
```

If you use the MC command to define an alias for a pathname, you must enclose the pathname in quotation marks when you define the macro because MacsBug is confused by the colons in the pathname—for example:

```
MC mylog  'Athena:MacsBug:Newlog'
```

If you now use the command LOG mylog, MacsBug creates the file Newlog in the MacsBug folder on the disk Athena and logs MacsBug output to it.

MacsBug expands all macros before it executes the command line. This means that you cannot define a macro and reference it on the same line, because the reference will be undefined at the time the macro is expanded. For this reason the following command line will generate an error; MacsBug tries to expand Save before executing the MC command that defines it:

```
MC Save CurrentA5; SL CurrentA5 Save
```

Using macros to save values

Macros give you a quick way to save values. For instance, you can enter

```
MC save PC
```

to save the contents of the program counter; then, you can enter

```
PC = save
```

to restore the contents. Note that this technique does not work with floating-point registers.

The macros you create using the MC command are only good until you shut down your Macintosh. You can create permanent macros using the 'mxbm' resource. The 'mxbm' resource also defines the macro FirstTime, which allows you to execute the commands you specify immediately after loading MacsBug, and the macro EveryTime, which allows you to define other commands that execute each time except the first time MacsBug is invoked. For additional information about how to create these macros using the 'mxbm' resource, see "Using Macros" in Chapter 8.

Use the MCC command to clear a macro. Use the MCD command to display all macros that match the current name. This command is handy if you want to know whether you're redefining an existing macro.

Examples

MacsBug recalculates the value for this macro each time you use it:

```
MC quick 'D0+D1*3'
Macro quick will expand to 'D0+D1*3'
```

MacsBug calculates the value for this macro when it is defined:

```
MC quicker D0 + D1 * 3
Macro quicker will expand to '00000015'
```

MCC — Macro Clear

Description The Macro Clear command clears the specified macro or all macros.

Syntax MCC [*name*]

name
specifies the name of the macro to be cleared. If you omit this parameter, the MCC command clears all macros.

See also MC, MCD

Example

The following command clears the macro named "quick":

```
MCC quick
quick cleared
```

MCD — Macro Display

Description The Macro Display command displays the specified macro or all macros whose names begin with the specified characters.

Syntax MCD [*name*]

name
specifies part of or a complete macro name. If you omit this parameter, the MCD command displays all currently defined macros.

See also MC, MCC

Considerations

The MCD command displays all macros, whether they were defined using the 'mxbm' resource or the MC command.

The MCD command displays two columns: the first column lists the macro name; the second column contains the macro expansion (*expr*).

If you specify a series of characters for *name*, the MCD command lists all macros beginning with those characters. Thus, the MCD command is useful in telling you whether a macro name is already defined.

Use the MCC command to clear a macro. For additional information about macros, see "Using Macros" in Chapter 8.

Example

```
MCD apf
Macro table
  Name                    Expansion
  ApF                     F ApplZone^ (ApplZone^^-ApplZone^)
  ApFW                    FW ApplZone^ (ApplZone^^-ApplZone^)
  ApFL                    FL ApplZone^ (ApplZone^^-ApplZone^)
  ApFP                    FP ApplZone^ (ApplZone^^-ApplZone^)
  ApFontID                0984
```

MR — Magic Return

Description If you have accidentally stepped into a JSR, BSR, or trap call that you meant to step over, executing the Magic Return command before executing any of the subroutine or trap code will execute the equivalent of a GT (Go Till) command to the instruction immediately after the subroutine or A-trap call.

Syntax MR [*param*]

param
is an integer used by the MR command to find the address where the return address is stored.

See also G, GT

Considerations

The MR command sets a temporary breakpoint at the first instruction after the call to the current procedure. It does this by replacing the return address on the stack with a MacsBug address. When the procedure returns, MacsBug gets control. It then performs an RTS in trace mode, breaking at the instruction after the call. The *param* value that you specify helps the MR command figure out where the return address is stored on the stack.

The *param* value you specify to the MR command depends on how far you've stepped into the procedure and whether your compiler uses the A6 register as a stack frame pointer:

- If the program counter points to the LINK instruction or what is otherwise the first instruction of the subroutine, enter MR with no parameters. In this case the return address is assumed to be stored on the top of the stack.

- If the program counter points after the first instruction and your compiler uses A6 as the stack frame pointer, you should specify A6 as the parameter to the MR command. For example, if you enter

    MR   A6

    the MR command looks for the return address at A6 + 4.

- If the program counter points after the first instruction and you are not using A6 as the stack frame pointer, then presumably you know where you're storing the return address and you can specify this address as an offset from A7. Thus, if you enter

    MR 8

    the MR command will look for the return address at A7 + 8.

- If the program counter points after the first instruction of a nested procedure, entering MR A6^ will set a breakpoint at the first instruction following the procedure that called your procedure.

Using the MR command to display function results

You can display the result of a function every time it's called by entering the command

BR *functionname* ' ; MR ; DW SP '

Whenever the breakpoint is reached, MacsBug executes the MR command and displays the top word on the stack (the function result). For functions that return long words, you should use the command

BR *functionname* ' ; MR ; DL SP '

For functions that return pointers, you could dereference the pointer and display the structure using a template; for example:

BR *functionname* ' ; MR ; DM SP^ *templatename* '

MR error messages

MacsBug checks to see that the address determined from the specified *param* value is a valid stack address and that it is a valid return address.

If the address is not in the range between A7 and CurStackBase^, MacsBug displays the message "This address is not a stack address."

If the address does not immediately follow a JSR, BSR, or A-trap instruction, MacsBug returns the message "The address on the stack is not a return address."

Example

In the following example, the USERBRK procedure is disassembled to show you that the program counter points after the first LINK instruction. That is, you've already stepped into the procedure.

```
USERBRK
    +0000   0041ADCA   LINK         A6,#$FFF8                       | 4E56 FFF8
    +0004   0041ADCE   _Debugger                      ; A9FF        | A9FF
    +0006   0041ADD0   *NOP                                          | 4E71
    +0008   0041ADD2   PEA          -$0008(A6)                      | 486E FFF8
    +000C   0041ADD6   _GetPort                       ; A874        | A874
    +000E   0041ADD8   CLR.L        -(A7)                           | 42A7
    +0010   0041ADDA   JSR          *+$0408           ; 0041B1E2    | 4EBA 0406
    +0014   0041ADDE   MOVE.L       (A7)+,D0                        | 201F
    +0016   0041ADE0   MOVE.L       D0,-$0004(A6)                   | 2D40 FFFC
    +001A   0041ADE4   UNLK         A6                              | 4E5E
    +001C   0041ADE6   RTS                                          | 4E75
```

If you now enter the command MR A6, MacsBug displays a message that tells you where it set the temporary breakpoint:

```
Breakpoint at DOCMD+0114
```

After disassembling the DOCMD procedure, you'll find that the program counter points to the first instruction after the call to the USERBRK procedure—just what you expect the MR command to accomplish.

```
Disassembling from 0041AD70
  DOCMD
    +00F6   0041AD70   DC.W         $FFFC             ; ????        | FFFC
    +00F8   0041AD72   JSR          $003A(A5)                       | 4EAD 003A
    +00FC   0041AD76   ORI.B        #$07,D1                         | 0001 0007
    +0100   0041AD7A   ORI.W        #$000E,D0                       | 0040 000E
    +0104   0041AD7E   ORI.B        #$10,CCR                        | 003C 0010
    +0108   0041AD82   ORI.B        #$18,(A4)                       | 0014 0018
    +010C   0041AD86   ORI.B        #$2E,(A4)+        ; '.'         | 001C 002E
    +0110   0041AD8A   JSR          USERBRK           ; 0041ADCA    | 4EBA 003E
    +0114   0041AD8E   *BRA.S       DOCMD+0140        ; 0041ADBA    | 602A
    +0116   0041AD90   JSR          SHOWATRA          ; 0041ADF0    | 4EBA 005E
    +011A   0041AD94   BRA.S        DOCMD+0140        ; 0041ADBA    | 6024
```

RAD — Toggle Register Name Syntax

Description The Toggle Register Name Syntax command allows you to specify the address and data registers in two different ways.

Syntax RAD

See also Registers

Considerations

By default, MacsBug expects the actual Motorola names for the address and data registers. So, if you want to enter a register on the command line, for example:

```
DM D0
```

you just type the name of the register. But D0 is also a valid hexadecimal number; if you want to enter the hexadecimal number, you must put a dollar sign in front of it; for example:

```
DM D0 + $D0
```

The RAD command allows you to select a naming convention that interprets D0 as a hexadecimal number. When this convention is in effect, you must put R in front of the register name to let MacsBug know you mean the register; for example:

```
DM RD0 + D0
```

Examples

```
RAD
```
An and Dn numbers enabled

```
RAD
```
An and Dn numbers disabled

RB — Reboot

Description   The Reboot command restarts the system. It unmounts the startup volume before restarting.

Syntax   RB

See also   RS

Considerations

For additional information about what unmounting does, see the description of the UnmountVol routine in the "File Manager" chapters of *Inside Macintosh,* Volumes II and IV.

MacsBug defines a number of commands that allow you to leave MacsBug: G, EA, ES, RS, and RB. For additional information about how to select the appropriate command, see Chapter 2, "Getting Started."

Example

RB

Registers

Description The Registers command allows you to display the value of a register or assign a value to a register.

Syntax *registerName* [= *expr* | := *expr*]

registerName
specifies the name of a 68000, 68020, 68030/68851, or 68881 register. By default, MacsBug uses the Motorola names for all registers. However, you might prefer to use an alternate syntax. See the description of the RAD command earlier in this chapter for additional information.

expr
is an expression whose value is assigned to the specified register. If you omit this parameter, the Registers command displays the current value of the specified register.

See also RAD

Considerations

Table 9-4 lists all registers and their names.

■ **Table 9-4** Register names

Microprocessor	Name	Function
68000	D*n*	Data register *n*
	A*n*	Address register *n*
	PC	Program counter
	SR	Status register
	SP	Stack pointer
	SSP	Supervisor stack pointer

(continued)

■ **Table 9-4** Register names (continued)

Microprocessor	Name	Function
68020	ISP	Interrupt stack pointer
	MSP	Master stack pointer
	VBR	Vector base register
	SFC	Source function code register
	DFC	Destination function code register
	CACR	Cache control register
	CAAR	Cache address register
68030/68851	CRP	CPU root pointer
	SRP	Supervisor root pointer
	TC	Translation control register
	PSR	PMMU status register
68881	FP*n*	Floating-point data register *n*
	FPCR	Floating-point control register
	FPSR	Floating-point status register
	FPIAR	Floating-point instruction address register

Examples

The following examples show the information MacsBug displays when you enter various register names:

```
D7
D7 = $0027C2EC    #2605804    #2605804     '•'••'
FPSR
FPSR = $00000000    #0     #0     '••••'
SP
SP = $0037FE9C    #3669660    #3669660     '•7••'
SSP
SSP = $E149F8FD    #3779721469    #-515245827     '•I••'
MSP
MSP = $E149F8FD    #3779721469    #-515245827     '•I••'
CACR
CACR = $00002101    #8449    #8449     '••!•'
```

RN — Set Reference Number

Description The Set Reference Number command restricts symbol references to the specified file.

Syntax RN [*expr*]

expr
evaluates to a hexadecimal integer that specifies the file's reference number. If you omit this parameter, the RN command uses the reference number of the current file, contained in the global variable CurMap.

See also SX

Considerations

You can use the HD command to find out the reference number of a file. Once you've specified a reference number with the RN command, subsequent symbol references are restricted to the file with the specified reference number.

Specifying 0 for *expr* restores the default situation where all symbols match.

The RN command is useful when you're dealing with multiple files that contain the same symbol names. When you're working with MPW tools, for instance, there might be multiple code segments with the same name.

Examples

In the following two examples, the RN command first restricts symbol references to file 0294 and then restores the default condition:

RN 0294
```
Only symbols with a file ref num of 0294 will be shown
```
RN 0
```
All symbols will be shown
```

RS — Restart

Description   The Restart command unmounts all volumes and restarts the Macintosh.

Syntax   RS

See also   RB

Considerations

See the description of the UnmountVol routine in the "File Manager" chapters of *Inside Macintosh,* Volumes II and IV, for additional information about unmounting.

MacsBug defines a number of commands that allow you to leave MacsBug: G, EA, ES, RS, and RB. For additional information about how to select the appropriate command, see Chapter 2, "Getting Started."

Example

RS

S — Step

Description The Step command either steps through the specified number of instructions or traces through your program until the specified condition is met.

Syntax S [n | expr]

n
is a hexadecimal integer specifying the number of instructions that you want to step through.

expr
specifies that the microprocessor step through instructions until the condition specified by *expr* is met.

See also SO

Considerations

If you do not specify a parameter, the S command simply steps through the next instruction. In this case, you can also use Command-S to specify the S command. If you use Command-S, MacsBug ignores any commands in the command line.

The S command traces into subroutine or A-trap calls when these are encountered. If you want to step over subroutine or A-trap calls, use the SO command. If you have unwittingly stepped into a subroutine or A-trap and want to get out, use the MR command. See the description of the MR command earlier in this chapter for additional information.

If you find you have entered a parameter to the S command that cannot be satisfied, use the ES command to terminate the tracing.

If the S command encounters a breakpoint while it is tracing through instructions, the break into MacsBug terminates the S command.

◆ *Note:* Stepping through certain MMU instructions can cause MacsBug to hang. If you're doing MMU programming, be aware that MacsBug executes many instructions while executing an S command and expects a valid memory map.

For additional information about tracing, see "Using MacsBug to Control Program Execution" in Chapter 7.

Example

The following example uses the S command to trace through five instructions:

```
S 5
Step (into)
  _SubPt
      +001C  81E74A    RTS                                | 4E75
  _GetMouse
      +0012  80F140    MOVE.L    (A7)+,(A7)               | 2E9F
      +0014  80F142    RTS                                | 4E75
      +01B8  80F2E6    MOVEM.L   (A7)+,D3/A3              | 4CDF 0808
      +01BC  80F2EA    UNLK      A6                       | 4E5E
```

SB — Set Byte

Description   The Set Byte command assigns a value to bytes, starting at the specified address.

Syntax   SB *addr value* [*value*] ...

addr
specifies the address where the SB command starts assigning the specified value to bytes.

value
specifies either an expression or a string. The string must be enclosed in single quotation marks.

See also   SL, SW

Considerations

If you specify an expression for *value,* the low-order byte of its value is used.

If you specify a string for *value,* the characters are placed in successive bytes. The string length is limited only by the length of the command line.

The SB command sets the dot command to the first byte set. If you press Return after executing an SB command, MacsBug displays the memory just set.

If you want to get some practice using any of the set memory commands (SB, SW, SL, or SM) without causing damage, use the HD command to find out the starting address of a free block in the heap and then use that address as the *addr* parameter to the command. Be careful not to write beyond the boundary of the block. Even if the next block is free, writing over its header will corrupt the heap.

▲ **Warning**   You set memory at your own peril. If you realize that you have specified the wrong address after executing a command that sets memory, it might be safest to use the RS or RB command and start over. ▲

Examples

In the following examples, the SB command sets memory at the specified address; pressing the Return key then displays memory at that address:

```
SB 002B04F8 'new memory'
{Return}
```
Memory set starting at 002B04F8
  002B04F8 6E65 7720 6D65 6D6F 7279 0000 0000 000C new memory••••••

```
SB 002B04F8 1 222 3333
{Return}
```
Memory set starting at 002B04F8
  002B04F8 0122 3333 6D65 6D6F 7279 0000 0000 000C •"33memory••••••

SC6 — Stack Crawl (A6)

Description The Stack Crawl (A6) command lists stack frame information from the oldest to the most current stack frame on the stack. You can use SC as an alias for SC6.

Syntax SC6 [*addr* [*nbytes*]]

addr
specifies the current frame address. If you omit this parameter, the SC6 command uses A6 for *addr*.

nbytes
addr + *nbytes* specifies the upper limit of the range. If you omit this parameter, SC6 uses CurStackBase^ for the upper limit.

See also SC7

Considerations

Information on the stack is normally arranged in units called stack frames. The use of stack frames allows the compiler to generate instructions that reference everything a routine creates and manipulates relative to one address, stored in register A6. The use of stack frames also allows MacsBug to determine the calling chain when one procedure calls another. Knowing what the calling chain is can be very useful when you're tracking down a bug.

By using the optional parameters, you can display the calling chain for a private stack where the top of the stack is specified by *addr* and the stack base is specified by *addr* + *nbytes*.

Although most C and Pascal compilers use register A6 as the frame pointer, register A6 is not often used as the frame pointer in assembly language or in ROM. Thus, it is not uncommon for SC6 to fail. But you should always try SC6 after a crash; it's an enormous help if it works. If SC6 fails, try the SC7 command.

The following listing shows sample output for the SC6 command:

```
SC6
Calling chain using A6 links
  A6 Frame   Caller
  0027BB5C   00218DC6   CONVERSI+0016
  0027BB54   00218D2A   DOMAINEV+003A
  0027BB0A   00218B72   DOCLICK+0038
  0027BAC4   00218AB6   DOMENUDI+002C
  0027BA98   003B418A
  0027B93C   0080F19E   _GetMouse+0070
```

The first row describes the oldest stack frame (procedure); the last row describes the newest stack frame (procedure). You can interpret the information in this listing as follows:

1. At address 00218DC6 the procedure CONVERSI stored an instruction (JSR or BSR) that called the DOMAINEV procedure.

2. At address 00218D2A the procedure DOMAINEV stored an instruction that called the DOCLICK procedure.

3. At address 00218AB6 the procedure DOMENUDI stored an instruction that called an unnamed procedure.

4. At address 003B418A an unnamed procedure stored an instruction that called the GetMouse trap.

The value of A6 when each of the calling procedures is current is listed in the first column.

If MacsBug does not know the procedure name, but the address is in a known resource, MacsBug displays the type of the resource, the number of the resource, the file in which the resource is stored, the name of the resource, and the offset within the resource where the instruction is found; for example:

```
Calling chain using A6 links
 A6 Frame   Caller
 top level  0040C910  'CODE 0001 0294 Main'+34FC
 00488A40   0040B588  'CODE 0001 0294 Main'+2174
 004889E0   0040A5C6  'CODE 0001 0294 Main'+11B2
 004888A6   0041CEB4  'CODE 0007 0294 Init'+0A3C
 00488866   004BD190
 00488832   00813C68  _DialogSelect+007C
 00488788   004BF22A
 00488770   004BF422
 00488736   0003FF5C
 004886F2   0080F19E  _GetMouse+0070
```

For additional information on stack frames, please see "Stack Frames" in Chapter 4.

SC6 error messages

The following conditions have to be met for the SC6 command to work:

- Register A6 or the specified *addr* is the address of a frame on the stack and it points within the range defined by register A7 and CurStackBase^. If this is not the case, the SC6 command returns the message "A6 does not point to a stack frame."
- The SC6 command makes similar assumptions about the optional parameters you supply. If these assumptions are not met, MacsBug displays the message "Bad stack: stack pointer must be even and <= stack base."
- Register A7 must be even and point to the top of the stack; it must also be less than or equal to CurStackBase^. If either of these conditions is not met, the SC6 command displays the message "Damaged stack: A7 must be even and <= CurStackBase."

Example

```
SC6
Calling chain using A6 links
   A6 Frame   Caller
   0027BB5C   00218DC6   CONVERSI+0016
   0027BB54   00218D2A   DOMAINEV+003A
   0027BB0A   00218B72   DOCLICK+0038
   0027BAC4   00218AB6   DOMENUDI+002C
   0027BA98   003B418A
   0027B93C   0080F19E   _GetMouse+0070
```

The following partial disassemblies show how calls are actually made, starting with the DOCLICK procedure.

```
Disassembling from 218b72
  DOCLICK
      +0024  218B5E    MOVE.W    (A7)+,D6                        | 3C1F
      +0026  218B60    MOVE.W    D6,D0                           | 3006
      +0028  218B62    BRA       DOCLICK+00B4    ; 00218BEE      | 6000 008A
      +002C  218B66    SUBQ.W    #$4,A7                          | 594F
      +002E  218B68    MOVE.L    -$0016(A6),-(A7)                | 2F2E FFEA
      +0032  218B6C    _MenuSelect               ; A93D          | A93D
      +0034  218B6E    MOVE.L    (A7)+,D7                        | 2E1F
      +0036  218B70    MOVE.L    D7,-(A7)                        | 2F07
      +0038  218B72    JSR       DOMENUDI        ; 00218A8A      | 4EBA FF16
Disassembling from 218ab6
  DOMENUDI
      +0018  218AA2    SUBQ.W    #$4,A7                          | 594F
      +001A  218AA4    MOVE.W    #$1770,-(A7)                    | 3F3C 1770
      +001E  218AA8    _GetMHandle               ; A949          | A949
      +0020  218AAA    MOVEA.L   (A7)+,A4                        | 285F
      +0022  218AAC    MOVE.W    D6,D0                           | 3006
      +0024  218AAE    BRA       DOMENUDI+007C   ; 00218B06      | 6000 0056
      +0028  218AB2    MOVE.W    D7,D0                           | 3007
      +002A  218AB4    BRA.S     DOMENUDI+0034   ; 00218ABE      | 6008
      +002C  218AB6    JSR       DOABOUTD        ; 00218A1C      | 4EBA FF64
Disassembling from 003b418a
  No procedure name
             3B4172    BEQ.S     *+$0008         ; 003B417A      | 6706
             3B4174    ORI.B     #$80,$0071(A0)                  | 0028 0080 0071
             3B417A    MOVE.L    CurrentA5,-(A7)                 | 2F38 0904
             3B417E    JSR       *+$39FA         ; 003B7B78      | 4EBA 39F8
             3B4182    MOVE.L    D0,D5                           | 2A00
             3B4184    MOVE.L    D4,-(A7)                        | 2F04
             3B4186    MOVE.L    D3,-(A7)                        | 2F03
             3B4188    MOVEA.L   A2,A0                           | 204A
             3B418A    JSR       (A0)                            | 4E90
```

SC7 — Stack Crawl (A7)

Description The Stack Crawl (A7) command displays a possible calling chain by listing the stack addresses where each caller's return address is stored.

Syntax SC7 [addr[nbytes]]

addr
specifies the current frame address. If you omit this parameter, the SC7 command uses A7 for *addr*.

nbytes
addr + *nbytes* specifies the upper limit of the range. If you omit this parameter, SC7 uses CurStackBase^ for the upper limit.

See also SC6

Considerations

If information on the stack is set up using stack frames, the SC6 command gives you much more reliable information about the calling chain than the SC7 command. If information is not set up using stack frames, use the SC7 command to display a possible calling chain.

By using the optional parameters, you can display the calling chain for a private stack where the top of the stack is specified by *addr* and the stack base is specified by *addr* + *nbytes*.

Not all values displayed by the SC7 command are necessarily valid, and you will want to do some additional checking to make sure that the locations listed by the SC7 command do indeed contain return addresses. For example, SC7 can return an invalid value if you execute an SC7 command just at the point where a procedure has allocated space for its local variables but has not initialized those variables. If an old return address is stored in the space allocated for one of the local variables, the SC7 command will report it to you as a return address, even though it is just leftover information from a procedure that has already finished executing.

When a JSR instruction executes, it saves the address of the following instruction on the stack before jumping to the new location. In the following example, before jumping to the DOCLICK procedure, the JSR instruction would save the address of the next instruction, BRA DOMAINEV+00A0, on the stack.

```
+0036  218D26    PEA      -$0020(A6)                        | 486E FFE0
+003A  218D2A    JSR      DOCLICK         ; 00218B3A        | 4EBA FE0E
+003E  218D2E    BRA      DOMAINEV+00A0   ; 00218D90        | 6000 0060
```

When the DOCLICK routine returns with an RTS instruction, it returns to the saved address; in this case, it returns to the instruction at 218D2E.

The SC7 command checks the stack from A7 to CurStackBase^ for possible return addresses: it checks that the value is even, that it is a valid ROM or RAM address, and that it is the address of an instruction immediately following a JSR, BSR, or A-trap instruction.

SC7 display

The SC7 command displays a calling chain in the same order as the SC6 command: from the oldest to the newest procedure called. Here is sample output from the SC7 command:

```
SC7
Return addresses on the stack
  Stack Addr   Frame Addr   Caller
    0027BB58    0027BB54    00218DC6    CONVERSI+0016
    0027BB50                002182C2    DOINITRO+0032
    0027BB30    0027BB2C    00218706    DOSETUPM+0054
    0027BB0E    0027BB0A    00218D2A    DOMAINEV+003A
    0027BAFA                003B441E
    0027BAC8    0027BAC4    00218B72    DOCLICK+0038
    0027BAB4                003B51CA
    0027BAB0                003B51C2
    0027BA9C    0027BA98    00218AB6    DOMENUDI+002C
    0027BA90                008119DA    _NewMenu+01EC
    0027BA8C                00810DA4    _DisableItem+0014
    0027BA78                003B1F40
```

- The first column contains the address on the stack where the return address (or what the SC7 command considers to be a likely candidate) is stored.
- The second column contains the value of A6 when the procedure that is being called is current. With respect to the listing above, the value 27BB0A turns out to be the value of A6 when the DOCLICK procedure is current.

- The last column contains the address of a JSR or BSR instruction and, if that instruction is part of a procedure or A-trap, the name of the procedure or A-trap and the offset of the instruction within the routine. If MacsBug does not know the procedure name, but the address is in a known resource, MacsBug displays the type of the resource, the number of the resource, the file in which the resource is stored, the name of the resource, and the offset within the resource where the instruction is found; for example:

```
'CODE 0007 0294 Init'+0A3C
```

If the SC7 command lists a frame address alongside the address of a return value, it is nearly certain that the address contains a genuine return value. You need only test the ones for which no frame address is listed.

SC7 error messages

The SC7 command assumes that register A7 is even and points to the top of the stack and that it is smaller than or equal to CurStackBase^. If this is not the case, MacsBug displays the message "Damaged stack: A7 must be even and <= CurStackBase."

The SC7 command makes similar assumptions about the optional parameters you supply. If these assumptions are not met, MacsBug displays the message "Bad stack: stack pointer must be even and <= stack base."

SHOW — Show

Description The Show command allows you to display any region of memory in the stack area of the status region, using one of several formats. By default the Show command displays the stack starting at the address stored in register A7 and shows any changes to the value of A7.

Syntax SHOW [*addr* | '*addr*'] [L | W | A | LA]

addr
specifies the address from which memory is shown. If you specify '*addr*', the specified address is evaluated each time the display is updated. If you specify *addr*, the specified address is evaluated when you execute the Show command, and the resulting value is shown until you change the Show options by executing another Show command.

L
specifies that memory be shown in long word format.

W
specifies that memory be shown in word format.

A
specifies that memory be shown in ASCII format.

LA
specifies that memory be shown in combined long word and ASCII format.

Considerations

The way you specify *addr* (with or without quotation marks) affects only the display of the address; if values in the memory range displayed change, MacsBug updates the display whether or not *addr* is in quotation marks.

Entering SHOW without parameters cycles between the four display formats. The Show command assumes you want information displayed starting at the last specified *addr*.

To restore the default display, enter

`SHOW 'SP' L`

The Show command is very useful, although it is undervalued and not well known. It puts the stack area of the MacsBug display at your disposal to display whatever value or values you need to keep track of as you're debugging or testing code.

Example

The following command shows routine parameters for routines using LINK instructions to set up the stack frame:

`SHOW 'A6 + 8'`

SL — Set Long

Description The Set Long command assigns a value to long words, starting at the specified address.

Syntax SL *addr value* [*value*] ...

addr
specifies the address where the SL command starts assigning the specified *value* to bytes.

value
specifies either an expression or a string. The string must be enclosed in single quotation marks.

See also SB, SW

Considerations

If you specify an expression for *value,* it is evaluated to a 32-bit value.

If you specify a string for *value,* the characters are placed in successive bytes. The string length is limited only by the length of the command line.

The SL command sets the dot command to the address of the first long word set. If you press Return after executing an SB command, MacsBug displays the memory just set.

If you want to get some practice using any of the set memory commands (SB, SW, SL, or SM) without causing damage, use the HD command to find out the starting address of a free block in the heap and then use that address as the *addr* parameter to the command. Be careful not to write beyond the boundary of the block. Even if the next block is free, writing over its header will corrupt the heap.

▲ **Warning** You set memory at your own peril. If you realize that you have specified the wrong address after executing a command that sets memory, it might be safest to use the RS or RB command and start over. ▲

Examples

In the following examples, the SL command sets memory at the specified address; pressing the Return key then displays memory at that address:

```
SL 002B04F8 'new set long memory'
{Return}
```
Memory set starting at 002B04F8
 002B04F8 6E65 7720 7365 746C 6F6E 6720 6D65 6D6F   new setlong memo


```
SL 002B04F8   1 222 3333
{Return}
```
Memory set starting at 002B04F8
 002B04F8 0000 0001 0000 0222 0000 3333 6D65 6D6F   •••••••"••33memo

SM — Set Memory

Description The Set Memory command assigns a value to long words, starting at the specified address.

Syntax SM *addr value* [*value*] ...

addr
specifies the address where the SM command starts assigning the specified *value* to bytes.

value
specifies either an expression or a string. The string must be enclosed in single quotation marks.

See also SB, SL, SW

Considerations

If you specify an expression for *value*, the size of the assignment made is determined by the size of *value*. You can set specific assignment sizes by using the SB, SL, or SW command.

If you specify a string for *value*, the characters are placed in successive bytes. The string length is limited only by the length of the command line.

The SM command sets the dot command to the address of the first long word set. If you press Return after executing an SM command, MacsBug displays the memory just set.

If you want to get some practice using any of the set memory commands (SB, SW, SL, or SM) without causing damage, use the HD command to find out the starting address of a free block in the heap and then use that address as the *addr* parameter to the command. Be careful not to write beyond the boundary of the block. Even if the next block is free, writing over its header will corrupt the heap.

▲ **Warning** You set memory at your own peril. If you realize that you have specified the wrong address after executing a command that sets memory, it might be safest to use the RS or RB command and start over. ▲

Examples

In the following examples, the SM command sets memory at the specified address; pressing the Return key then displays memory at that address:

```
SM 003E8BF4 'set memory'
{Return}
Memory set starting at 003E8BF4
 003E8BF4   7365 7420 6D65 6D6F  7279 019D 0000 0014   set memory••••••
```

```
SM 003E8BF4 1000 222 3333
{Return}
Memory set starting at 003E8BF4
Displaying memory from 003E8BF4
 003E8BF4   1000 0222 3333 6D6F  7279 019D 0000 0014   •••"33mory••••••
```

Note that if you specify the expressions used with the SB, SW, or SL commands with the SM command:

```
SM 003E8BF4 1 222 3333
```

MacsBug returns the error message shown below. MacsBug 6.2 implements the SM command differently than MacsBug 6.1.

```
Attempt to write the value 0222 to the odd address 003E8BF5
Warning: The command completed without using all parameters
```

SO — Step Over

Description   The Step Over command steps through the specified number of instructions or until the specified expression is TRUE.

Syntax   SO | T [*n* | *expr*]

n
is a hexadecimal integer specifying the number of instructions to step through.

expr
specifies that the microprocessor step through instructions until the condition specified by *expr* is met.

See also   S

Considerations

If you do not specify any parameters for the SO command, it simply steps through the next instruction. In that case, it might be easier to use the Command-T option, which accomplishes the same thing. Any commands sitting in the command line when you enter Command-T are ignored.

You can use T as an alias for SO.

In general the SO command behaves exactly like the S command except that it steps over traps, JSRs, and BSRs, treating them like a single instruction.

If you have entered a number that cannot be reached or an expression that cannot be satisfied, use the ES command to terminate stepping.

When stepping over a toolbox trap with the auto-pop bit set, MacsBug correctly returns to the address on the top of the stack at the time of the trap call (instead of to the address immediately after the trap).

If you step over a LoadSeg trap, MacsBug will stop at the first instruction of the loaded segment.

◆ *Note:* Stepping through certain MMU instructions can cause MacsBug to hang. If you're doing MMU programming, be aware that MacsBug executes many instructions while executing an S command and expects a valid memory map.

Example

The following command steps through five instructions:

```
SO 5
```
```
Step (over)
  No procedure name
          00A346    RTS                                          | 4E75
  _GetMouse
     +0176  80F2A4  MOVEA.L   (A7)+,A0                           | 205F
     +0178  80F2A6  _HUnlock                      ; A02A         | A02A
     +017A  80F2A8  CLR.W     (A3)                               | 4253
     +017C  80F2AA  BRA.S     _GetMouse+018       ; 4080F2BC     | 6010
```

SS — Step Spy

Description The Step Spy command calculates a checksum for a specified memory range or for a word at a specified address before executing an instruction. If the checksum value changes, the SS command invokes MacsBug.

Syntax SS *addr1* [*addr2*]

addr1
specifies that MacsBug should calculate a checksum for the long word at *addr1*. If you specify *addr2*, MacsBug calculates a checksum for the range of memory defined by *addr1* and *addr2*.

See also ATSS, CS

Considerations

Checksumming is a technique used by the debugger to determine whether the contents of memory have changed. The debugger adds all the values in the specified memory range and saves the result. After one or more instructions are executed (depending on whether checksumming is implemented by the ATSS, CS, or SS command), the debugger recalculates a sum for the same memory range and compares the new result to the saved result. If the values differ, MacsBug is invoked.

The SS command works fastest when you are calculating a checksum for *addr1*.

When you enter the SS command, the application begins to execute immediately. When the long word or memory range changes, MacsBug displays the debugging screen and clears the action set with the SS command. At this point, you know that the instruction that caused memory to change is the instruction preceding the instruction pointed to by the PC.

The SS command is very slow. The ATSS (A-trap Step Spy) command is much faster because it only checks memory before executing A-traps, whereas the SS command checks after each instruction. You can use the ATSS command to zero in on a range of instructions containing the instruction that is affecting the value that concerns you. When the ATSS command invokes MacsBug, you know that the A-trap that is about to execute is not responsible for the change in value. You also know that the instruction that you are looking for is either the previous A-trap or any instruction executed between the previous A-trap and the instruction pointed to by the PC. You can now use the SS command to find that instruction.

The SS command might also be useful to slow down certain routines—such as those that draw to the screen—so you can see how they work.

Example

The following example sets SS to checksum the long word at $9D6:

```
SS 09D6
Checksumming from 000009D6 to 000009D9
Step Spy checksum was changed at 4080EF38 _BlockMove+0096
 Step Spy cleared
```

SW — Set Word

Description The Set Word command assigns a value to words, starting at the specified address.

Syntax SW *addr value* [*value*] ...

addr
specifies the address where the SW command starts assigning the specified *value* to words.

value
specifies either an expression or a string. The string must be enclosed in single quotation marks.

See also SB, SL, SM

Considerations

If you specify an expression for *value,* the low-order word of its value is used.

If you specify a string for *value,* MacsBug places the characters in successive bytes. The string length is limited only by the length of the command line.

The SW command sets the dot command to the first byte set. If you press Return after executing an SB command, MacsBug displays the memory just set.

If you want to get some practice using any of the set memory commands (SB, SW, SL, or SM) without causing damage, use the HD command to find out the starting address of a free block in the heap and then use that address as the *addr* parameter to the command. Be careful not to write beyond the boundary of the block. Even if the next block is free, writing over its header will corrupt the heap.

▲ **Warning** You set memory at your own peril. If you realize that you have specified the wrong address after executing a command that sets memory, it might be safest to use the RS or RB command and start over. ▲

Examples

In the following examples, the SW command sets memory at the specified address; pressing the Return key then displays memory at that address:

```
SW   002B04F8    'new sw memory '
{Return}
Memory set starting at 002B04F8
 002B04F8   6E65 7720 7377 206D  656D 6F72 7920 2020   new sw memory


SW   002B04F8    1 222 3333
{Return}
Memory set starting at 002B04F8
 002B04F8   0001 0222 3333 6E67  206D 656D 6F72 790C   •••"33ng memory•
```

SWAP — Swap

Description The Swap command controls the frequency of screen swapping between MacsBug and the application. The way swapping takes place depends on whether you use the same screen for both your application and MacsBug or one screen for MacsBug and a different screen for your application.

Syntax SWAP

Considerations

If you are using the same screen for both MacsBug and your application, the SWAP command toggles between the following two modes:

- It traces through the specified instructions or A-traps, displaying the MacsBug screen after each instruction or A-trap has finished executing.
- It traces through the specified instructions or A-traps without displaying the MacsBug screen.

If you are using only one screen, you can get stuck if you choose the swapping mode and enter a step or trace command that includes no breakpoint. For example, if you toggle SWAP on and enter ATT, you will find yourself staring helplessly at a flickering screen, as MacsBug loops rapidly ever onward. You can stop it by pressing the NMI switch, or you can prevent the situation from arising in the first place by specifying a break at an instruction you know will execute or that you can cause to execute. For example, if you enter

`ATT; ATB MenuKey`

and then enter a Command-key combination that has some meaning to your application, you can invoke MacsBug and stop the tracing.

If you are using one screen for your application and a different screen for the MacsBug display, the SWAP command toggles between the following two modes:

- It traces through the specified instructions or A-traps, displaying MacsBug output on the other screen after each instruction or A-trap has finished executing.
- It traces through the specified instructions or A-traps while keeping the MacsBug display always visible on the other screen.

See Chapter 2, "Getting Started," for additional information about displaying MacsBug on a different screen.

Examples

If you use a single screen, the SWAP command displays the following messages:

```
SWAP
Display will only be swapped at a break
SWAP
Display will be swapped after each trace or step
```

If you use two screens, the SWAP command displays the following messages:

```
SWAP
MacsBug will remain visible always
SWAP
MacsBug will only be swapped at a break
```

SX — Symbol Exchange

Description The Symbol Exchange command toggles between allowing and not allowing symbol names in place of addresses.

Syntax SX [ON | OFF]

If you omit the parameter, the SX command toggles between the two modes. The default setting is ON.

See also IL, RN

Considerations

By default you can use a symbol name in place of an address in specifying a command parameter. MacsBug also displays the addresses of disassembled instructions as offsets from the beginning of the procedure to which they belong. To do this, MacsBug must translate symbol names into addresses in the first case, or addresses into offsets from symbol names in the second case. Since this process can be slow, MacsBug provides a way to disable it. Disabling it, of course, can slow *you* down, since you must then specify all addresses as absolute addresses.

Example

In the following example, the IR command disassembles the DOCLICK procedure. Then the SX command is used to turn symbols off, and the same code is disassembled once again. (Only part of the procedure is shown.)

```
IR doclick
```
Disassembling from doclick
DOCLICK
```
  +0000   218B3A    LINK      A6,#$FFCE           | 4E56 FFCE
  +0004   218B3E    MOVEM.L   D6/D7,-(A7)         | 48E7 0300
  +0008   218B42    MOVEA.L   $0008(A6),A0        | 206E 0008
  +000C   218B46    LEA       -$0020(A6),A1       | 43EE FFE0
  +0010   218B4A    MOVE.L    (A0)+,(A1)+         | 22D8
  +0012   218B4C    MOVE.L    (A0)+,(A1)+         | 22D8
  +0014   218B4E    MOVE.L    (A0)+,(A1)+         | 22D8
  +0016   218B50    MOVE.L    (A0)+,(A1)+         | 22D8
  +0018   218B52    SUBQ.W    #$2,A7              | 554F
  +001A   218B54    MOVE.L    -$0016(A6),-(A7)    | 2F2E FFEA
  +001E   218B58    PEA       -$0026(A6)          | 486E FFDA
```
SX

Symbols disabled

```
IR 218b3a
```
Disassembling from 218b3a
No procedure name
```
          218B3A    LINK      A6,#$FFCE           | 4E56 FFCE
          218B3E    MOVEM.L   D6/D7,-(A7)         | 48E7 0300
          218B42    MOVEA.L   $0008(A6),A0        | 206E 0008
          218B46    LEA       -$0020(A6),A1       | 43EE FFE0
          218B4A    MOVE.L    (A0)+,(A1)+         | 22D8
          218B4C    MOVE.L    (A0)+,(A1)+         | 22D8
          218B4E    MOVE.L    (A0)+,(A1)+         | 22D8
          218B50    MOVE.L    (A0)+,(A1)+         | 22D8
          218B52    SUBQ.W    #$2,A7              | 554F
          218B54    MOVE.L    -$0016(A6),-(A7)    | 2F2E FFEA
          218B58    PEA       -$0026(A6)          | 486E FFDA
```

TD — Display CPU Registers

Description The Display CPU Registers command displays all CPU registers in the output region of the MacsBug display.

Syntax TD

See also TF, TM

Considerations

Since most of the registers displayed in the status region of the MacsBug screen are continuously updated, you can use the TD command to record values between commands. You can also use the TD command to display the values of special registers in the 68020 and 68030 that are not shown in the status region of the MacsBug display.

Use the TM command to display the contents of the 68030 MMU registers; use the TF command to display the contents of the 68881 registers.

For additional information about the 68020 and 68030 registers display, consult the appropriate Motorola manual.

Example

```
TD
68030 Registers
  D0 = 00000000     A0 = A003E9D8     USP  = C93F9E97
  D1 = 00000007     A1 = 0027DE84     MSP  = E149F8FD
  D2 = FFFF0001     A2 = 0027DE84     ISP  = 0037FE9C
  D3 = 00000000     A3 = 0027DE84     VBR  = 00000000
  D4 = 0028FFFF     A4 = 0027DA30     CACR = 00002101    SFC = 7
  D5 = 00280000     A5 = 003BFFD8     CAAR = EF9FCFF2    DFC = 7
  D6 = 0038011C     A6 = 0037FEAC     PC   = A003E9DA
  D7 = 0027C2EC     A7 = 0037FE9C     SR   = SmXnzvc     Int = 0
```

TF — Total Floating-Point Register Display

Description   The Total Floating-Point Register Display command displays all 68881 registers.

Syntax   TF

See also   TD, TM

Considerations

The 68881 registers are not shown in the status region of the MacsBug display.

To display the 68000, 68020, or 68030 registers, use the TD command. To display the 68030 MMU registers, use the TM command.

For additional information about the 68881 registers, consult the Motorola manual.

Example

```
TF
68881/68882 FPU Registers
 FP0  = 4011 A1F74CA2 339C0EBF        3.31706394800000000e+5
 FP1  = 7FFF FFFFFFFF FFFFFFFF        NAN(255)
 FP2  = 7FFF FFFFFFFF FFFFFFFF        NAN(255)
 FP3  = 7FFF FFFFFFFF FFFFFFFF        NAN(255)
 FP4  = 7FFF FFFFFFFF FFFFFFFF        NAN(255)
 FP5  = 7FFF FFFFFFFF FFFFFFFF        NAN(255)
 FP6  = 7FFF FFFFFFFF FFFFFFFF        NAN(255)
 FP7  = 7FFF FFFFFFFF FFFFFFFF        NAN(255)
        EE MC            CC QT ES AE
 FPCR = 00 00     FPSR = 00 00 02 08  FPIAR = 00000000
```

TM — Total MMU Display

Description   The Total MMU Display command displays the MMU registers common to the 68851 and 68030 microprocessors.

Syntax   TM

See also   TD, TF

Considerations

The MMU registers are not shown in the status region of the MacsBug display.

You can use the TM command to determine whether a Macintosh II has a PMMU chip installed without opening the cover.

To display the 68000, 68020, or 68030 registers, use the TD command. To display the 68881 registers, use the TF command.

Example

The following command displays the MMU registers for a Macintosh with a 68030 microprocessor:

```
TM
68030 MMU Registers
  CRP = 7FFF000240800050        TC  = 80F84500
  SRP = 02480814FFFFEFC4        PSR = EE47
```

TMP — List Templates

Description The List Templates command lists all templates that match or partially match the specified name.

Syntax TMP [*name*]

name
is a string of characters. The TMP command displays the names of all templates that begin with *name*. If you omit *name*, the TMP command lists all template names.

Considerations

You use templates to control the way MacsBug displays data in memory.

You can use the names of templates defined by 'mxwt' resource 100 to display data structures created and maintained by toolbox or operating system managers. You can also create your own templates to display data structures created by your application. For additional information about the 'mxwt' resource and creating your own templates, see "Using Templates to Display Memory" in Chapter 4.

Example

The following command displays all currently loaded templates whose names begin with C:

```
TMP C
ControlRecord
ColorSpec
ColorTable
CGrafPort
CntrlParamBlockRec
```

WH — Where

Description The Where command returns information about the location of the specified trap, symbol, or address.

Syntax WH [*addr* | *trap*]

addr
specifies that you want information about the location of the instruction at *addr*.

trap
specifies the trap name or number whose location you want.

Considerations

Use the Where command after a crash to determine the procedure that's currently executing.

If you do not specify a parameter, the Where command uses the program counter for *addr*.

If you specify an address in ROM, the Where command looks for the preceding trap and displays the address of the instruction as an offset from the start of the trap. (Sometimes it returns the wrong trap name for ROM addresses.)

If you specify an address in RAM, the Where command tells you if the instruction is in a heap block and, if so, which heap block. The Where command also tells you the name of the routine containing the instruction at the specified address and the offset of the instruction from the start of the routine.

If you specify a trap name or number, the Where command tells you the corresponding number or name. The Where command also tells you whether the code for the trap is in ROM or in RAM. If the code is in RAM, the trap is patched.

If the specified address is in a block header, the Where command displays that information—for example:

WH 0027A0F4

```
Address 0027A0F4 is in the Application heap at 00279FB8
It is FFFFFFF8 bytes into this heap block (in the block header):
    Start     Length       Tag  Mstr Ptr Lock Prg  Type    ID    File       Name
  • 0027A0FC 00000016+02    R    0027A0F0      L
```

Note that in this case the number of bytes specified in the output represents a negative number. In this example FFFFFFF8 is –8. A negative number is used because the heap block begins with the first byte of the contents region, so the header region is at a negative offset from the beginning of the contents region.

Examples

WH 00218B3A

```
Address 00218B3A is in the Application heap at DOCLICK
It is 000008AE bytes into this heap block:
    Start     Length       Tag  Mstr Ptr Lock Prg  Type    ID    File       Name
  • 0021828C 00000B50+04    R    00218268      L    P   CODE    0002  0526
```

WH menuselect

```
Trap number A93D (_MenuSelect) starts at 003C02A2 in RAM
It is 0019F732 bytes into this heap block:
    Start     Length       Tag  Mstr Ptr Lock Prg  Type    ID    File       Name
    00220B70 00054FF0+00    F
```

WH getmouse

```
Trap number A972 (_GetMouse) starts at 4080F12E in ROM
```

Appendix A Command Summary

This appendix provides two listings of MacsBug commands: Table A-1 lists MacsBug commands by functional category; Table A-2 lists MacsBug commands in alphabetical order. The alphabetical listing also includes a description and syntax for each command.

The following conventions are used to describe MacsBug commands:

literal	Plain text indicates a word that must appear in the command exactly as shown. Special symbols (-, §, &, and so on) must also be entered exactly as shown.
italics	Italics indicate a parameter that you must replace with specific information.
[*optional*]	Brackets indicate that the enclosed elements are optional. Omit the brackets when you enter the command.
...	Ellipses (...) indicate that the preceding item can be repeated one or more times.
		A vertical bar (	) indicates an either/or choice.

Command names and filenames are not sensitive to case.

For more information about each command, see Chapter 9, "MacsBug Commands."

■ **Table A-1** MacsBug commands by functional category

Function	Commands
Flow control	G — Go GT — Go Till S — Step SO — Step Over SS — Step Spy MR — Magic Return
Breakpoints	BR — Breakpoint BRC — Breakpoint Clear BRD — Breakpoint Display BRM — Multiple Breakpoints
A-traps	ATB — A-trap Break ATT — A-trap Trace ATHC — A-trap Heap Check ATSS — A-trap Step Spy ATC — A-trap Clear ATD — A-trap Display ATR — A-trap Record ATP — A-trap Playback DSC — Discipline
Disassembly	IL — Disassemble From Address IP — Disassemble Around Address ID — Disassemble One Line IR — Disassemble Until End of Procedure DH — Disassemble Hexadecimal
Stack	SC6 — Stack Crawl (A6) SC7 — Stack Crawl (A7)

(continued)

■ **Table A-1** MacsBug commands by functional category (continued)

Function	Commands
Heap	HX — Heap Exchange
	HZ — Heap Zone
	HD — Heap Display
	HT — Heap Totals
	HC — Heap Check
	HS — Heap Scramble
Symbol	RN — Set Reference Number
	SX — Symbol Exchange
Memory	DM — Display Memory
	TMP — List templates
	DP — Display Page
	DB — Display Byte
	DW — Display Word
	DL — Display Long
	SM — Set Memory
	SB — Set Byte
	SW — Set Word
	SL — Set Long
Register	TD — CPU Registers Display
	TF — Total Floating-Point Register Display
	TM — Total MMU Display Registers
Macro	MC — Macro Create
	MCC — Macro Clear
	MCD — Macro Display
Exit MacsBug	RB — Reboot
	RS — Restart
	ES — Exit to Shell
	EA — Exit to Application

(continued)

■ **Table A-1** MacsBug commands by functional category (continued)

Function	Commands
MacsBug information	HELP — Help
	DV — Display Version
MacsBug output	LOG — Log (to a Printer or File)
	SHOW — Show
	SWAP — Swap
Miscellaneous	WH — Where
	F — Find
	CS — Checksum
	HOW — Display Break Message
	DX — Debugger Exchange
	RAD — Toggle Register Name Syntax

■ **Table A-2** MacsBug commands in alphabetical order

Command	Syntax and description
ATB	ATB[A] [*trap* [*trap*]] [*n* | *expr*] [';*cmd* [;*cmd*]...'] The A-trap Break command invokes MacsBug whenever the microprocessor encounters the specified A-trap.
ATC	ATC [*trap* [*trap*]] The A-trap Clear command clears actions set on all the specified A-traps with the ATB, ATT, ATHC, and ATSS commands.
ATD	ATD The A-trap Display command displays information about all actions currently set with the ATB, ATT, ATHC, and ATSS commands.
ATHC	ATHC[A] [*trap* [*trap*]] [*n* | *expr*] The A-trap Heap Check command checks the heap before executing the specified A-trap. If the heap is bad, MacsBug displays the debugging screen and an error message.
ATP	ATP The A-trap Playback command displays the information saved while trap recording is on. If trap recording is turned off, the ATP command displays information from the most recent ATR command.
ATR	ATR[A] [ON | OFF] The A-trap Record command turns trap recording on and off.
ATSS	ATSS[A] [*trap* [*trap*]] [*n* | *expr*], *addr1* [*addr2*] The A-trap Step Spy command calculates a checksum for a specified memory range or for a word at a specified address before executing the specified traps. If the checksum value changes, the ATSS command invokes MacsBug and does not execute the A-traps.
ATT	ATT[A] [*trap* [*trap*]] [*n* | *expr*] The A-trap Trace command writes information to the MacsBug output buffer whenever the mciroprocessor encounters the specified A-trap, without stopping the current program.

(continued)

■ **Table A-2** MacsBug commands in alphabetical order (continued)

Command	Syntax and description
BR	BR addr[n	expr][';cmd[;cmd]...'] The Breakpoint command sets a breakpoint at the specified address.
BRC	BRC [addr] The Breakpoint Clear command clears the breakpoint at the specified address.
BRD	BRD The Breakpoint Display command displays addresses where breakpoints are currently set.
BRM	BRM name The Multiple Breakpoints command allows you to set breakpoints using partial name matching.
CS	CS [addr[addr]] The Checksum command allows you to determine whether the contents at the specified address or within the specified memory range have changed.
DB	DB [addr] The Display Byte command displays the byte at the specified address.
DH	DH expr ... The Disassemble Hexadecimal command converts one or more hexadecimal values to assembler mnemonics.
DL	DL [addr] The Display Long command displays the long word at the specified address.
DM	DM [addr[nbytes| template	basic type]] The Display Memory command displays memory starting from the specified address.

(continued)

- **Table A-2** MacsBug commands in alphabetical order (continued)

Command	Syntax and description
DP	DP [addr] The Display Page command displays a page (128 bytes) of memory starting from the specified address.
DSC	DSC[A][X] [ON | OFF] The Discipline command turns the Discipline utility on and off. You use Discipline to check the validity of the parameters you pass to A-traps and the values returned to your applications by the A-traps.
DV	DV The Display Version command displays the version of MacsBug currently in use.
DW	DW [addr] The Display Word command displays the word at the specified address.
DX	DX [ON | OFF] The Debugger Exchange command disables user breaks.
EA	EA The Exit to Application command restarts the application from which MacsBug was invoked.
ES	ES The Exit to Shell command returns you to the current shell.
F	F[B | W | L | P] addr nbytes expr F addr nbytes expr | "string" The Find command searches for a specified pattern of bytes.
G	G [addr] The Go command allows you to leave MacsBug and resume program execution.

(continued)

■ **Table A-2** MacsBug commands in alphabetical order (continued)

Command	Syntax and description
GT	GT *addr* [';*cmd* [;*cmd*] ...'] The Go Till command executes your program until the program counter reaches the specified address.
HC	HC The Heap Check command tells you whether the information in the heap zone header or in any of the block headers in the current heap has been corrupted.
HD	HD [*qualifier*] The Heap Display command displays information about the blocks in the current heap.
HELP	HELP [*cmd*	*topic*] The Help command displays information about the given command or section.
HOW	HOW The HOW (Display Break Message) command redisplays the break message that was displayed when you initially entered MacsBug.
HS	HS [*addr*] The Heap Scramble command turns heap scrambling on and off. When heap scrambling is on, the Memory Manager moves all unlocked relocatable blocks whenever the move is legitimate—that is, during every A-trap call that can allocate memory directly or indirectly.
HT	HT The Heap Totals command displays information about the current heap.
HX	HX [*addr*] The Heap Exchange command selects the current heap.
HZ	HZ [*addr*] The Heap Zone command lists all heap zones starting at *addr*.

(continued)

■ **Table A-2** MacsBug commands in alphabetical order (continued)

Command	Syntax and description
ID	ID [*addr*] The ID (Disassemble One Line) command disassembles one line, starting at the specified address.
IL	IL [*addr*[*n*]] The IL (Disassemble From Address) command disassembles *n* lines starting from an address you specify.
IP	IP [*addr*] The IP (Disassemble Around Address) command disassembles a half page (64 bytes) centered around the specified address.
IR	IR [*addr*] The IR (Disassemble Until End of Procedure) command disassembles code from the address you specify until the end of the procedure containing the instruction at the specified address.
LOG	LOG [*pathname*	Printer] The Log to a Printer or File command sends MacsBug output to the specified text file or to an ImageWriter via the serial port.
MC	MC *name*'*expr*'	*expr* The Macro Create command creates a new macro with the given name that expands to the expression you specify.
MCC	MCC [*name*] The Macro Clear command clears the specified macro or all macros.
MCD	MCD [*name*] The Macro Display command displays the specified macro or all macros whose names begin with the specified characters.

(continued)

■ **Table A-2** MacsBug commands in alphabetical order (continued)

Command	Syntax and description
MR	MR [*param*] If you have accidentally stepped into a JSR, BSR, or trap call that you meant to step over, executing the Magic Return command before executing any of the subroutine or trap code will execute the equivalent of a GT (Go Till) command to the instruction immediately after the subroutine or A-trap call.
RAD	RAD The Toggle Register Name Syntax command allows you to specify the address and data registers in two different ways.
RB	RB The Reboot command restarts the system. It unmounts the startup volume before restarting.
Registers	*registerName* [= *expr*	:= *expr*] The Registers command allows you to display the value of a register or assign a value to a register.
RN	RN [*expr*] The Set Reference Number command restricts symbol references to the specified file.
RS	RS The Restart command unmounts all volumes and restarts the Macintosh.
S	S [*n*	*expr*] The Step command either steps through the specified number of instructions or traces through your program until the specified condition is met.
SB	SB *addr value* [*value*] The Set Byte command assigns a value to bytes, starting at the specified address.

(continued)

■ **Table A-2** MacsBug commands in alphabetical order (continued)

Command	Syntax and description
SC6	SC6 [*addr* [*nbytes*]] The Stack Crawl (A6) command lists stack frame information from the oldest to the most current stack frame on the stack. You can use SC as an alias for SC6.
SC7	SC7 [*addr* [*nbytes*]] The Stack Crawl (A7) command displays a possible calling chain by listing the stack addresses where each caller's return address is stored.
SHOW	SHOW [*addr*	'*addr*'] [L	W	A	LA] The Show command allows you to display any region in memory using one of several formats. By default the Show command displays the stack starting at the address stored in register A7 and shows any changes to the value of A7.
SL	SL *addr value* [*value*] ... The Set Long command assigns a value to long words, starting at the specified address.
SM	SM *addr value* [*value*] ... The Set Memory command assigns a value to long words, starting at the specified address.
SO	SO	T [*n*	*expr*] The Step Over command steps through the specified number of instructions or until the specified expression is TRUE.
SS	SS *addr1* [*addr2*] The Step Spy command calculates a checksum for a specified memory range or for a word at a specified address before executing an instruction. If the checksum value changes, the SS command invokes MacsBug.
SW	SW *addr value* [*value*] ... The Set Word command assigns a value to words, starting at the specified address.

(continued)

■ **Table A-2** MacsBug commands in alphabetical order (continued)

Command	Syntax and description
SWAP	SWAP The Swap command controls the frequency of screen swapping between MacsBug and the application. The way swapping takes place depends on whether you use the same screen for both your application and MacsBug or use one screen for MacsBug and a separate screen for your application.
SX	SX [ON	OFF] The Symbol Exchange command toggles between allowing and not allowing symbol names in place of addresses.
TD	TD The TD (Display CPU Registers) command displays all CPU registers in the output region of the MacsBug display.
TF	TF The Total Floating-Point Register Display command displays all 68881 registers.
TM	TM The Total MMU Display command displays the MMU registers common to the 68851 and 68030 microprocessors.
TMP	TMP [name] The List Templates command lists all templates that match or partially match the specified name.
WH	WH [addr	trap] The Where command returns information about the location of the specified trap, symbol, or address.

Appendix B Error Messages

This appendix lists MacsBug error messages in alphabetical order.

64-bit registers not allowed in expressions

All expressions are evaluated as unsigned 32-bit values; floating-point registers and some MMU registers cannot be evaluated in this context.

68881 not installed

The TF command functions only if the system has a 68881 installed. This error also occurs if you try to display or set an individual floating-point register.

A6 does not point to a stack frame

The SC6 command assumes that register A6, or the parameter if specified, is the address of the first frame on the stack. It must point within the range specified by register A7 and CurStackBase.

Addresses must be even

Any command that takes an address parameter can get one of these errors. The first is a 68000 bus error exception, and the second is an address error exception.

Address range must be entered before comparisons

The CS command remembers a range of memory to checksum; subsequent CS commands compute the checksum and compare it against the previous value. If no address range has been previously specified, entering CS without parameters will return this message.

All step points cleared

Bad stack: stack pointer must be even and <= stack base

This message is returned by SC or SC7 when the stack pointer is bad.

bkLim does not agree with heap length

Walking through the heap block by block must terminate at the start of the trailer block, as defined by the bkLim field of the zone header.

Block length is bad

The block header address plus the block length must be less than or equal to the trailer block address. Also, the trailer block must be a fixed length.

Count must be greater than zero

Any command that takes a count (such as BR or ATB) requires it to be greater than 0.

Damaged stack: A7 must be even and <= CurStackBase

The stack commands (SC6 and SC7) must have a memory range to constrain the search for frames or return addresses. They assume that register A7 is even and points to the top of the stack, and that the global variable CurStackBase points to the bottom of the stack.

Divide by zero error
This error is returned when an expression attempts to divide a number by zero.

Entry will not fit in the table
MacsBug stores information about breakpoints, step commands, and A-trap commands in a single table. Note that it's possible to receive this message while entering one type of action for the first time (a breakpoint, for instance), since other types of actions may have already filled this table.

Expression evaluation caused data read fault

Floating point not allowed in expressions

Free bytes in heap do not match zone header
The zcbFree field in the zone header must match the total size of all the free blocks in the heap.

Free master pointer list is bad
Free master pointers in the heap are chained together, starting with the hFstFree field in the zone header and terminated by a NIL pointer.

Low address must be less than or equal to high address
The CS command requires an ordered address range.

Macro expansion exceeds maximum command line length
Macros are expanded in the command line buffer. This is a fixed-length buffer determined by the width of the command line on the current display.

MacsBug code has been changed
The MacsBug code has been corrupted. Reinstall MacsBug.

MacsBug stack overflowed

Master pointer does not point at a block
The master pointer for a relocatable block must point at a block in the heap.

MMU not installed
The TM command functions only if the system has a 68851 or 68030 installed. This error also occurs if you try to display or set an individual MMU register.

No blocks of this type found
The HD command was instructed to display only blocks of a specific kind, and none were found.

Nonrelocatable block: Pointer to zone is bad
Block headers of nonrelocatable blocks must contain a pointer to the zone header.

PC is not inside a procedure
The ":" character can be used to represent the address of the start of the procedure displayed in the program counter window. If you enter ":" and no symbol information can be found for the program counter, this error message will be displayed.

Relative handle is bad
The relative handle in the header of a relocatable block must point to a master pointer.

Start of link chain does not point to a stack frame

Syntax error
This is a catch-all error message; it's used in cases where the error is obvious given the context of the command. Possibilities include the following:

- An expression contains a value and an operator but no second value.
- A nested expression does not have matching parentheses.
- An address qualifier other than .B, .W, or .L has been given.
- An illegal character is in the command line.
- The ATSS command does not include an address range.
- The format parameter for the SHOW command is other than L, W, A, or LA.
- The F command does not have the correct number of parameters.
- The value being assigned to a floating-point register is illegal.
- A toggle command has been passed a parameter other than ON or OFF.
- The HD command qualifier is not valid.

Templates cannot expand more than 8 levels
Template definitions can themselves contain template definitions, and so on. Expansion is limited to eight levels. Since it's unlikely that a structure would contain this many levels, this message may indicate a template definition that contains a recursive path.

The address on the stack is not a return address
The MR command must know where the return address for the current procedure is located on the stack, since it replaces this address with an internal MacsBug address. MacsBug checks that the address it replaces is in fact a return address. A return address is defined as an address immediately following a JSR, BSR, or A-trap instruction. (All forms of JSR and BSR are recognized.)

There is no current procedure

The string passed to DebugStr is paged to disk

The template contains an unrecognized basic type
The field of the template currently being displayed is not a valid basic type; see the description of the TMP command for a list of all possible types.

This address is not a stack address
The MR command can optionally take a parameter specifying where on the stack the return address for the current procedure is located. This address must be even and within the range specified by register A7 and CurStackBase.

Unable to access that address

Unrecognized symbol
Any command that takes a symbol as a parameter can receive this error if a valid symbol name could not be found in the heap and the name is not a valid trap name.

Value expected
Some commands will supply default parameters when no parameter is specified. This error can be returned by commands that require certain parameters.

Zone pointer is bad
The zone pointer for the current heap (SysZone, ApplZone, or user address) must be even and in RAM. In addition, the bkLim field of the header must be even and in RAM and must point after the header.

Appendix C Macintosh Error Codes

This appendix lists error codes returned by the Macintosh system software. There are three groups of codes:

- "Sad Macintosh" codes are displayed if the system detects a hardware failure during startup.
- System Error Handler alerts result from a fatal error and are displayed in the Bomb box or, if MacsBug is installed, as the first message displayed by MacsBug in the output region.
- Operating system errors are returned by the system to the program; it is up to the program to respond to these.

"Sad Macintosh" codes

"Sad Macintosh" errors are presented in two groups: one for the Macintosh Plus, which also includes the Macintosh 128K, 512K, and 512KE, and one for all other Macintosh computers.

Codes for the Macintosh Plus Computer

- **Table C-1** "Sad Macintosh" error codes for the Macintosh Plus Computer

ID	Description
01*xxxx*	ROM test failed.
02*xxxx*	RAM test (bug subtest) failed.
03*xxxx*	RAM test (byte write) failed.
04*xxxx*	RAM test (mod3 test) failed.
05*xxxx*	RAM test (add uniqueness) failed.
0F0001	Bus error.
0F0002	Address error.
0F0003	Illegal instruction.
0F0004	Zero divide.
0F0005	Check instruction.
0F0006	Trap instruction.
0F0007	Privilege violation.
0F0008	Trace mode error.
0F0009	Line 1010 error.
0F000A	Line 1111 error.
0F000B	Other exceptions.
0F000C	Nothing.
0F000D	NMI (interrupt button).
0F0064	Couldn't read system file.

Codes for other Macintosh computers

Unlike those for the Macintosh Plus, "sad Macintosh" codes for other Macintosh computers consist of two 8-digit hexadecimal numbers, displayed one above the other.

■ **Table C-2** "Sad Macintosh" codes for all Macintosh computers other than the Macintosh Plus

ID	Description
xxxx0001 xxxxxxxx	ROM test failed
xxxx0002 xxxxxxxx	RAM test failed
xxxx0003 xxxxxxxx	RAM test failed
xxxx0004 xxxxxxxx	RAM test failed
xxxx0005 xxxxxxxx	RAM test failed
xxxx0006 xxxxxxxx	VIA1 chip failed
xxxx0007 xxxxxxxx	VIA2 chip failed
xxxx0008 xxxxxxxx	ADB failed
xxxx0009 xxxxxxxx	MMU failed
xxxx000A xxxxxxxx	NuBus failed
xxxx000B xxxxxxxx	SCSI chip failed
xxxx000C xxxxxxxx	IWM chip failed
xxxx000D xxxxxxxx	SCC chip failed

(continued)

- **Table C-2** "Sad Macintosh" codes for all Macintosh computers other than the Macintosh Plus (continued)

ID	Description
xxxx000E xxxxxxxx	Data bus test failed
xxxx000F 00000001	Bus error
xxxx000F 00000002	Address error
xxxx000F 00000003	Illegal instruction error
xxxx000F 00000004	Divide-by-zero error
xxxx000F 00000005	Check instruction error
xxxx000F 00000006	cpTrapCC, TrapCC, or TrapV error
xxxx000F 00000007	Privilege violation
xxxx000F 00000008	Trace
xxxx000F 00000009	Line A error
xxxx000F 0000000A	Line F error
xxxx000F 0000000B	Unassigned error
xxxx000F 0000000C	Coprocessor protocol violation error
xxxx000F 0000000D	Format exception
xxxx000F 0000000E	Spurious interrupt
xxxx000F 0000000F	Trap 0 to 15 exception

(continued)

■ **Table C-2** "Sad Macintosh" codes for all Macintosh computers other than the Macintosh Plus (continued)

ID	Description
xxxx000F 00000010	Interrupt level 1
xxxx000F 00000011	Interrupt level 2
xxxx000F 00000012	Interrupt level 3
xxxx000F 00000013	Interrupt level 4
xxxx000F 00000014	Interrupt level 5
xxxx000F 00000015	Interrupt level 6
xxxx000F 00000016	Interrupt level 7
xxxx000F 00000017	Coprocessor BRA or SET on unordered condition
xxxx000F 00000018	Coprocessor inexact result
xxxx000F 00000019	Coprocessor divide by 0
xxxx000F 0000001A	Coprocessor underflow
xxxx000F 0000001B	Coprocessor operand error
xxxx000F 0000001C	Coprocessor operand error
xxxx000F 0000001D	Coprocessor NAN
xxxx000F 0000001E	MMU configuration
xxxx000F 0000001F	MMU illegal operation
xxxx000F 00000020	MMU access level violation

System Error Handler alerts

If these errors are reported by the Bomb box, they are identified by an ID number in the lower-right corner of the box; if they are reported by MacsBug as a break message, they are identified by their ID number as well as an error string. This section describes some of the possible causes for these errors.

■ **Table C-3** System Error Handler alerts

ID	String	Description
1	dsBusErr	Bus error: an attempt to read from or write to an address that doesn't exist. For instance, if you have 2 MB of RAM in your Macintosh, and you try to read the byte at 3 MB, you may get a bus error. You may not stop at the exact instruction that contained the error—you could stop one or two instructions away from it. Because of their hardware design, the Macintosh Plus and Macintosh SE almost never get bus errors; instead, the nonexistent address is "wrapped around" to an address that does exist. What address that will be is difficult to predict.
2	dsAddressErr	Address error: a word or long word reference to an odd address. An address error can be caused by two things. All machine instructions are an even number of bytes long and must start on an even-numbered address. If the PC ever gets set to an odd address, you will get an address error. On 68000 processors only, all word and long word accesses must be to even addresses (this is not true of single-byte accesses); otherwise, your program will crash. On 68020 and 68030 processors, word and long word accesses can be at any address, but they are faster if they are on even addresses.
3	dsIllInstErr	Illegal instruction: the 68000 received an instruction it didn't recognize. Not all hexadecimal numbers are valid machine code instructions. If the processor hits a value that is not a valid machine code instruction, you will get an illegal instruction error. The most likely cause of this error is that you jumped from the program code into a random memory location that contains garbage. A less common cause of this error is related to the hardware you're using. Some instructions are valid on a 68020 or 68030 but not on a 68000. If you hit such an instruction on a Macintosh Plus or Macintosh SE, you will get an illegal instruction error.

(continued)

■ **Table C-3** System Error Handler alerts (continued)

ID	String	Description
4	dsZeroDivErr	Zero divide: signed divide (DIVS) or unsigned divide (DIVU) with 0 divisor was executed.
5	dsChkErr	Check error: check register against bounds error was executed and failed. Pascal compilers put in code to make sure that array indexes are not larger than the array itself, to prevent you from running off the end of the array. (Strings are just arrays, so they are checked this way too.) If the code the compiler puts in finds an error, it generates a check error. C compilers don't do this.
6	dsOvFlowErr	TrapV exception (also known as an overflow error): TRAPV instruction was executed and failed. Usually (but not always) this indicates an overflow on an operation. It is a very rare error.
7	dsPrivErr	Privilege violation: the application tried to get into restricted OS memory. Also a very rare error.
8	dsTraceErr	Trace exception: the trace bit in the status register was set accidentally. Another rare error.
9	dsLineAErr	Line 1010 exception: the A-trap dispatcher is not working. Another rare error.
10	dsLineFEr	Line 1111 exception: a floating-point instruction tried to execute on a machine without a floating-point processor.
11	dsMiscErr	Miscellaneous exception: all other 68000 hardware exceptions. Cosmic rays. If it happens repeatedly, have your hardware checked.
12	dsCoreErr	Unimplemented core routine. This just means that you've hit an unimplemented A-trap—that is, an A-trap number that's not used, so no code exists for it.
13	dsIrqErr	Spurious interrupt: the interrupt vector table entry for a particular level of interrupt (usually level 4, 5, 6, or 7) was NIL. Cosmic rays. If it happens repeatedly, have your hardware checked.
14	dsIOCoreErr	I/O system error: File Manager dequeue failed.
15	dsLoadErr	Segment Loader error: a GetResource call to read a segment into memory failed. This is caused either by a bad file or by running out of memory.
16	dsFPErr	Floating-point error: error in the floating calculations.

(continued)

■ **Table C-3** System Error Handler alerts (continued)

ID	String	Description
17	dsNoPackErr	Can't load package 0: package 0 not present (List Manager); a GetResource call to load a 'PACK' resource failed. Your System file may be trashed, or you may be out of memory.
18	dsNoPk1	Can't load package 1: package 1 not present; a GetResource call to load a 'PACK' resource failed. Your System file may be trashed, or you may be out of memory.
19	dsNoPk2	Can't load package 2: package 2 not present (Disk Init); a GetResource call to load a 'PACK' resource failed. Your System file may be trashed, or you may be out of memory.
20	dsNoPk3	Can't load package 3: package 3 not present (Standard File); a GetResource call to load a 'PACK' resource failed. Your System file may be trashed, or you may be out of memory.
21	dsNoPk4	Can't load package 4: package 4 not present (SANE floating point); a GetResource call to load a 'PACK' resource failed. Your System file may be trashed, or you may be out of memory.
22	dsNoPk5	Can't load package 5: package 5 not present (SANE transcendentals); a GetResource call to load a 'PACK' resource failed. Your System file may be trashed, or you may be out of memory.
23	dsNoPk6	Can't load package 6: package 6 not present (International Utilities); a GetResource call to load a 'PACK' resource failed. Your System file may be trashed, or you may be out of memory.
24	dsNoPk7	Can't load package 7: package 7 not present (Binary-Decimal Conversion); a GetResource call to load a 'PACK' resource failed. Your System file may be trashed, or you may be out of memory.
25	dsMemFullErr	Can't allocate requested block: out of memory. This is the error the ROM returns when it runs out of memory deep inside itself, in places that are impossible to back out of.
26	dsBadLaunch	Segment Loader error: a GetResource call to read code segment 0 failed. Probably the file you double-clicked isn't an application or has been trashed.
27	dsFSErr	File system map destroyed: someone attempted to access an invalid block. Hope you remembered to back up your disk!

(continued)

■ **Table C-3** System Error Handler alerts (continued)

ID	String	Description
28	dsStknHeap	Stack overflow error: the stack grew so large that it intruded into the heap, thus corrupting the heap. This situation was detected by the stack sniffer. Not all stack overflows are caught by the stack sniffer. You can trash the heap without getting this error, but you'll crash sooner or later. One possible cause of this error is recursion that goes much deeper than you expect or whose stack frames are very large.
30	dsReinsert	"Please insert the disk:" File Manager alert; request to reinsert off-line volume. Not an error.
31	dsNotThe1	Not the requested disk.
32	memTrbBase	Memory Manager failed.
33	negZcbFreeErr	ZcbFree is negative: you trashed the heap zone header.
34–53		Memory Manager errors.
40	dsGreeting	"Welcome to Macintosh" greeting. Not an error.
41	dsFinderErr	File named Finder couldn't be found on the disk.
42	shutDownAlert	"You may now switch off your Macintosh safely" dialog box. Not an error.
51	dsBadSlotInt	Unserviceable slot interrupt.
81	dsBadSANEopcode	Bad SANE opcode: floating-point package was given bad instructions.
84	menuPrgErr	Menu purge error: a menu resource currently in use was purged.
85	dsMBarNFind	Menu Manager error.
86	dsHMenuFindErr	Menu Manager error.
87	wDEFnFnd	WDEF not found: system couldn't load the default window definition procedure resource.
88	cDEFnFnd	CDEF not found: system couldn't load the default control definition procedure resource.
98	dsNoPatch	Can't patch for particular model Macintosh: System file does not contain ROM patch resources for your Macintosh model. You may be using a system that's older than your computer.
99	dsBadPatch	Can't load patch resource: error generated while loading the ROM patch resource. System file may be corrupted.
32767	dsSysErr	General system error. A fatal error occurred, but the system doesn't know which one.

Operating system errors

Operating system errors are presented in roughly ascending ID order and grouped according to manager.

Note that the following tables include operating system errors introduced with system software version 7.0. These are denoted by an asterisk. It is possible that some of these might change with the final release of system software version 7.0.

OS Event Manager error

- **Table C-4** OS Event Manager error

ID	Name	Description
1	evtNotEnb	Event not enabled at PostEvent.

Serial driver errors

- **Table C-5** Serial driver errors

ID	Name	Description
1	swOverrunErr	Serial driver overrun error
16	parityErr	Serial parity error
32	hwOverrunErr	Serial hardware overrun
64	framingErr	Serial framing error

Slot Manager errors

■ **Table C-6** Slot Manager errors

ID	Name	Description
1	siInitSDTblErr	Slot init dispatch table couldn't be initialized.
2	siInitVBLQsErr	VBL queues for all slots couldn't be initialized.
3	siInitSPTblErr	Slot priority table couldn't be initialized.
10	sdmJTInitErr	SDM jump table couldn't be initialized.
11	sdmInitErr	SDM couldn't be initialized.
12	sdmSRTInitErr	Slot Resource Table couldn't be initialized.
13	sdmPRAMInitErr	Slot PRAM couldn't be initialized.
14	sdmPriInitErr	Cards couldn't be initialized.
*–32768	svTempDisable	Temporarily disable card but run primary init.
*–32640	svDisabled	Reserve range –32640 to –32768 for Apple temp disables.

SCSI Manager errors

■ **Table C-7** SCSI Manager errors

ID	Name	Description
2	scCommErr	Communications error (operations timeout).
3	scArbNBErr	Arbitration failed during SCSIGet; bus busy.
4	scBadparmsErr	Bad parameter or TIB opcode.
5	scPhaseErr	SCSI bus not in correct phase for attempted operation.
6	scCompareErr	SCSI Manager busy with another operation when SCSIGet was called.
7	scMgrBusyErr	SCSI Manager busy with another operation when SCSIGet was called.
8	scSequenceErr	Attempted operation is out of sequence, such as calling SCSISelect before doing SCSIGet.
9	scBusTOErr	Bus timeout before data ready on SCSIRBlind and SCSIWBlind.
10	scComplPhaseErr	SCSIComplete failed; bus not in Status phase.

Printing Manager errors

■ **Table C-8** Printing Manager errors

ID	Name	Description
128	iPrAbort	Application or user requested abort.
−1	iPrSavPFil	Saved a spool file.

General system errors

■ **Table C-9** General system errors

ID	Name	Description
0	noErr	Success.
−1	qErr	Queue element not found during deletion.
−2	vTypErr	Invalid queue element.
−3	corErr	Core routine number out of range.
−4	unimpErr	Unimplemented core routine.
−8	seNoDB	No debugger installed to handle debugger command.

Color Manager errors

■ **Table C-10** Color Manager errors

ID	Name	Description
−9	iTabPurgErr	From Color2Index/ITabMatch
−10	noColMatch	From Color2Index/ITabMatch
−11	qAllocErr	From MakeITable
−12	tblAllocErr	From MakeITable
−13	overRun	From MakeITable

(continued)

■ **Table C-10** Color Manager errors (continued)

ID	Name	Description
−14	noRoomErr	From MakeITable
−15	seOutOfRange	From SetEntry
−16	seProtErr	From SetEntry
−17	i2CRangeErr	From SetEntry
−18	gdBadDev	From SetEntry
−19	reRangeErr	From SetEntry
−20	seInvRequest	From SetEntry
−21	seNoMemErr	From SetEntry

Device Manager errors

■ **Table C-11** Device Manager errors

ID	Name	Description
−17	controlErr	Driver couldn't respond to this Control call.
−18	statusErr	Driver couldn't respond to this Status call.
−19	readErr	Driver couldn't respond to Read calls.
−20	writErr	Driver couldn't respond to Write calls.
−21	badUnitErr	Driver reference number didn't match unit table.
−22	unitEmptyErr	Driver reference number specified NIL handle in unit table.
−23	openErr	Requested read/write permission didn't match driver's open permission; attempt to open RAM Serial Driver failed.
−24	closErr	Permission to close .MPP driver was denied.
−25	dRemovErr	Tried to remove an open driver.
−26	dInstErr	DrvrInstall couldn't find driver in resource file.
−27	abortErr	I/O call aborted by KillIO. Publisher has written a new edition (Edition Manager).
−28	notOpenErr	Can't read, write, control, or status; driver was not opened.
−29	unitTblFullErr	Unit table has no more entries.
−30	dceExtErr	DCE extension error.
128	iIOAbort	I/O abort error (Printing Manager).

Macintosh File System (MFS) errors

■ **Table C-12** MFS errors

ID	Name	Description
–33	dirFulErr	File directory full.
–34	dskFulErr	All allocation blocks on the volume are full.
–35	nsvErr	Volume not found.
–36	ioErr	I/O error.
–37	bdNamErr	Bad filename or volume name (perhaps zero-length).
–38	fnOpnErr	File not open.
–39	eofErr	Logical end-of-file reached during read operation.
–40	posErr	Tried to position the file pointer before the start of the file (read or write).
–41	mFulErr	Memory full (open), or file wouldn't fit (load).
–42	tmfoErr	Too many files open.
–43	fnfErr	File not found; Folder not found; Edition container not found; Target not found.
–44	wPrErr	Volume is locked by a hardware setting.
–45	fLckdErr	File is locked.
–46	vLckdErr	Volume is locked by a software flag.
–47	fBsyErr	File is busy; Section doing I/O.
–48	dupFNErr	Duplicate filename (rename).
–49	opWrErr	File already open with write permission.
–50	paramErr	Error in user parameter list: Parameters didn't specify an existing volume (File Manager). Bad positioning information (Disk Driver). Bad drive number (Disk Initialization Package).
–51	rfNumErr	Path reference number specifies nonexistent access path.
–52	gfpErr	Error during GetFPos.
–53	volOffLinErr	Volume not on line (was ejected).

(continued)

■ **Table C-12** MFS errors (continued)

ID	Name	Description
–54	permErr	Not a subscriber; software lock on file.
–55	volOnLinErr	Drive volume already on line at MountVol.
–56	nsDrvErr	No such drive; specified drive number didn't match any number in the drive queue.
–57	noMacDskErr	Not a Macintosh disk; significant bytes are wrong.
–58	extFSErr	Volume in question belongs to an external file system, file system identifier is nonzero, or path reference number is greater than 1024.
–59	fsRnErr	Problem during rename.
–60	badMDBErr	Bad master directory block; must reinitialize volume.
–61	wrPermErr	Write permissions error; not a publisher.

Font Manager errors

■ **Table C-13** Font Manager errors

ID	Name	Description
–64	fontDecError	Error during font declaration.
–65	fontNotDeclared	Font not declared.
–66	fontSubErr	Font substitution occurred.

Low-level disk errors

- **Table C-14** Low-level disk errors

ID	Name	Description
–64	lastDskErr	Last of the range of low-level disk errors.
–64	noDriveErr	Drive not installed.
–65	offLinErr	Read/write requested for an off-line drive.
–66	noNybErr	Couldn't find 5 nibbles in 200 tries.
–67	noAdrMkErr	Couldn't find valid address mark.
–68	dataVerErr	Read verify compare failed.
–69	badCksmErr	Address mark checksum did not check.
–70	badBtSlpErr	Bad address mark bit slip nibbles.
–71	noDtaMkErr	Couldn't find a data mark header.
–72	badDCksum	Bad data mark checksum.
–73	badDBtSlp	Bad data mark bit slip nibbles.
–74	wrUnderrun	Write underrun occurred.
–75	cantStepErr	Step handshake failed.
–76	tk0BadErr	Track 0 detect does not change.
–77	initIWMErr	Unable to initialize IWM.
–78	twoSideErr	Tried to read second side on a one-sided drive.
–79	spdAdjErr	Unable to correctly adjust disk speed.
–80	seekErr	Track number wrong on address mark.
–81	sectNFErr	Sector number never found on a track.
–82	fmt1Err	Couldn't find sector 0 after track format.
–83	fmt2Err	Couldn't get enough sync.
–84	verErr	Track failed to verify.
–84	firstDskErr	First of the range of low-level disk errors.

Clock chip errors

■ **Table C-15** Clock chip errors

ID	Name	Description
−85	clkRdErr	Unable to read same clock value twice.
−86	clkWrErr	Time written didn't verify.
−87	prWrErr	Parameter RAM written didn't read-verify.
−88	prInitErr	InitUtil found the parameter RAM uninitialized.

Serial Communications Controller (SCC) errors

■ **Table C-16** SCC errors

ID	Name	Description
−89	rcvrErr	SCC receiver error (framing, parity, OR).
−90	breakRecd	Break received (SCC).

AppleTalk errors

■ **Table C-17** AppleTalk errors

ID	Name	Description
*−91	eMultiErr	Invalid address or table is full.
−91	ddpSktErr	DDP error in socket number: socket already active, not a well-known socket, socket table full, or all dynamic socket numbers in use.
−92	ddpLenErr	DDP datagram or ALAP data length too big.

(continued)

■ **Table C-17** AppleTalk errors (continued)

ID	Name	Description
*–92	elenErr	Packet too large, or first entry of the write-data structure did not contain the full 14-byte header.
–93	noBridgeErr	No network bridge for nonlocal send.
–94	LAPProtErr	Error in attaching/detaching protocol: attach error when ALAP protocol type is negative, not in range, or already in table, or when table is full; detach error when ALAP protocol type isn't in table.
–95	excessCollsns	Excessive collisions on write.
–97	portInUse	Driver open error; port already in use.
–98	portNotCf	Driver open error; parameter RAM not configured for this connection.
–99	memROZErr	Hard error in ROZ.
–99	memROZWarn	Soft error in ROZ.

Scrap Manager errors

■ **Table C-18** Scrap Manager errors

ID	Name	Description
–100	noScrapErr	Desk scrap not initialized.
–102	noTypeErr	No object of that type in scrap.

Storage allocator errors

■ **Table C-19** Storage allocator errors

ID	Name	Description
−108	memFullErr	Not enough room in heap zone.
−109	nilHandleErr	Handle was NIL in HandleZone; GetHandleSize fails on baseText or substitutionText.
−110	memAdrErr	Address was odd or out of range.
−111	memWZErr	WhichZone failed (applied to free block); GetHandleSize fails on baseText or substitutionText.
−112	memPurErr	Tried to purge a locked or nonpurgeable block.
−113	memAZErr	Address in zone check failed.
−114	memPCErr	Pointer check failed.
−115	memBCErr	Block check failed.
−116	memSCErr	Size check failed.
−117	memLockedErr	Tried to move a locked block (MoveHHi).

Hierarchical File System (HFS) errors

■ **Table C-20** HFS errors

ID	Name	Description
−120	dirNFErr	Directory not found.
−121	tmwdoErr	No free WDCB available.
−122	badMovErr	Moved into offspring error.
−123	wrgVolTypErr	Wrong volume type (operation not supported for MFS).
−124	volGoneErr	Server volume disconnected.
−127	fsDsIntErr	Internal file system error.

Alias Manager error

■ **Table C-21** Alias Manager error

ID	Name	Description
*–128	userCanceledErr	User canceled out of an operation status.

Menu Manager errors

■ **Table C-22** Menu Manager errors

ID	Name	Description
–126	mBarNFnd	System error code for MBDF not found.
–127	hMenuFindErr	Couldn't find HMenu's parent in MenuKey.

Color QuickDraw and Color Manager errors

■ **Table C-23** Color QuickDraw and Color Manager errors

ID	Name	Description
*–125	updPixMemErr	Insufficient memory to update a pixmap.
*–145	noMemForPictPlaybackErr	
*–147	rgnTooBigError	Region too big or complex.
*–148	pixMapTooDeepErr	PixMap record is deeper than 1 bit per pixel.
*–149	mfStackErr	Insufficient stack.
–150	cMatchErr	Color2Index failed to find an index.
–151	cTempMemErr	Failed to allocate memory for temporary structures.
–152	cNoMemErr	Failed to allocate memory for structure.
–153	cRangeErr	Range error on colorTable request.

(continued)

■ **Table C-23** Color QuickDraw and Color Manager errors (continued)

ID	Name	Description
−154	cProtectErr	colorTable entry protection violation.
−155	cDevErr	Invalid type of graphics device.
−156	cResErr	Invalid resolution for MakeITable.
−157	cDepthErr	Invalid pixel depth.

Resource Manager errors

■ **Table C-24** Resource Manager errors

ID	Name	Description
*−188	resourceInMemory	Resource already in memory.
*−189	writingpastEnd	Writing past end-of-file.
*−190	inputOutOfBounds	Offset or count out of bounds.
−192	resNotFound	Resource not found.
−193	resFNotFound	Resource file not found.
−194	addResFailed	AddResource failed.
−195	addRefFailed	AddReference failed.
−196	rmvResFailed	RmveResource failed.
−197	rmvRefFailed	RmveReference failed.
−198	resAttrErr	Attribute inconsistent with operation.
−199	mapReadErr	Map inconsistent with operation.

Sound Manager errors

■ **Table C-25** Sound Manager errors

ID	Name	Description
–200	noHardware	No hardware support for the specified synthesizer.
–201	notEnoughHardware	No more channels for the specified synthesizer.
–203	queueFull	No room in the queue.
–204	resProblem	Problem loading resource.
–205	badChannel	Invalid channel queue length.
–206	badFormat	Handle to 'snd ' resource was invalid.
*–207	NotEnoughBufferSpace	Insufficient memory available.
*–208	badFileFormat	File is corrupt or unusable, or not AIFF or AIFF-C.
*–209	ChannelBusy	Channel is busy.
*–210	buffersTooSmall	Buffer is too small.
*–211	channelNotBusy	Channel not currently used.
*–212	noMoreRealTime	Not enough CPU time available.
*–213	badParam	A parameter is incorrect.
*–220	siNoSoundInHardware	No sound input hardware available.
*–221	siBadSoundInDevice	Invalid sound input device.
*–222	siNoBufferSpecified	No buffer specified.
*–223	siNoCompletionRoutine	No completion routine specified.
*–224	siHardDiskTooSlow	Hard drive too slow to record.
*–225	siInvalidSampleRate	Invalid sample rate.
*–226	siInvalidSampleSize	Invalid sample size.
*–227	siDeviceBusyErr	Sound input device is busy.
*–228	siBadDeviceName	Invalid device name.
*–229	siBadRefNum	Invalid reference number.
*–230	siInputDeviceErr	Input device hardware failure.
*–231	siUnknownInfoType	Unknown type information.
*–232	siUnknownQuality	Unknown quality.

Slot Manager errors

Errors –290 to –320 might be generated during system initialization; if they are, they will be logged into the sInfo array and returned each time a call to the Slot Manager is made for the card that generated the error.

Errors –330 to –351 might be generated at any time after system initialization and will not be logged into the sInfo array.

■ **Table C-26** Slot Manager errors

ID	Name	Description
–290	smSDMInitErr	SDM couldn't be initialized.
–291	smSRTInitErr	Slot Resource Table couldn't be initialized.
–292	smPRAMInitErr	Slot Resource Table couldn't be initialized.
–293	smPriInitErr	Cards couldn't be initialized.
*–299	nmTypeErr	Invalid qType—must be ORD(nmType).
–300	smEmptySlot	No card in this slot.
–301	smCRCFail	CRC check failed for declaration data.
–302	smFormatErr	Format of the declaration ROM is wrong.
–303	smRevisionErr	Revision level of the declaration ROM is wrong.
–304	smNoDir	Directory offset is NIL.
–305	smLWTsBad	Long word test failed.
–306	smNosInfoArray	SDM was unable to allocate memory for the sInfo array.
–307	smResrvErr	A reserved field of the declaration ROM was used.
–308	smUnExBusErr	Unexpected bus error.
–309	smBLFieldBad	A valid ByteLanes field was not found.
–310	smFHBlockRdErr	F-Header block could not be read.
–311	smFHBlkDispErr	F-Header block could not be disposed of.
–312	smDisposePErr	An error occurred during execution of _DisposPointer.
–313	smNoBoardsRsrc	No board sResource.
–314	smGetPRErr	An error occurred during execution of _sGetPRAMRec.
–315	smNoBoardId	No board ID.
–316	smInitStatVErr	InitStatus_V field was negative after Primary Init.
–317	smInitTblErr	An error occurred while trying to initialize the Slot Resource Table.
–318	smNoJmpTbl	Slot Manager jump table could not be created.

(continued)

■ **Table C-26** Slot Manager errors (continued)

ID	Name	Description
–319	smBadBoardID	Board ID was wrong; reinitialize the PRAM record.
–320	smBusErrTO	Bus error timeout.
–330	smBadRefID	Reference ID was not found in the given list.
–331	smBadsList	IDs in the given sList are not in ascending order.
–332	smReservedErr	A reserved field was not 0.
–333	smCodeRevErr	Revision of the code to be executed by sExec was wrong.
–334	smCPUErr	CPU field of the code to be executed by sExec was wrong.
–335	smsPointerNil	sPointer is NIL; no list is specified.
–336	smNilsBlockErr	Physical block size of an sBlock was 0.
–337	smSlotOOBErr	Given slot is out of bounds or does not exist.
–338	smSelOOBErr	Selector is out of bounds.
–339	smNewPErr	An error occurred during execution of _NewPointer.
*–340	smBlkMoveErr	_BlockMove error.
–341	smCkStatusErr	Status of slot is bad (InitStatus_A, V).
–342	smGetDrvrNamErr	An error occurred during execution of _sGetDrvrName.
*–343	smDisDrvrNamErr	Error occurred during _sDisDrvrName.
–344	smNoMoresRsrcs	No more sResources.
–345	smGetDrvrErr	An error occurred during execution of _sGetDrvr.
–346	smBadsPtrErr	A bad sPointer was presented to an SDM call.
–347	smByteLanesErr	Bad ByteLanes value was passed to an SDM call.
*–348	smOffsetErr	Offset was too big (temporary error).
–349	smNoGoodOpens	No opens were successful in the loop.
–350	smSRTOvrFlErr	Slot Resource Table overflow.
–351	smRecNotFnd	Record not found in the Slot Resource Table.

Notification Manager error

■ **Table C-27** Notification Manager error

ID	Name	Description
−299	nmTypErr	Wrong queue type.

Device Manager errors

■ **Table C-28** Device Manager errors

ID	Name	Description
−360	slotNumErr	Invalid slot number.
−400	gcrOnMFMErr	gcr format on high-density media error.
−500	rgnTooBigErr	Region too big error.
−501	teScrapSozeErr	Scrap item too big for text edit record.
−502	hwParamrErr	bad selector for _HWPriv.

Edition Manager errors

■ **Table C-29** Edition Manager errors

ID	Name	Description
*−450	editionMgrInitErr	Edition Manager not initialized by this application.
*−451	badSectionErr	Not a valid SectionRecord.
*−452	notRegisteredSectionErr	Not a registered SectionRecord.
*−453	badEditionFileErr	Edition file is corrupt.
*−454	badSubPartErr	Can not use subparts in this release.

(continued)

■ **Table C-29** Edition Manager errors (continued)

ID	Name	Description
*–460	multiplePublisherWrn	A publisher is already registered for that container.
*–461	containerNotFoundWrn	Could not find editionContainer at this time.
*–462	containerAlreadyOpenWrn	Container already opened by this section.
*–463	notThePublisherWrn	Not the first registered publisher for that container.

Process Manager errors

■ **Table C-30** Process Manager errors

ID	Name	Description
*–600	procNotFound	No eligible process with specified process serial number.
*–601	memFragErr	Not enough room to launch application with special requirements.
*–602	appModeErr	Memory mode is 32-bit, but application is not 32-bit clean.
*–603	protocolErr	Application made module calls in improper order.
*–604	hardwareConfigErr	Hardware configuration is not correct for call.
*–605	appMemFullErr	Partition size specified in 'SIZE' resource is not big enough for launch.
*–606	appIsDaemon	Application is background only.

Event Manager errors

■ **Table C-31** Event Manager errors

ID	Name	Description
*–607	bufferIsSmall	Buffer is too small.
*–608	noOutstandingHLE	No outstanding high-level event.
*–609	connectionInValid	Connection is invalid.

Memory Manager errors

■ **Table C-32** Memory Manager errors

ID	Name	Description
*–620	notEnoughMemoryErr	Insufficient physical memory.
*–621	notHeldErr	Specified range of memory is not held.
*–622	cannotMakeContiguousErr	Cannot make specified range contiguous.
*–623	notLockedErr	Specified range of memory is not locked.
*–624	interruptsMaskedErr	Called with interrupts masked.
*–625	cannotDeferErr	Unable to defer additional user functions.

Data Access Manager errors

■ **Table C-33** Data Access Manager errors

ID	Name	Description
*–800	rcDBNull	The data item was NULL.
*–801	rcDBValue	Data available or successfully retrieved.
*–802	rcDBError	Error executing function.
*–803	rcDBBadType	Next data item not of requested data type.

(continued)

■ **Table C-33** Data Access Manager errors (continued)

ID	Name	Description
*–804	rcDBBreak	Function timed out.
*–805	rcDBExec	Query currently executing.
*–806	rcDBBadSessId	Session ID is invalid.
*–807	rcDBBadSessNum	Invalid session number.
*–808	rcDBBadDDev	Couldn't find the specified database extension, or error occurred in opening database extension.
*–809	rcDBAsyncNotSupp	The database extension does not support asynchronous calls.
*–810	rcDBBadAsynchPB	Invalid parameter block specified.
*–811	rcDBNoHandler	There is no handler for this data type installed for the current application.
*–812	rcDBWrongVersion	Wrong version number.
*–813	rcDBPackNotInited	The InitDBPack function has not yet been called.

Help Manager Errors

■ **Table C-34** Help Manager errors

ID	Name	Description
*–850	hmHelpDisabled	Help is not enabled.
*–853	hmBalloonAborted	Mouse was moving or not in rectangle.
*–854	hmSameAsLastBalloon	Menu and item are same as previous menu and item.
*–855	hmHelpManagerNotInited	Help menu not set up.
*–857	hmSkippedBalloon	Help message record specified a skip balloon.
*–859	hmUnknownHelpType	Help message record contained a bad type.
*–861	hmOperationUnsupported	Bad method parameter.
*–862	hmNoBalloonUp	No balloon showing.
*–863	hmCloseViewActive	User using Close View won't let you remove balloon.

PPC Toolbox errors

- **Table C-35** PPC Toolbox errors

ID	Name	Description
*–900	notInitErr	PPC ToolBox not initialized.
*–902	nameTypeErr	Invalid or inappropriate locationKindSelector in locationName.
*–903	noPortErr	Unable to open port or bad portRefNum.
*–904	noGlobalsErr	The system is hosed; better restart.
*–905	localOnlyErr	Network activity is currently disabled.
*–906	destPortErr	Port does not exist at destination.
*–907	sessTableErr	Out of session tables; try again later.
*–908	noSessionErr	Invalid session reference number.
*–909	badReqErr	Bad parameter or invalid state for operation.
*–910	portNameExistsErr	Port is already open, perhaps in another application.
*–911	noPortTableErr	User name unknown on destination machine.
*–912	userRejectErr	Destination rejected the session request.
*–915	noResponseErr	Unable to contact application.
*–916	portClosedErr	The port was closed.
*–917	sessClosedErrr	The session has closed.
*–919	badPortNameErr	PPC port record is invalid.
*–922	noDefaultUserErr	No owner's name in Network Setup Control Panel.
*–923	notLoggedInErr	The default userRefNum does not yet exist.
*–924	noUserRefErr	Unable to create a new userRefNum.
*–925	networkErr	An error has occurred in the network; a very rare error.
*–926	noInformErr	PPCStart failed because destination did not have inform pending.
*–927	authFailErr	Unable to authenticate user at destination.
*–928	noUserRecErr	Invalid user reference number.
*–930	badServiceMethodErr	Illegal service type or not supported.
*–931	badLocNameErr	Location name malformed.
*–932	guestNotAllowedErr	Destination port requires authentication.

File ID errors

- **Table C-36** File ID errors

ID	Name	Description
*–1300	fidNotFound	File ID not found.
*–1301	fidExists	File ID already exists.
*–1302	NotAFileErr	Specified file is a directory.
*–1303	DiffVolErr	Files on different volumes.
*–1304	catChangedErr	Catalog has changed and CatPosition might be invalid.
*–1305	desktopDamagedErr	Desktop database files are corrupted. The Finder will fix this, but if your application is not running with the Finder, use DTReset or DTDelete.
*–1306	sameFileErr	Can't exchange a file with itself.
*–1307	badFidErr	File ID is dangling or doesn't match with file number.

AppleTalk Name Binding Protocol (NBP) errors

- **Table C-37** NBP errors

ID	Name	Description
–1024	nbpBuffOvr	Buffer overflow in LookupName.
–1025	nbpNoConfirm	Name not confirmed on ConfirmName.
–1026	nbpConfDiff	Name confirmed for different socket.
*–1027	nbpDuplicate	Duplicate name already exists.
–1028	nbpNotFound	Name not found on remove.
–1029	nbpNISErr	Error trying to open the NIS.

AppleTalk Session Protocol (ASP) errors

■ **Table C-38** ASP errors

ID	Name	Description
–1066	aspBadVersNum	Server couldn't support this ASP version.
–1067	aspBufTooSmall	Buffer too small.
–1068	aspNoMoreSess	No more sessions on server.
–1069	aspNoServers	No servers at that address.
–1070	aspParamErr	Parameter error.
–1071	aspServerBusy	Server couldn't open another session.
–1072	aspSessClosed	Session closed.
–1073	aspSizeErr	Command block is too big.
–1074	aspTooMany	Too many clients.
–1075	aspNoAck	No acknowledge on attention request.

AppleTalk Transaction Protocol (ATP) errors

■ **Table C-39** ATP errors

ID	Name	Description
*–1096	reqFailed	SendRequest failed; retry count exceeded.
–1097	tooManyReqs	Too many concurrent requests.
–1098	tooManySkts	Too many responding sockets.
–1099	badATPSkt	Bad responding socket.
–1100	badBuffNum	Bad response buffer number specified.
–1101	noRelErr	No release received.
*–1102	cbNotFound	Control block not found.
–1103	noSendResp	AddResponse issued before SendResponse.
–1104	noDataArea	Too many outstanding ATP calls.
*–1105	reqAborted	Request aborted.
*–1273	errOpenDenied	Open request denied by recipient.

(continued)

■ **Table C-39** ATP errors (continued)

ID	Name	Description
*–1274	errDSPQueueSize	Send or receive queue is too small.
*–1275	errFwdReset	Read terminated by forward reset.
*–1276	errAttention	Attention message too long.
*–1277	errOpening	Attempt to open connection failed.
*–1278	errState	Bad connection state for this operation.
*–1279	errAborted	Request aborted by dspRemove or dspClose function.
*–1280	errRefNum	Bad connection reference number.
*–3101	buf2SmallErr	ALAP frame too large for buffer or DDP datagram too large for buffer.
–3102	noMPPError	MPP driver not installed.
–3103	ckSumErr	DDP bad checksum.
–3104	extractErr	NBP couldn't find tuple in buffer.
–3105	readQErr	Socket or protocol type invalid or not found in table.
–3106	atpLenErr	ATP response message too large.
–3107	atpBadRsp	Bad response from ATPRequest.
–3108	recNotFnd	ABRecord not found.
–3109	sktClosedErr	Asynchronous call aborted because socket was closed before call was completed.

AppleTalk Filing Protocol (AFP) errors

■ **Table C-40** AFP errors

ID	Name	Description
–5000	afpAccessDenied	AFP access denied.
–5001	afpAuthContinue	AFP authorization continue.
–5002	afpBadUAM	Unknown user authentication method (UAM) specified.
–5003	afpBadVersNum	AFP Bad version number.
–5004	afpBitmapErr	AFP bitmap error.
–5005	afpCantMove	AFP can't move error.

(continued)

■ **Table C-40** AFP errors (continued)

Id	Name	Description
−5006	afpDenyConflict	AFP deny conflict.
−5007	afpDirNotEmpty	AFP directory not empty.
−5008	afpDiskFull	AFP disk full.
−5009	afpEofError	AFP end-of-file error.
−5010	afpFileBusy	AFP file busy.
−5011	afpFlatVol	AFP flat volume.
−5012	afpItemNotFound	AFP item not found.
−5013	afpLockErr	AFP lock error.
−5014	afpMiscErr	AFP miscellaneous error.
−5015	afpNoMoreLocks	AFP No more locks.
−5016	afpNoServer	AFP no server.
−5017	afpObjectExists	AFP object already exists.
−5018	afpObjectNotFound	AFP object not found.
−5019	afpParmErr	AFP parameter error.
−5020	afpRangeNotLocked	AFP range not locked.
−5021	afpRangeOverlap	AFP range overlap.
−5022	afpSessClosed	AFP session closed.
−5023	afpUserNotAuth	AFP user not authorized.
−5024	afpCallNotSupported	AFP call not supported.
−5025	afpObjectTypeErr	AFP object type error.
−5026	afpTooManyFilesOpen	Too many AFP files open.
−5027	afpServerGoingDown	AFP server going down.
−5028	afpCantRename	AFP can't rename.
−5029	afpDirNotFound	AFP directory not found.
−5030	afpIconTypeError	AFP icon type error.
−5031	afpVolLocked	Volume is read-only.
−5302	afpObjectLocked	Object is M/R/D/W inhibited.

SysEnvirons errors

- **Table C-41** SysEnvirons errors

ID	Name	Description
−5500	envNotPresent	SysEnvirons trap not present (System file earlier than version 4.1); glue returns values for all fields except systemVersion.
−5501	envBadVers	A nonpositive version number was passed—no information returned.
−5502	envVersTooBig	Requested version of SysEnvirons call was not available.

Gestalt Manager errors

- **Table C-42** Gestalt Manager errors

ID	Name	Description
*−5550	gestaltUnknownErr	Could not obtain the response.
*−5551	gestaltUndefSelectorErr	Undefined selector.
*−5552	gestaltDupSelectorErr	Selector already exists.
*−5553	gestaltLocationErr	Function not in system heap.

Picture utilities errors

■ **Table C-43** Picture utilities errors

ID	Name	Description
*–11000	pictInfoVersionErr	Wrong version of the PictInfo structure.
*–11001	pictInfoIDErr	Internal consistency check for PictInfoID is wrong.
*–11002	pictInfoVerbErr	The passed verb is invalid.
*–11003	cantLoadPickMethodErr	Unable to load the custom pick procedure.
*–11004	colorsRequestedErr	The number of colors requested was illegal.
*–11005	pictureDataErr	The picture data was invalid.

Power Manager errors

■ **Table C-44** Power Manager errors

ID	Name	Description
*–13000	pmBusyErr	Power Manager IC stuck busy.
*–13001	pmReplyTOErr	Timed out waiting to begin reply handshake.
*–13002	pmSendStartErr	Power Manager IC did not start handshake.
*–13003	pmSendEndErr	During send, Power Manager did not finish handshake.
*–13004	pmRecvStartErr	During receive, Power Manager did not start handshake.
*–13005	pmRecvEndErr	During receive, Power Manager did not finish handshake.

Appendix D Procedure Names

This appendix describes how a procedure must be defined in order for MacsBug to recognize it.

Procedure definition

Whenever possible, MacsBug accepts and returns addresses as procedure names and offsets. MacsBug finds names by scanning relocatable heap blocks for valid procedure definitions. A procedure definition, in the simplest case, consists of a return instruction followed by the procedure's name.

A procedure is defined as follows:

- LINK A6—This instruction is optional; if it is missing, the start of the procedure is assumed to be immediately after the preceding procedure, or at the start of the heap block.
- Procedure code
- RTS or JMP(A0) or RTD
- Procedure name
- Procedure constants

The procedure name can be a fixed length of 8 or 16 bytes, or of variable length. Valid characters for procedure names are a–z, A–Z, 0–9, underscore (_), percent (%), period (.), and space. The space character is allowed only to pad fixed-length names to the maximum length.

With fixed-length format, the first byte is in the range $20 through $7F. The high-order bit may or may not be set. The high-order bit of the second byte is set for 16-character names, clear for 8-character names. Fixed-length 16-character names are used in object Pascal to show class.method names instead of procedure names. The method name is contained in the first 8 bytes, and the class name is in the second 8 bytes. MacsBug swaps the order and inserts the period before displaying the name.

With variable-length format, the first byte is in the range $80 to $9F. Stripping the high-order bit produces a length in the range $00 through $1F. If the length is 0, the next byte contains the actual length, in the range $01 through $FF. Data after the name starts on a word boundary. Compilers can place a procedure's constant data immediately after the procedure in memory. The first word after the name specifies how many bytes of constant data are present. If there are no constants, a length of 0 must be given.

Examples of procedure definitions

Here are some examples of valid assembly-language procedure definitions:

```
; Variable-length name with no constant data.

Proc1        PROC
             LINK    A6, #0
             UNLK    A6
             RTS
             DC.B    $8C, 'VariableName'
             DC.W    $0000
             ENDP


; Fixed 8-character name.

Proc2        PROC
             LINK    A6, #0
             UNLK    A6
             RTS
             DC.B    $80 + 'F', 'ixed   '
             ENDP


; Fixed 16-character name.

Proc3        PROC
             LINK    A6, #0
             UNLK    A6
             RTS
             DC.B    $80 + 'M', $80 + 'e', 'thod Class   '
             ENDP
```

Appendix D Procedure Names 409

Appendix E MacsBug Internals and Discipline Interface

This appendix describes how MacsBug installs itself, how it forces exceptions, and how it interfaces with Discipline or—by extension—with any other program.

How MacsBug installs itself

Support for debuggers is provided beginning with the 128K ROM. When a system error or 68000 exception occurs, the ROM code examines the global variable MacJmp to obtain the address of the debugger's entry point. MacJmp might contain additional information, depending on whether you are running under a 24-bit or 32-bit Memory Manager.

If you are running under a 24-bit Memory Manager, the high-order byte of MacJmp is a flags byte that contains the following information:

Bit	Meaning
7	Set if debugger is running.
6	Set if debugger can handle system errors.
5	Set if debugger is installed.
4	Set if debugger can support the Discipline utility.

The lower 3 bytes of MacJmp are used to store the address of the debugger's entry point.

If you are running under a 32-bit Memory Manager, the flags byte is moved to address $BFF and the long word at MacJmp becomes a full 32-bit address that points to the debugger's entry point.

When a debugger installs itself, it should set bit 5 in the flags byte to indicate it is installed, and, if it supports Discipline, it should set bit 4 as well. It must do this under either a 24-bit or 32-bit Memory Manager, although, as mentioned above, this information will be stored in different locations.

How MacsBug is implemented

If a debugger is installed and an exception occurs, the register set is saved in the global variable SEVars, and a call is made to the address in MacJmp. When the debugger returns, the register set is restored and execution resumes at the address in the program counter.

While active, MacsBug installs a bus error handler to catch any illegal memory references. MacsBug does not install an address error handler since it can check whether addresses are even before accessing them.

MacsBug itself forces two kinds of exceptions. The first is used to set breakpoints. MacsBug replaces the first word in an instruction with a TRAP instruction; when the program reaches this point, an exception is generated. The second is used in tracing instruction execution while single-stepping. MacsBug forces an exception by setting the Trace bit of the status register before executing an instruction.

MacsBug installs its own trace exception handler when any of these conditions is true:

- At least one ROM breakpoint is set.
- A breakpoint was set at the PC when execution resumed. The instruction must be executed before the breakpoint can be reinstalled.
- A Step command is in progress.
- A Step Spy command is in progress.

The SO (Step Over) command steps over JSR and BSR instructions by executing the call with the Trace bit set, replacing the return address with an address inside MacsBug, and then proceeding normally. The SO command steps over a trap call by copying the trap instruction into MacsBug and proceeding from that point.

MacsBug installs its own A-trap exception handler when any of these conditions is true:

- An A-trap command is active.
- The Extended Discipline utility is enabled.
- Heap scrambling is enabled.
- MacsBug steps into a trap call.

The Debugger and DebugStr traps do not preserve the status register (SR). These traps are directed to MacsBug by the dispatcher, which tosses the contents of the SR immediately upon entry.

Since interrupts are turned off, MacsBug gets keystrokes by polling for a keyboard interrupt and then calling the interrupt routine at Lvl1DT+8. MacsBug fields the event by temporarily installing its own PostEvent handler.

MacsBug assumes the screen buffer on a Macintosh Plus or Macintosh SE is at address $3FA700, accommodating external monitors that change ScrnBase. MacsBug always appears on the internal display.

On all Macintosh II computers, MacsBug uses the first item in the gDevList as its display. The device must support 1-bit mode, and the display is limited to 640 by 480 to conserve memory.

While swapping the user and MacsBug displays on multibit displays, MacsBug calls SetMode and SetEntries (using the Control trap) to set a bit depth of 1 and a black-and-white color table.

How MacsBug interfaces with Discipline

Discipline is a set of routines that the debugger calls to get information before or after a trap call. If the parameters are bad, Discipline returns a text string. The debugger halts program execution and displays the message.

The address of the debugger's entry point is stored in MacJmp. The long word preceding the entry point, points to a structure allocated by the debugger and filled in by both the debugger and Discipline. The structure contains version information, a jump table of Dsicipline function addresses, and a pointer to Discipline's global data. All jump table addresses are 32-bit addresses. Table E-1 describes the fields of this structure.

■ **Table E-1** Discipline and debugger information

Field	Offset	Description
Version information	+0	Debugger signature: filled in by debugger. MacsBug sets this to MT.
	+2	Debugger version: filled in by debugger. MacsBug sets this to 1.
	+3	Discipline interface version supported by debugger: filled in by debugger. MacsBug sets this to 1.
	+4	Discipline signature: Discipline sets this to LB.
	+5	Discipline version: Discipline sets this to 1.
	+6	Discipline interface version provided by Discipline: Discipline sets this to 1.
Jump table		The debugger initializes jump table entries to zero; Discipline fills in the addresses when it is installed. If the CheckBeforeCall entry is set to a non-NIL value, the debugger assumes Discipline is installed.
	+8	CheckBeforeCall
	+12	CheckAfterCall
	+16	Configuration
Data pointer	+20	Discipline global data pointer: filled in by Discipline. This storage location is provided by the debugger so that if Discipline is implemented as an INIT, it can access its data through this hook.

Jump table entries

Each entry in the jump table is the address of a procedure the debugger can call. All calls must use Pascal calling conventions. This means the Discipline routines should pop the parameters from the stack. Discipline must also preserve registers D3–D7 and A2–A6.

Discipline should set up its own A5 and A7 worlds. Discipline can use a small amount of the debugger stack (never more than 1K) to do this.

Calling Discipline

The debugger should provide a command to turn Discipline on or off or to configure Discipline—for example:

DSC [ON | OFF | *text*]

Typing DSC without parameters would toggle Discipline on and off. Typing DSC with ON or OFF as parameters would turn Discipline on and off respectively. The debugger uses the Configuration routine to pass a pointer to a null-terminated string containing ON, OFF, or the remainder of the command line whenever the user enters DSC.

The Pascal definition for the configuration routine is

```
FUNCTION Configuration (parameters: CStringPtr): CStringPtr;
```

The Configuration routine returns a pointer to a null-terminated text string. If the result is not NIL, the debugger displays the text. The text can have embedded carriage returns to display multiple lines.

Once the user has turned Discipline on, all A-traps are routed through the debugger before the dispatcher is called. Before dispatching a trap, the debugger calls the CheckBeforeTrap function. The definition for CheckBeforeTrap is

```
FUNCTION CheckBeforeTrap (trapNumber: INTEGER; registers:
     Pointer; VAR resultCode: INTEGER; VAR checkAfter:      BOOLEAN):
     CStringPtr;
```

The CheckBeforeTrap function returns a pointer to a null-terminated text string. If the result is not NIL, the debugger halts the program and displays the text. The text can have embedded carriage returns to display multiple lines. Discipline uses the *resultCode* parameter to indicate what it thinks is wrong with the call. A result code of 0 is the same as a NIL result string. All other result codes are defined by Discipline.

The *trapNumber* passed to Discipline by the debugger should be masked with $A0FF for operating system traps and $ABFF for toolbox traps. The PC in the register file points to the trap word that was encountered.

Discipline can examine the registers by looking at the register file pointed to by the *registers* parameter. The register file is made up of 18 long words, with information ordered as shown in Table E-2.

If the debugger can break after the trap call, it sets the *checkAfter* parameter to TRUE. The debugger should not break after the trap call if the call is made from ROM to RAM since this won't work with patched traps. The debugger should also ignore the LoadSeg trap. If Discipline wants to check after the trap and the debugger can break, then *checkAfter* is left unchanged. If Discipline does not want to check after the trap, it must set the *checkAfter* parameter to FALSE.

The definition for the CheckAfterTrap function is

```
FUNCTION CheckAfterTrap (trapNumber:  INTEGER; registers:  Pointer;
      VAR resultCode:  INTEGER):  CStringPtr;
```

The parameters to this routine are the same as those to the CheckBeforeTrap function.

- **Table E-2** Contents of register file

Offset	Contents	Offset	Contents
0	D0	32	A0
4	D1	36	A1
8	D2	40	A2
12	D3	44	A3
16	D4	48	A4
20	D5	52	A5
24	D6	56	A6
28	D7	60	A7
		64	PC
		68	SR (high-order word)

Glossary

24-bit addressing: A memory management scheme under which the microprocessor can access up to 24 MB of address space.

32-bit addressing: A memory management scheme under which the microprocessor can access up to 4 GB of address space.

32-bit clean: (adj.) a program that does not use the high byte of an address to store data.

addressing mode: A method used by the microprocessor to compute the value of an operand.

address register: One of eight locations within the microprocessor normally used to store addresses. Some of these registers are used for specific purposes: A7 designates the top of the stack, A6 is used to reference items in a stack frame, and A5 is used to reference application global variables and the jump table.

address space: A range of accessible memory.

assembler: A language translator that converts a program written in assembly language (source code) into an equivalent program in machine language (object code). The opposite of a **disassembler.** Compare **compiler.**

assembly language: A low-level programming language in which individual machine-language instructions are written in a symbolic form that's easier to understand than machine language. Each assembly-language instruction produces one machine-language instruction. Because assembly-language programs require very little translation, they can be very fast. See also **machine language.**

asynchronous I/O: The capability to perform an I/O operation while its calling process continues to run. With synchronous I/O, the calling process "sleeps" until the I/O operation is finished.

block: A contiguous, page-aligned region of computer memory of arbitrary size, allocated by the Memory Manager. Also called a memory block. See also **free block, nonrelocatable block, relocatable block.**

colon address: A MacsBug variable that contains the starting address of the current procedure.

command line: The area of the MacsBug display used to enter commands and perform base conversions and arithmetic calculations.

compiler: A language translator that converts a program written in a high-level programming language (source code) into an equivalent program in some lower-level language such as machine language (object code) for later execution. Compare **assembler.**

data register: One of eight locations within the microprocessor normally used to store data.

dcmd: A code resource type that you can use to extend or modify the MacsBug command set. You can use standard dcmds, shipped with MacsBug, or you can write your own.

disassembler: (1) A language translator that converts a machine-language program into an equivalent program in assembly language, which is easier for programmers to understand. The opposite of an **assembler.** (2) A program that examines data in memory and interprets it as a set of assembly-language instructions. Assuming that the data is object code, a disassembler gives the user the source code that could have generated that object code.

dot address: A MacsBug variable that contains the last address used by certain commands.

driver: A program, usually in a System Folder, that lets a peripheral device and a computer send and receive files. Printer drivers control printers; a hard disk driver controls exchanges between a hard disk and a computer.

effective address: The address where the value of the operand is stored. The way to find the effective address depends on the addressing mode used.

error handler: Code to which the microprocessor transfers control in the event of a fatal error. This could be the System Error Handler or a resident debugger like MacsBug if one is installed.

EveryTime macro: A macro that is executed every time except the first time MacsBug is invoked. Compare **FirstTime macro.**

exception: An error or abnormal condition detected by the processor in the course of program execution; includes interrupts and traps.

exception handler: A routine that gains control whenever an exception to normal processing occurs.

exception processing: The means used by the microprocessor to handle unusual conditions caused by the hardware or by the software that must be addressed before normal processing resumes.

exception vector: The first 256 bytes of RAM ($00 0000 through $00 00FF) as used by the 68000 processor. These locations contain the addresses of routines that gain control whenever an exception to normal processing occurs. Exceptions include such events as a reset, an interrupt, or a trap.

FirstTime macro: A special initialization macro that loads and executes automatically when MacsBug loads during system startup. Compare **EveryTime macro.**

free block: A contiguous region in the application or system heap that has not yet been allocated.

glue: In-line glue is code inserted at compile or link time to implement very simple system routines without going through the trap dispatcher. Library glue, which resides in interface libraries, is used to pass values to and receive values from register-based routines.

handle: A pointer to a master pointer; it designates a relocatable block in the heap by double indirection.

heap: The area of memory in which space is dynamically allocated and released on demand, using the Memory Manager.

heap zone: An area of memory initialized by the Memory Manager for heap allocation.

high memory: (1) The upper limit of addressable memory. (2) A region in memory near the upper limit of addressable space. (3) A region near the top of RAM.

high-order: (adj.) Describes the most significant part of a numerical quantity. In normal representation, the high-order bit of a binary value is in the leftmost position; likewise, the high-order byte of a binary word or long word quantity consists of the leftmost 8 bits. Compare **low-order.**

high-order byte: The more significant half of a 2-byte quantity. In the 68000 microprocessors used in the Macintosh family, the high-order byte is stored first. Compare **low-order byte.**

high-order word: The more significant half of a long word. In normal representation, the *high-order word* of a long word is in the leftmost position. Compare **low-order word.**

interrupt: (1) An electronic attention-getter; a signal sent to the microprocessor that is intended to force the microprocessor to stop its current activity and accept input from the device that sent the interrupt. (2) A temporary suspension in the execution of a program that allows the computer to perform some other task, typically in response to a signal from a peripheral device or other source external to the computer. (3) An exception that's signaled to the microprocessor by a device to notify the microprocessor of a change in condition of the device, such as the completion of an I/O request.

interrupt handler: A routine that services interrupts. A program, associated with a particular external device, that executes whenever that device sends an interrupt signal to the computer. The interrupt handler performs its tasks during the interrupt, then returns control to the computer so it may resume program execution.

interrupt priority level: A number identifying the importance of the interrupt. It indicates which device is interrupting and which interrupt handler should be executed.

interrupt switch: A switch marked with a circled V (or the word "Interrupt" on the Macintosh Plus). Pressing this button generates a level 7, nonmaskable interrupt, which is why it is often called the NMI key. (On the Macintosh Plus or Macintosh SE, it can generate a level 4, 5, 6, or 7 interrupt.) The microprocessor handles this interrupt by invoking MacsBug. See also **interrupt.**

interrupt vector: A pointer to an interrupt handler.

jump table: A table constructed in memory by the System Loader from all jump table segments encountered during a load. The jump table contains all references to dynamic segments that may be called during execution of the program.

low memory: (1) The lowest limit of addressable memory. (2) A region in memory near 0.

low-order: (adj.) Describes the least significant part of a numerical quantity. In normal representation, the low-order bit of a binary number is in the rightmost position; likewise, the low-order byte of a binary word or long word quantity consists of the rightmost 8 bits. Compare **high-order.**

low-order byte: The less significant half of a 2-byte quantity. For Macintosh computers the high-order byte is stored first and the low-order byte second. Compare **high-order byte.**

low-order word: The less significant half of a long word. In normal representation, the *low-order word* of a long word is in the rightmost position. Compare **high-order word.**

machine language: The form in which instructions to a computer are stored in memory for direct execution by the computer's microprocessor. Each model of microprocessor (such as the 6502 or the 68000) has its own form of machine language. See also **assembly language.**

macro: A name that you can substitute for an address, expression, or series of commands on the MacsBug command line.

NIL: (adj.) Pointing to a value of 0. A memory handle is NIL if the address it points to is filled with 0's. Handles to purged memory blocks are NIL.

nonrelocatable block: A block whose location in the heap is fixed and can't be moved during heap compaction.

output region: The area of the MacsBug display used to display information in response to the commands you enter.

package: A set of routines and data types that forms a part of the toolbox or operating system and is stored as a resource. On the original Macintosh, all packages were disk-based and brought into memory only when needed; some packages are now in ROM.

partition: A locked relocatable block allocated for a **process.** The partition for an open application contains the application's heap, stack, A5 world, and jump table.

420   MacsBug Reference and Debugging Guide

patch: (v.) (1) To replace one or more bytes in memory or in a file with other values. The address to which the program must jump to execute a subroutine is patched into memory at load time when a file is relocated. (2) To replace a piece of ROM code with other, RAM-based system code by means of a new entry into the trap dispatch table. (n.) A resource of type 'PTCH' containing the patched code.

PC region: The area of the MacsBug display in which the address of the next instruction to be executed and the disassembly of that instruction are shown.

PC register: A location within the microprocessor used to store the address of the next instruction to be executed.

pointer: An item of information consisting of the memory address of some other item. For example, Applesoft BASIC maintains internal pointers to the most recently stored variable, the most recently typed program line, and the most recently read data item, among other things.

process: An open application—for example, the Finder, an application launched by the user, or an application running in the background only.

programmer's switch: A two-pronged switch consisting of an interrupt switch, used to invoke MacsBug, and a reset switch, used to restart the Macintosh. See also **interrupt switch.**

relocatable block: A block that can be moved within the heap during compaction.

stack: A portion of memory that is used for temporary storage of operating data during operation of a program. The data on the stack is added (pushed) and removed (pulled or popped) in last-in, first-out (LIFO) order.

stack-based routine: A toolbox or operating system routine that receives its parameters and returns its results, if any, on the stack.

stack frame: The area of the stack used by a routine for its parameters, return address, local variables, and temporary storage.

status region: The area of the MacsBug display used to display information about the system at the time that MacsBug is invoked.

status register: A location within the microprocessor used to store information about the operation that has just been executed. (Also called the condition code register.)

synchronous I/O: The calling process "sleeps" until the I/O operation is finished. Compare **asynchronous I/O.**

trap dispatcher: The part of the operating system that examines a trap word to determine what operation it stands for, looks up the address of the corresponding routine in the **trap dispatch table,** and jumps to the routine.

trap dispatch table: A table in RAM containing the addresses of all toolbox and operating system routines in encoded form.

trap number: The identifying number of a toolbox or an operating system routine; an index into the trap dispatch table.

trap word: An unimplemented instruction representing a call to a toolbox or an operating system routine.

virtual memory: A method of expanding available memory through the use of software rather than by installing additional hardware. A program running under virtual memory can access the entire logical memory of the computer as if it were RAM, except for blocks of memory reserved for the system heap, ROM, NuBus cards, and a resident debugger.

Index

Cast of Characters

* (asterisk) 15, 66
    in disassembly display 68
: (colon) 206
$ (dollar sign) 207
. (period) 68, 205
(pound sign) 50, 204
; (semicolon)
    as command separator 203
    in disassembly display 68
~ (tilde) 20

A

A0 register 126, 163
A5 register 121, 131, 132
    at interrupt time 153
    pointer to current grafPort 187
    use of by ROM 21
A6 register. *See* stack frames
A7 register. *See* stack pointers
absolute addressing 41
addresses
    colon 206
    dot 205
    exercise locating 33
    expressed as offsets 205
    invalid 186
    return 124
    specifying 204
    starting of current procedure 206
    storage in memory 74
addressing modes
    absolute 41
    address register direct 42
    address register indirect 43
    address register indirect with
        displacement 46
    address register indirect with
        postincrement 44–45
    address register indirect with
        predecrement 44–45
    data register direct 42
    immediate 49
    implied 50
    indexed indirect with
        displacement 47
    PC-relative 48
    summary 40
address register direct addressing 42
address register indirect
    addressing 43
address register indirect with
    displacement addressing 46
address register indirect with
    postincrement addressing
    44–45
address register indirect with
    predecrement addressing
    44–45
address space 72
    division of 77
AP macro 216
AppleShare 19
application partition 113
ApplLimit low-memory global
    variable 33, 83
ApplZone low-memory global
    variable 32, 83
arithmetic operators 206, 209
assemblers 36
assembly-language code
    reading 36–69
    sample program 59–62
    vs. source code 62
assembly-language instructions
    branching 55
    integer arithmetic 51
    without operands 50
    program control 52
    stack frame 58
    syntax 38
    unimplemented 134, 135

assertions 185
asterisk (*) 15
    in disassembly display 68
ATB (A-trap Break) command
    232–235
ATC (A-trap Clear) command
    236–237
ATD (A-trap Display) command
    238–239
ATHC (A-trap Heap Check)
    command 240–241
ATP (A-trap Playback) command
    242–243
A-traps vs. toolbox routines *See also*
    operating system routines.
    action table 155
    breaking on, in a package 233
    called by application 157
    changing address of 138, 139
    commands, dedicated to 154
    displaying actions set on 238–239
    excluding from range 236
    glue. *See* glue
    name and number of 135
    name conflicting with procedure
        name 207
    numbers 141
    numbers and names of 156
    in packages 158
    patches. *See* patches
    processing of 135, 151
    in a range 157
    recording 244–245
ATR (A-trap Record) command
    244–245
ATSS (A-trap Step Spy) command
    246–247
ATT (A-trap Trace) command
    248–250
auto-pop bit 196
A/UX

423

installing MacsBug under 10
invoking MacsBug under 24

B

base conversion 30
bomb box 2
Boolean operators 206
BRA instructions 53
branching 53
branching indicator 15, 54
BR (Breakpoint) command 251, 254
BRC (Breakpoint Clear)
    command 255
BRD (Breakpoint Display) command
    256–257
break message 15
    example 28
breakpoints
    clearing 255
    displaying 256
    how MacsBug implements 252
    inactivating user breaks 23
    marker in disassembly display 68
    setting 194–198
        in C++ program 258
        in ROM 252
        from source program 22
BR macro 215
BRM (Multiple Breakpoints)
    command 258–259
BSR instructions 53
BufPtr low-memory global
    variable 33, 83

C

calling chain 128–129
case, upper and lower xxii
checksumming 260
'CODE' resources 56
code segment 57
colon (:) 206
colon address 206
Command-B command 211
Command-D command 205
command line 202
    buffer 14, 211
        exercise using 30
    editing 14, 211
    entering commands 203

    exercise using 31
    extending 207
    features of 14
    insertion point 203
    use for base conversion 208
    use for calculations 30, 208, 209
commands
    A-trap, summary of 154
    canceling execution of 203
    command-line editing 211
    dcmd. *See* dcmds
    disassembly, summary of 66
    display of output of 15
    entering 14, 203
    expressions in 206
    formatted output 221
    heap blocks 107
    heap, summary of 103
    last address used by 205
    macro. *See* macros
    memory, summary of 75
    overview 202–229
    parameter types 204
    pausing execution of 203
    program control, summary
        194–198
    referring to registers in 88
    register, summary of 89
    saving output of 25
    specifying an address in 204
    specifying parameters to 204
    summary of by function 354
    syntax conventions 203
    syntax summary 357
    use of names in 207
command syntax. *See* notation
    conventions
Command-S command 320
Command-T command 337
Command-V command 211
compilers 36
    procedure definitions 408
condition code register.
    See status register
'C++' resources 27
CS (Checksum) command 260
CurrentA5 low-memory global
    variable 33, 83, 132
current grafPort 187

CurStackBase low-memory global
    variable 33, 83, 118

D

data register direct addressing 42
DB (Display Byte) command 261
'dcmd' resources 219.
    See also dcmds
dcmds
    building 229
    creating 223
    debugging 229
    defined 219
    introduced 27
    listing installed 222
    restrictions on 228
    standard 220
    using 219
Debugger Prefs file
    installing 10
    updating 13
    working with 26–27
Debugger routine 21, 22, 63, 271
debuggers
    Discipline interface 414
    interaction with
        operating system 4
    source-level vs. low-level 4
    support for 412
debugging screen 13–19
    output region 15–16
    PC region 14–15
    status region 16–19
debugging strategies. *See also*
    Discipline; errors
    checking code on all
        machines 186
    checking source code 190
    creating a memory map 32
    finding invalid pointers 193
    symptom vs. cause of crash 188
    using assertions 185
    using signals 184
decimal numbers 50, 204
DebugStr routine 22, 63, 271
    to call Discipline 179
    to display variables 198
desk accessories 169
    testing with Discipline 180

device control entry (DCE) 165–167
  unit table 167
Device Manager 159, 165
DevList macro 216
DH (Disassemble Hexadecimal)
    command 262
disassemblers 36
disassembling
  object code 262
  where to start 68
disassembly display 67
Discipline 20, 173–180
  configurations 179
  how it works 174
  installing as an application 175
  installing as an INIT 174
  MacsBug interface with 413–416
  interpreting output 177
  restrictions on using 180
  to test startup code 179
  using from MacsBug 178
DL (Display Long) command 263
DM (Display Memory) command
    90, 264–266
  exercise using 31
dollar sign ($) 207
dot address 205
double-page fault 88
Down Arrow key 16
DP (Display Page) command 267
drive queue 160
drivers 159, 164–171
  device control entry 165–167
  information about 170
  SCSI 165
  that execute asynchronously 164
  unit table 167
DrvQHdr low-memory global
    variable 160
drvr dcmd 170, 220
'DRVR' resources 165
DSC (Discipline) command 268
DSErrCode low-memory global 183
DV (Display Version) command 269
DW (Display Word) command 270
DX (Debugger Exchange) command
    23, 271

E

EA (Exit to Application)
    command 272
effective address 39
equality operators 206
error codes
  sad Macintosh 372–375
  System Error Handler 376
error handler 134
  defined 2
error handling routines 184
error handling 2
error messages
  to HC command 282
  MacsBug 366–369
  to MR command 312
  operating system 380–405
  to SC6 command 326
  to SC7 command 330
errors
  address 186
  bus 189, 192
  checking operating system 183
  fragmented memory 191
  illegal address 189
  illegal instruction 189
  invalid pointers 191
  returned by Memory
      Manager 184
  returned by Resource
      Manager 184
  stack overflow 194
  uninitialized variables 191
error trapping 184
Esc key 20
ES (Exit to Shell) command 273
EveryTime macro 219
exception handler 2
exception processing 134–137
  handling interrupts 151
  introduced 2
exceptions, A-trap. See A-traps
exception vectors 135, 192
expressions
  in MacsBug commands 206
  order of evaluation 206

F

fatal error 2
FCB (file control blocks) 162
FCBSPtr low-memory global
    variable 162
F (Find) command 274, 277
file control blocks (FCBs) 162
file dcmds 162, 220
File Manager 159, 164
file system 159
  B*tree files 162
  I/O queue 163
  routines 163
FirstTime macro 219
'FKEY' resources 21
floating-point register 19
FSQHdr low-memory global
    variable 163
functions, displaying
    results of 127, 253

G

G (Go) command 278
GetDrvQHdr routine 160
GetPort routine 187
GetTrapAddress routine 139
GetVCBQHdr routine 161
GG macro 215
global variables, allocating
    space for 121
glue
  in-line vs. library 144
  replacing A-trap 141
grafPort, current 187
GS macro 58, 215
GT (Go Till) command 279–280
GTO macro 215

H

handles 106
  dangling 111
  finding invalid 186
  NIL 111
HC (Heap Check)
    command 281–283
HD (Heap Display) command
    284–286
  interpreting display of 108

heap blocks 104
   format 104
   free 106
   header 105
   kinds of 105
   logical size vs. physical size of 105
   nonrelocatable 105, 108
   pointers and handles to 106
   relocatable 106
       properties of 106
       purgeable 107
   resource blocks 117
   starting address 105
   that cannot be moved 108
heaps. *See also* heap blocks
   corruption, cause of 110
   defined 101
   displaying partially damaged 285
   embedded 116
   format of 103
   fragmentation 109
   header 103
   identifying embedded 295
   in multiple-application
       environment 102, 113, 117
   in single-application
       environment 102
   system 115
   trailer 103
   24-bit vs. 32-bit 116
heap zones. *See* heaps
help, displaying topics 210
HELP (Help) command 287
   exercise using 29
high-order byte 75
high-order word 75
history buffer 16
HOW (Display Break Message)
      command 289
HS (Heap Scramble) command
      113, 291
HT (Heap Totals) command
   interpreting display 107, 292
HX (Heap Exchange) command 293
HZ (Heap Zone) command
      294–296
   in multiple-application
       environment 116

I

ID (Disassemble One Line)
      command 297
IJ macro 216
IL (Disassemble From Address)
      command 299–300
immediate addressing 49
indexed indirect addressing with
      displacement addressing
      mode 47
indirection operators 206, 209
INITs
   debugging 3
   testing with Discipline 179
installing MacsBug 10
   under A/UX 10
   installation message 10
   overriding for one session 10
   preventing 10
instructions. *See also* assembly-
      language instructions
   stepping through MMU 337
interrupt handlers 134, 153
interrupt masks 152
interrupts 151–154
   display of interrupt level 19
   interrupt handler 134
   mask 152
   priority levels 152
   types of 152
   VBL 152
interrupt switch 21, 152
interrupt time
   restrictions on code 153
   VBL tasks 154
intersegment calls 56–58
intrasegment calls 56
invoking MacsBug 19–24
   under A/UX 24
   from source program 22
   using 'FKEY' resource 21
   using programmer's switch 20
I/O, synchronous vs.
      asynchronous 163
IOPB template 163
IP (Disassemble Around Address)
      command 301–302
IR (Disassemble Until End of
      Procedure) command 303

J, K

JMP instructions 53
JSR instructions 53
jump table 56
   location of 131–132

L

least significant byte 75
leaving MacsBug, summary of
      commands 24
LINK instruction 58, 125
LoadSeg routine 58
LockMemory routine 88
LOG (Log to a Printer or File)
      command 4, 25, 305–306
   use of under A/UX 24
logical address space 85
low-level debugging
   defined 2
   overview 1–5
   reasons for 3
low-memory global variables 81, 83
   restrictions in using 100
low-order byte 75
low-order word 75

M

machine language 36
Macintosh File System.
      See file system
Macintosh system software, use of by
      debuggers 4
Macintosh XL 1
MacJmp low-memory global
      variable 412
macros
   commands for 213, 307–310
   creating permanent 217–218
   EveryTime 219
   FirstTime 219
   introduced 213
   ranges for F command 276
   standard 214–217
   using to save values 308
MacsBug
   can't access 192
   displaying on different
      monitor 11

getting out of 24
getting started exercise 28–34
how implemented 412
installing. *See* installing MacsBug
invoking. *See* invoking MacsBug
machine dependencies 1, 5
memory use by 4
new features introduced
 in 6.2 5–8
software dependencies 1
MacsBug error messages 366–369
 display of 15
master pointers 106
MaxApplZone routine 194
MC (Macro Create) command
 307–308
MCC (Macro Clear) command 309
MCD (Macro Display)
 command 310
MC68851 Memory Management
 Unit (MMU) 1
MC68881 floating-point
 coprocessor 1
MemErr low-memory global
 variable 111, 184
memory 101. *See also* registers
 application's use of 100
 checksumming 199
 commands that set and
  display 75
 compaction and reservation 109
 exercise for displaying 31
 fragmentation of 109, 193
 high 73
 holding 88
 kinds of 72
 locking 88
 low 73
 maps. *See* memory maps
 overview 72
 regions of 77, 83
 storage convention 75
 templates. *See* templates
 units 74
 use of by MacsBug 4
 virtual 18, 85–88
memory configuration marker 18
memory management
 in multiple-application
  environment 113–117

24-bit vs. 32-bit mode 18, 84
 under system 7.0 84–88
 virtual memory 18, 85–88
Memory Manager
 results from calls 184
 use of at interrupt time 153
memory maps 77–83
 exercise creating 32
 using low-memory global
  variables to create 81, 83
MemTop low-memory global
 variable 33, 83
microprocessors. *See also* registers
 pipelining 189
 processing states of 134
 summary of registers 316–317
 supported by MacsBug 1
MMU instructions, stepping
 through 320
MMU register 19
mnemonics 36
monitors 11
most significant byte 75
Motorola 68000 1
MR (Magic Return) command
 127, 311–313
'mxbc' resources 27
'mxbi' resources 27
 changing size of history buffer 16
 changing size of PC region 14
'mxbm' resources 27, 214
'mxwt' resources 27

N

names, conflicting references 207
NIL handles 111
NIL pointers 111
NMI key (interrupt switch) 21, 152
nonmaskable interrupt 21
notation conventions xxii
numbers
 base conversion 208
 conflicting references 207
 convention for display xxii, 208
 conventions about entering 204
 converting 30
 hexadecimal representation 75
 negative 31, 50
 representation of 30

O

object code
 disassembling 262
 vs. source code 36
operands 38. *See also*
  addressing modes
operating system errors 380–405
operating system routines vs.
 toolbox routines 143
operators
 in assembly-language
  instructions 38
 in MacsBug commands 206
optimization 3
output region 15–16

P, Q

packages 158
'PACK' resources 158
parameters
 application 131
 Pascal storage convention for 124
 Pascal vs. C conventions for 130
 VAR 130
partitions 113
Pascal compiler directive 130
patches
 custom 139
 by INITs 140
 installing 138
 multiple layers of 140
 restrictions on 140
 that replace old trap 138
PBGetFCBInfo low-memory
 global variable 162
PC register. *See* program counter
PC-relative addressing modes 48
physical address space 85
pipelining 189
pointers
 dangling 111
 dereferencing 209
 finding invalid 186, 193
 finding references to 275
 indirection operator 206
 in low memory 32
 NIL 111
pound sign (#) 49, 204
pre-patching 139

Index **427**

printf dcmd 220, 221
procedures
    listing names of 205
    stepping out of 127
process 113
Process Manager 113
    fragmenting its heap 115
program counter 89
    display of contents 14
programmer's switch 20
    use of under A/UX 24

R

RAD (Toggle Register Name Syntax) command 207, 314
RB (Reboot) command 315
registers 88–89
    A0 126, 163
    A5. See A5 register
    A6. See stack frames
    A7. See stack pointer
    address 89, 117–118
    commands that display 19
    conflicting name references 207
    data 89
    displaying and setting values of 316–317
    display of 19
    list of 316–317
    PC 89
    status 89
    use of by operating system routines 143
Registers command 316–317
ResErr low-memory global variable 184
ResErrProc low-memory global variable 184
resource chains 117
Resource Manager 165
    results from calls to 184
return address 124
RN (Set Reference Number) command 318
ROMBase low-memory global variable 33, 83
ROM calls. See A-traps
routine names, in disassembly display 67

routines, implementing. See stack frames
routine selector 158
RS (Restart) command 319
RTS macro 215

S

SADE (Symbolic Applications Debugging Environment) 4
S (Step) command 320
SB (Set Byte) command 322
SC (Stack Crawl) command 190
ScrnBase low-memory global variable 83
SCSI Manager 159
SC6 (Stack Crawl [A6]) command 324–326
SC7 (Stack Crawl [A7]) command 328–330
Segment Loader 57
semicolon (;)
    as command separator 203
    in disassembly display 68
SetPort routine 187
SetTrapAddress routine 139
SHOW (Show) command 17, 331
signals 184
'SIZE' resources 113
SL (Set Long) command 333
SM (Set Memory) command 335
SO (Step Over) command 337
    using to step over LoadSeg trap 58
source code
    vs. assembly-language code 62
    vs. object code 36
SS (Step Spy) command 339–340
stack
    balance 185
    display 119
    management 117–130
    overflow 194
    pushing and popping items 120
    use of in implementing A-traps 142
stack frames 58, 122–129
    calling chain 128–129
    defined 118
stack pointers. See also stack

    contents of 17
    display 119
stack sniffer 194
status register 89
    display of 19
Strip Address routine 18
SW (Set Word) command 341
SWAP (Swap) command 11, 12, 343
SX (Symbol Exchange) command 345
symbol display 68
symbol dump 68
symbols
    disabling display of 345
    display command 205
    MacsBug display of 205
    procedure definitions 408
    restricting references to 318
SysBeep routine 190
System Error Handler 2, 4
    alerts 376
System files, file control blocks 162
system routines. See A-traps
    testing parameters to. See Discipline
system software version 7.0 84–88
SysZone low-memory global variable 31, 83, 116

T

TargetZone MacsBug variable 116
T (Step Over) command 337
TD (Display CPU Registers) command 19, 347
templates 90
    with DM command 90
    exercise creating custom 97
    IOPB 163
    linked lists in 94
    predefined 91
    types to define 93
    use of basic types to define 93
    ways to create 92
TF (Total Floating-Point Register Display) command 19, 348
theCPort macro 215
thePort macro 215
theWindow macro 215

TheZone low-memory global
    variable 116
32-bit addressing 84
tilde (~) 20
TM (Total MMU Display)
    command 19, 349
TMP (List Templates)
    command 91, 350
'TMPL' resources 27
trace, custom A-trap 234
trap dispatcher 134, 136
    defined 2
trap dispatch table 137, 156
trap recording 182
traps. *See* A-traps
24-bit addressing 84
two's complement arithmetic 50.
    See also numbers

U

unit table 167
UNLK instruction 58, 126
UnloadSeg routine 57
Up Arrow key 16
user breaks, disabling 271
UserZone MacsBug variable 295

V

variables, displaying value of 198
VAR parameters 130
vbl dcmd 153, 154, 220
VBL Manager 153
VBLTask record 154
VBL tasks 154
VBLTasks macro 216
VcbList macro 216
VCBQHdr low-memory global
    variable 161
vector number 135, 136
vector table 135
vertical blanking. *See* interrupts
Vertical Retrace Manager 154
virtual memory 85–88
virtual memory marker 18
vol dcmd 161, 220
volume queue 161
volumes, information about 161

W, X, Y, Z

WH (Where) command 33, 140, 351
WindList macro 216

THE APPLE PUBLISHING SYSTEM

This Apple manual was written, edited, and composed on a desktop publishing system using Apple Macintosh® computers and Microsoft Word. Proof pages were created on Apple LaserWriter® printers. Final pages were created on the Varityper VT600 imagesetter. Line art was created using Adobe Illustrator. POSTSCRIPT, the page-description language for the LaserWriter, was developed by Adobe Systems Incorporated.

Text type and display type are Apple's corporate font, a condensed version of ITC Garamond. Bullets are ITC Zapf Dingbats. Some elements, such as program listings, are set in Apple Courier.

Writers: Joanna Bujes and David Shayer
Developmental Editor: Sean Cotter
Illustrator: Peggy Kunz
Production Supervisor: Teresa Lujan
Formatter: Liz Vasti

Special thanks to the Software Developer Training Group, which is responsible for developing many of the exercises and doing much of the ground-breaking work that finally led to this book. Much thanks also to Leo Baschy, Richard Clark, Judy Kettenhofen, and Keith Nemitz for their very patient explanations, and thanks also to Dave Bice for his enthusiastic support for this project.